Twentieth-century Sexuality

A History

Angus McLaren

BLACKWELL
Publishers

First published in 1999

2 4 6 8 10 9 7 5 3 1

Blackwell Publishers Ltd
108 Cowley Road
Oxford OX4 1JF
UK

Blackwell Publishers Inc.
350 Main Street
Malden, Massachusetts 02148
USA

British Library Cataloguing in Publication Data

A CIP catalogue record for this book is available from the British Library.

Library of Congress Cataloging-in-Publication Data

McLaren, Angus.
Twentieth-century sexuality : a history / Angus McLaren.
p.   cm.
Includes bibliographical references (p.   ) and index.
ISBN 0–631–20812–7 (hbk : alk. paper)
ISBN 0–631–20813–5 (pbk : alk. paper)
1. Sex customs—History—20th century.   2. Sex—History—20th
century.   3. Sex (Psychology)—History—20th century.   4. Sex and
history.   I. Title.   II. Title: 20-Century sexuality
HQ16 .M35   1999
306.7′09′04—dc21   98–33145
CIP

Typeset in 10½ on 12pt Garamond
by Graphicraft Limited, Hong Kong
Printed in Great Britain by TJ International Ltd, Padstow, Cornwall

This book is printed on acid-free paper.

Contents

Acknowledgements

This book is about the panics and pleasures associated with sexuality in the twentieth century. In adding the finishing touches to the manuscript I could not help but note that writing a book also entails a variety of panics and pleasures. A number of commentators have actually suggested that the two activities have a good deal in common. In the mid-nineteenth century the French novelist Gustave Flaubert warned a younger colleague that energies expended in amorous encounters could diminish one's creative abilities.

> But be careful not to injure your intelligence in relationships with ladies. You will lose your genius at the end of a womb . . . Keep your priapism for style, f__ your ink pot, calm yourself with meat, and be convinced, as Tissot (of Geneva) said (*Traité de l'onanie*, page 72, see the engraving), that the loss of one ounce of sperm, is more fatiguing than that of three litres of blood. (Gustave Flaubert, *Correspondence*, L. Conard, Paris, 1929, vol. 2, p. 312)

A century later Edmund Bergler asserted in *The Writer and Psychoanalysis* that 'writer's block' – Bergler coined the term – was due to unconscious psychic masochism. As will be seen in the following chapters, I believe that such ideas – as half-baked as they might be – are of interest in that they tell us something about the cultural preoccupations, if not the sexual practices, of their particular time period. And, as suspicious as I am about comparing sexual to other forms of human behaviour, I have to admit that as I soldiered on with this ambitious project I at times regarded myself as a masochist, the commissioning editor as a sadist, and the audiences, to whom I exposed portions of the work, as voyeurs. I also experienced the customary panics involved in writing. Did I have an argument? Could I prove it? Would I ever finish?

The chief pleasure in producing such a study comes in finally being able to thank all those who assisted in its production. I owe special thanks to those who took time out from their own projects to look over mine. Arlene McLaren and Dany Lacombe read early portions of the manuscript; Michael Finn, Becki Ross and Mariana Valverde perused an entire draft. They all sent along valuable critiques and words of encouragement. Lesley Hall in London, Christine Delphy in Paris, and Bruno Wanrooij in Florence produced useful references and citations. Brian Dippie subjected the pages of my present work, like all the earlier ones, to his slashing red pen. He and Donna continued to provide warm hospitality, non-stop conversation and insightful suggestions.

For efficient assistance I have relied on the staffs of the inter-library loan office at the University of Victoria, the Law Library and the Woodward Medical Library at the University of British Columbia, the Wellcome Institute for the History of Medicine, the British Library, the British Library Newspaper Repository at Colindale, the Bibliothèque Nationale, the Kinsey Institute Library, and the various libraries of Harvard University. At the University of Victoria Ted Wooley was an understanding Chair and Karen McIvor an ever helpful departmental secretary. The generosity of the Social Science and Humanities Research Council of Canada made possible the numerous research trips that this project required. Arlene was as ever my main critic and supporter. Jesse kept me from taking myself or the project too seriously.

Introduction

Sensational stories focusing on new sexual dangers sweep across the 1990s. Seducers, the press informs us, are employing the powerful sedative rohypnol – the 'date rape pill' – to have their way with young women, male sperm counts are dropping, adultery has become commonplace, marital fertility is declining and teenage pregnancy rates are up, divorce continually on the rise, age of first intercourse ever lower, sexual deviancy spreading like wildfire and AIDS poised to bring retribution for unnatural acts that violate sexual decency. The dangers posed by sexual intercourse, according to the tabloids, now rival its pleasures.

Such moral panics are, despite what the journalists might claim, not new; they can be traced back to the nineteenth century and beyond. Those familiar with the 1890s panics over syphilis, 'white slavery', male neurasthenia, 'race suicide' and 'Oscar Wilde types' can only regard the current crop of warnings with a distinct sense of *déjà vu*. Yet some things have changed. Today's media, while claiming to be shocked by the subversiveness of carnal desires, deluge the public with explicit sexual imagery to sell everything from Calvin Klein jeans to Black and Decker power drills. Sexuality, bewail the conservatives, has 'invaded' every aspect of public life. Sexual identity has indeed become a key defining category in the twentieth century. Whereas at dinner parties it used to be discreetly asked if someone was working class or Catholic, it is more likely today to be 'Is he gay?' 'Is he her first husband?' 'How did they have their children?' 'Is she taking oestrogen?' 'Does he use Viagra?' More importantly, the media now carry – in tandem with the barrage of cautionary tales warning of the dangers of deviant sexuality – a range of stories that present new sexual scripts. Gay men who have 'come out' and women 'in recovery' from rape or sexual abuse have increasingly made their voices heard. What motivates the tellers of such candid accounts is the late twentieth-century preoccupation with the importance of consciousness and identity. In ending the silence in which intimate human relations have so long been enveloped such healthy confessions will, it is argued, finally reveal the 'truth' about sex.[1]

The temptation is to conclude that the emergence of these new narratives is a symptom of the final unshackling of the libido, that essential, unchanging drive or passion that the Victorians so pointlessly attempted to contain. This study begins with the opposite assumption. The term 'sexuality' only surfaced a little over a century ago.[2] The basic premise of this book is that sexuality – commonly taken to be a biological given – is socially constructed.[3] 'Sex', as one researcher has rightly noted, 'is not a natural act.'[4] Sexuality has been remade by each generation and to understand such transformations necessarily requires placing its discussion in its social and cultural context.

Over the past few years friends have said to me: 'How can you write a history of sexuality? And of both Europe and North America? How are you going to decide on what to include and what to leave out?' I was initially as sceptical of such an overly ambitious project as they were. Given the avalanche of specialized studies which pour from the presses devoted to gays, lesbians, prostitution, pornography, rape, gender-blending, divorce and adultery, is there any need for yet another book about sexuality? I ultimately concluded that there was, since so many current studies are historically impoverished. Authors preoccupied by the sexual debates of the end of the millennium appear for the most part to be unaware of the genealogy of the discussion in which they are engaged. This book attempts to provide a brief yet insightful overview of twentieth-century sexual beliefs and practices. My hope is that, in presenting the ways in which sexual boundaries were constructed and contested in the past, this study may play a helpful part in contextualizing the current round of sexual debates. As an historical study, it necessarily refuses to naturalize or universalize either heterosexuality or homosexuality, but seeks to appreciate the ways in which race, class, generation and gender preoccupations constituted what sexuality has meant to Western culture.

The amount of geography that this book attempts to cover has worried my friends as much as the number of topics it touches on. Unlike most studies of sexuality, this book is geographically eclectic, examining developments in Europe, Britain and North America. I hope that it will become clear that there is much to be gained by taking such a broad view. Too many studies of sexuality have, as Theodore Zeldin pointed out, embraced the notion of national stereotypes – that Germans were given to sadism, the French to philandering, the British to restraint. Similarly, many Americans believe that their nation's discomfort in dealing with such issues as abortion or gay rights is unique. I am not suggesting that strong national traditions do not exist, but that a preoccupation with them can blind us to the more important sex and gender conventions that the nations of Western Europe and North America share.[5]

In producing a study of twentieth-century sexuality in the Western world I have necessarily synthesized a good deal of secondary material. I both rely on and critique much of the enormous literature that has already been devoted to modern sexuality. Despite Michel Foucault's assertion that it was wrong-headed to imagine that the Victorians were repressed and we are liberated, the notion that modernization somehow 'freed' sexuality has proved to be tenacious.[6] It is still often claimed that a 'sexual revolution' took place in the twentieth century, the most important symptom of which was the final severing of sex and reproduction. If such a revolution occurred the obvious question is why, in the late 1990s, the issues of pornography, prostitution, abortion, sexually transmitted diseases and homosexuality are still so hotly debated? The answer is that old forms of restraint were no doubt displaced but new methods of containment emerged. This book is accordingly not a 'progressive' history that tells of the replacement of old puritanical standards by new humane ones, of old myths being usurped by new scientific facts. Rather, I am interested in the more complex question of how the lines dividing private and public realms were repeatedly drawn, fought over and redrawn. I will be looking at attempts at sexual rebellion, contestation and control; in short I will try to provide a 'political' history of sexuality. Did shifts in sexual behaviour occur? Were they contested? How did changing family forms, economic demands and state policies influence change? What stories did contemporaries tell to prevent or account for change?

The book's underlying concern is the question of why at some times, but not at others, certain issues – such as child sexual abuse or prostitution or homosexuality – created moral panics. And why were race, religion, class and gender differences often related to specific sexual practices? The study's working hypothesis is that such cautionary tales were employed by the powerful for the surveillance, disciplining and silencing of the marginal. Take the charged labels used in the 1970s to describe the American 'explosion' in 'teen' pregnancies. Such language, in laying blame and pathologizing individual conduct allowed adults to maintain the subordination of the young. It licensed experts to talk in the name of their wards. At the same time this playing up of 'hormones' and 'youthful rebellion' deflected attention away from real problems, such as the high rates of unemployment and poverty facing unwed African-American mothers.

Examining such panics over sexuality allows one to get into the mind set of an epoch. The dominant morality did not of course accurately reflect actual social conduct, but it could and did restrain it. One only has to think about the ways in which politicians sensitive to media-generated panics turned their wrath on birth control, abortion and venereal disease clinics or launched campaigns to root out pornography and prostitution. Yet one must keep in mind that by privileging the official discourse there is the danger of ignoring those that could not be so freely expressed. It is relatively easy to determine what role models heterosexual males might have aped in the inter-war decades; to do the same for homosexual men requires greater ingenuity. Similarly, abortion was a condemned criminal act for much of the period under consideration, but it is vital to understand how women's networks passed on information on which methods to use and how sympathetic doctors could be approached. Accordingly, this investigation – in addition to unpacking the official line on sexuality – seeks to unearth other hidden, yet often equally powerful discourses.

Moral panics were not simply repressive. One purpose moralists unconsciously pursued in producing stereotypes was no doubt to head off explorations of competing models of sexual behaviour, but panics could unintentionally spread subversive information. Even the negative stereotype became a model for the dissatisfied and ill at ease to emulate. Oscar Wilde's trial in 1895 popularized a certain style of homosexuality; the prosecution in the 1920s of Radclyffe Hall's *The Well of Loneliness* publicized the existence of a type of lesbianism; reports of divorce cases informed the public of how liaisons were sustained. Notions of sexual identity, even when imposed by the powerful seeking to marginalize and exclude the deviant, could spark a sense of community, precipitating the enunciation and defence of once tabooed desires. This study does not assume a simple clash between good and evil, freedom and oppression. The victims of some moral panics on occasion launched their own. For example, early twentieth-century birth controllers who were accused of precipitating 'race suicide' retaliated by asserting that only cheap contraceptives could prevent the 'feckless breeding of the unfit'.

As should be clear by now, the investigation of 'sexual stories' plays an important role in this study. At times of moral panic cautionary tales told by those worried by new developments enjoyed a cultural hegemony. With hindsight it is easy to be dismissive of the alarms raised by such prudes and uncritical of the tales spun by those who sought to legitimate change. Marie Stopes informed the world that, though university educated, over a year had passed before she fully realized that her marriage had not been consummated. Shamed by her own ignorance she wrote *Married Love* (1918) and dedicated her life to improving marital happiness. Margaret Sanger, who became the world's most famous birth control advocate, explained in her autobiography that she was motivated by the trauma of witnessing in 1912 the death of a woman due to a botched abortion. Sanger decided there and then 'to do something to change the destiny of mothers whose miseries were vast as the sky'.[7] Alfred Kinsey began his investigations into human sexuality, so he told his readers, after being asked in the late 1930s by Indiana University to give a non-credit course on marriage. As a zoologist he was shocked to discover the lack of hard data available on human sexual behaviour and was accordingly forced to launch the surveys which would win him such notoriety. These inspiring stories were, my students are always disappointed to learn, just that, 'stories' crafted to legitimate a specific course of action. Stopes was not as sexually naïve as she pretended; Sanger was not propelled by the death of one poor New York mother directly into launching a birth control campaign; and Kinsey was collecting data on sexuality well before being asked to by his university.[8]

Such debunking revelations do not mean that these stories should be dismissed. The importance of both these progressive accounts and the popular cautionary tales is that they performed an obvious function. A current generation of historians has taken the 'narrative turn', that is, rediscovered the cultural significance of story-telling. Jean-Paul Sartre preceded them in observing in his novel *Nausea*, 'A man is always a teller of tales, he lives surrounded by his stories and the stories of others, he sees everything that happens through them; and he tries to live his life as if he were recounting it.'[9] Sexuality, this study argues, has been continually shaped and reshaped by social and economic forces. Stories, myths and parables were needed to make sense of the myriad of changes occasioned by modernization. If a culture is to be understood it is necessary to know why at a particular time certain sexual stories or images were produced and accepted and how they were related to larger social developments. Such stories – even if they were fictions, products of cultural shifts – could in turn precipitate a further round of social change. The impact that the 'coming out' story had on a generation of gay men and lesbians springs to mind. Art copies life, but life also copies art. This study will accordingly frame the accounts provided by historians, sociologists and sexologists of changing patterns of sexual behaviour with the stories which were both a cause and effect of such changes.

Sexuality has long remained such a sensitive issue, I will argue, because it was colonized, exploited and employed as a code word for other concerns. The intent – conscious or not – of the purveyors of sexual panics when constructing a 'sexual other' was to alert the public to the *social* rather than the strictly sexual threat posed by the 'deviant'. It was not private acts that the panics were chiefly about but their public repercussions. The sexual 'other' was at times constructed along class lines – the promiscuous lower orders threatening the self-controlled and propertied. Or the 'other' was racialized – blacks, Jews and Hispanics for White Americans, 'continentals' for the English, and Arabs for the French. Sexuality did not invade society; society invaded sexuality. If not for the existence of the pimp, prostitute, pornographer, abortionist, adulterer, homosexual, paedophile, queer, lesbian and nymphomaniac spawned by our commercialized urban culture, so the censorious story-tellers asserted, life would be safer, sexuality would not be polluted. In adopting a social constructionist argument, I assume that, given the tenacity of class, gender, race and ethnic divisions, those seeking to control and discipline the marginal will continue to produce accounts to exploit the 'dangers' purportedly posed by sexual practices and desires.

This study cannot cover every topic. The circumstances in which people did 'it' is difficult to determine. The study will draw on sex surveys such as Kinsey's to give some idea of researchers' findings about where, when and how people had sex. Quantitative data will only be used in a coitus interruptus fashion; inserted briefly in the text and quickly withdrawn. The study will focus more on what was said about sex. The sex surveys will themselves be 'read' as yet another cultural product. There is an obvious gap between the literature – be it descriptive or prescriptive – and actual behaviour. This is not an admission of defeat. The study's working assumption is that ideology and behaviour were related; that the discourse became part of the reality it described. I will be looking at meanings and representations of sexuality to attempt to see how earlier generations understood it. Accordingly, I will draw on medical, scientific, religious and legal sources. I will also exploit popular literary accounts – cartoons, jokes, plays, novels and films. Particular attention will of course be paid to sex and marriage manuals which in effect codified sexuality. In case all this sounds too dispassionate, it is worth stressing that, though I will be approaching sexuality from a social constructionist point of view, attempting to understand how it was socially defined and how such discussions were often used as a means of regulation, I will also seek to get not only into people's minds but under their clothes, to know what they did both in and out of bed. If there are any heroes in this account they are not the sex experts, but the ordinary women and men who, despite the admonitions of their 'betters', tenaciously sought by a variety of means to pursue their own particular sexual agendas.

Where to begin? I start this study in chapter 1 with an analysis of the sexual panics precipitated by the First World War. The conflict did not simply conjure up new sexual worries; the apparent gravity of the situation gave greater credibility to moralists who had for some time argued that sexual misdemeanours imperilled national well-being. Even before the war many were worried by the apparent sexualization of youth and marriage and in particular how, thanks to contraception, the declining identification of sexuality with reproduction was made possible. Using the war as a benchmark, I then turn in chapter 2 to the issues raised by the apparent restlessness of young people and the 'new women'. An attempt is made to explain why the policing of the sexuality of the young became such a twentieth-century preoccupation. Courtship ideally led to marriage. Unlike the passionless Victorians, the life of the twentieth-century married couple was supposedly more loving. The liberal view held that women were now to have sexual feelings, but they were ideally to be channelled into a traditional heterosexual marriage. An analysis of the eroticization of marriage and the intentions of the writers of the marriage manuals is provided in chapter 3. Marriage in turn was supposed to lead to children but fertility rates fell through most of the century. In chapter 4 I unpack the inter-war debates over abortion and contraception, paying particular attention to the role class played in determining the 'right' and 'wrong' ways of limiting family size.

Chapters 2–4 deal with the inter-war sexual practices of the 'normal'. Chapter 5 is devoted to the discovery of 'perverts' and the attempts to explain their behaviour by the 'sex doctors', the psychoanalysts and the sexologists. The question posed is were these experts seeking to extend greater freedoms to sexual minorities or seeking to inculcate new, internalized methods of self-control? Sigmund Freud is most associated with the modern type of sexual ideology based on middle-class individualism, self-management and privatization. Why he was preoccupied with 'frigidity' and how such concerns were exploited in conservative backlashes against the feminism of the 1930s is pursued in chapter 6. The fascist and Nazi condemnations of abortion and homosexuality are considered in the context of the eugenic pre-occupations of the inter-war period. The purpose of the review in chapter 7 of the demogogues' successful exploitation of repressive fears is to serve as a reminder that the history of sexuality is not simply a story of inevitable progress.

The study then traces the shift of sexological investigations following the Second World War to the United States. An exploration in chapter 8 of Kinsey's surveys provides an entrée into the post-war sexual world and a consideration of why conservatives felt that the story-book, happy 1950s' families were under siege. Remarkably radical discussions of sexuality took place in the 1950s, and this leads to the appraisal in chapter 9 of the myth and the reality of the 1960s' 'sexual revolution'. The rise of both the women's and gay movements are necessarily plotted as both causes and effects of a decade of political radicalism. The 1980s witnessed a swing to the right in Britain and North America. In chapter 10 an analysis of the moral panic over AIDS is used to query the notion of an end-of-the-millennium 'backlash' against the sexual liberalism associated with the 1960s. Those most enamoured of a free market place – which increasingly used sex to sell its products – were vociferous in their demands for restrictions on 'deviants'. But why were gays, lesbians and feminists divided by the issue of 'identity politics' and the question of sexuality's pleasures and dangers? And did such ideological debates have any impact on sexual practices?

As the century wears on, the number of sexual surveys and sexual scripts increases; so too does the contemporary historian's difficulty in providing satisfactory accounts of their genesis and interpretation. This study will no doubt raise as many questions as it answers, which is as it should be. Beginning with the premise that there is no 'truth' about sex to be discovered, the book seeks simply to review some of the key ways in which sexuality has been experienced and explained in the twentieth century. Unlike the prophets of doom who currently exploit the AIDS epidemic, this study does not claim primordial importance for sex, but the book does assume the significance of sex. As W. C. Fields aptly observed, 'Sex is not the most important thing in the world, but there is nothing quite like it.'

1

'The Cult of the Clitoris': Sexual Panics and the First World War

In June of 1918, a libel suit fought out in London's Central Criminal Court brought to the surface the bizarre rumour that sex-starved English women, deprived by the war of male companionship, were turning to lesbianism. The affair centred on Oscar Wilde's play *Salomé*. Though it had been first put on in France in 1896 and later made into an opera by the German composer Richard Strauss, it had been banned in England by the Examiner of Plays, who regarded it as 'half Biblical, half pornographic'.[1] When news got out that the Canadian dancer Maud Allan was to appear in a private performance of *Salomé* in April of 1918 Captain Harold Spencer attacked her in the columns of a scurrilous tabloid called the *Vigilante* with an article sensationally entitled 'The Cult of the Clitoris'. In it Spencer made the astounding claim that Wilde's play was not only immoral but its current production part of a German plot to undermine British wartime resolve. Not surprisingly, Allan sued for libel.[2]

The three-day trial produced a string of ludicrous and amazing scenes. Noel Pemberton Billing, independent MP and publisher of the *Vigilante*, defended the truth of the cited article. Though he had a German wife he asserted in court that English society was riddled with perverts and fifth columnists forced by 'corruption and black-mail' to serve the Germans.[3] The suborned included choir boys, cabinet ministers and dancing girls. A female bigamist was willing to testify that the government had ordered her to compromise Pemberton Billing by luring him to a male brothel. His star witness, Captain Spencer, claimed that he had seen in Albania a mysterious 'Black Book' in which the Germans had written both the names of the 47,000 English perverts whom they could employ as secret agents and the locations of the massage parlours, baths and public houses where they congregated. Sodomy, sadism and lesbianism were, he asserted, prac-tised by German spies to bring the English people into 'bondage'.[4] He explained that he had entitled his article 'The Cult of the Clitoris' to warn the public of the 'circle of vicious women', including the 'hereditary degenerate' Maud Allan, that was attempting by various means, such as the putting on of immoral entertainments, to sap England's strength.

The 'Black Book' of course did not exist and Captain Spencer – a man who suggested that a sexually excited woman suffering from 'an enlarged and diseased clitoris' might try to have sex with an elephant – was quite mad. Nevertheless, the jury cleared Pemberton Billing and Spencer of the libel charge and the public cheered their victory.[5] Maud Allan's counsel thought he could laugh away the absurd notion that enemy forces were seeking to pervert English society. Such was the persuasiveness of wartime sexual fears and ignorance that he was proved wrong.

Panics

A number of historians have asserted that the First World War, which in so many ways shattered the Victorian world, necessarily led to a reappraisal of traditional views of sex and gender.[6] The Maud Allan trial, as peculiar as it was, serves as a forcible reminder that the war did not lead in any simple and direct fashion to a liberalizing of sexual mores. Across Europe millions of young men died; families were dislocated; religious beliefs declined. The war violently ushered in a world of science, technology and mechanization. But in both Berlin and London the fear that traditional sexual standards could not stand up to such an onslaught led the anxious to be all the more zealous in their defence of them. One result was the plethora of cautionary tales. The French and English not surprisingly produced a string of atrocity stories, attributing to the 'Hun' a penchant for the raping and mutilation of the defenceless. As the 'Black Book' furore indicated, however, the chief preoccupation of moralists on both sides of the lines was the sexuality of women and youths. Fear of shifting gender and generational relationships underpinned a surge of stories targeting adulterous wives, 'good time girls' and 'war babies'.

When conservatives bemoaned the decline of morality what primarily preoccupied them was the notion that women were taking advantage of the dislocations occasioned by the conflict to free themselves of old restraints. The respectable reluctantly accepted the fact that the demands of the wartime economy necessitated the recruitment of thousands of women to occupy themselves with what heretofore had been called 'men's work'.[7] What the respectable opposed were the apparent symptoms of sexual emancipation that followed. As women freed themselves of the restrictive clothing of the Edwardian period to take up their new tasks, the fear was that they would shed much of their moral decorum as well.

The newspapers reported that the outbreak of hostilities led to a releasing of sexual restraints. Why should young people refrain from sexual pleasures when there was no telling how long they might live? Women purportedly jumped into the arms of young men on the way to the front. Women's police patrols, established to provide better surveillance of the prostitutes who always trawled for soldiers, found themselves also dealing with 'highly painted teenagers', 'good time girls' and housewives supposedly seized by 'khaki fever'.[8] British soldiers were as likely to contract venereal disease from an 'amateur' as from a professional.[9] In the eyes of the respectable the line separating good and bad girls was increasingly blurred. Misogynists even accused nurses of seeking an erotic charge in caring for the wounded. Nursing – which according to Vera Brittain had a 'glamorous' nature – at the very least reversed gender roles inasmuch as strong women found themselves caring for weak men.

The war, according to official reports, placed family life under great stress. The jump in marriages in 1914–15 was hardly reassuring. Evidence soon appeared showing that hasty marriages often could not stand the strain of lengthy absences. Divorce rates soared at the end of the conflict. In Germany, for example, the number of divorces jumped from 15,000 a year for the period 1909–13 to 40,000 in 1923.[10] The difficulties of re-establishing a relationship after a long separation underlay most break-ups, but moralists focused on the notion of the wife betraying her husband as he heroically risked his life at the front. Infidelity was so rife as to be almost a laughing matter. In central Europe the story was told of a movie manager who warned his audience that an armed trooper on leave was about to enter the theatre in search of his wife and her lover. Twenty-three couples immediately bolted for the exit.[11] It was bad enough that women might betray their husbands with the men unfit for service left at home. In England newspapers complained that women also consorted with well-paid American troops. In Germany the government was outraged to discover women fraternizing with prisoners of war. The nationalists encountered their worst nightmare, however, when the colonial powers brought black soldiers to Europe. Racists attributed to such recruits a natural taste for 'white meat' and lamented European women's morbid desire for such encounters and the cocaine and morphine with which they were associated.[12] France's stationing of Senegalese troops in the Rhineland following the Treaty of Versailles was hysterically denounced by racists in England as well as in Germany as an incitement to rape.

Rising illegitimacy rates were pointed to by the anxious as evidence of the increasing numbers of faithless women. The German rate rose from 9.77 per cent in 1913 to 13.10 per cent in 1918.[13] In England commentators also noted by 1915 a surge in the birth of bastards. *The Shield* reported that 'war babies' – by which it meant illegitimate children – who were usually delivered by young women had an infant mortality rate twice that of the average.[14] If the illegitimacy rate were not higher it was because many women had recourse to abortion. In France the claim that many women were seeking to free themselves of a pregnancy which resulted from their being raped by Germans led even conservatives to defend abortion as appropriate for those whom they regarded as the 'war wounded'.[15] Women who simply wished to terminate an undesired pregnancy were denounced by doctors and churchmen as contributing to 'race suicide'. This fanciful preoccupation with women's 'betrayal' of both their country and their sex finally and logically enough led to the construction of the notion of the 'lesbian spy'. In England it was out of such fantasies that Captain Spencer spun his story of the 'Black Book' and Maud Allan's lesbian cult. He was no doubt inspired in part by the fact that on 15 October 1917 the French government had executed Mata Hari, who had purportedly participated in sexual orgies as part of her espionage work for the Germans.[16]

It was not surprising that male commentators should have projected on to women their sexual fears, but as the war raged on disturbing evidence appeared that the men at the front were also falling prey to immoral urges. The war and the sacrifices that it would entail had been initially hailed by many as healthy antidotes to the materialism of the modern age. On both sides of the line nationalists presented the conflict as a test of true manliness and called on youth to demonstrate the manly virtues of courage, toughness and self-sacrifice.[17] Those who had been worried by the blurring of gender lines believed that the war would return the sexes to their 'natural' roles. The virile male would fight; the woman would guard the hearth and home. Men, for a time free of the cloying interference of females, would find in the forces a chaste and virtuous male camaraderie. The army drilled them, cut their hair and put them into uniforms to bond them and make them look bigger and stronger. The popular press presented the nation's 'men' as potent and masculine warriors; the enemy as cruel and vacillating degenerates.[18] Accordingly, the allies spoke of the kaiser's 'rape' of Belgium and a French professor of sexology could gravely inform his readers that research proved that the Germans had a marked predilection for sadism.[19] British propaganda presented the Germans as 'Huns' – half Asiatic brutes – given to slicing the breasts off helpless women.[20] Traditionally the English attributed the spread of vice to contact with continentals, especially the French. Hence the English references to French kisses, French letters and so on. But as France was a wartime ally, Anglo-Saxons now targeted the Germans as the dangerous sexual 'other'. The French for their part regarded most of their neighbours as more prone to homosexuality than themselves – referring, for example, to the *vice italien* and the *moeurs arabes*. They tended to regard the English public school, with its ritual beatings, as a particularly fertile breeding ground for sadism and masochism, but now had to show more discretion.[21]

As the war went on each side continued to insist on the moral superiority of its troops despite troubling evidence to the contrary. Under the constant barrage of artillery fire in the trenches of Flanders thousands of erstwhile brave soldiers broke down and behaved like 'hysterical women'. Shell shock, viewed as a manifestation of a dangerous loss of manliness, was initially treated with the utmost brutality.[22] Sigmund Freud's psychoanalytic approach proved successful in dealing with such cases. If the military finally accepted the diagnosis of 'war neurosis' and allowed for less punitive treatments of shell-shocked men, it was not a symptom of a softer attitude towards malingering or the embracing of a new view of true masculinity: the military accepted a psychological diagnosis primarily to individualize the problem and thereby prevent mass mutinies.[23]

Other disquieting discoveries forced themselves to the attention of investigators. The modern war machine, in subjecting millions of conscripts to close scrutiny, turned up in every army unanticipated evidence of sexual deviancy. Traditionalists could understand that even 'normal' recruits would shock civilians with their filthy jokes and scatological humour.[24] Less easy to explain were reports that transvestites showed up at enlistment centres in dresses or that bigamists were discovered when more than one wife demanded a man's pension. Some men were made into sadists by the morbid demands of authority and even the army found that their addiction to cruelty bordered on the pathological.[25]

Soldiers were discovered engaging in every imaginable form of sex from 'circle jerks' and bestiality to rape. The military tried to ignore evidence that the conscious and unconscious erotic relations which developed among masses of men separated from women led some, when drunk, to engage in 'pseudo-homosexual acts'.[26] It savagely persecuted the self-conscious homosexuals or 'urnings' who were discovered in U-boats, cavalry regiments and engineering divisions.[27]

An American study insisted that homosexuals diminished army moral though some had in fact enlisted to prove their bravery.[28] A common ploy of propagandists was to attribute such sexual deviancy to the enemy. Since German writers led by Iwan Bloch and Krafft-Ebing had been among the first to discuss homosexuality, British commentators such as the anti-semite Arnold White portrayed Germany as a haven for degenerates. Alfred Douglas, who had been both Oscar Wilde's lover and the translator of *Salomé* from French into English, turned violently against his past passions, poetically proclaiming: 'Two filthy fogs blot out the light: / The German and the Sodomite.'[29] The editor of the *Morning Post* heartily agreed:

> These perversions of sexual passion have no home in the healthy mind of England. They have, like scum on water, a floating root in the international population which drifts between capital and capital. It is like a pestilence of which sporadic cases and even epidemics are sometimes brought to our shores; but it is abhorrent to the nature of this nation.[30]

Prostitution, because it was viewed as the chief cause of the spread of venereal disease, posed in practical terms the armies' biggest sexual problem. The continental states had long regulated prostitutes and licensed brothels.[31] In Paris, brothels continued to serve a purported million customers a year in the twentieth century. France only ended the 'neo-regulationism' of prostitution in 1946. England's attempt to employ its own Contagious Diseases Act for such purposes was dropped in 1886 after feminist and moral purity activists protested against the blatant sexism of a policy that subjected women but not men to forcible medical inspection. In the course of the war 400,000 cases of venereal disease were reported in the British army which led it to reinstitute a policing policy.[32] Section 40d of the Defence of the Realm Act 1914 made it an offence for any woman with venereal disease to have 'sexual intercourse with any member of the armed forces or any of his majesty's allies'.[33] Similarly, the United States authorities, who were at first outraged by the French government's supplying brothels for its troops, rethought their position. Vice reformer Raymond B. Fosdick was hopeful that American boys could be continent and protected from venereal disease if provided with athletic distractions and if prostitutes – likened to mosquitoes carrying yellow fever – were eliminated. Thirty-two states ultimately passed compulsory medical inspection laws that resulted in over 18,000 women being incarcerated.[34] Once in France, however, the American military came to the conclusion that preventive methods had to be employed even though the moralists might howl that this was tantamount to condoning vice. It was a simple fact that the New Zealand army with its 'dangle parades' and provision of condoms had proved the effectiveness of prophylaxis. When informed of such discussions, the Secretary of War's shocked response was 'For God's sake don't show this to the President or he'll stop the war.'[35]

Continuities

With hindsight it can be recognized that the sexual fears engendered by the war were greatly exaggerated. Those who harped on about the dangers posed by flighty or seductive women were simply responding to the prospect of social disorder by the old misogynist tactic of attributing all their nation's failings to feminine interference. The truth was that in every country women's organizations threw themselves into the war effort. The League of German Women's Associations was for its part as nationalistic as Mrs Pankhurst's suffragists were in Britain. Women's war work impressed some contemporaries and shocked others, but it represented a continuation of economic and social changes that could be traced back decades earlier. Mills and factories had employed large feminine workforces since the early nineteenth century and indeed in France the war marked the zenith of women's labour participation. In Germany there was not so much a change in the numbers employed as in their visibility.

The notion that such changing social patterns threatened to undermine morality was an old charge. An anti-suffragist like Walter Heape had warned just prior to the war that the 'awakening of women' led some to seek to break the 'iron fetters of nature'.[36] Sexual mores did not change all that much during wartime. The talk of 'war babies' and declining fertility were both greatly exaggerated. Fertility rates had been declining in the United States and France for most of the nineteenth century, and in countries such as Britain and Germany where the drop was noticed after 1870, the pronatalists adopted the tactic of primarily blaming women for the fall.[37] 'The woman who flinches from childbirth', declared President Theodore Roosevelt of the United States, 'stands on a par with the soldier who drops his rifle and runs in battle.'[38]

The pessimistic also lamented the fact that the war dashed many women's hopes of marrying and fulfilling their natural role of wife and mother. Many men, of course, did not return and the huge losses at the front skewed the demographic pyramid, producing millions of 'surplus women'. In Germany's case two million soldiers were killed, leaving 600,000 widows, a million orphans and close to a million and a half so-called 'white widows' – the young women who had lost their prospective mates. France suffered a similar fate.[39] But the 'new woman' – by which was meant a college-educated or economically independent woman – was not a product of the war. 'New women' had been castigated by moralists since the 1890s. Those terrified by the spectre of lesbianism pointed out that some educated women did not marry and female couples formed what in the United States were called 'Boston marriages'. The reality was that an educated middle-class woman had to decide between having a profession and a husband. No doubt some women who opted for a profession and spinsterhood developed new modes of female interaction, some platonic, some sexual. In the nineteenth century women could, because of the separate sphere ideology, envisage living their entire lives with other women. With twentieth-century society increasingly pressuring the young to marry and pathologizing same-sex relationships, it could hardly be claimed that the war 'freed' the young woman's libido.[40]

The first fantasy of commentators, frightened at the prospect of the war turning the world upside-down, was that the conflict would empower women and render men passive. Their second nightmare was that racial barriers would be breached. The fear that surfaced in the war that black men would rape white women was the most blatant example of male projection.[41] In fact, in the southern United States – as in some European colonies – many white boys had their first sexual experience with black girls.[42] Young white men were expected to be sexually active while white women had to remain chaste. This wartime preoccupation with race is best understood when located against the backdrop of the racial tensions occasioned by the first stirrings of decolonization and the arrival of a massive wave of African-American migrants in the northern states in the first decades of the twentieth century. The lynchings in the southern United States that took several thousand African-American lives were the most dramatic evidence of such racial fears. In 1909 a *New York Times* reporter noted that Europeans were only now recognizing the danger of allowing their daughters to consort with blacks. 'It has long been a common and repulsive spectacle in German cities to see white girls and women walking down the street arm in arm with American and African negroes, and appearing in their company at restaurants, cafés and theaters.'[43] Women and non-whites, it was believed, were restive.

The war also changed men, but a good deal less than the fearmongers predicted. Soldiers paraded their coarseness and vulgarity but their letters and diaries revealed a good deal of prudery and a domestic longing for a return to their families.[44] Many men – such as the Provençaux consigned to Breton regiments – did not find in the ranks the much ballyhooed solidarity and fraternity. The homoeroticism which purportedly lurked in the trenches was rarely encountered. Whatever male intimacy occurred was a carry-over of the harmless pleasures previously met with at home in public schools, the scouts and men's clubs. Heterosexuality was not seriously challenged in the trenches and the majority of men appear to have reverted to women as soon as they could.[45]

Most of the stories of wartime debauchery similarly proved to be mythical. Civilians feared the return of millions of sex-crazed soldiers, but after the horrors of the trenches a cosy family life was what the troops found most tantalizing. Birth and marriage rates climbed dramatically after the war to make up for those postponed during the years of combat. In Germany, for example, there were 956,251 births in 1918 and 1,299,404 in 1919, though by 1923 the long-term trend in the decline of fertility had resumed.[46]

Numbers of young men probably had their sexual innocence prolonged by the conflict which prevented them from marrying and kept them cooped up at the front. Yet given their living conditions some soldiers no doubt experienced some liberalization of their sexual mores while in uniform. Little romance was found in brothels but some soldiers had their first sexual experience with a prostitute. One young man calmly reported to his mates that it was 'not as good as I thought. It's a bit like pulling your thing, but you have someone to talk to.'[47] Most soldiers did not have casual sex if only because they feared venereal disease. The idea that 'innocent' women might be infected by men who consorted with prostitutes had been played up by moral purity types for some time. In 1913 Christabel Pankhurst had claimed in *The Great Scourge and How to End It* that 80 per cent of men were infected with venereal diseases, something that even other moralists thought a 'warped' view.[48] Despite the sensational figures that were bandied about during the war, the rates of venereal disease in many forces such as the British army and the German navy were actually lower than they had been in peacetime.

Social Hygiene

When *Ghosts*, Henrik Ibsen's play dealing with syphilis was produced in London in 1891, it was described in the press as: 'as foul and filthy a concoction as has ever been allowed to disgrace the boards of an English theatre'.[49] The war, in gathering together huge masses of young men, forced upon the public and military authorities the extensive discussion of such heretofore tabooed subjects as the treatment of venereal disease, the policing of brothels and the distribution of prophylactics. Following the war and the 1917 revolution, the Soviet Union launched a series of radical sex reforms including the legalization of abortion.[50] Similar experiments were briefly carried out in Hungary. In New York's Greenwich Village the bohemians' defence of 'free love' was accordingly described by its critics as the 'Bolshevism of sex'.[51] As indicated above, however, most of the sexual challenges which contemporaries believed had been produced by the war can be traced back much earlier and their subsequent progress followed a complex course. Nevertheless, most post-war commentators, hankering after a return to old certainties, found it all too easy to attribute every perceived decline in national health or social stability to the conflict's undermining of bourgeois morality.

Would women return to their domestic, maternal roles? Conservatives, attempting to shore up gender boundaries, bewailed the appearance of the independent 'new woman' and the androgynous flapper who adopted fashions that seemed to repudiate her womb and breasts. The assumption was that with looser clothes came looser morals. In France Raymond Radiguet's *Le Diable au corps* (1923) created a sensation in coldly narrating a woman's betrayal of her soldier husband.[52] Veterans attacked the book just as in Germany they bitterly condemned the women who had 'stolen' their jobs.[53] In English courts male juries demonstrated their sympathy for veterans who had been thrown over by their spouses. In June 1920 Edwin Semmens, a demobilized soldier, shot his adulterous wife in the face, telling a friend later, 'I have shot my wife and spoiled her beauty.' Though two sympathetic medical experts argued that Semmens's malaria was to blame for sending him 'over the borderland', the judge instructed the jury that the question of intent was not at issue. Nevertheless, to his indignation and to Semmens's own bewilderment, the jury returned a not guilty verdict.[54] Even the avant-garde post-war writings of D. H. Lawrence and Ernest Hemingway reflected fears of selfish female sexuality. Such responses were understandable given that many equated sexual potency with courage. What fate, some wondered, awaited the thousands of men who in the war had been rendered impotent or suffered genital injuries.[55]

If the war blurred gender lines, the authorities were upon its conclusion all the more insistent that women be relegated to their 'traditional' tasks.[56] French officials saw the need for healthy families and a high birth rate after the great losses of men and the disruption of families.[57] Conservatives everywhere sought to reconstruct a normality that never existed. Those who launched jeremiads against sexual immorality were really talking in coded terms about what they perceived to be a breakdown in social order, deference and authority. Defeated Germany in particular looked to the post-war world for a restoration of order and discipline.[58] The Free Corps, by mutilating and torturing 'dirty' women suspected of supporting the left during the first chaotic years of the Weimar Republic, provided the most extreme example of the political right's equation of sexuality and subversion.[59]

The war also raised the question as to how many men would prove themselves unable to face up to the brutal challenges of the modern world. Well before 1914 degeneration fears were rife. In Britain they came to the surface when the recruitment drives during the Boer war of 1899–1901 revealed that thousands of volunteers were physically unfit. Following the First World War many wondered if the thousands of cripples, amputees and shell-shocked that the conflict had produced would find mates.[60] Intellectually, the conflict, which had been entered into with much macho talk of 'playing the game', gave birth to a culture of resignation and introspection.[61] The bloodletting was taken by many as a sign of the end of an age of reason. Those male cultural rebels of the pre-war period, such as Wilde, Proust and Gide, who had embraced hedonism and castigated the repressive morality of the Victorians, were hailed by the progressives of the 1920s as prophets. Yet for every writer who embraced modernism there were many more who trotted out old but reassuring jingoistic arguments.[62] And if some sophisticated readers of Freud felt that repression was out of fashion and sexual experimentation in vogue they were far outnumbered by those who were alarmed by such ideas.[63]

Would youths know their place? Europe had experienced a total war in which even children had been taught to hate their neighbours.[64] At the same time it had been a generational conflict in which the young had been sacrificed for the old. Nevertheless, the post-war press, filled with stories of children running wild, called for the more stringent disciplining of hooligans, hoodlums and 'problem girls'. The inspection and surveillance of the male body which the war legitimated as well as its military drills and exercises were carried over into the peacetime world through cadet corps, scouts and schools.[65] Pleasure-seeking, dance-crazed youths with too much money and time on their hands, predicted the anxious, would inevitably drift into sexual immorality. If gymnasiums and playing fields failed to steer juveniles away from such temptations more forceful measures would have to be adopted.

Would vice be controlled? The army's preoccupation with venereal disease and prostitution was a carry-over of previous peacetime concerns. Feminists such as Maud Royden had argued that economic distress drove the young woman into prostitution, a point also made by George Bernard Shaw in *Mrs Warren's Profession* (1910): 'It's far better than any other employment open to her.'[66] Conservatives and moral purity activists, who launched the so-called 'white slave' panic, preferred to believe that innocents were shanghaied into the trade by either foreigners or criminals. The obvious intent of the reformers leading the attack against drink and prostitution was not simply to eradicate immorality, but to domesticate and better control workers and immigrants. Poor women, whose sexual standards did not match those of the bourgeoisie, risked being labelled prostitutes. And although three-quarters of the men prosecuted in the United States under the 1910 Mann Act were native born, the police targeted perceived foreigners, Jews and Italians as the most likely pimps. The act was also used to prevent black men consorting with white women. Jack Johnson, hated by racists for having replaced a white man as the heavy-weight boxing champion of the world, was tried and sentenced to a year in jail for purportedly transporting a woman across state lines for 'immoral' purposes.[67]

The question posed by syphilis and gonorrhoea was how respectable society could combat such diseases without appearing to sanction the practices that were believed to produce them. 'It is better', argued one British commentator, 'that venereal diseases should be imperfectly combated than that, in an attempt to prevent them, men should be enticed into mortal sin which they would otherwise avoid.'[68] Progressive doctors responded that the well-being of the community depended on government-supported inspections and treatment. Accordingly, the campaigns against venereal disease in the Anglo-Saxon countries were marked in the first decades of the century by a swing away from moral purity rhetoric that centred on guilt and towards social hygiene programmes that stressed prevention. In the United States John D. Rockefeller established in 1911 the Bureau of Social Hygiene, while in England feminists joined with doctors in 1915 to create the Association for Moral and Social Hygiene. Such groups argued that venereal disease was a medical, not a moral problem. Accordingly, the Royal Commission on Venereal Disease, which reported in 1916 that something over 10 per cent of the male population was infected, called for government-supported clinics.[69] Yet relatively little was accomplished. The Medical Women's Federation still condemned treatment centres for making casual sex safe.[70] Some doctors continued to terrorize and lecture the public though others called for the sexual education of the young.[71] The 'scientific' approach was particularly pushed by eugenicists who advanced the notion that prostitutes were either feeble-minded or degenerate.[72] The respectable press shied away from discussing 'sexual' issues, though any programme that presented 'racial' improvement as its goal was guaranteed serious consideration. Similarly, the most progressive social hygiene lectures to which troops were subjected tended to return to the old theme of the woman as temptress. In 1923, when a twenty-one-year-old Englishman was found guilty of strangling to death the nineteen-year-old woman who had given him venereal disease, the ex-servicemen's association succeeded in drawing up a petition with 50,000 signatures which won his reprieve.[73] The case was known as the 'Damaged Goods' trial, echoing the title of the film shown to troops warning them of the temptations of prostitutes.[74]

Conclusion

In taking millions of men away from their families the First World War, conservatives warned, had seriously eroded male power. Prior to 1914 discussions of sexuality were already coloured by the alarming notion that conventional gender roles were under attack. The spectre of sadists, lesbians and sodomites that the Maud Allan trial conjured up would continue to haunt the respectable. In summing up the case, *The Times* asserted that it was a monstrous libel to claim that England harboured 47,000 perverts. At the same time the editor admitted that moral laxity was spreading.

> But the tolerance of evil is a fertile breeding-ground of suspicion. No public man or woman can afford unnecessary contact with questionable companions. In the days before the war there was growing in London, beyond any sort of question, that passion for excitement and for the latest novelty which is always the familiar beginning of a corrupt society.[75]

The editor thus implicitly acknowledged that the conflict, in crystallizing certain sexual fears, had simply speeded up long-term developments.

By starting an account of twentieth-century sexuality with an examination of the panics precipitated by the First World War and the responses made to them, one is provided with a vantage point from which to view the developments which both preceded and followed it. Contemporaries tended to attribute almost every disturbing moral change to the disruptions caused by the war. The mobilization of the civilian populations which took place in Europe no doubt weakened family structures and gender roles. The body lost much of its mystery as millions of recruits were subjected to medical inspection and discipline. Sexuality was spoken of more openly than it had ever been in the past, related as it was to the health, productivity, racial purity and military strength of the nation.[76] Reproduction assumed a crucial importance with a host of new experts – led by eugenicists, feminists, doctors and birth controllers – calling for an unprecedented public surveillance of childbearing.

Some conservatives continued to find the very discussion of sexual matters unseemly. Sex reformers – more interested in efficiency than morality – broke the conspiracy of silence by replying that such issues as sex education, marital happiness, homosexuality and birth control were too important to ignore. Following the line set by those campaigning against venereal disease, they argued that replacing the older moral purity model with a modern hygienist model of social control would best assure both personal happiness and public order. This did not mean that the biomedical approach purged itself of references to 'immorality' or 'promiscuity' or dangerous 'others'.[77] As will be seen in the following chapters, the sex reformers would produce their own cautionary tales.

The pursuit of sexual modernity would go furthest in the defeated powers – Germany and Russia – where the destruction of the older social hierarchies allowed greater scope for experimentation. In the West, the most original accounts of the sexual shifts produced by the war – the stories of the liberating effect of women's war work produced by Vera Brittain and Radclyffe Hall and the tales of the homoeroticism experienced in the trenches by poets such as Siegfried Sassoon and Wilfred Owen – would only have an impact long after the guns were silenced. It would be an exaggeration to speak of some sudden liberalization of mores. The sexual panics occasioned by the First World War gave birth to many new and sophisticated means of repression. Yet inasmuch as the war focused unprecedented attention on sexuality it did mark the end of an era. Childhood sexuality, marital unhappiness, family limitation and the perversions had all been discussed before, but the war, in devouring millions of men, brought home to the state and the public the vital importance of reproduction. War, Clemenceau had declared, was too important to be left to the generals. A host of twentieth-century experts would add that sexuality was too important to leave to chance.

2

'Hypersexual Youths': Premarital Sex and the Sex Educators

'What are you up to in there, you swine! Open the door at once!' According to Fritz Wittels this was the sort of command that anxious adults, fearing the ravages of masturbation, were known to shout through the bathroom door at their children. As a Freudian, Wittels was concerned that parents and priests in the first decades of this century were continuing to manifest an unhealthy hostility towards all signs of childhood sexuality.[1] His story reflected the progressive view that if adults were effectively to channel their children's passions they would have to abandon the brutal methods of the nineteenth century. The increasingly lengthy cast of sexually preoccupied characters – the masturbator, the adolescent, the troubled youth, the flapper, the wayward girl – who peopled the accounts of early twentieth-century investigators reveals how preoccupied adults were by the sex lives of the young.

Childhood

Though nostalgic writers of the 1920s claimed that the childhood 'age of innocence' had been imperilled as a result of the war, in fact the very notion that children should be sexual innocents was a relatively recent development. Only in the nineteenth century had important social changes such as the introduction of compulsory education and restrictions on child labour led to the age grading that the middle classes quickly assumed was 'natural'.[2] In the early modern world one's fate had been largely determined by social status – it was expected that the propertied would have lives distinctly different from the poor. By 1900, however, experts claimed that there was a biologically determined, 'appropriate' age to be in school, to be courting, to marry.[3] Among the most striking examples of the policing of age grading was the insistence that children be kept in ignorance about sex. The nineteenth-century fear of educating children too early was often successful in inculcating an unfamiliarity with the basic facts of life.[4] One woman raised in an Essex village at the turn of the century recalled that in her family there was no discussion of reproduction.

> When your sister was born you'd be about six or seven?
> Yes.
> Was it concealed from you how babies were born and that sort of thing?
> I hadn't the faintest idea – I didn't know how babies were born then, no.
> Where did you think your sister came from then?
> Well, the old story that we were taught, under some gooseberry bushes.[5]

Early twentieth-century autobiographies are full of similar accounts of both the deflecting of embarrassing questions of children and the policing of the morals of youth. Some girls claimed to be completely ignorant of sexual functioning right up to marriage. One wonders if middle-class girls really were ignorant or simply playing a role. Girls in convent schools were certainly kept under constant surveillance. But their desires were elicited rather than repressed by warnings not to watch themselves while urinating, not to look up other girls' skirts, not to rub or touch their privates. Many memoirists recall the birth of a younger sibling precipitating questions which parents sought to divert. Mysterious problems were conjured up in children's minds by vague though vociferous parental castigations of filth, immorality, vice, the 'unnatural' and the 'unspeakable'. Children were left puzzled, curious and often worried. Boys wondered why adults said it was vulgar to keep their hands in their pockets. Girls pondered why each night mother would ask 'Where are your hands?' Why were they supposed to be above the covers? Children exchanged whatever information they stumbled on; they learned not to ask adults awkward questions.

The late Victorians, by their very insistence on the notion that childhood was an age of innocence during which any interest in sexual matters was unhealthy, inadvertently forced the 'discovery' of childhood sexuality. Logically enough their first concern was the masturbating child. In condemning masturbation the middle class fixated on the notion that children were unwittingly falling victims to the very privacy and individualism which middle-class adults so highly valued. The hedonistic autonomy sponsored by the rise of consumer capitalism thus by a cruel irony returned, in the guise of infantile self-abuse, to haunt the bourgeoisie.[6] The nineteenth-century adage that if one 'spent' one's physiological capital, the result would be physical and psychological exhaustion was parroted well into the twentieth century.[7] Self-abuse, the gloomy claimed, was more sapping than normal intercourse because it could be repeated whenever desired. At the very least, asserted tracts with titles such as 'The Mishandled Sex Life', premature pleasures took the bloom off one's later love life.[8]

Mothers were accordingly advised to train their offspring early. 'Tell them that little children, sometimes when they do not know this, form the habit of handling themselves and as a result they become listless and sick, and many times idiotic and insane, or develop epileptic fits. This will so impress them that they will not fall easily into the bad habit.'[9] Baden-Powell called masturbation 'beastliness' and included in *Scouting for Boys* various suggestions on how best to counter the contagion of self-abuse. F. Arthur Sibly, a headmaster who claimed to have received hundreds of letters from school children, struck a similarly sour note. He located himself in the 'Muscular Christian' camp of Alfred Lyttelton, A. C. Benson, Clement Dukes and Baden-Powell and as an enemy of the quacks who tried to exploit sexual fears. He declared that nocturnal emissions were not normal and even condemned self-consciousness as the symptom of an 'unclean inner life'. The 'prevalence of impurity among boys' he attributed to a lack of adult direction. Self-abuse, he warned, wore out the nerves and brain, led to short, enfeebled lives and was responsible for seductions, prostitution and divorce.

Even refined, middle-class boys, stated Sibly, fell prey to their 'foul desires' due to the instruction of brothers, friends, servants or 'street boys'. Traitorous nurses stroked toddlers to put them in a good temper. Once a sufferer became addicted to such practices their fate was sealed. Some died, some contracted St Vitus's Dance. Sibly could spot such victims. He had once been puzzled by a boy who was shy, artistic, conscientious and a 'duffer' at games. Sibly could now, he boasted, instantly detect the problem. 'With my present experience I should have known him to be a victim of self abuse.'[10] Sibly said that he had only known two boys who were totally ignorant of the vice, and cited Rugby's medical officer who claimed that 95 per cent of public school boys were abusers. Few who spoke of the ravages caused by masturbation explained how such a deadly vice could be so prevalent. Sibly, following William Acton and G. Stanley Hall, called for less discretion and more straight talk from parents to prevent their sons from becoming 'vicious'. If boys were not saved they would go on to make terrible marriages. Raising his rhetoric to ludicrous heights, Sibly concluded by asking: 'Who would not rather that his daughter were killed in her innocence than that she should be doomed to such a fate?'[11]

What did boys think of such warnings? George Orwell suffered from a sort of social amnesia in believing that turn-of-the-century young people were unperturbed by the passions and that magazines like *Chum* and *Magnet* made no mention of sex.[12] A glance at the responses in the 'Letters to the Editor' column provides evidence that there were worried young readers.

> BAD HABITS (J. B.) Are we not constantly warning our readers against this manhood-sapping habit? We can do no more. If boys choose to kill themselves, the sin is theirs. We do our duty. Consult your doctor. The sooner the better, too.

> MORE NERVOUSNESS (Rufus) – Nervousness and shyness are on the increase, owing partly to boys' evil habits (in secret) and to the taking of quack medicines. No physic will cure you. Only entire regeneration of health, such as is being so often explained in these pages.[13]

The medical world was not much more sophisticated in its response to childhood sexuality. Freud, it is generally believed, stood out from his colleagues in attributing the exhaustion, weaknesses and timidity of his male patients to psychological problems rather than to self-abuse. Henry Campbell and Arthur Cooper, with their dire predictions about the dangers of masturbation, and F. W. Mott with his warnings of the perils posed by the loss of the 'highly phosphorized nucleo-proteids contained in the sperm', seem far removed from the measured introspection of Freud's better known works. Yet, as Freud made clear in *An Autobiographical Study*, his 'momentous step' in starting out on his own path of discovery was made in linking the hysteria of his patients to their onanism.[14]

Some doctors, like James Paget in England, pooh-poohed the dangers of masturbation.[15] F. R. Sturgis, professor of medicine at the City University of New York who dedicated a 1902 study to the 'sexual cripples of the United States', went so far as to joke about 'the homely pleasure of the hand'.[16] The majority of physicians at the turn of the century thought it safer to adopt far more conservative positions. Indeed, circumcision was popularized in the United States in the twentieth century in part because doctors regarded the operation as a way of preventing self-abuse.

Progressives

But by the first decades of the twentieth century childhood sexual experimentation was beginning to find some defenders. Havelock

Ellis attacked the fear-mongering associated with self-abuse, and intimated that only extreme cases posed any real problem. Ellis, noting that in 1892 Silvio Venturi had spoken of masturbation as a seed that would eventually grow into adult heterosexual love, agreed that masturbation was not a serious problem. Freud spoke of the 'primacy of the phallus' but if one only looked closely, Ellis quipped, it was obvious that real toddlers believed in the 'primacy of the thumbs and toes'.[17]

In France 'Dr Caufeynon' provided, in *L'Onanisme chez l'homme*, an equally balanced account of masturbation. The author, after noting that the ancients were untroubled by the vice, observed that only after the appearance of the works of Tissot in the late eighteenth century were excitement, imagination and heredity targeted as causes of self-abuse. Admitting that because of 'sympathy' excessive masturbation could be harmful to the whole body, the book concluded by asserting that work and exercise were better than the terror and mechanical restraints brandished by some nineteenth-century doctors and that, in any event, boys almost always dropped such habits once they discovered women.[18]

W. F. Robie, an American physician, provided in his casebooks the remarkably candid accounts of hundreds of patients' early sexual experiences. Robie noted that his observations supported many of Freud's contentions concerning childhood sexuality. Thumb-sucking, Robie conceded, was sometimes sexual in nature. Most children's first conscious sexual experiences came from watching animals, pressing their thighs against a desk, being hugged by a nurse.[19] A fifty-two-year-old woman told Robie that she had not masturbated as a child but was excited by seeing cats mating.[20] Robie's patients, unlike Freud's, had few memories of events prior to the age of five or six and provided little evidence of suffering from an Oedipal complex. Robie presented children's first sexual hurdle as having to deal with self-stimulation. One man recalled finding that climbing trees excited him and he decided it must be a good thing.[21] A girl found that sliding down banisters gave her similar pleasure. Some recalled that French playing cards were pleasantly arousing. Many were taught to masturbate by friends.[22] One confidant recalled that when he was twelve older boys had the younger suck them off, sometimes putting sugar on their prepuces.[23] A twenty-seven-year-old American college graduate recalled in 1916: 'When eight years of age witnessed a boy of thirteen get up a step-ladder behind a mare and attempt intercourse. Thought this a good idea.'[24] Mrs R. C., a fifty-year-old patient of Robie, confessed that she and her sister, when eight and nine, sucked the penises of two little boys aged four and five which led to feelings of shame. She was later haunted by the notion that insanity would result from masturbation. Her doctor was hardly helpful. He made a practice of kissing his female patients and went so far as to put his penis on Mrs R. C.'s vagina.[25]

Robie was unusually frank in his acceptance of masturbation. He stressed that most of his confidants who had practised it had suffered no ill effects. He noted it was certainly less risky than intercourse which could result in venereal disease.[26] He knew that the Freudians did not approve of auto-erotic practices and some went so far as to suggest that their adult male patients find relief with prostitutes. Robie declared that this was an unethical suggestion inasmuch as in doing so the patient ran real risks.[27]

Robie reported cases of some youths being preyed on by their elders. But here again the long-term effects of sexual predation were, he concluded, sometimes hard to judge. A man who went on to be a successful lawyer reported that an older judge had once gone down on him.[28] Robie interviewed one woman who recalled: 'from earliest memory father practised tickling clitoris with tongue and with fingers whenever he could get opportunity. Great aversion to this, but some sensation aroused by it.'[29] Until the age of eleven or twelve she thought that all fathers acted the same way. She did observe that she differed from other girls in one aspect; they could show their fathers affection but she for some reason could not. Eventually her mother discovered what was going on; in fact, all the daughters had been similarly treated and she threatened to leave her husband unless it stopped. Robie's patient claimed that these incestuous activities had left no ill effects though she did admit that she had to fantasize to have pleasure with her husband.

Children frequently had to be taught to be ashamed of their sexual knowledge. Their sexual activities were usually discovered by parents inadvertently.[30] Since their sexual interaction with adults was usually only reported by the traumatized in subsequent therapeutic sessions or court cases, the impression was given that they were always passive victims. Many young people were abused and sexually exploited but there is evidence that in some cases natural curiosity and at times even self-serving calculation could play a role in such encounters. Investigators who assumed that every child was an 'innocent' were not so much seeking to protect the young as to deny the complexities of childhood sexuality.

Gauging the impact of injunctions against self-abuse and early sexual experiences is a difficult undertaking. Doctors dealt mainly with the confessions of those who found sexuality a problem. One fifty-year-old male confessed to Robie that he was so afraid that self-abuse

would bring on insanity that he tied down his penis.[31] Quack literature offering cures for intemperance undoubtedly aroused some
while it scared off others. Marie Stopes, the British birth control advocate, received many letters from men worried that their habit would
destroy their sex life.[32] Many took on board the arguments of pessimistic doctors and quacks though obviously the problem of an addiction to self-abuse would only be mentioned by those worrying about
it. Although Stopes herself tried to be reassuring, she did argue that
masturbation undermined males' sexual sensitivity. Far more negative
views regarding masturbation were still in wide circulation throughout
the inter-war period. The writers of the sex education books of the
1940s thought themselves progressive in arguing that the anxieties created by the fear of being a masturbator were worse than masturbation itself. No one lauded the positive pleasures of self-abuse.

Young people learned how to be ignorant. Common myths that
children worried about in England in the 1940s included the idea
that kissing could lead to pregnancy, that self-abuse caused a loss
of blood, and that the baby came out of the stomach.[33] Exactly how
'ignorant' children in fact were is difficult to determine. The assumption is often made that evidence of the 'facts of life' was something
that farming and working-class children, living in cramped living
conditions, would have had difficulty in ignoring. But a woman born
in Italy in 1918 recalled 'We grew up knowing nothing about sex or
learning the wrong way. It isn't true that we in the countryside understood because we were close to nature. Yes, we saw animals [do it],
but we didn't understand.'[34] Oral history accounts tell us that in England boys called the penis the 'little man', 'willy', 'dick', 'chopper'
or 'mouse'. The girl had a 'Mary', 'winkie' or 'ha'penny' (half-penny),
hence the cautionary ditty:

> Keep your hand on yer ha'penny
> Cover it well with your palm
> Keep yer hand on yer ha'penny
> And you'd never come to no harm.[35]

Knowledge was gained on the street or, as adults would have it, 'in
the gutter'. Inevitably every boy had a smutty friend who spread
information and passed on jokes or magazines. Yet ignorance and
shame clouded many young people's understanding. Children had to
pretend when with more worldly friends that they knew more than
they actually did. By the time they were adolescents they did not
want to be instructed by parents; to be offered such advice was taken
as an embarrassing intrusion.

Youth

Late nineteenth-century social observers of youth tended to worry more about boys than about girls. Young women, it was assumed, simply had to be prepared for marriage whereas young men had to be trained for more important and complex roles in the worlds of labour, the military and politics.[36] The American psychologist G. Stanley Hall raised the alarm that boys were put at risk in an urban environment.[37] Such new preoccupations with protecting young men fuelled the late nineteenth-century campaigns against smoking, dancing, drinking, lurid dime novels, and what one observer called the 'gangrene of pornography'.[38] Moral entrepreneurs such as René Beranger in France and Anthony Comstock in the United States created repressive leagues calling for censorship.[39] In France pornography in particular was seen as fuelling the threats of national degeneration and depopulation.[40] If one were to believe such propagandists, young men on the continent were exposed outside *lycées* and at *fêtes patronales*, at cafés-concerts and theatres to a constant barrage of temptations and seductions. Salacious material came in the forms of cards, photographs, newspapers, books, stereoscopes and cinematographs. Boys were offered, in publications that carried advertisements for *moyens anti-conceptionnels* and abortifacients, the purchase of everything from lewd slides to fully inflatable rubber women.[41] Immorality led to debauchery; overexcitation to sadism, heterosexual excesses finally to homosexuality. Pornography was declared to be even more dangerous than antimilitaristic propaganda to new nations; the debauched not only failed to reproduce, they became rebels or 'Apaches' who drifted into criminality. For the Republic to survive, claimed the moral purists, let alone prove its moral superiority to other regimes, it was necessary to silence those seeking to drag young men down into immorality.[42]

The conservatives, despite their exaggerated fears, at least broke the silence surrounding sexual issues. The sex education books of Sylvanus Stall, a Lutheran minister, Emma Drake and Mary Wood Allan were international best-sellers. Stall's *What a Young Boy Should Know*, which brandished the threats of idiocy and death for masturbators, was incredibly popular.[43] It was translated into many languages including Urdu, Arabic, Hindi, Bengali and Korean.[44] In France, Paul Good, who claimed that his book *Hygiène et morale: étude dédiée aux jeunes gens* (1898) had sold 585,000 copies in seventeen languages, attacked the old idea that youth has to sow wild oats. Citing experts such as Dr Adrien Proust, the novelist's father, he argued that early sexual experiences led to ill health, tuberculosis and failed exams.[45]

Those interested in protecting the race had to battle with the argument that youth had 'to have it'.[46]

According to a 1919 text by Mary Scharlieb and F. Arthur Sibly, adolescence went on to about the age of twenty-five when the individual was 'approximating to the adult type'.[47] The young girl was mentally and morally 'soft' so liable to 'irreparable damage'. The young working-class girl unfortunately had 'too little to learn' about sex. Her middle-class counterpart was bewildered but the authors noted that society now had franker and healthier discussions of sexuality than had been the case forty years before. The concerned parent stressed order, obedience and self-restraint. Some days the adolescent girl needed rest but her parents were not to let her day dream. She had to be saved from herself and prepared by useful employments for her role. 'The highest earthly ideal for a woman is that she should be a good wife and a good mother.'[48] All her training was to be directed to that end. She needed – in addition to reverence for her body – a knowledge of physiological facts; otherwise marriage would come as a 'shock'.

Curiously enough Sibly did not seek to counter self-abuse by encouraging boys to interest themselves in girls. He sneered at young men's 'ludicrously indiscriminate and exaggerated susceptibility to female attractions'.[49] In fact, he claimed that a boy 'if he gets into the habit of exchanging glances with girls who are socially inferior' would be prone to immorality.[50] In this regard Sibly shared with people like Baden-Powell the notion that there was a 'girl problem' from which boys had to be protected. Sibly went so far as to suggest that young men be subjected to hypnotism to save them from the attractions of sexuality. Some, he knew, regarded it as a Svengali trick.

> Altogether the time for hypnotic suggestion in education is not yet, but the day must come when its use is recognised not only in the physical cases such as nocturnal emissions and constipation, but in all cases in which the will power is practically in abeyance, as in bad cases of impurity.[51]

In the late twentieth century one naturally associates sexuality with youth but this is a fairly recent phenomenon. For the social observers of the nineteenth century the 'youth problem' had been posed by the potential criminality of working-class delinquents; only in the 1920s was the term applied to sexually adventurous middle-class youths.[52] Traditionally young people had policed their own morality through such institutions as the charivari.[53] In the twentieth century they were increasingly supposed to be in school under the tutelage of adults. In fact, it was only in the 1900s that one could say that the majority of young people in the Western world experienced the curious stage of life known as 'adolescence' in which one was sexually mature but still treated as a child. The word itself had only been coined in the 1880s by the American G. Stanley Hall. Hall used the recapitulation theory of evolution in *Adolescence* (1904) to popularize the notion that youths went through a second birth. He warned that at this time, when they were most impressionable, they had to be protected against falling victim to the sexual temptations offered by the city.[54] Hall was only one of many commentators to call for the dependency of the young to be prolonged. As a result of recently enforced laws on compulsory education and protective labour legislation, working-class as well as middle-class young people were increasingly prevented from entering the workforce until much later than had traditionally been the case. Moral purity campaigners even made some attempts to have the age of consent raised and to restrict marriage. Underlying these new fears of precocity was the notion, popularized by nineteenth-century writers such as Orson Fowler and Elizabeth Blackwell, of the 'convertibility of energy'. Youthful energy, if used up in sex, it was claimed, would result in a depletion of mental resources.[55] 'Manliness', argued educators, was best developed for boys in schools and colleges where they would be isolated from the dangerous sexuality of the urban world. Sports were encouraged to work off steam. In the age of Edgar Rice Burroughs and Teddy Roosevelt good, clean 'fun' of the sporty, outdoors variety was vaunted as a way of countering compromising contacts with females. Baden-Powell, having condemned masturbation, went on to describe girls as another threat to male innocence. Boys, he asserted, if they were to do their duty to the race, had to postpone gratification.

Temptation was all the greater in the early 1900s as both boys and girls were reaching puberty at an earlier age. The onset of the girl's period posed special problems. Reformers gave accounts of girls kept in ignorance of menstruation and accordingly so alarmed at its appearance that they feared bleeding to death. Some sat in the snow to stop the blood; others secretly washed their soiled clothing.[56] Doctors no longer prescribed bed rest for their middle-class patients but sanitary products were slow to enter the market. Sanitary towels or 'jam rags' were home-made, washed and re-used well into the twentieth century. In Britain the first commercial brands were sold under the names of Silcot, Mene, Southalls and Dr Whites; in the 1940s Boots introduced disposables which by the 1950s were being sold in machines. But tampons, introduced in 1936, were opposed by some Catholics for fear that they would break the hymen.[57] The age of sexual maturity of girls in the nineteenth century had been marked by wide variations. Well-fed, middle-class young women had their first periods at about fourteen, several years before their poorer sisters. In the twentieth century the age of menarche dropped and the class disparities began to shrink. Yet adults sought to protect girls more than in the past; working-class parents were, for example, less likely to send them out to work as domestics. The ideal was for them to remain at home until marriage. Both boys and girls were more iso-lated from the adult community by longer years of schooling and increasingly shut out of the job market. The irony was that in seeking to protect youths from the real world adults failed to note that the passions were all that some young people were left to explore. The rise of youth culture was a way of establishing an identity half-way between that of the child and the adult. It could be claimed that parents who accepted the tenets of a world of consumerism that lauded the pursuit of personal gratification should not have been surprised that their more adventurous children turned to sexual experi-mentation, but of course they were.

Some parents were not sure whether same-sex experimentation was any more or less troubling than heterosexual adventures. The term 'heterosexual' only came into popular usage in the 1920s. In the early decades of the century there was a good deal of openness about adolescent same-sex 'crushes' or passions. Auguste Forel, the Swiss sexologist, who had advanced the argument that 'compen-satory' masturbation was permissible, stated that 'essential Onanism' was problematic as it led on to homosexuality.[58] The comforting argument that cases of 'inversion' (as homosexuality was known) were mere schoolboy flings that could be cured by marriage was asserted by Pierre Garnier.[59] Court authorities certainly did not regard boy victims of same-sex seductions as suspiciously and judgement-ally as they did female rape victims. Kinsey's figures for the 1930s – admittedly drawn from a skewed sample – revealed a rise in male homosexual experiences from 16 to 30 per cent.[60] Such figures were not available in the inter-war period, but anxieties about male hetero-sexuality led to the defensive creation by fiction writers such as Sinclair Lewis of the caricatured effeminate homosexual as the antithesis of the real man.[61]

A 1924 Student Christian Movement book noted that girls were slower to realize their sexual desires and were often first infatuated by other girls. These 'grand passions' could go too far. Such same-sex relations the author condemned as a sort of regression. 'It cannot give a woman children. It leaves part of her hungry.' Neverthe-less, because war losses left Britain with a million 'excess' women he imagined that many women would live together and might even adopt children.[62] In America Katherine Bement Davis's pioneering 1929 sex survey revealed the importance of women's homosexual experiences. Twenty-six per cent had indulged in 'overt practices' but subsequently moved on to a heterosexual life with no 'evil consequences'.[63] Bibby, the English sex educator, who noted that many girls had 'crushes' on female teachers, was less sanguine.[64] He declared homosexuality 'a real deviation' which he felt was due partly to sex segregation in schools.

As opportunities for youths to meet expanded in the twentieth century so too did attempts to police them. In rural areas encounters were made at fairs and in towns via the new leisure activities of skating, swimming and bicycling parties. Young people met at the seaside in summer, at skating parties in winter, at Bank Holiday week-end fêtes. Churches promoted sports events and Sunday School outings. Vaudevilles and melodramas offered racier settings. In the first decade of the century the movie-house became the new leisure centre that required no special dress. By 1910 one-quarter of New York's population was attending on a weekly basis. Some reformers hailed the movie-house as safer than the saloon; others feared the promiscuity which they imagined would take place in the semi-darkness.

Dances particularly preoccupied the censorious. Young girls in New York danced in the street and as adolescents went to dance halls in pursue of excitement, romance and glamour. The city boasted five hundred dance halls in 1910. The earliest were attached to saloons but purpose-built ballrooms emerged in the first decade of the twentieth century. Middle-class observers, such as the members of the anti-vice Committee of Fourteen, were appalled by the lack of propriety paraded in such institutions. The respectable associated such places with prostitutes and 'taxi dancers'. The failure of the middle class either to discriminate between prostitution and legal sex or to be able to tell by appearance who was a prostitute and who was not was understandable. For working-class young women fancy dress and display were increasingly important; the hats, high heels, make up, lipstick and plucked eyebrows all conferred status. It was also true that the 'tough dancing' styles that became popular emerged from the sporting houses. Older styles such as the waltz were replaced by close dancing that allowed the man to handle his partner and elicit 'sexual excitement'.[65] The respectable particularly attacked jazz as over-stimulating.

Middle-class establishments had tables and barriers to prevent the promiscuous mixing one found in a dance hall. Respectable young women went on a 'date'. Working-class girls were more likely to be 'picked up' at a dance hall. In New York they were called 'charity girls' because they were purported to barter sexual favours for a night out of amusement, fun and entertainment. Such a barter economy promised pleasures but on occasion posed dangers. Mixed messages might be misunderstood. A chance encounter could be the beginning of a romantic relationship or it might result in a blurring of the line separating rape and consensual sex. As the men treated, they expected some remuneration and possible sexual reciprocation. Some working-class girls did barter their favours; they were 'game', their morals were flexible, but they did not see themselves as prostitutes. They would not allow sex on a first date; on a subsequent one perhaps. They were aware of the risks and looked to friends for protection from exploitation. The fact that such independent young women could actually go out by themselves was what most bothered middle-class observers. They were outraged by what they took to be young women's immorality; workers were more realistic. Given wage disparities, male financial support was essential if young women were to have any social life. The same was true in Britain where one man recalled, 'Really, we were pretty poor like, you know! Really in them days, you know, we couldn't afford to take a girl out, in a way of speaking. And in them days, as we are talking about, the, the boy was supposed to pay for girl tut' pitchers, and a bar o' choc'lat'.'[66] Young people who 'kept company' but could not afford a dance or film had to seek privacy in parks, fields, back alleys and family parlours.

Courtship

In this context of concern about restless adolescents, social critics condemned what they took to be the decline of traditional forms of courtship. Though young women were put more at risk by the erosion of traditional sexual boundaries they were the ones targeted in the barrage of works describing and condemning the new sexual mores. Young women were kept under close surveillance. In Viennese working-class households, for example, girls were not given the house key so that they had to be home before the family retired. For middle-class Americans, the 'date' in which a man took the woman out, displaced the tradition of 'calling' in which men visited women at their parents' home. Particularly in the large city, the 'date' and its petting techniques emerged in the first decades of this century and courtship evolved from a female- to a male-controlled ritual. In European women's magazines advice columns began to give suggestions on how to flirt and kiss.[67] In America, middle-class youths escaped chaperonage in the automobile and made the shift, as one historian has put it, 'from front porch to back seat'.[68]

The young middle-class man, with more economic power, having taken a date out, anticipated sexual favours. Traditionally the legitimate extent of intimacy was fixed by the rules of the community, but to some the lines between 'good' and 'bad' girls appeared to blur. A sense of the shifts in attitudes of youth towards sexuality was found in the earliest sex surveys, the queries sent to well-known progressives like Judge Ben Lindsey and the letters to the personal advice columns. Youths expected greater heterosexual freedom but a common complaint was that the greater flexibility of the dating system made it harder for both women and men to be 'good'.[69] Nevertheless, the majority of middle-class youths retained the ideal, if not the practice, of premarital chastity.

For young men the Victorian model of masculinity that stressed self-control, discipline and delayed gratification was slowly replaced by new notions of elegant manliness, personified by Rudolph Valentino's *The Sheik* (1921). Thomas Mann was pleased to note that the German youths of the 1920s were 'no longer martial, stiff-backed, with heels clicked together, and heavily moustached'.[70] Yet middle-class males, unlike their female counterparts, could still, without fear of loss of reputation, enter the sexual underworld and cross class barriers. Harlem was a magnet for white Americans seeking a freer, exotic sexual milieu. Similarly in Europe such adventures in rougher neighbourhoods were appealing as sexual mores in the working class were thought to be advanced and less inhibited and popular districts more tolerant of pornography, prostitution and homosexuality.[71] Working-class dance halls, patronized by middle-class males, served as a conduit by which new sexual fashions in dance percolated up to the bourgeoisie.

The 1920s saw much talk about the waning of the double standard and the new male models of gentle eroticism and athleticism provided by Valentino and Fairbanks, but the sexual double standard did not disappear; indeed, young men enjoyed greater freedoms. Typically, the young man who assaulted one of Robie's confidantes sensed no loss of face when his advances were rebuffed. 'At nineteen, when working in a hotel, a young man asked her to go for a walk. In a secluded place he threw her down and jumped upon her, but she screamed and he desisted. He asked her what she went to walk for, anyway, and later asked her to name some girl who would go out with him.'[72] The laws policing rape, seduction and abduction targeted males but in general boys were permitted greater sexual latitude. There was no concept of a 'loose' man.

The Flapper

Many held the First World War responsible for undermining youth's sexual morality. Those who in the early 1900s were concerned by masturbation and premarital sex went on to condemn in the 1920s nude bathing, the modern dance craze, jazz, and bobbed hair. Their fixation on the 'new woman', flapper, flirt, *demi-vierge* and 'hyper-sexual female' indicated that women's sexuality was considered particularly dangerous. French commentators noted just before the war that the term 'flirt' had been introduced to France.[73] The term was employed by commentators made nervous by evidence that women were mixing more with men and brazenly using their sexuality to make relationships. 'Flappers' were critiqued for adopting styles that exposed their arms and legs and for otherwise being socially aggressive. It is likely that young women were changing more than young men; contemporaries certainly thought so. When a post-war drug panic was sparked in England by the death of the socialite Billie Carleton, the report of her friendship with blacks and use of cocaine was the press's coded way of expressing fears of female autonomy and sexuality.[74] Similarly, the titillating appeal of the fast, young characters played by film stars Clara Bow and Louise Brooks in the 1920s stemmed from the notion that the relationship of the 'gold-digger' or designing woman and an older, wealthy man bordered on prostitution. Adults worried that young women were drawn to movies that glamourized vice, just as young men were to movies that glorified violence.[75]

Even women who had fought for the vote prior to the war were critical of the new female generation's purported fixation on sexuality. After observing the young women of the 1920s, Lorine Pruette cited the line 'freedom for women is God's greatest gift to men' as a warning that the flapper's supposed independence actually put her at risk. The young woman expressed a tough-mindedness and breezy casualness but was she in fact more hard-boiled, cooler and more direct than her predecessor? Was her mind as 'free as her legs'? Pruette dismissively categorized the flapper as a perennial adolescent who gamely envisaged having 'a job or two, a man or two, a child or two, and none of them will be as good as she feels in her heart she deserves'.[76]

Mary Ware Dennett agreed that the young people of the 1920s were 'not only yelping noisily about freedom, but they are ostentatiously showing the world that they dare all sorts of exhibitionism which only a few years ago was rare enough to be extraordinary'.[77] Yet underneath their hard-boiled exteriors she believed they were anxious. After a first sexual fling they felt only dissatisfaction. Dennett hoped to bring romance back to youth. They needed some sense of the 'beauty' of sex to feel happy rather than just wicked. The idea that young women in the 1920s, bombarded by discussions of sex, were apparently knowing but in fact confused was also expressed by Phyllis Blanchard. She thought she detected a conservative shift with girls going back to long dresses while their elders were in short skirts.[78]

Lorine Pruette doubted the rebelliousness of the young women of the 1920s, arguing that they were goaded on by mothers who had not been kissed enough in their youth who sought vicariously to enjoy their daughters' high jinks. She also suggested that the dissemination of psychoanalysis was making fathers nervous of caressing their own daughters who in turn were driven prematurely into heterosexuality. Did the lifting of old taboos actually increase happiness? She thought not, presenting a sad picture of a party of drunk, 'soggy, sodden college students' left on their own by their parents. She thought progressives like Judge Lindsey were wrong to believe that youth wanted to experiment; in reality they were just following the herd instincts of mass society.[79] The middle-aged were abandoning the young – for example, by giving up chaperonage – rather than the young striking off on their own. Youth was forced to be free. 'Is that all?' she claimed girls soon asked, finding that compulsory pleasure was as bad as coercive repression.

Pruette cited figures from Phyllis Blanchard and Carlyn Manasses's study to show how confused young women were about sexuality.[80] Only 20 per cent disapproved of smoking but their sample of 252 girls was split on the propriety of drinking. Twenty per cent accepted petting as part of a normal date. Ninety-two per cent said premarital sex was either immoral or unwise but over half admitted that they would not disapprove of a friend who indulged.[81] Seventy per cent would accept a fiancé having had earlier experiences and 49 per cent would tell him of theirs. Most favoured divorce and 80 per cent planned on using birth control. All believed in companionate marriage though 45 per cent believed it would have to offer economic security as well. They still saw as their goal in life being a good wife and mother. What Pruette most regretted was that the young women of the inter-war period knew nothing of the struggles of the feminists.

> But the flapper knows nothing of that tedious world against which the old-line feminists rebelled. She knows nothing of the fight and cares less. 'Feminism?' she asks nonchalantly. 'Oh, you mean anti-man stuff? No, I'm not a feminist.' Nothing is so dead as the won causes of yesterday; there is no reason why she should think of herself as a feminist; she has inherited feminism.[82]

Most of the evidence suggests that youth's desire in the inter-war period was fairly traditional. The goal of sexual intimacy was marriage and so promiscuity was condemned by the young while premarital sex was condoned. A 1930s study of 1,300 American college students revealed that 25 per cent of the women were non-virgins and another 37 per cent were willing to take the jump. Forty-nine per cent said they accepted the morality of sex before marriage if it was an act of love.[83] Men, the researchers found, felt pressured to prove themselves sexually, though, unlike women, they were not castigated for pursuing pleasure. Young women continued to anticipate employing sexuality to confirm a romantic attachment. Their sexuality was their 'social capital' which had to be invested wisely. Simple desire was not motivating such youths; they regarded sexual encounters not as ends in themselves but as essential means by which women pursued the traditional coupling process.

Sex Education

Following the First World War and the fright over the high levels of venereal disease discovered among the troops, social hygienists propounded the need for sex education to protect the race. Most of this literature was fear-mongering. Canadian girls were instructed that those who were 'accustomed to self-control' were safe but those who flaunted a 'love of excitement or ignorance of certain of the fundamental facts concerning sex laws' were at risk.[84] The conservative line was continued in the inter-war period by writers such as Meyrick Booth who declared that the moral crisis in Britain was as important as the economic depression. Booth attacked Dr J. B. Watson for suggesting that people act like animals, Bertrand Russell for defending sexual experimentation, Judge Lindsey for describing the 'barbaric licence' of petting parties, and Sigmund Freud for seeking to replace reason with 'instinctivism'.[85] Booth, following Keyserling and other conservative theorists, held that women's dominance in the United States led to a mother complex and the 'infantilism' of men, and cited D. H. Lawrence to prove that males and females were qualitatively different.[86]

Youth, claimed Booth, had lost its traditional moral moorings. Girls, no longer fearing pregnancy, pursued sex. And because they increasingly received the same education as boys a 'pseudo-masculinism' resulted that ill prepared young women for motherhood.[87] What Booth regarded as 'artificial' equality had produced a race of celibate Amazons. Feminism, by encouraging women to enter the workforce, 'encouraged this home destroying process'.[88] Family allowances, he predicted, would further undermine the responsibilities of parents and obliterate the notion of illegitimacy.

Leslie D. Weatherhead in *The Mastery of Sex* (1931) trotted out the old monetary metaphor to warn promiscuous youth. He lamented the fate of the man who had 'dribbled away in harmful frivolity something that belongs to another who may be keeping herself for him with far finer self-control. The gold he spends like this belongs to her and when she comes to him as his wife he finds he has not quite so much in the bank of love to give.'[89] Weatherhead backed up this injunction with the even sadder story of 'Martin' who, having rashly indulged in sex, guiltily committed suicide. Yet Weatherhead was actually in favour of sex education. Silence was a mistake, he claimed, since uneducated youth could stumble into sin; the psychological problems that resulted were as bad as the moral ones. He argued that women not instructed by parents as children about the facts of life were less likely to have successful sex lives. He advanced figures to show that 84 per cent of those so instructed before the age of six were orgasmic as opposed to only 4 per cent instructed after the age of twelve.[90] Weatherhead said that companionship was healthy; flirting was not. He likened it to dropping a match into an explosives room. Yet he stressed that one should not talk of 'bottled-up' energy; what were needed were sacrifices and he hoped that soon England would have a 'Youth Movement' like Germany's to provide healthy companionship.[91] The desire of moralists such as Weatherhead to make all youths – the middle class as much as the working class – more dependent was manifested in the creation by adults of groups such as the YMCA, YWCA, Band of Hope, Boys' Brigade, Scouts and their socialist equivalents, such as the Red Falcons in Austria. 'Our youth', declared an Austrian socialist, sounding very much like his conservative counterpart, 'must be prepared to fight against the sex drive when it challenges the demands of socialist morality.'[92]

More progressive views on sex education began to appear in the 1920s. Dennett noted that much sex education had used fears of venereal disease 'to scare and browbeat young people into continence'. She considered it an insult that the purity types – the 'emotionally illiterate' – should stoop to such tactics in books with such morbid titles as *Why We Must Behave*.[93] Judge Ben Lindsey of Colorado won notoriety by arguing that sexual experimenting be regarded as natural. Yet in the United States Max Exner's popular pamphlets, produced for the YMCA, *The Question of Petting* (1926) and *Education for Marriage* (1933) were moralistic in tone.[94] Such works tended to begin with the notion that embarrassed parents were failing to provide the facts of life and that boys needed education, girls protection. Social as

well as gender relationships were reinforced. Sex education was produced by the middle class and directed at the working class.

Some radicals did take culture into account. Scott Nearing, after a
1925 visit to the Soviet Union, declared that there the child was at last
free.[95] Margaret Mead undermined G. Stanley Hall's views on the set
stages of youth. In her famous study of Samoan young people she
pointed out that the pressures of adolescence were not universal but
linked to particular cultures.[96] She lamented the fact that in the civilized world physical facts were denied and there were few of the rites
and rituals that provided the girl with social recognition. Society had
plans for her but she was not allowed to know her own body; she
was simply a pawn in the social scheme.[97] The French sex reformer
Dr René Allendy agreed, lamenting the psychic and physical ignorance of French girls. There were, he claimed, in the 1940s still convent schools in Paris in which girls slept in camisoles and with their
hands tied to prevent masturbation.[98] Yet advances were being made.
By the 1930s American magazines carried articles with titles like 'Your
Teenage Daughter' in which a mother reported that she told her
fifteen year old all about 'sex physiology, the nature of marriage, birth
control, and how to look after herself before she had a baby'.[99]

In Germany leftists and feminists led the call for sex education.[100]
Women who were opposed to state-organized prostitution were the
sort to support such programmes. Germany was especially progressive in calls for sex education in schools prior to the First World War.
Some lectures were given following the war, the north being more
liberal than Bavaria. In Weimar Germany, communists called for sex
education by the age of fourteen; the Nationalists opposed it. Though
the chief concern behind such campaigns was to combat venereal
disease and preach abstinence, they were attacked by the churches
and Pope Pius XI expressly condemned them in *Decretum de Edu-
catione Sexuali* (1929) and *De Eugenica* (1931). Even Social Democrats hoped that sex education would inculcate purity.[101] Socialists
expressed fears that boys would be drawn away from political action
by smoking, drinking and pornography, while girls in domestic service, if not seduced, would be tempted by the appeals of dancing and
tawdry clothes.[102] Max Hodann, a socialist doctor, went the furthest to
reach youth with a realistic message in books such as *Where Children
Come From* (1926).[103] Wilhelm Reich – following his idiosyncratic
notions of the importance of the orgasm – wanted intercourse made
available to youth for the purposes of combating masturbation.[104]

The Anglo-Saxon nations were not as advanced. One expert informed his 1941 readers that wet dreams were not dangerous but
to avoid excitement a young man should avoid girls. 'Take up some

hobby', he suggested, 'preferably an open-air one, such as gardening, or poultry-keeping.'[105] Young men entering the British army in the Second World War were provided with a pamphlet that described their sexuality as a sacred trust that was not to be abused. They should mix with members of the opposite sex but never compromise them. The tract, written by a padre, adopted a brisk, manly tone. If wet dreams were posing a problem the youth was told to 'take it in your stride'. 'Self-relief' was a 'very hopeless imitation of the sex act' and physically and morally detrimental. The author recommended 'sun-baking' since the body was something to be improved and the daily cold shower if desire had to be damped down.[106] In the 1940s Britain did have sex education experts like Cyril Bibby who were calling for less moralistic lessons. Their goal was not to terrorize youth by tales of venereal disease or sexual abuse but to give clear information that would lead to rational decision-making. Parents, Bibby asserted, felt awkward and were relieved when teachers assumed the task of sex educators. But even a progressive like Bibby was unhappy with school children's sniggering, their passing of obscene notes, their lavatory wall drawings associating sex with defecation and their 'morbid' interest in nude photos. He believed that showers and swimming, by familiarizing the young with their own bodies, would raise the moral tone.[107] Such themes of 'repressive tolerance' were carried on by *The Journal of Sex Education* which appeared in Britain in 1948 edited by Norman Haire.

Even the cinema was turned to the purposes of sex education. In the United States Ivan Abrahamson made a number of sexual hygiene films including *Enlighten thy Daughter* (1917) and *The Sex Lure* (1917).[108] As early as 1919 such movies were being spoofed. A cartoon in a 1919 issue of the German humour magazine *Simplicissimus* portrayed a visibly pregnant young woman fending off her enraged father and distraught mother with the defence 'You must forgive me, my dear parents! It happened while we were shooting an educational film!'[109]

'It'

Where else were young people doing 'it'? The vast range of laws regulating dance halls, fairs and drinking establishments, the police's right to move people off the street or arrest them for vagrancy, and the restrictions on contraception and criminalization of abortion all restricted sexuality. A common assertion in the 1920s was that contraception, by making risk-free sex available to the young, changed

the very notion of sexuality.[110] Paula Fass agrees that premarital
sexuality, so fraught with frustrations and dangers, was necessarily
condemned until protection was available.[111] What she does not mention is that birth control was still illegal in many countries and that
reformers like Margaret Sanger in America had to carry out protracted
struggles against the criminalization of contraception. Most couples
still had to rely on simple withdrawal. The boy would tell the girl 'it
will be alright', meaning that he would withdraw before ejaculating.
Some girls thought they were safe the first time as the hymen was
not broken or if they were standing up.[112] Despite such perils the
evidence suggests that rates of premarital sex rose sharply in the
1920s and then plateaued until the next jump in the 1960s.[113] Later
surveys showed that men resorted less frequently to prostitutes in
the inter-war period and that more petting and premarital intercourse
occurred.[114] Working-class couples had sex in back alleys, parks and
in parents' houses. They 'snogged' in fields, cemeteries, railway tunnels
and in the back rows of cinemas. For middle-class youth the automobile provided a magical world of privacy, though it was hardly
unprecedented if one remembers nineteenth-century references made
by French novelists to sex in closed carriages.

Was there a great split between the rough and respectable concerning sex? In the late nineteenth century the poorest did marry
earliest. Those with professional aspirations had to defer gratification. Lengthy engagements were encouraged in the nineteenth century because it was assumed that they would lead to more stable
marriages, but at times they had the unintended consequence, as
breach of promise cases made clear, of leaving some women in
the lurch.[115] When courtships resulted in pregnancy in the middle
class the result was either marriage or a suit for seduction. Among
the working class, parents tended to be more accepting of sexual
intimacy as long as it led on to marriage. If not, there was a problem. Despite late marriages, illegitimacy dropped in England from
6 per cent in 1850 to 4 per cent by 1900; premarital pregnancies
dropped from 40 per cent of first births in 1800 to 20 per cent in
1900.[116] The claim made by some English historians that this decline,
which continued on into the twentieth century, was due to abstinence
rather than to contraception can only be sustained if one regards
coitus interruptus as a form of abstinence.[117]

The percentage of sexually active young women clearly rose in
the early twentieth century. Was this exploration and experimentation linked to changes in education, employment opportunities, birth
control, suffrage? The notion was generally accepted at the time that
independence in the outside world complemented a young woman's

search for sexual independence. Later surveys revealed that 50 per cent of American women had lost their virginity prior to marriage.[118] Yet it was still held that women 'had' sex and men 'took' it.[119] The line continued to be drawn between 'good' girls and 'bad' girls. Only men were supposed to have an active sex life. A boy was expected to 'sow his wild oats', a girl was not.

A 'bad' boy was a criminal; a 'bad' girl was sexually adventurous. In short, society 'sexualized' the young woman's morality.[120] African-American girls, white social workers assumed, would naturally be sexual. But a white girl who was sexually adventuresome risked in the 1920s being labelled 'hypersexual'.[121] Much of what we know about young women's sexuality comes from the courts which were so preoccupied by 'wayward girls' and girls 'in trouble'.[122] Reformatory records reveal that incorrigibility laws were used by families to put sexually troublesome daughters away. Such laws were on the statute books in New York state as early as 1886. Bad girls were punished as delinquents in Canada under the Juvenile Delinquency Act of 1908. Wayward or unmanageable children under twenty-one could be sent to reform school. No specific crime had to be committed; simply the suggestion that a girl might exhibit signs of 'sexual precocity' could be sufficient reason to lock her up. The act's stated intent was 'to check [delinquents'] evil tendencies and to strengthen their better instincts'.[123] The 'saucy' or 'bold' or 'forward' girls risked being targeted as 'tramps'. Likewise in Britain 'larking about in the streets with the lads' came to be seen as dangerous.[124]

Elite women played a central role in the new moralism by which philanthropists and the religiously inclined pathologized single parenthood.[125] The irony was that many charity workers were themselves not married and did not have children. Indeed, their own unusual lives – some lived in stable unions with other women – might explain why they were so zealous in condemning 'fallen' girls and evil men. A young woman who failed the ultimate morality test by producing an illegitimate child could only obtain support from a charity maternity home by declaring her repentance.[126] In the United States the term 'unwed mother' became a code word for black and working class. By the 1930s, single mothers were subjected to neurotic labelling and regarded as a discrete abnormal group. Religious workers had referred to them as the 'fallen'. Social workers in the 1930s saw them as 'feeble-minded' or 'sexual delinquents'. The young women's own sense of their experiences were often shaped by the melodramatic script of seductions and betrayals carried in the pulps such as *True Story*. Welfare workers were not impressed. They regarded them no longer just as victims, but as presenting a biological danger to society. Psychiatric and psychological explanations of their actions were increasingly offered and eugenicists argued that sterilization was the obvious logical means to end the reproduction of the unfit.

Conclusion

John Gillis has argued that between 1890 and 1960 youth lost status. The irony was that youth was regarded as 'special' just when it was being cut off from the adult world. The notion of adolescence being an especially sensitive stage of life had great staying power. Experts offered advice on how restless boys could be made dependent and adventurous girls 'feminized'. The sex experts who chronicled and policed youth culture – ranging from conservatives like Dr Mary Scharlieb and the researchers of the Bureau of Social Hygiene to progressives like Judge Ben Lindsey, Katherine Bement Davis and Victor Marguerite – though differing in many ways, all sought to discipline the hormones and habits of the young. The preoccupation with keeping youth pure manifested itself in the work of the sex educators – from Sylvanus Stall, Emma Drake and Mary Wood Allan in turn-of-the-century America to Cyril Bibby in 1940s Britain and in movements ranging from the Scouts, Boys' Brigade, YMCA and YWCA to the Student Christian Movement. Adults were not always clear what they wanted. On the one hand, they punished and ostracized wayward youths if they crossed boundaries; but, on the other, adults encouraged independence and experimentation as part of growing up.

In the inter-war period parents and children appeared to have less in common and emotional tensions between the generations rose.[127] In response, youth became more rebellious and introspective, and developed its own dress, music, magazines and petting techniques. By the 1920s many of the forms of working-class sexual behaviour that had led to girls being labelled as 'hypersexual' had spread to the middle classes and became increasingly normalized. Yet what the letters written to birth controllers and personal advice columnists and the findings of sex surveyors and investigative journalists reveal is that, in fact, youth was not 'sex mad' and its detractors' employment of such terms chiefly served to deflect attention from the social problems posed by the young in an increasingly urban, industrialized world. The social crisis was 'read' by the middle class as a sexual crisis. Such a story attempted to collapse all youth problems into the problem of sexuality. Even the 1930s Depression failed to convince conservatives that social problems were the cause of sex problems rather than the reverse.

3

'Selfish Beasts': Marriage Manuals and the Eroticization of Marriage

In publishing in 1916 his archive of oral and written interviews, W. F. Robie, an American progressive physician, produced a fascinating account of early twentieth-century marital sexuality. Robie himself collected the sex histories of sixty-one males and thirty-four females, indirectly those of thirty-seven males and eleven females, and by letter those of thirteen males and two females. He also had at hand five hundred reports sent in by doctors.[1] His interviewees were doctors, clergymen, teachers, artisans and their wives, sisters and daughters. He insisted that they were not the ill but the 'normal' and the industrious. As such Robie saw himself following Havelock Ellis, the English sexologist, and taking a different path from the majority of medical researchers who only reported on the abnormal. New studies were needed, according to Robie, because the world was plagued by sterility, low fertility, divorce, venereal disease and what he called the 'unattracted woman'. If sex were seriously investigated ways would be found so that many of these evils could be avoided.

Robie was a rationalist who believed that fear and ignorance underlay most sexual problems. Couples were only further confused if they read dangerous quack literature such as Joseph W. Howe's *Excessive Venery* (1883).[2] Citing the example of a twenty-seven-year-old man who reported that he had only been relieved of his sexual fears by reading a reassuring text, Robie asserted that there was a crying need for sex education carried out in an enlightened fashion.[3] Robie's hopeful message was that most sexual malfunctions stemmed from ignorance and excessive prudery. There were, however, some scientists, sensualists and socialists who were, in his opinion, going too far in attacking marriage. Robie felt proper restraints were needed. Sex education, not 'free love', offered the cure for marital ills.

As a sexual enthusiast who believed that a good sex life was necessary for one's general well-being, Robie began his patient's treatment with explanatory talks on the harmlessness and prevalence of masturbation.[4] Turning to marriage he informed the man that his first duty was to satisfy his wife. Foreplay was necessary. He noted that a particularly sensitive forty-two-year-old female patient said she only had to be kissed to experience orgasm.[5] Robie's main contention was that the husband had to make sure that his wife climaxed, preferably by penetration but digitally if necessary.[6] The husband of a Mrs E., a forty-three-year-old woman who had clitoral but not vaginal orgasms, believed something was wrong. And she confessed to feeling that she was not a 'true wife'. Told that her husband employed coitus interruptus, Robie directed him to use a condom, digital stimulation and to 'ride high'. The husband and wife reported that the changes led to happiness.[7] Even an impotent man could be a good husband. A fifty-two-year-old woman informed Robie that her husband always manipulated her breasts and clitoris to bring her to orgasm. 'He was very considerate and saw to it that she had complete satisfaction in intercourse. Almost invariably had orgasm.'[8] Even in middle-age and after her husband's death she still had strong sexual feelings, Robie reported approvingly, due to 'watching the young people and to reminiscences'. Women in turn, Robie instructed, had to know how to pleasure their husbands.[9] Robie pooh-poohed the notion that intercourse during pregnancy was dangerous. He reported that some of his female patients felt even stronger desires when pregnant.[10] He was convinced that the abandonment of sexual activities at menopause brought on senility.[11]

For centuries past, Western writers had produced an enormous literature devoted to love, courtship and seduction. Save for tragedies, such accounts of the stratagems of the single were expected to conclude with the depiction of a marriage. Married life itself was not necessarily regarded as bliss. Talleyrand had defined marriage as 'two bad tempers during the day and two bad smells during the night'.[12] Another French wit held that 'When you stop loving your wife, that is when marriage really begins.'[13] In the twentieth century marriage was supposed to be sexually satisfying and experts daringly took it upon themselves to proceed to describe what happened – or should happen – after the bedroom door was closed. New story-tellers emerged: sexual enthusiasts and therapists like Robie, marriage experts and marital counsellors. They introduced the public to a new cast of characters, including the frigid wife and the uncaring husband, and set the married couple a new goal – the simultaneous orgasm. Many of these writers regarded themselves as radicals and were certainly perceived as such by conservatives. Nevertheless, the most inter-esting aspect of this new literature, as provocative and liberating as it appeared at the time, was the way in which it produced a sexual script tailored to strengthen existing family relationships.

The notion that wives and husbands would judge the well-being of their relationship by finding – perhaps with the help of experts – sexual passion and pleasure in marriage was a relatively new idea. The older religious view was that the primary purpose of marriage was the bearing of children. Catholic writers clung to the notion well into the twentieth century. One French author, for example, thought the church deserved praise for allowing persons to marry who were physically incapable of having children. He noted that the Vatican also generously tolerated the marriage of women past child-bearing age who, though they were 'finished', went on having sex, crudely likening them to Napoleon's frozen grenadiers at Eylau who, though dead, had remained standing.[14]

Protestants conceded that love and sexuality played important parts in family life, but the subject was one about which the respect-able could or would say very little. Nineteenth-century doctors, while willing to write extensively on abnormal sexuality, particularly on such issues as prostitution and venereal disease, were reluctant to discuss 'normal' marital sex. Dr Lushington, when asked by the Con-sistory Court of London in 1845 to define 'sexual intercourse', had replied 'This is a most disgusting and painful inquiry but it cannot be avoided.'[15] Many Victorians found something indecent in even ima-gining the married having sex. Elizabeth Blackwell, England's first woman doctor, in calling for early marriage to prevent immorality, felt it necessary to provide the assurance that this would not provide an opportunity for marital 'licence'.[16] Even in the 1920s a British sex manual promised that, though containing accurate information, it was 'free from the taint of sensuality or erotic sentiment'.[17]

The older view, that sexual intercourse was primarily justified by procreation and was even within marriage a potentially destructive force, had remarkable staying power. Dr Emma F. Angell Drake's *What a Young Wife Ought to Know*, first published in the United States in 1901 and reprinted on into the 1940s, warned against marital excesses.[18] Dr Paul Goy, a French physician, concurred that it was dangerous to speak of people's 'sexual needs' as though they had some natural legitimacy. If the passions were not bridled or subordin-ate to social duties the result would be vice and promiscuity.[19] Such views did not disappear but were overwhelmed in the early twen-tieth century by those of increasing numbers of 'sexual enthusiasts' who made the novel claim that society was best served by liberating rather than repressing the pleasures of marital sex. In fact, the happiness and stability of a marriage was, these commentators argued, primarily based on a couple's sexual compatibility. Doctors began to acknowledge that marital happiness was as important an issue as social hygiene.

The reformers shrewdly won over a middle-class readership that would have been alarmed by any suggestion that animal appetites be unleashed by cloaking the discussion of sex in a terminology that was both romantic and religious. In Britain Marie Stopes described her task as helping to shift marriage from being 'brutal and hopeless and sodden' to something 'rapturous, spiritual and vital'. In the United States Margaret Sanger similarly argued in *The Pivot of Civilization* (1922) that married women would be freed through rather than from sex.[20] Sex was presented by such propagandists in terms akin to those employed by religious mystics as a means by which apparently passive women could exploit their redemptive powers. Intercourse did not have to be just a meeting of bodies; it could and should be a spiritual union. The freeing of the married from their sexual fears and worries, the reformers claimed, had to be regarded as a socially responsible and life-serving act.[21]

Marriage

Although the sexual enthusiasts saw themselves launching a daring sex revolution against the Victorians, the evidence suggests that the sex lives of ordinary married men and women evolved at a placid pace. The median age of marriage did not change too much, but increasingly in the twentieth century there did emerge a right age at which to marry – that is, before thirty. What also shifted was the percentage marrying; it rose to include about 95 per cent of women. The extent of premarital sex crept up as well. Everyone claimed in public that they were supporters of the virginity of brides when in fact a growing percentage abandoned it. This was not done lightly. The woman who had no property had to consider her virginity as part of her social 'capital' and so had to be cautious in her decision-making. Would she, in giving up herself, capture her beau or lose his respect? If she became pregnant would he abandon her? Some assurances were needed. Family and friends sought to see that promises were made, declarations given and vows exchanged.

The court records pertaining to working-class illegitimacy show that sexual relations usually only commenced after a relationship had lasted months if not over a year. Temptations increased the longer a marriage had to be delayed. The tradition held on in some peasant areas that sex was allowed before marriage to test the fecundity of the female. Once a marriage was arranged, but before the actual wedding, the parents did not object if relations commenced. Workers and small shopkeepers were equally liberal. The early twentieth-century bourgeoisie put a high value on the virginity of women, but arranged marriages declined.[22] Passion became more important and sexual favours were taken by courting couples as gages of intimacy. This evolution made refusal by the young woman – who, if obdurate, ran the risk of being called frigid – more difficult.[23] A popular French sex manual asserted in 1908 that the double standard still existed, but few brides were completely ignorant.[24] The French accordingly referred to them as the *demi-vierges*. In France it has been estimated that probably about 20 per cent of women had prenuptial sex at the turn of the century and 30 per cent during the inter-war period.[25] Similar figures based on North American data reveal that as the century wore on more and more women arrived at marriage with some sexual experience.

The middle classes employed the honeymoon as a way of easing into marriage. By the 1870s Niagara Falls had become the archetypal North American destination for newly weds. Traditionally, the community had put the couple to bed and sought evidence of a successful coition; now the middle-class couple secluded itself and so announced the heightened importance the community accorded conjugality. New concerns for privacy and discretion purportedly underlay this seclusion but, as countless 'honeymoon jokes' showed, the effect of the self-conscious departure of the couple likely exaggerated rather than attenuated their sexual embarrassment.[26] Most workers could not afford a honeymoon and simply made do with a wedding night party. In Britain by the 1940s couples from the ranks of skilled labour were earning enough to take a short wedding excursion which would likely consist of a weekend at a seaside resort. But for working young people – many of whom had to move in with parents – the emphasis on separation and the establishment of a new nuclear family that the honeymoon symbolized made little sense. Nor did marriage signify for working-class women such a sharp demarcation between the stages of daughter and wife. Most had already joined the ranks of labour and many had had premarital sexual relations. Life for them did not change as abruptly as it did for their newly married middle-class sisters.[27]

Most couples presumably passed easily and uneventfully into the ranks of the married. Happy families leave few records and we consequently know little of their sex lives. Marriage for the less fortunate brought with it unhappiness, disappointment and shocks. Simple economic necessity forced some working-class women into marriage or concubinage. Investigators found that even wives who had freely chosen their fate were often exhausted by work, children and pregnancies. Their husband's sometimes excessive sexual demands were one more burden. 'I shouldn't mind married life so much', reported one woman, 'if it wasn't for bedtime.'[28] Husbands in all ranks of society were more likely than wives to complain of the sexual inadequacy of a spouse, and her refusal of sex was often given by men as reason for separation or divorce. Women wanted 'love'. Middle-class women in particular who had been led to believe that they would find complete emotional fulfilment in marriage, on discovering themselves in a disappointing relationship, asked the classic question: is that all there is?

Advice

Marie Stopes was such a woman, but she did something about it. Stopes (1880–1958) grew up in an enlightened upper middle-class family. She was the first Englishwoman to receive a doctorate in palaeobotany, but was not unhappy that many assumed that 'Dr Stopes' was a physician. Stopes's story was that in 1912, after a year of marriage to a Canadian botanist, it slowly dawned on her that all was not well. She was shocked to discover that a well-educated woman such as herself did not realize at first that her husband was impotent and that her marriage had not been consummated. Only in 1914 did she start proceedings for an annulment. More importantly, shamed by her own blindness, she began the serious study of sexuality. The product of this research was her book *Married Love*. It appeared in 1918 and was an overnight sensation, going through seven printings and eventually selling more than a million copies.[29]

There is a good deal of evidence that undermines Stopes's claims to have been sexually naïve.[30] What cannot be disputed is that the enormous popularity of her book was due, not to its account of 'the facts of life', but to the romantic spirit in which the information was presented. Stopes noted that nineteenth-century sex manuals spoke primarily about restraint and not near enough about married couples' need for a regular, satisfying sex life. Her main argument was that a happy marriage was one in which the husband continued to court and woo his wife. She accordingly dedicated her next book, *Enduring Passion*, to 'married lovers'.[31] They had to adore each other, she insisted; no other relationship was as rich in interests and possibilities. Sexual compatibility provided their essential bond and it followed, Stopes declared, that the single bed was the enemy of marriage.[32] She went on to explain in some detail how the man's duty, in the comforting confines of the marital double-bed, was to pleasure the woman so that she along with him obtained orgasm.[33]

Stopes's first concern was for the family which she presented as the foundation stone of a stable society. Few would have denied that the economic well-being of families was important, but what preoccupied Stopes was their emotional well-being. Her goal was the creation of the stable and sexually happy couple in which the husband would be sensitive and caring. She elaborated the idea of a woman's sensuality being dominated by a 'fundamental pulse' that the man would have to learn to interpret. The sex act, in her romantic view, had to be a '*mutual* affair, not the mere indulgence of a man'. She set her readers the goal of achieving mutual orgasm or what she referred to as the 'co-ordinated function'. In unlocking the passions, she promised, one would shift marriage to a higher plane. Her model man and wife were 'young, happy, and physically well-conditioned'.[34] Only a woman so prepared would be able to enjoy what Stopes referred to as 'Radiant Motherhood'.

Stopes was one of the first of the modern marriage counsellors who made it obligatory for the twentieth-century husband and wife to 'adore' each other, to be 'married lovers' constantly 'wooing' each other, when not reading up on how it was to be done. In passing, she condemned lesbianism and masturbation, not on moral grounds, but because they reduced the woman's ability to have a 'real union'. Stopes thus became one of the main architects and defenders of modern heterosexuality. Her concern for the couple's 'synchronized orgasm' reflected a new twentieth-century conception of female sexuality. Michael Gordon has suggested that the first reference to the synchronized orgasm appeared in George W. Savory, *Marriage: its Science and Ethics* (1900) in which it was argued that it resulted in superior offspring.[35] In past centuries both doctors and clerics had declared the female orgasm important because they believed that to ensure conception it was necessary for the woman to climax.[36] Now experts were arguing that the chief importance of the orgasm was not in abetting fertility but in serving as the basis of a couple's happy marriage.[37]

With this greater interest in the woman's sexual needs came a greater concern for sexual technique. The writers of sex manuals slowly laid out all the various techniques of fore- and after-play – words, touch, pacing. The most popular of the inter-war texts was Theodore van de Velde's *Ideal Marriage: its Physiology and Technique* (1926) which, with its stress on 'love play' and 'after-glow', became a world-wide romantic best-seller.[38] Van de Velde, a Dutch gynaecologist who had himself abandoned an unhappy marriage to run off with a younger woman, asserted that his task was to provide information which would relieve suffering and offer joy. Like Stopes, he insisted that the man had to go on courting his wife for their entire married life and set out the stages by which the couple could reach the goal of simultaneous orgasm.

Van de Velde described in detail the importance of the erotic kiss in foreplay. Kisses on the mouth and deep kissing, it might be recalled, were not accepted by all in the nineteenth century and regarded by some as more erotic than genital touching.[39] He then succeeded, by employing language that did not offend the middle class, to describe and defend previously tabooed sex practices. Fellatio and cunnilingus, asserted van de Velde, were perfectly acceptable as long as they were employed for arousal. Clitoral stimulation he also explained. The ultimate goal was the woman's achievement of a vaginal orgasm. If the woman was successfully aroused the man's orgasm in turn would trigger hers; indeed, van de Velde believed that the woman could actually feel her spouse's ejaculate. If the woman did not climax the man was instructed that he could then resort to digital excitation. And finally, after orgasm, van de Velde instructed his male readers how they should again demonstrate their devotion by not simply slipping off to sleep but by indulging in 'after-play'. The book's ethos was summed up in the title of one chapter: 'The Husband as Permanent Lover of his Wife'.

Writers across the Western world competed with each other in declaring the importance of sexual compatibility in marriage. Havelock Ellis in Britain, Léon Blum and Edouard Toulouse in France, Ellen Key in Sweden and Paolo Mantegazza in Italy all called for the sexual education of women.[40] In 1927 the family sociologist Ernest R. Groves offered at the University of North Carolina the first American courses on marriage preparation. In the past, asserted Groves, only prostitution offered sexual pleasure without any 'duties'; now birth control made it also possible in marriage which made it all the more important that the relationship be grounded on love.[41]

The marriage manuals' avowed purpose was to end sexual ignorance. Each had its horror story to tell. In Berlin Iwan Boch claimed on the basis of interviews that up to 40 per cent of women were frigid and that their lack of sexual appetite was due to their husbands' incompetence. One German mother informed her daughter that prostitutes were women who had sex for money and 'even enjoy it'.[42] Some people found it difficult to consummate marriage. Six of the twelve middle-class women who responded to Celia Duel Mosher's early twentieth-century survey reported that they had only consummated their marriage from ten days to one year after their wedding.[43] More than one British doctor suggested that women take up horse riding to ready themselves for the ordeal. Jeanne Deflou argued in 1906 that, while French workers had marriages of inclination, bourgeois marriages continued to be arranged. Men often simply slept with their wives to produce children and sought pleasure elsewhere. Bourgeois girls were sequestered. She cited a *fabricante de lingerie* who stated that some families in the Faubourg Saint Germain included in the bride's trousseau special night-dresses 'equipped, about mid-length, with a specially designed opening which allows for maximum avoidance of carnal contact without preventing conception'.[44] English women were similarly kept in ignorance. 'When I was married', reported one, 'I was totally in the dark respecting this part of my nature, and when my first baby was within a few minutes of the portals of existence, I positively did not know where it was coming from.'[45] Males in the inter-war period also needed enlightening. Many men informed Marie Stopes that they did not know that women had orgasms. One upper middle-class man reported that when he had first observed one 'he was frightened and thought it was some sort of fit.'[46] Several correspondents of Stopes mentioned failure to consummate, sometimes out of ignorance, sometimes in order to avoid pregnancy.[47] Kenneth Walker, in reporting that he was consulted by a forty-year-old solicitor who for a year did not realize that his marriage had not yet been consummated, stated that gynaecologists in the 1940s still came across such evidence of sexual confusion.[48]

Stopes's defence of post-menopausal women's sexual needs and van de Velde's calm assertion that there was nothing wrong with having sex during menstruation, though some might abstain for aesthetic reasons, must have come as a revelation to many readers.[49] Yet if the means adopted by the writers of the marriage manuals appeared radical, their goal – the defence of the existing family structure – was fairly conservative. The main rationale of the marriage manual was to rejuvenate marriage and so more tightly bond the couple. The author of *When Married Life Gets Dull* (1911) typically stressed the need for romance in married life. Some men reportedly asked what was the point in running after a bus that one had already caught, but the author advised the husband to help out a bit with family chores, remembering that he was a man and 'my wife is only a poor weak woman'. The woman for her part was enjoined to do all she could to 'keep her husband still a lover'. If she did not there was always the chance he would go off looking for 'cheap simplicities'.[50] By reinvigorating marriage, one thereby prevented divorce, adultery and prostitution. Sex, once seen as potentially threatening to family life, was now presented as its glue. According to Marie Stopes, 'The only secure basis for the present-day state is the wedding of its units in marriage; but there is rottenness and danger at the foundations of the state if many of the marriages are unhappy.'[51] Ettie Rout, the New Zealand social hygienist, struck the same note in declaring in *Safe Marriage: a Return to Sanity* (1922) that a marriage deprived of joy was 'easily the most dangerous of all our social institutions'.[52]

Such writers tended to view the failure to have children as a sign of sexual incompatibility that could lead to the collapse of the family. Good sex would result in keeping up the fertility rate. Even Marie Stopes, best known as a birth control advocate, declared that parenthood was a 'duty' best carried out by the 'normal, healthy and loving'.[53] One rationale for providing sex education was that it would make childbirth less frightening. In France, which had the lowest birth rate in Europe, the marriage manuals were especially pronatalist. Georges Anquetil and Jane de Magny described maternity as a demonstration of women's 'patriotism'.[54] That husbands were brutal was bad enough but that they should limit family size by subjecting their wives to 'conjugal frauds' was, asserted Michel Bourgas, unspeakable.[55]

But the sex experts advised some not to marry. One guide asserted that it was not advisable for homosexuals, fetishists and habitual masturbators to wed. Sexually anaesthetic or neurotic women were advised to remain celibate.[56] Their sort should not reproduce. The writers of marriage manuals made it clear that they were providing information to defend 'normal' sexuality. They especially celebrated potent male heterosexuality. They tended to believe that labourers, being less civilized, were more potent. Working-class men, claimed Stopes, did not suffer from premature ejaculations.[57] She asserted that in the upper and professional classes about one-third of wives had non-virile husbands.[58] Her advice was for them to avoid alcohol and 'hard brain work'. Margaret Sanger likewise challenged her male readers to prove by their passionate love-making that they had not fallen victim to effeminization.

The tone of the marital manuals was resolutely heterosexual. Van de Velde described normal forms of intercourse as a 'Holy Ground' as opposed to the 'Hellgate of the Realm of Sexual Perversions'. Eustace Chesser asserted that the enjoyment of 'normal erotic techniques' would in fact protect one from sliding into perverse activities.[59] The 'byways of sex' where 'sets' of perverts lurked could thus be avoided. He cautioned that one should not mock or punish sexual abnormals; like other handicapped persons they suffered from a sickness. 'He-women' and 'she-men' were not born bad, but had a predisposition that led on to their pathological state. Some, Chesser admitted, had qualities that might 'compensate' for their disability.[60] The danger was that at schools 'innocents' might be contaminated by such types and later even the married were at risk of seduction. 'If you choose deliberately to experiment outside of the area of normal sexual activity you run the risk of becoming perverted.'[61] Why, asked the writers of the sex manuals, given all the varieties of normal sex now open to them, would anyone risk dangerous experimentation with deviant practices?

Male and Female Responsibilities

In freely employing such terms as 'normal' and 'abnormal', the sex manuals reassured their readers that existing gender divisions were biologically determined. And yet at first glance this literature appeared to attack male power. Stupid husbands were upbraided for being crass or brutal.[62] Stopes, for example, presented the stereotypical picture of the careless and unfeeling husband 'raping' his young bride on their wedding night. It was no wonder that such a man, likely used to prostitutes, would be angered and confused by the apparent coldness and unresponsiveness of his virgin bride.[63] Stopes estimated that 70–80 per cent of women were deprived of orgasm because of the speed of unthinking men; wives were left frustrated and husbands exhausted by over-indulgence. In some ways such attacks on male passion were not particularly new. In 1895 B. O. Fowler had followed other Victorian writers in condemning 'lust' in marriage. The fact that a woman could be subjected to the sexual needs of her husband – 'a human gorilla' – who insisted on his 'marital rights' he condemned as an 'awful harlotry'. Indeed, Fowler asserted that prostitutes were freer than wives inasmuch as the former at least dictated the terms of the sale of their sexual favours.[64] The originality of twentieth-century writers was their insistence, not that men should sexually restrain themselves, but that they should learn how to please their partners.

The sex manuals did not suggest that male and female roles would change. Their authors took it as a given that men were innately aggressive and women passive. Readers were informed that male sexuality was a constant physiological function whereas the woman's was 'intermittent'. What was asked was that the man learn to control himself by adopting learned techniques. Michel Bourgas employed a telling metaphor in jesting that a man who complained of the frigidity of his wife resembled the musician who attributed his lack of success to his instrument.[65] In van de Velde's words, the doctor was the guide, the husband the initiator and the wife the pupil.[66] The general expectation was still that the man should be older than the wife; indeed, van de Velde assumed that the new husband would be sexually experienced and the bride a virgin. The sex experts sought to win over men by assuring them that their greater sexual knowledge would strengthen rather than undermine their position in the household.

Stopes, like van de Velde, challenged men to turn their 'vital energy and nerve force' to creative purposes. She popularized the notion that the man who took the time to ensure the satisfaction of his mate would be rewarded. Was the working-class male more thoughtless than his middle-class counterpart? This was assumed by many writers but not proved. Blundering men were found in all strata; they were not cruel but ignorant. Such clumsy fellows had to be instructed on how to employ 'love play' to arouse women for union. Various suggestions were offered to deal with the problem of premature ejaculation.[67] One doctor curiously argued that a problem associated with circumcision was that it delayed orgasm. No doubt more disturbing was his claim that this 'amputation' could be viewed as a psychological wounding that could lead to impotence.[68]

The sex educators targeted men as a reaction to the First World War's epidemic of impotence and sterility and in the hope that properly trained males would spurn pornography, prostitution and the perversions. The marriage manual writer told them they could be better in bed and assured them they could pleasure women. They were promised that in satisfying their wives their own satisfaction would be all the greater. The model husband who emerged from these texts was a healthy, vigorous animal.[69] This sexually educated man would practise a new form of restraint, pertaining not to the number of his sex acts but their quality. His job, in the words of one writer, was to keep his head; his wife's job was to lose hers.[70] The marriage manuals, which at first glance appeared to critique masculinity, concluded by exalting male power and potency.

The writers of sex manuals usually portrayed themselves as defenders of oppressed femininity outraged by male brutality. They recognized the existence of female desire but still supported the notion that the woman was to be passive and awakened to her own sexuality by her spouse. There appeared to be an inherent contradiction in the assertion that the woman had her own sexual needs but could not fully express them autonomously. A number of writers claimed that the problem was that many women had been rendered frigid by a repressive society. A phrenologically inclined sex expert of the 1890s estimated that only 10 per cent of women allowed themselves to enjoy sex because 'it indicates a lack of feminine virtue to feel desire for sexual intercourse at all, and it is something to be proud of if you never felt such impulses.[71] He opposed such prudery but was still cautious about unleashing female desire. He did hazard the suggestion that the young woman 'ascertain the opinions of your future husband upon the subject of sexual indulgence'.[72] His advice to wives was that intercourse should be sought only once a fortnight, never during pregnancy and no sooner than six weeks after birth. The over-passionate wife was warned that her demands could exhaust her spouse or drive him to the use of harmful stimulants.

Stopes agreed that middle-class repressions produced frigid women. The signs of male desire were obviously visible to all; those of the female were more mysterious. Women were themselves ignorant of their own 'rhythmic sex-tide' and it was this 'fundamental pulse' that the man had to discover. Such knowledge would provide men with the 'key' which would unlock the female passions and lead to the hoped-for synchronized orgasm or 'co-ordinated function'.[73] Married sex would then be a 'mutual affair, not the mere "indulgence" of a man'.[74] He would, however, still be the dominant partner. Indeed, Stopes believed that the woman's very physiological well-being depended on receiving the man's semen.[75]

Hailed by many for its daring broaching of such issues as oral sex and the varieties of coital position, van de Velde's book was also marked by an inherent conservatism. Every non-orgasmic stimulation of the wife, warned the doctor, could cause injury.[76] The woman astride her husband experienced great pleasure but the position was unhealthy as it imposed on the male an unnatural passivity.[77] The fear of female sexuality continued to be met with in the marriage manuals of the 1940s. Asking 'Why should the Devil have all the best tunes?', Eustace Chesser suggested that if necessary the woman should use the methods of the prostitute on occasion to arouse the male.[78] But Chesser's assumption, like that of his peers, was that normally the man would take the lead and educate his wife. Such writers always took male standards as the norm, equating the clitoris to the penis, but never the other way round.[79] Even manuals that talked about female sexual frustrations focused primarily on men's sexual abilities, not women's.[80]

This literature came close to suggesting that marriage and heterosexual happiness were obligatory. Traditional proverbs such as 'Old maid, old rag' had long disparaged the spinster.[81] Now doctors advanced the argument that every woman should have a sex life and lamented the 'tragedy' of the unmarried.[82] Robie cited his German colleague Dr Max Marcuse in stating that abstinence posed actual physiological dangers.[83] Once married, the woman had, in order to prove her femininity, to achieve orgasm. Schedules were set up; one marriage guide stating, for example, that the normal woman should climax within ten minutes.[84] Freudians like Wilhelm Stekel asserted that only the homosexual woman – wishing to dominate and afraid to submit – refused to reach orgasm, at least with men. Such women were not fit to be mothers because the frigid mother was, according to the Freudians, responsible for the homosexuality and incestuous fixations of adolescents. Girls who did not receive a careful education would eventually swell the ranks of the frigid, the suffragists and the man-haters.[85]

Antony Ludovici, an iconoclastic misogynist, took just the opposite line and attacked the writers of marriage manuals for what he took to be the excessive sensitivity they showed to women. Based on his personal experience with English, French and German females, Ludovici asserted that a woman who insisted on reaching orgasm was too 'masculine'.[86] If there were sexual problems it was because men – prevented from being able to enjoy what he called a premarital 'safe-sex experience' – became clumsy masturbators. Naturally such sex-starved fellows in turn became infatuated with the first woman they met. As far as the male was concerned it was not true, asserted Ludovici, that 'love is blind' but that 'tumescence is blind'.[87] The normal woman did not seek such a release. Her desire was simply to reproduce and the man was a mere means to an end. That was why women were not interested in male beauty. Accordingly, Ludovici defended arranged marriages on eugenic grounds. The fact was that people in any event almost always married members of the same class and talk of 'love', he asserted, simply mystified the process. 'A train from Brighton', he concluded tartly, 'might as well rhapsodise about the irresistible attraction of Victoria Station.'[88] Ludovici's views were eccentric but serve as a reminder that the sexual enthusiasts did not go unopposed. The religious attacked what they saw as the defence of lust. The prudish were alarmed by public discussions of sexuality which they felt should be confined to the home. Misogynists critiqued a literature which they claimed undermined existing gender roles.

Influence

What people think is often as important as what they do and much sexual behaviour is necessarily learnt. From whom did the married learn their lessons? From the self-appointed sex experts? We know that in the early twentieth century the general public had greater access to sex information than ever before. In North America five-cent tracts, such as *What Married Women Should Know* in Haldeman-Julius's Little Blue Books series, sold by the thousands from the 1920s on.[89] Did the behaviour and attitudes of married couples reflect the changing fashions in such writings or were they largely impervious to such debates? The truth is that it is very difficult to gauge the impact of the marital manuals.

Thanks to the huge correspondence Stopes's activities engendered we do know at least what her readers worried about.[90] A good proportion of her letters were from men, obviously intent on improving their marital relations. For example, an Alberta man wrote to ask her in 1934 if the use of contraceptives would lower sexual sensitivity and if premature ejaculation could be cured.[91] A Canadian woman, who kept her copy of *Married Love* in a brown paper cover marked on the outside *The Way of an Eagle,* typically hailed Stopes's books for providing essential information and clearing up a good deal of ignorance.[92]

Most people, of course, neither purchased sex manuals nor wrote to their authors. The evidence does seem to suggest, however, that sexual mores did evolve. The ideal of companionate marriage emerged though the reality was slow in coming. In particular, in the working class the expectation was that the roles of partners would be quite different and there would not be the same amount of emotional intensity as between middle-class couples. The latter did show an increasing concern for the quality of their relationship and the notion that the spouse should be a 'lover' had wide currency. Respectable women in the nineteenth century had been embarrassed to undress in front of their husbands. In Catholic countries they continued in the inter-war period to ask their confessors if it was decent, but with the short skirts and bathing costumes of the 1920s the female body was revealed and began to lose its mystery.[93] Vaginal examinations, which had once outraged respectable women, became commonplace.[94]

In the inter-war period there was growing appreciation of both partners being pleasured. Kissing, restricted by the Victorians, became banal. The ritual of foreplay, consisting of touching and caressing the breasts and genitals, was increasingly insisted on by wives. Sex now sometimes took place with the lights on. Yet the assumption was still made that male and female sex interests differed. Men wanted sex more frequently than women. Every other day was taken as the norm; every day was regarded by women as excessive. Women did not want to have sex during their period. Men were initiators in oral sex and when it was refused in marriage sought it with mistresses and prostitutes. Women were more opposed to anal than to oral intercourse.[95] Religious condemnations of 'unnatural acts' no doubt had some influence on their thinking, just as improvements in hygiene made acceptable greater experimentation. Women still did not admit to their desires as readily as men. Among the working class and especially in Catholic Europe the two female models were the vivacious young woman and the sexless mother. Once married, it was expected that the woman would give up the revealing clothes, make-up and dancing associated with girlhood. John Gillis reports that a Preston woman, born in 1900, never went out when she was pregnant. 'I used to be ashamed, because I knew they would think what I'd been doing and I used to think it was terrible.'[96]

Yet attitudes towards sexuality did evolve. Men and women were less ashamed and more willing to admit their desires. The couple was eroticized. It was no longer necessary to talk about doing something 'dirty'. Stopes and others at least provided a vocabulary that made previously unspeakable topics able to be discussed. Sex might not have lost its mystery but with medicalization a secular, scientific and sin-free discourse was made available.[97] The general theory – usually associated with Freud's work – which held that men and women's nature was essentially libidinal and which provided the possibility of both thinking about sexual passions and wishes and desiring to control, rule and satisfy those needs was, in the inter-war period, very much in the air.

Anxieties

In 1934 a young Ontario woman sent a letter to Stopes asking for a copy of her first international best-seller *Married Love* (1918). 'I am about to be married', the correspondent explained, 'and I am anxious that my married life will be as perfect as I can make it, and my fiancé is as anxious as I am that we enter into marriage intelligently.'[98] This woman shared with many in the Western world the great expectations that perfect happiness would be provided by marriage. Marie Stopes and Margaret Sanger perhaps went furthest in defending the emancipatory powers of sex but the notion that the quality of a married couple's sex life could serve as the barometer of their relationship had a wide resonance. It has to be stressed how new the idea was that the main purpose of marriage was to provide sexual pleasure and companionship. It was a symptom of the fact that the term 'family' was coming to mean in the first instance simply the married couple. Their relationship came first and their parenting and child-rearing responsibilities were secondary. As the world became more complex, middle-class families in particular were shorn of the instrumental roles – in providing economic, health and education services – that they had in the past.[99] Therefore, by default, sex was increasingly presented as pivotal to the success of marriage. Accordingly, one witnessed a progressive shift from the notion of the Victorian 'passionless' wife to the twentieth-century sensual partner. The companionate model was pressed into the service of propping up the nuclear family.

In advancing 'sexual emancipation' as the new morality of the twentieth century, the sex reformers, according to Christopher Lasch's pessimistic account, sacrificed monogamy and virginity in order to save marriage. The spouse's chief task was now not that of father or mother but sex partner. Sex was taught; orgasms were 'achieved'.[100] This triumph of the helping professions in America, led by people like Judge Lindsey who supported such reforms of marriage, Lasch regarded as a tragedy. The 'family' was reduced to its emotional functions; parenthood was made secondary as was child-rearing. The stress on 'happiness' and 'adjustment' represented pseudo-emancipation. Old forms of restraint, claimed Lasch, were simply replaced by new ones.

Lasch's pessimism could be supported by evidence that in the course of a few decades one had moved in Western culture from a society in which abstinence was obligatory to one in which orgasm was obligatory. Eustace Chesser's *Love without Fear* (1941) contained the gloomy message that only one-twelfth of husbands were aware of the right sexual technique, the majority of wives never knew 'supreme joy' and 80 per cent of marriages were 'failures in the true sense'.[101] Similarly bleak data revealed that one-quarter of women had been repelled by their first sexual relationship.[102] Robert Latou Dickinson, the American sex researcher, found that seventeen of fifty patients did not achieve orgasm and 40 per cent were dissatisfied with their sex lives.[103] Janet Chance, having asserted that a woman should have two or three orgasms per session, conceded that 'A husband's job is not an easy one.'[104] The sense of sex as a 'job' was captured in Kenneth Walker's advice on the need just before marriage for couples to have a 'routine medical overhaul', described in the same tones as having a car's oil changed.[105] Walker asserted that the doctor was the man best prepared to deal with a tough hymen and even if it posed no special problem 'a gentle dilation' was a good idea as it ensured the ease of the male and the comfort of the female. If she planned on using birth control her cap should be fitted weeks before.[106]

The experts on marital sexuality thus provided mixed messages. On the one hand, they described sex as something akin to a spiritual discipline inasmuch as it promised a sort of religious ecstasy. On the other hand, their setting of daunting new performance targets led to the notion of 'sex as work'.[107] It was no wonder that Stopes's correspondent noted above described herself as 'anxious'. The marriage manuals banished many fears but undoubtedly created new ones. The danger, however, is to exaggerate the influence of such texts. Prior to the Second World War most doctors were clearly as uncomfortable as their patients when it came to discussing sexuality. Ordinary men and women for their part were not passive consumers of the marriage experts' doctrines. Those husbands and wives who perused marriage manuals made their own idiosyncratic readings, no doubt taking what they needed and ignoring that which was deemed irrelevant. The evolution of the sexual habits of the vast majority of the married population was more reflective of general cultural shifts towards individualism than of the particular and often peculiar injunctions of the sex experts.

4

'Race Suicide': Birth Control, Abortion and Family Stability

Sometime prior to 1916 a Mrs F. was so disgusted by the messiness of her husband's contraceptive techniques, which consisted of either ejaculating after withdrawing or resorting to inter-femora intercourse, that she had him talk to Dr W. F. Robie. The doctor was proud later to announce that once he had convinced the man to use condoms the couple's marital love was so successfully rekindled that the wife had up to nine orgasms in a row.[1] Though few could hope for such impressive results, Robie asserted that much marital unhappiness stemmed from contraceptive worries, and he supported his contention by providing numerous examples of the problems recounted by his patients.[2] Coitus interruptus left the woman a physical wreck. The douche was awkward and unhealthy. One husband refused 'to wear a protector' and Robie had to suggest that he refrain from ejaculating until the woman used her hand to bring him off after his withdrawal.[3] Dr C., who was worried about the ethics of using a condom, had to be assured by Robie that he was not a degenerate and advised that any discomfort would be removed if he used a slightly looser sheath and his wife douched for added protection.[4]

Robie, though he catalogued the range of contraceptives, was not intent on lowering the birth rate. He regarded children as the 'cement' of a conjugal union and believed every woman should bear from two to twelve offspring.[5] Like many of the early twentieth-century sex reformers he defended the use of contraceptives because he believed that the happiness of a couple's sex life could only be assured if they did not have to worry about an unwanted pregnancy. There is a good deal of evidence showing that women's fear of becoming pregnant effectively checked their experiencing any sense of sexual freedom. If a conception posed a threat to their health or to the wellbeing of the family how could they be expected – as instructed by the new sex manuals – to give themselves up completely to the pursuit of sensual pleasure? Some, believing the old myth that conception could not take place if the woman did not climax, desperately sought to stifle their passions by 'holding back'.[6] Most felt the need to be permanently on guard and each month waited with hopeful trepidation for the signs of their period.

Whether or not the accounts left by Robie were literally true is not as important as the fact that the public defence of birth control had become respectable. In Europe a number of male physicians like Robie, sympathetic to women's plight, set out at the turn of the century well-rounded defences of family planning. For example, Dr Anton Nyström, in *La Vie sexuelle et ses lois* (1910), asserted that it was the woman's right to decide on the number of children she desired, and after condemning coitus interruptus he went on to provide the pros and cons of a number of 'preservatives': condoms, sponges, pessaries, tampons and douches.[7] It was left, however, to two women – Margaret Sanger and Marie Stopes – to be most responsible for the popularization of the notion that birth control had to be made available to the masses, because without it a happy sex life was not possible.

Birth Controllers

Margaret Sanger (1879–1966), raised in a progressive atmosphere, was a New York housewife with a vague desire to do something with her life.[8] Her father was a socialist and feminist; her husband, an architect, was active in the Socialist Party. In 1911 Sanger moved to New York City and in her capacity as a nurse began to discover the plight of poor women burdened by a series of unwanted pregnancies. At the same time she shifted her support from the Socialist Party to the more radical Industrial Workers of the World in which some members advanced birth control as a revolutionary creed. Sanger later chose to date her conversion to birth control not to the time of her contact with Emma Goldman, a political radical whom she came to see as a rival, but to the day she witnessed the abortion-related death of a Mrs Sachs. Sanger's brilliance lay in seizing the moral high ground. She coined the term 'birth control' as a positive description of family limitation to replace the old, gloomy economic label, 'neo-Malthusianism'. She thus began to separate the issue of fertility restriction from some of its nineteenth-century political and economic associations.

Her first efforts to win mass support had limited success. Fortunately, Sanger's tract, *Family Limitation* (1914), which described for the benefit of working-class couples the use of douches, condoms and pessaries, was prosecuted by the federal government which created unexpected positive publicity. She began to seek court confrontations and her name soon became known across the country.[9] She started out on her first lecture tour in 1916, turning the defence of birth control into a free speech issue. She also established a birth control clinic in Brooklyn for which she was arrested and jailed. In response, she founded the American Birth Control League and began a campaign for legislative reform to permit the opening of medically supervised clinics for the poor. She herself was not to open another until 1923. Meanwhile Marie Stopes set up her clinic in London in 1921.

Stopes, as noted in chapter 3, had first won notoriety by writing a marriage manual, *Married Love* (1918). Her main argument had been that the married woman had as much right to sexual pleasure as her spouse. Stopes only noted the issue of birth control in passing, but in the huge number of letters she received from her readers learned that the inability to limit fertility was the source of much marital misery.[10] In response, she brought out another book at the end of 1918, *Wise Parenthood*. In this second text she directly broached the issue of birth control by providing diagrams of the reproductive organs and descriptions of a variety of contraceptives. She realized after a year or so that it was not sufficient to describe to poor mothers various forms of fertility control. They had to be made accessible. Doctors, dispensaries, chemists and local health officials made it clear that they did not see it as their duty to provide cheap devices for the working class; as a result, in March 1921 Stopes opened her Mothers' Clinic in Holloway Road, London. The purpose of the clinic was to show to public officials how such services could be carried out. The clinic was to serve primarily as a model and the chief aim of Stopes's Society for Constructive Birth Control and Racial Progress, also established in 1921, was to pressure government officials into taking over the responsibility for such work.[11]

Stopes and Sanger shared many of the same concerns. They both were alarmed by the high maternal and infant mortality rates associated with large families and exploited the eugenic concerns for the need to improve the 'quality' of the race. Knowing that the middle class already restricted births, they sought to make accessible to lower-class women the contraceptives limited as yet to the better off. They both stressed the need for clinics supported by the government and directed by trained personnel to educate the public in contraceptive use. But, most important of all, they sought, on the one hand, to downplay the old pessimistic economic arguments usually trotted out by the neo-Malthusians in favour of birth control and, on the other, to purge the movement of any associations with sexual or political radicalism. Stopes and Sanger believed that the challenge was to make limitation of family size appear not simply economically necessary but morally acceptable. To do this they developed the positive argument that contraception was not only compatible with pleasure but essential if the woman's passions were to be allowed full expression.

The letters written in their thousands to Stopes and Sanger provide striking first-hand accounts of the motives of those seeking birth control information. Women confessed to living in dread from month to month, of having their sex lives blighted by fear of pregnancy, of actually avoiding orgasm in the hope that they could thereby avoid conceiving. These apparently candid confessions have to be used with care, however, because the writers unconsciously knew what they had to say. A 'script' for the correspondent seeking help had in effect been created by Stopes and Sanger and others who popularized new notions of modern sexuality. The writer usually was a married woman with children. She would state that others clearly had access to contraceptive information that she did not. Some methods had already been employed but had proved unreliable. If a doctor had been approached for help he had not responded to her pleas. Turning to specifics, she asked if the pessary was reliable or the condom dangerous; did contraceptives lower sexual sensitivity; could premature ejaculation be cured? Her central concern was to limit family size to avoid jeopardizing the health and well-being of both herself and her existing children.[12] But what was especially striking was the writers' insistence that they sought contraceptive information not out of simple economic self-interest, but so that they could become better wives and mothers.

These women were concerned with the 'romance' in their marriages. They accepted the idea that the 'safeguarding of passion [was] of critical import for marital adjustment'.[13] Clearly a new, twentieth-century role of sensuous wife and conscientious mother had been created that could only be fulfilled if family size were limited. Of course, with a decline in family size the role of wife became more significant and that of mother less. But a 'sentimentalization' if not 'sacrilization' of childhood also occurred in Western societies just as the number of births declined.

The middle-class family had by the twentieth century given up to outside agencies most of the provision of health and educational services. Its household was smaller, having fewer children and having shed the many relatives, servants and occasionally lodgers it once had sheltered. 'Home' was where one now expected only to find domestic happiness. In the past such high expectations of connubial bliss were uncommon. Now a new image of the sensual, married woman was advanced throughout the media which portrayed her marrying young, being passionately attached to her spouse, and raising no more than two or three children. Implied, but rarely mentioned, was the fact that only contraception would permit the resolution of the inherently contradictory implications of the cult of domesticity. That the small, privatized family had already arrived was implied by the very fact that advice on intimate sexual matters was now sought by some middle-class women, not from neighbourhood friends or female relatives, but from marriage manuals, magazine columns, doctors or a stranger like Stopes or Sanger living perhaps thousands of miles way. Many of the letter writers openly confessed their sexual ignorance and lamented not having a mother or female confidante to turn to.

Stopes and Sanger sold so many books and received so many letters because they appeared to have the answer to the question of how the twentieth-century woman could reconcile the conflicting pressures in her life. The war had highlighted women's contribution to every country's national effort and was followed in many states with the reward of the franchise. There seemed, to the fearful, to be some basis for talking of a blurring of sex distinctions. The war certainly did break down much of the resistance to the public discussion of such sexual issues as venereal disease and birth control. But if the reading public was more enlightened in the 1920s one should not exaggerate the impact of feminism, psychoanalysis or sexology on the mass of the population. Nor should it be assumed, as it often has been in references to women bobbing their hair and taking up smoking, that in the post-war world gender roles were radically changed.[14] Indeed, as if in response to the modest extension of political and economic rights made to women (to which were attributed rising divorce and falling fertility rates), social commentators took up the new cultural emphasis on the inescapable sex differences promulgated by psychoanalysists, sociologists and sexologists.

At the turn of the century new concepts of female desire and pleasure were constructed and the notion of 'normal' sexual behaviour elaborated. 'Biological needs' were defined by sexologists like Havelock Ellis who provided ammunition for an acknowledgement of a woman's right to pleasure that had been demanded by feminists such as Emma Goldman and Ellen Key.[15] Birth control played a key part in such scenarios in that it provided a release from the fear of pregnancy and therefore undermined old arguments in defence of abstinence. But women were not to be 'freed' of their traditional responsibilities. Such contraceptives were not meant for the unmarried;

they were to be used rather to shore up a stable, heterosexual relationship. Indeed, most of the sex and marriage manuals sought to define the male and female roles more narrowly so that more efficient parenting would result. In an unexpected swing away from Victorian mores, sex manuals implied – as was seen in chapter 3 – that it was now not simply a woman's right, it was her duty, to enjoy sex. Her failure to achieve orgasm was presented as a threat to family stability and therefore to society.[16] In a world in which pregnancy did not have to be feared any lack of heterosexual ardour could be taken as sign of either frigidity or latent homosexuality.[17]

Class and Politics

It is unlikely that the appeals to 'romance' made much headway in labouring districts. Working-class women could not fully escape, however, the new stress on woman as efficient wife, mother and homemaker. As part of the effort to compensate for the losses of the First World War a barrage of propaganda was spread by child-savers in favour of 'mothercraft' and 'well-baby clinics'.[18] Middle-class mothers led the way in seeking to meet the high standards of mothercraft set by such reform-minded child experts as Dr Frederick Truby King with his complicated schedule of mandatory nursings. Working-class parents were said by investigators to 'spoil' their children; that is, irrationally care for them, and therefore in need of instruction in mothering. The inhabitants of tenements were forced to suffer the intrusive inspections of social workers and health visitors; a typical report of one American investigator announced that Italian immigrant mothers did not love their children 'in the right way'.[19]

Given their higher fertility it was also assumed that working-class women did not love their husbands in the right way either. Many working-class men continued to see unfettered sex as their 'right'. Working-class wives tended to value 'careful', decent, sober husbands more than passionate spouses. The fact that every conception was not welcomed could be seen in the terms working-class women employed for pregnancy: being 'caught', having a 'bun in the oven' or 'up the spout'.[20] To her astonishment, Stopes found that working-class women wanted to know how to make their husbands less rather than more passionate.

> The demand for a simple pill or drug to solve such troubles [she wrote] is astonishingly widespread. After lecturing to working-class audiences, in the question time, and even more when talking individually

to members of the audience afterwards, I am surprised by the prevalence of the rumour that there are drugs which can safely be taken
to reduce the man's virility, and that such drugs act directly and only
on the sex organs. I think it may not be out of place, even in a book
specifically addressed to educated people, to explode this popular
fallacy, and warn everyone that *no reliable drug of this nature exists.*[21]

Working-class life did change in the inter-war period. Many traditional forms of women's work – particularly in agriculture – declined.
But in the cities a surge in white-collar employment required an
army of 'respectable' working-class women who, though ceasing to
work after marriage, had snatched a brief taste of independence. A
concern to retain some margin of freedom was reflected in the 'feminist' line advanced in some of the letters to Stopes by women stating
that they had the right to control their own bodies. 'Birth-control
use', notes Linda Gordon, 'almost always represented, in fact, a raised
self-evaluation of women's own work as child-raisers, a change that
increased women's self-identification as workers, even without being
wage labourers.'[22] But letters were also written to Sanger and Stopes
by concerned working-class men, and in the women's correspondence husbands were increasingly praised for being 'careful' or 'considerate'.[23] The older, male work-centred culture, revolving around
mine or factory, pub and football club, was slowly being eroded.
As men's work became more regimented and sedentary, they looked
increasing to their families for emotional fulfilment. As working
hours were reduced, holidays provided and housing improved, married men were 'domesticated' and spent more leisure time with their
wives. They took greater interest in their children as their numbers
declined. Working families, in acknowledging the importance of educational qualifications, accordingly became more child-centred. Poverty
became associated with the large family in a way in which it never
had been before.

Diana Gittens has argued that in England the working-class
couples who were most successful in limiting family size tended to
be the ones with a more home-oriented, communicative, negotiated
relationship.[24] Their first desire was to protect the health of the
mother; their second to assure the family budget. Working-class women
until at least the Second World War relied on neighbours for advice
and the chemist for contraceptives. They did not feel at ease in discussing their fertility either with a doctor or with the staff at a birth
control clinic.[25]

Middle-class couples were more likely than working-class couples
to employ contraceptives and to adopt them early in marriage to

postpone or space births. Working-class women tended to have the number of children they desired and then turned to some method to stop. It was not so much that they had a predetermined idea of a perfect number; they just decided when they had had enough. A German socialist like Eduard Bernstein recognized early on that their limitation of family was not due simply to adherence to the Malthusian wage fund theory. The decline in labouring families size was due to a whole range of changes in lifestyles and living conditions, including new types of housing, furnishings, leisure activities, entertainment and education.[26]

The nineteenth-century Malthusian League had supported fertility control on economic grounds. Birth control for Stopes and Sanger was essentially an instrument that, by sparing the woman unwanted pregnancies, would permit the emergence of the happy, sensual family unit in which she could have the leisure of delighting in motherhood.[27] It followed that the contraceptives Stopes and Sanger favoured could not be any that violated this image of the rational, caring couple. The myth of domesticity they conjured up must have drawn the interest of working-class women; their lives would necessarily have improved if their husbands became more responsible spouses. Stopes and Sanger shattered some myths – such as the old belief that coughing could prevent conception – but then proceeded to condemn most of the fertility control measures already employed by working men and women.[28] They condemned abstinence in describing the single bed as the enemy of marriage. Extended nursing, widely employed to space births, was damned as weakening for the mother.[29] And what of coitus interruptus? Across the Western world the poor primarily relied on this method, though as one researcher in the American South reported, few knew the technical term. One woman ventured 'Well, I always say that when you chew tobacco, it don't make so much mess if you spit it out the window.' Another described the same method in the words of advice which had been given her by an older woman, 'If you don't want butter, pull the dasher out in time!'[30] Despite its extensive employment, Stopes declared coitus interruptus to be extremely unreliable and physically and psychologically dangerous. According to Sanger, it prevented 'the satisfactory fulfilment of the act of physical communion, and produces a nervous reaction fatal to the well-being of both participants'.[31] It not only left the woman psychologically tense; Stopes also held the curious belief that it had deleterious physiological side-effects. 'The woman, too, loses the advantage (and I am convinced that it is difficult to overstate the physiological advantage) of the partial absorption of the man's secretions, which must take place through

the large tract of internal epithelium with which they come in contact.'[32] Moreover men, she asserted, could be lured into dangerous
over-indulgence by the simplicity of withdrawal. The douche Stopes
opposed as possibly harmful; she described the sheath as unromantic
and unaesthetic.[33]

Were there, wrote one woman to Margaret Sanger, 'any real sure-
enough things women can do to keep from having children?'[34] In
their beseeching letters written to the birth control advocates women
of all classes made it clear that they wanted more effective contraceptive protection; the question was could they use what was available?
Stopes's favoured method of contraception (which allowed the purported absorption of 'male secretions') was the cervical cap. Sanger
backed the use of the diaphragm. There was a clear feminist argument
underlying their preference for such contraceptives. The condom and
coitus interruptus were, asserted Sanger, 'of no certain avail to the
wife because they placed the burden of responsibility solely upon the
husband – a burden which he seldom assumed. What she was seeking
was self-protection she could herself use, and there was none.'[35]

But female contraceptives had to be fitted by a physician. In opting
for such techniques, Sanger and Stopes necessarily also had to argue
in favour of the establishment of clinics in which such fittings could
be provided for working-class women. The hope was that the clinics
would, on the one hand, serve to distance birth control from the
shady world of rubber goods shops and, on the other, attract the
support and interest of doctors.[36] The flaw in such a strategy was
that most doctors refused to have anything to do with birth control,
and the few clinics that were established had difficulty in attracting
working-class women, intimidated if not repelled by their male,
middle-class, medical aura. Stopes and Sanger condemned the very
contraceptive measures the working class found easiest to use and
exalted those that, though the most 'effective', were the least likely to
be employed.[37] And, ironically, while they called for greater male
responsibility they opposed coitus interruptus, the contraceptive practice which required the greatest degree of male cooperation. They
chided working women for assuming, as many did, that men would
take the initiative in contraception.

Enid Charles pointed out that it was strange, given the fact that the
two main methods of birth control – coitus interruptus and the condom – were male methods, that researchers increasingly focused on
women who attended clinics. The condom was, she noted, a remarkably successful contraceptive and the horror stories told about the
effects of coitus interruptus were wildly exaggerated. Stopes, Charles
further observed, overstated the success of the female methods she

supported by not reporting as failures those women who ceased coming to her clinics.[38] Foremost in Stopes's mind was not so much the acceptability and reliability of the contraceptive, but the desire to make marriage a 'mutual affair'.

Male methods predominated in France, which, though it had no organized birth control movement, had the lowest fertility rate in Europe.[39] Following the bloodletting of the First World War, the French National Assembly in 1920 declared contraception in principle illegal. The legislation did nothing to increase family size. French population growth was, with the exception of Ireland's, the slowest in Europe. Between 1900 and 1939 it increased 3 per cent while Germany's grew 36 per cent, Italy's 33 per cent and the United Kingdom's 23 per cent. And even the growth that France enjoyed was a result, as many had gloomily predicted, of foreign immigration. Total population increased from forty million in 1914 to forty-two million in 1939, but the numbers of foreigners – led by Italians, Belgians and Spaniards – exceeded two million. A mild 'baby-boom' in 1920–25 raised the birth rate back to a pre-war level of 19.7 per thousand, but in 1926–30 it fell to 14.8 per thousand, leaving the nation with the lowest fertility in the world.[40]

Depopulation was seized upon by French nationalists as a code word for decadence.[41] Successfully playing on the tensions, anxieties and fears of those who believed that the social status quo was in danger, the right accused the defenders of birth control of being responsible for a vast number of troubling concerns ranging from the emergence of the independent woman to the declining ability of the nation to defend itself.[42] This campaign against birth control was largely fuelled by hypocrisy. Middle-class male politicians who bewailed the nation's low fertility had for the most part small families themselves, and the 1920 law outlawing the sale and discussion of birth control devices made no mention of the two main male forms of contraception – coitus interruptus and the condom.[43] Many deputies who voted for the legal repression of contraceptive information, though they must have known that such legislation could have little impact on population growth, could only content themselves with the knowledge that such laws would at least silence the sexual subversives. The post-First World War government's preoccupation with the birth rate launched what was to become for much of the rest of the twentieth century a national obsession.[44]

In the United States and Britain in the inter-war period birth control movements won the support of wealthy philanthropists interested in maintaining social order, whereas in France the neo-Malthusians found themselves marginalized. Paul Robin, France's best-known defender of contraception, had committed suicide just before the First World War.[45] His leading disciples such as Eugène and Jean Humbert who publicly defended birth control in the 1920s and 1930s, were hounded out of public life by the authorities.[46] Dr Madeleine Pelletier, a lone defender of abortion, was silenced and imprisoned.[47] Some discreet supporters of contraception, including Dr Jean Dalsace and Bertie Albrecht, joined the *Association d'Études Sexologiques*, but their academic papers had little impact on the general public. Eugenicists were not numerous in France and did not, like their counterparts in neighbouring nations, rally to support neo-Malthusian doctrines.[48]

Yet, given the nation's low birth rate in the 1920s and 1930s, no one could ignore the fact that the majority of French couples were seeking, often by dangerous means, to restrict family size.[49] Even the Catholic church found it impossible to remain indifferent to such desires. In conservative Brittany coitus interruptus was spoken of openly from the 1920s onward; a considerate husband, it was said, 'knew how to wipe his nose'. Churchmen hoped that they could, by trumpeting the legitimacy of a 'natural' form of contraception such as the rhythm method, keep otherwise faithful Catholics in the church.[50] Progressive politicians also felt compelled to respond. The laws forbidding the diffusion of birth control information so patently discriminated against working-class couples that the Socialists, though reluctant to embrace the issue, in 1933 proposed ending the punitive 1920 legislation. They initially had the support of the Communists but the latter reversed their stand in 1938. The party's hostility to discussion of birth control was to be maintained in the years following the Second World War. Though supporting abortion reform, Communist spokespersons were still hostile to birth control propaganda, associating it as they did with socially conservative neo-Malthusian arguments. As late as the 1950s, Maurice Thorez would declare that those who spoke constantly about the importance of birth control were simply looking for a way of masking capitalism's responsibility for poverty.[51]

Abortion

Stella Browne, Britain's most vocal proponent of the decriminalization of abortion in the inter-war period, held the 'cant of contraception' partly responsible for society's refusal to admit that some women would always need to terminate a pregnancy.[52] Abortion was relied on by many as a back-up method of birth control. 'I have worked in a factory eleven years', wrote a working woman to Margaret Sanger, 'and the majority of women of my acquaintance procure abortion as their means of family limitation, regardless of the suffering and ill-health which it produces.'[53] Women continued to try to abort themselves by taking all kinds of drugs. Alice Jenkins recalled in the 1950s that even as a child she knew what it meant when one woman said of another, '*She takes things.*'[54] In France the question of whether the women raped by Germans should be permitted to abort brought the issue into the public arena following the First World War.[55] The French Assembly in fact passed draconian laws against both abortion and birth control propaganda.[56] Nevertheless, abortion was common with information on how help could be obtained circulating via women's networks across class lines.[57] In inter-war Austria abortion was widespread and the poorest workers, because of poverty, actually had smaller families than the artisans.[58] In Germany, though Marriage Consultation Clinics provided birth control information, it was claimed that the number of abortions climbed from 300,000 prior to the war to a million in the 1920s and resulted in between 5,000 and 8,000 abortion-related deaths a year.[59] Three-quarters of the women involved were married.[60] In England Dr Janet Campbell shocked the public with reports that not only were abortion deaths numerous but that they were driving up the maternal mortality rate from 3.91 per thousand births in 1921 to 4.41 per thousand in 1934. Abortion-related deaths increased from 10.5 per cent to 20 per cent of all maternal deaths between 1930 and 1934.[61] Edward Griffith cited figures in the mid-1930s that suggested there were two million abortions a year in the United States with 15,000 resulting in deaths, whereas in the Soviet Union, where abortion had been decriminalized, Moscow had 80,000 abortions a year and not a single mortality.[62] Marie Stopes informed *The Times* in 1931 that in a three-month period she had received 20,000 requests for information on where to procure abortion.[63]

All these figures have to be treated with extreme caution but there is no doubt that abortion was widespread. Nevertheless, supporters of birth control insisted on their hostility to the inducement of miscarriage. Bernarr McFadden, the American physical culture faddist, attacked abortion as the 'American crime' which could only be ended by free access to birth control. Eugenic needs, he believed, made it necessary to prevent conceptions; unwanted children were likely to become criminals. So for economic and health reasons the United States had to follow Europe in allowing doctors to give contraceptive advice. The selfish woman should not be allowed to abort. Her husband had to show 'sufficient manhood and force of character' to stop her.[64] Stopes and Sanger were similarly hostile.

By the 1930s it was clear that in the first trimester medical abortion was as safe (indeed safer once sulphonamides were available) than delivery at term. Dilation and curettage was the most common method utilized. The old argument in defence of the law based on risk to the mother was thereby undermined. Now it was the criminalization of abortion itself which, by driving women into the arms of abortionists employing vaginal salves, instruments and uterine syringes, was putting women in danger. The Depression forced the abortion rate up to new heights. Dr W. D. Cornwall wrote that in Canada,

> I think most general practitioners can testify to the increasing frequency with which they are approached to terminate undesired pregnancies. Pregnancy is looked upon as an economic and social disaster. I note that England has recorded the lowest birth rate in 1932 for many decades. If it were possible to compile statistics it would be shown that abortion among the intelligent has increased tremendously.[65]

In the United States Frederick J. Taussig reported that something like a fifth of all pregnancies ended in abortion.[66]

The idea that the woman less than three months' pregnant who sought to 'put herself right' was committing a crime was clearly not accepted by a large section of the female public. Havelock Ellis stated that women felt no regret and could not understand the legal and medical opposition to abortion. In Britain the Birkett Committee on abortion reported in 1937 that 'Many mothers seemed not to understand that self-induced abortion was illegal. They assumed it was legal before the third month, and only outside the law when procured by another person.'[67] Working-class women clung to the traditional view that life was not present until the fetus 'quickened'. They took pills, not to abort, but 'to bring on a period'. That they did not intend to harm a new life was indicated by their abandonment of such tactics once quickening was perceived. The abortionists who aided them were sometimes exploitative charlatans, but often neighbourhood women who provided services as much out of kindness as for any monetary gain. Of the forty-four interviewed in Holloway Prison in the 1950s by Moya Woodside, all had been married, all but three had children, thirteen were grandmothers, and twenty-two were over sixty years of age. There were few crimes in which one would expect to find so many elderly women involved. Woodside noted that they viewed their activities not as 'criminal' but as gestures elicited by 'compassion and feminine solidarity'.[68] Such support was rarely given by the medical authorities; hospitals relegated women with suspicious miscarriages to the harsh treatment of the 'naughty ward'.[69] For some women, abortion was a primary, rather than a back-up, method of birth control. An investigator of a Liverpool slum reported that the Catholic resident of Ship Street:

> regards birth control as a sin but abortion before the age of three months a perfectly legitimate measure . . . though so few of the Mums use contraceptives the majority have at some time or another tried to bring on an abortion. Pills, jumping down stairs, etc., are perfectly legitimate up to the end of the third month, after which the woman stops in case she hurts the baby.[70]

The legalization of abortion in Russia following the 1917 revolution proved the safety of the procedure but confirmed in the mind of its opponents its association with the forces subverting existing class and sex relations.[71] In the West the abortion laws were clearly class biased because a well-off woman could usually find a doctor who would justify her need for a therapeutic abortion. In fact, there were, as improvements in obstetrics increased the chances of safe deliveries, fewer and fewer medical justifications for such intervention. The abortion issue emerged increasingly as an issue of women's rights and the campaign for decriminalization began to find advocates. Dorothy Dunbar Bromley argued in 1934 that America could avoid 8,000 maternal deaths a year by legalizing abortion at least until adequate contraceptives were made available.[72] In England Stella Browne declared 'The right to prevent the conception of life must logically and justly include the right to remove the life-seed which has been fertilised against the mother's will, either through accident or intention.'[73] To fight for liberalization Browne, along with Alice Jenkins and Janet Chance, formed the Abortion Law Reform Society in 1936.[74]

By the 1920s there were also some English lawyers and doctors willing to express their own unhappiness with the 1861 law on abortion. The statute was an obvious embarrassment to the police who recognized that abortion was largely condoned and prosecutions were unpopular. Eugenically minded judges in the 1930s wondered aloud why impoverished mothers should be punished for seeking to avoid the birth of congenitally unhealthy children. And physicians in both Britain and the United States – who for the most part believed that abortion was 'wrong' but sometimes 'necessary' – worried that their freedom to provide or withhold therapeutic abortions would be jeopardized if they were subjected to the dictates of either their patients or the courts.[75] Doctors, on the one hand, loathed being pressured by their patients; on the other hand, they knew that if they did not provide such services others would. Professional control in both

England and America was maintained by progressive physicians' continual broadening of the definition of 'health' – in particular by adding psychiatric indications – so that abortion would always be justified on medical rather than on social grounds.

A woman three days overdue wrote to Stopes in August of 1923 complaining that *Wise Parenthood* only dealt with 'pre-conception', and went on to threaten 'If I do not get anyone with *knowledge* to help me, I shall try other means, as I feel I shall go mad if I have to go through it all again.'[76] In her clinic established off the Holloway Road Stopes had her staff take an oath against providing any information on inducement of miscarriage. In *A Letter to a Working Woman* (1923) Stopes set out her arguments against such tactics. She envisaged the woman 'caught' and then 'So you do, or try to do, a desperate thing; you try to get rid of the baby before it has "gone too far".' This, she informed her readers, was 'what is called an abortion' and was opposed to both law and nature. Some might feel the law to be wrong, conceded Stopes: 'I know that many thousands of you feel all this is cruel and unjust, but I want to tell you that the law is not cruel, and that it is not unjust.'[77]

Margaret Sanger received so many enquiries about abortion that she had a form letter made up stating that she could not respond to such requests. It has been argued that she presented herself as a campaigner against abortion as a way of claiming a moral impulse for her work; certainly both she and Stopes sought for tactical purposes to draw a sharp line between contraception and abortion.[78] But working-class women made it clear in their letters that, though they feared the risks posed by abortion, they did not accept the idea that the employment of one method of birth control required the sacrifice of the other; rather, they saw both having a place on a continuum of fertility control measures.

The fact that working-class women wanted to provide themselves with the greatest possible degree of flexibility in dealing with reproductive decisions was reflected in their use of language. They did not usually employ the term 'abortion' because it clearly conjured up the image of a doctor carrying out an operation, something qualitatively different from the traditional means of limiting family size. In France the obstruction would be described as something one would *faire passer* or *faire descendre*. The fetus was regarded neither as human nor as a baby but as *ça*. In England the woman described herself as attempting to 'restore her menses' or 'make herself regular'. Likewise, women did not say they had 'conceived', which had an irremediable ring to it; they said they were 'caught' or had 'fallen', 'am that way again', 'my monthly courses are ten days late', 'am a month over my time', 'am two months on the road', 'am four months on the way', all of which implied a process which could or could not be terminated.[79]

Stopes and Sanger made slow headway in their attempts to turn working women towards complicated methods of contraception.[80] Birth controllers often chose to interpret such intransigence as evidence of 'ignorance'. What they ignored was that the ideological baggage with which middle-class contraceptive methods were lumbered often deterred their acceptance by the working class. Labouring families clearly wanted more effective contraceptives, but they would have to become almost middle class in mentality to use many that the birth controllers offered. Stopes and Sanger envisaged a model family in which the far-sighted and prudent husband would employ or assist his wife in employing mechanical means of contraception for the purposes of ensuring the family's upward economic mobility. The rational mother would not work outside the home but devote herself to her appropriate maternal, child-rearing duties. For advice on the suitable method of fertility control the couple would turn to their friendly, progressive physician. He would explain to them not only the efficacy of the medically fitted cap or diaphragm but the dangers of other methods of contraception and the immorality of abortion.

The dangers the birth controllers saw in abortion and coitus interruptus were as much social as physiological. Such tactics represented not the harmonious couple but two separate sexual cultures in which the man demanded his 'rights' and the woman relied on her female friendship network for support; they epitomized not the consumption-oriented, far-sighted, rational middle class, but the short-sighted, risk-taking working class. Abortion conjured up the image of relying, not on the doctor, but on the neighbourhood wise woman. The ambition of Stopes and Sanger was to remake not only the fertility control decision but the family that made it. The modern marriage could only be saved, declared the birth controllers (and like-minded progressives in favour of sex education and liberalization of divorce), if it evolved towards the companionate model.[81]

Doctors and Priests

Stopes and Sanger 'medicalized' contraception in part to attract the legitimating support of doctors. In 1922 Stopes established a Medical Research Committee with the intent of enlisting such backing. But if the clinic appealed to some doctors it did not appeal to many patients. By 1930 the sixteen clinics and two private consultants in Great Britain had seen a mere 21,000 clients, and despite Stopes's claims of success their failure rates were high.[82] The caps and diaphragms proved too demanding to be consistently employed. The vast majority of the population continued to rely on traditional methods. Arguably the greatest good served by the birth control clinics was in tabulating and publicizing both the threats posed to women's health by their frequent attempts at abortion and the physical disabilities associated with childbirth. Of her first 10,000 clients, Stopes reported that 1,321 had slit cervixes, 335 serious prolapses and 1,508 internal deformations.[83] Doctors seriously concerned with maternal health could hardly ignore such shocking statistics. But one way of side-stepping the issue of contraception was for doctors to assert that maternal mortality and morbidity rates could be brought down by the medicalization of birthing. Such a campaign was remarkably successful. In England hospital deliveries climbed from 15 per cent in 1927 to 54 per cent in 1954; in America the rate was even higher. Women, told that such institutions offered superior care, naturally sought access to them. Doctors believed that they could minimize the risks of childbearing in such a setting; in fact, given the greater chance of instrumental intervention, it is doubtful whether hospital births were safer than home deliveries.[84]

The birth controllers constantly warned women to spurn the contraceptive advice of ill-informed local gossips and instead turn to trained professionals. But English doctors, though the 1911 census revealed that they had the smallest families of all occupational categories, long opposed discussion of contraception. In the 1920s eminent British physicians still described the subject as a 'highly nauseous' one that could only attract the 'prurient-minded'. Women who employed contraceptives were condemned as selfish and self-centred. Mechanical contraceptives were attacked by purportedly well-trained gynaecologists as 'sordid and unnatural' and posing 'physiological dangers'.[85] 'The professional and well-to-do practice it [contraception]', a Saskatchewan correspondent of Sanger's American Birth Control League wrote in 1923, 'as in any other city in the US. An increasing number of people are applying to the doctor for birth control information.'[86] The problem was that doctors would not respond. They might advise the spacing of births, but few would say how.

Some doctors were simply opposed to birth control on moral grounds but in England and North America the profession as a whole was obviously afraid of the loss of respectability that an association with Stopes and Sanger might entail, worried by confusions over abortion and contraception, and simply ignorant of contraceptive techniques. The graduates of the London School of Medicine for Women were as ill informed as their male counterparts. 'A young woman doctor, being interviewed for her first assistantship, was asked for her views on birth control. She replied tentatively that she had always thought large families rather jolly, and was relieved when this appeared to be the right answer.[87] Even after British welfare centres began in the 1930s to provide birth control information, doctors had little to contribute and did not take the initiative in broaching the subject with patients. Edward F. Griffith, MRCS, who believed that birth control could end much juvenile delinquency and marital discord, complained that men disliked putting on sheaths and appreciated the cheapness of simple withdrawal. Some women's hope that the man would be 'careful' simply resulted in unwanted births. Because they were shy and embarrassed they acquired cheap unreliable caps from their chemist rather than being properly fitted by a doctor.[88] In England the first medical training lectures on contraception were started in 1936 but were neglected by the majority of schools well into the 1950s.[89]

In the United States the medical profession was even slower to support birth control. The very fact that clinics had been established by Sanger and others allowed doctors to send their patients to them for diaphragm fittings rather than engage themselves in such unglamorous activities. Doctors presented themselves as defenders of public morality and were concerned that if they appeared to be critics of society their medical schools would lose the support of wealthy philanthropists. Nevertheless, Sanger continued to woo the medical profession by demonstrating that her Clinical Research Bureau could provide valuable data on the health histories of its clients. Dr Robert Latou Dickinson finally succeeded in having the American Medical Association pass a 1937 resolution acknowledging the importance of contraception and calling for its teaching in medical schools. This did not mean that doctors had become enthusiastic defenders of contraception. The Depression had simply forced them to provide grudging acknowledgement of the importance of the issue. Most continued into the 1960s to argue that the healthy woman was the childbearing woman.[90]

Nevertheless, in the 1930s a breakthrough of sorts was made in the public acceptance of birth control. This change has usually been attributed to the remarkable propaganda work of Marie Stopes and Margaret Sanger. They did succeed in presenting birth control as a positive force that would serve both the interests of individual couples in improving their health and happiness and the interests of the state in scientifically improving the quality of the race. For these reasons the birth controllers disarmed much of the opposition of the Protestant churches and the medical profession. More important, however, was the realization by these organizations that the social, cultural and economic forces that had led the majority of ordinary men and women to restrict family size simply could not be reversed.

The churches had, by the 1930s, little to say in opposition. The Anglican bishops at the Lambeth Conference of 1908 referred to contraception as 'preventive abortion', but the eugenically minded clergy were slowly won over by the birth controllers' utilitarian argument that contraception would spare society high social costs.[91] Stopes and Sanger received a good number of requests for information from Protestant ministers and their wives who both employed it and helped disseminate such advice in isolated communities.[92] Pius XI's encyclical, *Casti Connubi* (On Christian Marriage), which was in part a response to the Anglicans' tepid acceptance of contraception announced at the 1930 Lambeth Conference, crystallized the Catholic church's opposition to 'artificial' fertility regulation. But, at the same time, the new rhythm method elaborated by Knaus and Ogino in 1929 was publicized by the church and sanctioned by the Vatican. 'A knowledge of a woman's rhythm', wrote Leo J. Latz in a church-approved text, 'enables married people to know *when*, by performing the married act, they are co-operating with God in the procreation of a new human being.'[93] Use of the rhythm method allowed the regulation of family size to take place 'naturally' and would, Latz hoped, be a way of winning back Catholics who were over-represented among the birth control clinics' clients.[94] One way out for the woman who wanted both to use reliable contraception and to remain a good churchgoer was to find a liberal confessor.[95]

In England maternal and child welfare centres were, after the Labour victory of 1929 and as a result of the vigorous lobbying of feminist and birth control societies, allowed to give out birth control information if warranted for medical reasons. By 1937 only ninety-five of 423 centres did provide such information but an important breakthrough had been made. Moreover, the Anglican church and the British Medical Association conceded that birth control could be sanctioned if a further pregnancy were deemed detrimental to a mother's health. In Canada a 1937 court case sanctioned the distribution of birth control information when done for the 'public good'.[96] In the United States the seizure by customs of a shipment of diaphragms led federal appeals court justice Augustus Hand to strike down the provisions of the 1873 Comstock law that prevented the use of the mail by physicians to provide contraceptives or contraceptive advice.[97]

Stopes and Sanger offered new sentimental justifications for family limitation and elaborated an oft-times florid vocabulary with which to describe the reasons it would be sought. They successfully used books, public lectures and courtroom forums to spread their message. But all the birth control clinics combined provided only a tiny fraction of the population with new means of regulating fertility and the main motive for employing them remained the old one of economic survival. Pronatalists continued to castigate the immorality of birth control; they could not bring themselves, however, to attack the class and income inequities that impoverished large working-class families.[98] Fear of poverty drove the fertility rate down to a new historical low in the depths of the Depression; the simple acknowledgement of such social realities underlay the public acceptance of birth control. Social conservatives and eugenicists were finally forced to support birth control if only in the hope of reducing welfare expenditures. In the United Kingdom the crude birth rate (number of births per 1,000 of the population) dropped continuously from 34.1 per 1,000 in 1870–2 to 24.5 per 1,000 in 1910–12 to 15.8 per 1,000 in 1930–2.[99] In America the cohort of women marrying in the 1920s produced fewer children than any other between the 1880s and the 1950s.[100] The fertility of the working class fell faster than that of the middle class but differentials in family size and contraceptive method remained.

Methods

The evidence collected at the birth control clinics revealed that coitus interruptus was the main form of contraception employed by the mass of the population. In England the percentage of couples utilizing appliance methods of birth control grew between 1910 and 1930 from 9 to 40 per cent for the middle class and from 1 to 28 per cent for the working class.[101] Indeed, there appears to have been a peak in the use of non-appliance methods in the 1920s and only then a shift to new techniques. In the 1930s the most popular methods used in Britain, in order of use, were: withdrawal, sheath, safe period and pessary. The First World War had clearly popularized the use of condoms though primarily for protection from venereal disease. They were long associated with prostitution or extramarital affairs which, along with their expense and discomfort, served to impede their domestic use. Even Ettie Rout, a New Zealand expert on venereal disease who supervised a 'tolerated house' in Paris during the First World War, was hostile to the condom which she said 'destroyed contact' and thereby inhibited pleasure.[102] By the 1930s they were made of more comfortable latex rather than rubber. In France condoms were offered for sale by herbalists, pharmacists and midwives. Barbers in England sold but did not advertise them.

Many men did not like using contraceptives. 'Rubber check pessaries', complained one Englishman, 'remind me of one having a bath with top hat and spurs on.'[103] Male methods of contraception were slowly supplanted by female methods; the process took place earliest in the United States where by the 1930s employment of the cap, douche and rhythm was already high.[104] The cervical cap, invented in the late 1830s, was popularized by Stopes in the 1920s. It could be left in for up to a month but required medical fitting. The diaphragm and cream were especially popular among the middle class. It was estimated that in the 1950s one in three American wives employed this method. The problem was that since the spring-rim vaginal diaphragm required medical fitting few working-class women found it satisfactory and a low success rate resulted.[105]

In Belgium Fernand Mascaux argued that for the proletariat simplicity and cheapness were essential; cotton wool dipped in vinegar or lemon juice could provide a vital margin of protection.[106] An appreciation of the social forces that inhibited the use of contraceptives was best represented by A. R. Kaufman. He began his Canadian birth control work in the 1930s by funding clinics that fitted diaphragms. He soon became impatient with the low success rate that he realized was due to the medicalization of the process. He withdrew his support from the clinics and instead began to send out from his Parents Information Bureau kits of condoms and contraceptive creams. A less effective form of contraceptive, if used, was clearly more successful than its rivals that were not used.[107] In the United States Clarence James Gamble (of the soap dynasty) followed a similar path in experimenting with the mass delivery of simple contraceptives such as lactic-acid jelly.[108] Social conservatives like Kaufman and Gamble were sensitive to the argument that welfare costs could be kept down by limiting the size of working-class families. It was for them not a question of women's rights, but of class concerns.

Some new methods of birth control were produced in the early twentieth century; none proved satisfactory. Surgical sterilization of men and women was made possible in the 1890s, but usually only carried out for eugenic reasons on the mentally ill. The accurate plotting in the 1920s of ovulation by Ogino and Knaus resulted in the publicizing of a new rhythm method; although superior to its nineteenth-century counterpart, its high failure rate led to its being dubbed 'Vatican roulette'. Similar frustrations met German researchers who before the First World War began work on intra-uterine devices that prevented the implantation of the fertilized egg. The first were made of silk but in the 1920s Gräfenberg announced his invention of a ring made of gold and silver. Stopes provided some patients with a similar device she called the 'gold pin'. The dangerous internal irritations caused by such methods created a host of medical problems that limited their employment.[109]

Where scientists failed businessmen stepped in. Calverton stated that in the late 1920s though medical schools did not teach birth control techniques, businesses made huge profits from the sale of contraceptives. In the city of Baltimore alone each year two and a quarter million contraceptives were sold in drug stores, confectioneries and dry goods establishments and by the two hundred salesmen who canvassed neighbourhoods.[110] Taking advantage of the demand for contraceptive protection, commercial houses produced a wide range of spermicidal creams and jellies. Rendells, Norforms, Sanitabs, Zonite and Zonitors were all advertised as offering contraceptive security. But because of the questionable nature of the merchandise there were no brand names or government regulations; customers had no guarantees of the products' efficacy. In one study carried out in the United States one-half of the condoms tested were found to be defective.[111] Some douches, whose makers claimed that they could protect 'married happiness', might have contained spermicidal agents but often were no more than vaginal deodorants. Disinfectants such as Lysol and Dettol that could, according to their discreet marketers, be turned to the same purposes proved to be dangerously irritating. Despite such shortcomings, the 'feminine hygiene' industry became a multimillion dollar business with an estimated $250 million a year spent in the United States on such products in the 1930s.[112]

Conclusion

In introducing a birth control discussion with the claim that the 'safeguarding of passion is of critical import for marital adjustment', Robert Latou Dickinson captured the essence of the sex reformers' reasons for embracing contraception.[113] Women who attempted to limit their fertility had once been attacked as 'selfish' enemies of the family. The birth controllers turned the argument around and claimed that the greatest threat to family happiness was posed by women's fear of pregnancy. Interestingly enough, this argument was primarily popularized and made respectable by women activists: Marie Stopes in Britain, Margaret Sanger in the United States, Aletta Jacobs and Maria Rutgers-Hoitsema in The Netherlands. Contraception, they asserted, was necessary not just as a means of limiting family size, but as the basis for the romantic and companionate family and ultimately the woman's enjoyment of 'Radiant Motherhood'. There was evidence that supported some of these claims. One study of 153 women using the cap found that forty-seven reported that the use of the birth control device increased their sexual pleasure, while ten believed it diminished it.[114] Most women employing contraception no longer had their sexual pleasure blighted by a sense of 'fear'.

By the 1930s the majority of Western women approved of birth control.[115] But *Britain and her Birth-Rate*, a Mass Observation study published in 1945, revealed that the birth controllers' message had still not reached all members of the community. A twenty-one-year-old woman with four children was quoted as saying, 'Oh, there's enough babies in Poplar [a working-class London borough] if it's babies you want. I wish I knew how to stop them.'[116] Women such as her accepted their fate; others tried 'being careful', by which they meant insisting on their husband withdrawing, but as a twenty-nine-year-old mother of three admitted ruefully, 'You gets excited and forgets yourself.'[117] Despite the limited access to reliable contraceptives, the birth rate was brought down. Pursuit of marital romance played some part but such a preoccupation was a luxury for couples worrying about how to feed an additional child. Because of social and economic changes working-class women could simply no longer envisage bearing large numbers of children. Their feelings were summed up by one who concluded 'I don't want to be like my mum.'[118] Such women would for much of the twentieth century continue to rely on traditional means to control their fertility – despite rather than because of the advice of the sex experts.

5

'Perverts': Mannish Women, Effeminate Men and the Sex Doctors

Having followed the experts' inter-war discussion of the sexuality of the 'normal', it is now necessary to backtrack to fill in their account of the 'abnormal'. In fact, doctors had produced reports of what they regarded as the curious sexual activities of the deviant long before they investigated the apparently humdrum behaviour of the married. Late nineteenth-century experts set out the taxonomies of a host of 'perverts' – homosexuals, sadists, masochists, fetishists and exhibitionists. This classification and definition of sexual pathologies represented in part a new medicalization of sexuality. Since classical times pretty much the whole range of sexual *practices* had been categorized, but in the late nineteenth century certain sorts of *persons* – the homosexual, the masochist, the sadist – were discovered or, one might say, invented. Before, deviants were silenced or their mutterings ignored; now, careful reports were kept of their incriminating statements. In the works of sexologists who demanded confessions from their clients erupted into the print 'the speaking pervert'.[1] What doctors now declared to be important was not so much what one did as what one was; having adopted an essentialist model they shifted attention from 'doing' to 'being'. Ian Hacking has argued that, by this process, 'a kind of person came into being at the same time as the kind itself was being invented. In some cases, that is, our classifications and our classes conspire to emerge hand in hand, each egging the other on.'[2]

Early sexology was as much a literary as a scientific undertaking. A French criminal anthropologist like Alexandre Lacassagne noted Dostoevsky's insightful comments on the correlation between beatings and sexual arousal and went on to say that Emile Zola's *La Bête humaine* was a 'wonderful confirmation of the notion which links sex and violence'.[3] Alfred Binet similarly drew many of his references to fetishes from fiction. The tabloids, police files, decadent novels and psychiatric journals of the *fin de siècle* all shared the same morbid fascination with the perversions. This literature was sparked not so much by any new threat that sexual minorities might pose as by the fear that the artificial nature of urban society was weakening 'normal' men and women's respect for appropriate gender roles.[4]

After sketching in these earlier developments, this chapter will examine why twentieth-century sex doctors prided themselves on being both more sympathetic to their subjects and more scientific than their nineteenth-century predecessors. As will be shown, some members of the sexual minorities would find in the new investigations material that could be turned to their own purposes. Nevertheless, all the sex doctors continued to craft their accounts carefully. Even their patients' confessions unconsciously followed a familiar script.

Pierrette

Sometime in the early 1930s Pierre Vachet, a Parisian psychiatrist, began treating a slender, blond, blue-eyed young man who, claiming to have the soul of a woman, felt himself being driven mad by society's insistence that he dress and act like a man. 'Pierrette', as Vachet called him in his account of the case, had been a timid boy. Teased constantly as 'the girl', he was unhappy at his *lycée* and hated his school uniform. By twelve he was clearly interested in women's clothing. He ceased to feel humiliated when he imagined himself a woman and this obsession slowly grew. He began to take advantage of fêtes, masquerades, costume parties and amateur theatricals to put on women's clothes. He gradually came to believe that he had a *libido féminine* and to realize that his desire was actually to be a woman. He found himself drawn to men though, he hastened to add, not specifically in a sexual sense. 'It was just the desire to please men', he explained, 'to flirt with men, especially to reveal my weakness to men.'[5]

Pierrette went through both cycles of cross-dressing and attempts to give up the practice. He seems to have abstained from masquerading while at university. At twenty-three he even tried to establish his 'normality' by attempting to have sex with a Parisian prostitute in a hotel off one of the grand boulevards. She failed to arouse him and concluded, he was proud to recall, that he 'would certainly be successful as a girl'.[6] In the winter of 1927–8 he returned to his passion of cross-dressing and by 1930 had come to the decision to give up completely his life as a man. As he relinquished his masculinity he felt himself going through an unexpected psychological transformation. No longer timid but active and energetic, he felt himself actually braver as a woman than he had been as a man. On one memorable occasion he seized the bridle of a panicked horse that was menacing a woman and child, an action he declared he would normally not have contemplated. The psychological satisfaction he received from wearing women's clothing was such that he no longer had the need to masturbate. It was at this stage that Pierrette sought the help of Dr Vachet. He did not want to be 'cured', but aided. Would the doctor, Pierrette asked, explain to his family his need to live his own life as he saw fit?

Vachet was won over by the evidence that Pierrette's cross-dressing was non-threatening. The fact that Pierrette was so accepting of normative gender roles was, the doctor pointed out, curiously reassuring. The patient's transgender obsession was divorced from same-sex desires. Pierrette claimed that he was not a homosexual and did not like men who sought sex with other men. He did have a male friend but insisted that nothing sexual took place between them. He did admit to kissing men; that was all. He insisted that he only liked 'normal men'. Pierrette read up on the sexological literature to provide proof that he was not a homosexual.[7] A dislike of women was taken by many doctors as a symptom of homosexuality and he pointed out that he was neither sexually excited by men nor hostile to women. Indeed, he insisted that he liked the sexual and non-sexual attitudes of women and especially envied attractive females. Pierrette embraced a particular chaste form of femininity. He did admit to being a flirt and even rivalrous with women over men's admiring glances. This jealousy he ironically advanced as further proof of his distaste for same-sex relations. It would have been impossible, he insisted, to flirt with a man he knew to be a homosexual because the other man would be looking for the male behind the dress. Pierrette insisted that he was disgusted by effeminate male attire and that when dressed as a man he was not himself at all effeminate. He claimed to have even abandoned masturbation because he regarded it as a masculine vice.[8]

As a woman he occupied himself with the 'normal' feminine tasks of shopping, cooking and cleaning. When dressed as a man he had led a disorderly and chaotic existence. He never felt at ease or truly himself in his masculine attire. In men's clothing he sensed himself an intruder in his own apartment. He hated his 'masculine mask' and in particular evidence of a beard. He described to Vachet having vivid nightmares of his whiskers growing backwards through his skull into his brain and spent up to ten hours every two weeks shaving and plucking himself smooth.

Vachet was reassured by the fact that when dressed as a woman Pierrette was a model of femininity. As a woman he clothed and made himself up discreetly. He moved easily about town. He did not feel he 'dressed' as a woman but rather that when in female clothing he had become himself. He was finally free. Pierrette nevertheless felt a lack of love and maternity. He saw himself as a sterile female. Transvestism was not enough. He obviously could not perform sexually as a woman; his hope was one day to have reconstructive surgery. Vachet talked to the young man's family and convinced them his mania was inoffensive. With his help Pierrette eventually won over his parents to his having his own apartment where, after work, he could indulge himself. In his own 'home' – Vachet used the loaded English word conjuring up domestic calm – the young man was ecstatically happy.

Degeneration

Vachet's sympathetic account of Pierrette represented how far the treatment of deviants by sex experts had advanced by the 1930s. Unlike their British and North American counterparts, continental doctors had since the early nineteenth century played the role of a 'medical police' in the regulation of prostitution. Sexology – the science of sexuality – emerged in the last decades of the nineteenth century as magistrates in European courts increasingly called upon medical experts to aid them in understanding a variety of sex crimes that were more difficult to fathom than simple rape or sodomy. The prosecutions of such crimes required that the boundaries separating permitted and forbidden, 'normal' and 'abnormal', sexual practices be rigidly drawn. The problem was that otherwise respectable individuals were frequently found to be guilty of such acts. Urban middle-class society's attempt to impose its moral norms on the entire community was partly responsible for this development. Some sexual acts – exhibitionism, for example – that had been casually tolerated in an agrarian society were not to be permitted in an urban milieu. More important was the middle-class polarization of acceptable forms of feminine and masculine deportment. Male sexuality in particular had become 'codified' in the course of the nineteenth century in such a way as to deny any place for same-sex attraction.[9] Doctors, as members of the middle class, were largely oblivious to such cultural factors, however, and believed an objective science of sexuality could be constructed by first cataloguing the range of deviant sexual practices and then advancing explanations for them.[10]

Late nineteenth-century medical scientists investigating sexual behaviour believed that they, like their fellow social scientists, were
simply observing and reporting 'facts', but they in fact produced a
literature that was both descriptive and prescriptive. In asserting what
was 'abnormal', they were also declaring what was 'normal.' The new
scientific norms of male and female sexuality which were propounded
were thus not simple 'discoveries': they were products of the middle-
class demand for reassurances that the separation of the sexual spheres
was firmly grounded in biology. Such reassurances were needed because social transformations such as the changing nature of men's
work, the reduction of the birth rate and women's entry into higher
education and the professions appeared in the eyes of the anxious to
have undermined much of the explanatory powers of older notions
of masculinity and femininity.

Western society had, of course, long condemned as unnatural a
number of specific sex acts; sodomy, for example, was in the nineteenth century in a number of countries still punishable by death.
Churchmen said that such vices were simply due to sin and immorality. Medical scientists demonstrated their modernity by claiming that
the perversions were the result of biological rather than moral flaws.
Perverts were seduced into engaging in abnormal acts because of a
hereditary predisposition; they were degenerates whose failings were
symptomatic of the depletion of male energy in an over-civilized
world. The luxurious and feverish life in the city with its excesses of
food and drink led to physical debilitation, psychiatric troubles and
finally sexual perversions.[11] George M. Beard, the American physician
who popularized the notion of neurasthenia, argued that perverts were
either born or acquired their vice as a result of over-indulgence.[12]
Ambroise Tardieu, the most important of the French forensic experts,
described pederasts in the context of either the criminality of bachelors
or the loss of reason of the married and the respectable. He, like
Richard von Krafft-Ebing, his German counterpart, tried to demonstrate that 'morbid love' was related to anatomical anomalies.[13] Such
doctors, assuming that perverts would bear the stigmata of their perversion, necessarily paid great attention to the culprit's physiology.
One trained in pathological anatomy was supposed to be able to spot
the signs of either active or passive homosexuality. The active homosexual, Tardieu informed his readers, would have a very thin, dog-
like penis, while the passive would have a funnel-shaped anus.[14] So
common were such beliefs that a British specialist in legal medicine
tried to draw a laugh from his audience by telling the story of 'a
police surgeon deputy [who] examined the penis of the passive and
the anus of the active agent, a mistake it is well to avoid'.[15] Other

doctors claimed the pervert would carry lesions on the genitals or the brain.[16]

French and German specialists in the 1880s began to produce more sophisticated interpretations of sexual perversion, a key argument being that the aberrant act simply represented the particular stage of a deviant's development.[17] These doctors, in regarding the act as a mere symptom and in paying greater attention to the specific type of individual who carried it out, accordingly turned away from biological and towards psychological explanations. Whereas it had been once said in a tautological way that a pervert was one who performed perverse acts, now researchers such as Valentine Magnan declared that the importance of such acts was that they were due to a diseased central nervous system and symptomatic of a morbid category of person.[18] Perverts suffered, claimed the doctors, from congenital rather than acquired illnesses; they were irresponsible yet could be cured. Some perverts – in particular the humiliated fetishists – were presented by the doctors as often causing more pain to themselves than to the community.[19] Most importantly, progressive doctors asserted that a variety of deviant practices, once regarded as 'choices' made by the sinful or immoral, were actually involuntary symptoms of the individual's entire personality. Thus the sex experts created in the latter decades of the nineteenth century an entirely new nomenclature to describe the species they had discovered: the 'exhibitionist', the 'transvestite', the 'voyeur', the 'homosexual', the 'sadist' and the 'masochist'. Countless pseudo-scientific treatises popularized the notion that whole subcultures were populated by potentially dangerous 'others'.[20]

The doctors could not help but advance their professional self-interests in their exhaustive cataloguing of the perversions. By claiming that the treatment of perverts was a medical rather than a criminal issue they enlarged medicine's terrain. In policing the vague boundaries separating abnormal and normal sexual practices they moved on from treating psychotics and asylum patients to the counselling of free, fee-paying neurotics. The new generation attacked Tardieu's claims about the 'stigmata' as mere inventions and pointed out that some patients had an absolutely normal anatomy.[21] The nervous system could, the argument now went, always override one's organic predisposition.[22] A doctor could, following this logic, detect a deviant, not because of any particular action, but by evidence of perverse desires. With this shift from biological to psychological explanations the notion of the 'sexual instinct' which Charles Darwin had popularized was revealed not to be as simple as once thought. Doctors such as Albert Moll and Sigmund Freud asserted that in order to explain irrational behaviour, a variety of different drives had to be distinguished.[23] Vachet followed Freud – whose views are analysed in chapter 6 – in arguing that even a kiss, inasmuch as it deviated from the mouth's primary aim, could be construed as a failing. For such a doctor a vice was any act or desire that in becoming tyrannical or obsessive jeopardized an individual's health and mental equilibrium.

Sexology

The style of reasoning which assumed that a sexual perversion was an illness over which the patient had no control did not simply displace the older notion that the immorality of the deviant was due to either seduction or degeneration. Many writers combined both approaches. Richard von Krafft-Ebing, whose encyclopaedic *Psychopathia Sexualis* (1886) was the most influential of the late nineteenth-century catalogues of sexual mental diseases, was a case in point. In the first editions of his work he took a pathological approach to the 'abnormal,' and labelled homosexuals as degenerates. His thinking evolved over time and in the later editions he presented them as unable to control themselves. A similarly confused account was presented by G. Frank Lydston who asserted in 1904 that the United States had 215,000 degenerates.[24] In Chicago, he claimed, male sex perverts have 'so increased in numbers that they have formed large colonies with well-known resorts'.[25] In these congregated men whose effeminacy and inferior physique signified a degenerative reversion to type. What caused deviancy? On the one hand, Lydston stressed the dangerous impact of early impressions and warned that boys should not be allowed to associate intimately; on the other hand, he argued that the passions were passed on by heredity which explained why imprisoning perverts was doomed to failure.[26]

Auguste Forel, the turn-of-the-century Swiss sexologist, similarly pointed out that the line separating acquired and inherited vices was difficult to determine. Homosexuality was, Forel claimed, worse than the other perversions because the object, not just the means of pleasure, was wrong.[27] Homosexuals were, he claimed, attracted mostly by normal men; but had to be content with like-minded fellows in their *confrérie secrète*. They wanted their 'marriages' recognized but were all, according to the doctor, unbalanced, promiscuous, pathologically inclined and hereditarily tainted. The few honest homosexuals whom Forel felt deserved respect were those who were so disgusted by other perverts that they committed suicide.[28] But Forel concluded his diatribe by stating that, though minors needed protection, homosexuality did not pose as many problems to society as did prostitution. He further argued that it was a mistake for homosexuals to try to cure themselves by marrying and pointed out that the laws that targeted them were too severe. Blackmailers who exploited such legislation often drove their victims to kill themselves.[29]

The public defenders of homosexuality who appeared in the latter decades of the nineteenth century embraced the notion that same-sex desires were congenital, not acquired. This notion underlay Karl Maria Benkert's coining of the terms 'homosexual' and 'heterosexual' in 1869.[30] Carl Heinrich Ulrichs in the 1860s spoke of a female soul in a male body, but insisted that the 'urning' – the term invert was also used for homosexuals – was simply a special type of normal man, not a feminized male as some like Forel would argue.[31] In England Edward Carpenter developed a similar theory of an 'intermediate sex' that was an outcome not of degeneration, but of a psychological blending of the masculine and feminine.[32]

Most informed commentators agreed that the laws against homosexuality increased rather than diminished crime. In England the false charges of a homosexual nature that soldiers and policemen commonly made to extort money, A. S. Taylor noted, often led to suicide.[33] France, Italy and some of the southern German provinces did not criminalize adult same-sex acts. The Western world's most vigorous sex reform movement emerged in Germany in response to its imperial government's imposing on the entire country, following the unification of the nation in 1871, article 175 of the draconian Prussian Criminal Code.[34] Magnus Hirschfeld led the homosexual rights campaign against article 175 through a Scientific-Humanitarian Committee.[35] Hirschfeld, a homosexual himself, insisted that homosexuality was not a perversion but a distinct variation of masculinity which was embraced by about 3 per cent of the population.[36] He also investigated cross-dressing (which he insisted was a distinct sexual variety not always accompanied by homosexual desires) and was responsible for coining the term 'transvestism'.[37] A tireless activist and researcher, he investigated almost every aspect of sexuality, in 1908 founded the first sexological journal and, with Iwan Bloch, in 1913 began the Medical Society for Sexology and Eugenics. Bloch, a Berlin dermatologist, who coined the term *Sexualwissenschaft* or sexology, stressed the importance of cultural as well as biological forces in determining sexual preferences. He attacked degeneration theorists who bandied about such vague terms as 'nervous' and 'over-civilized' and adopted a relativist, ethnographic approach in his researches. Modern society was, according to Bloch, by its attempts at imposing a common morality on every citizen, subjecting the individual to unprecedented moral coercion. The irony, in his view, was that many perversions spread because the respectable had been too successful in preventing the free expression of sexual desires. If they could not be manifested in a healthy fashion they would emerge in a pathological form.[38]

In the English-speaking world Havelock Ellis forwarded the idea that the passions of the 'abnormal' were not as bizarre as they might first appear and could be located on the extremes of a normal continuum of the desires. Ellis, an impotent urolagnist (an individual who experiences pleasure in watching others urinate) whose first wife was a lesbian, was understandably sympathetic to sexual minorities.[39] He countered the pathological approach of earlier chroniclers of sexuality, presenting his material in an accessible and sympathetic fashion. He repeatedly used the traditional notion of 'courtship', which assumed heterosexual male aggressiveness and female passivity, to explain deviant relationships. He thus presented sadism as an excessive form of normal male aggressiveness, transvestism as an excessive demonstration of the male's love of the female and exhibitionism as an excessive form of wooing. Unlike rape or sexual assault, most perversions harmed no one and in any event, according to Ellis, they were more symptomatic of lack of arousal rather than of excessive passion.

Turning to homosexuality, Ellis, like his progressive European counterparts, concluded that it was a congenital, not an acquired, condition. Some individuals were born inverted, Ellis noted, just as others were born colour blind. In the many case studies he collected he stressed the fact that the passion could be intense and high-minded.[40] Following on from Darwin, who had introduced the notion of the instincts as biological, unlearned responses, Ellis pointed out the futility of punishing deviants. He argued that anyone who thought about it would have to concur that sexuality was usually not simply linked to the instinct to reproduce. Giving full rein to his mania for indexing and cross-indexing data, he provided in his monumental *Studies in the Psychology of Sex*, written between 1897 and 1928 – a work that foreshadowed the investigations of Alfred Kinsey – a panoramic portrayal of the vast range of sexualities in which healthy men and women had indulged.[41]

If, as the psychologists demanded, sexual deviants were not to be imprisoned but treated, what might they expect? The sort of therapies an enlightened doctor might impose on a patient was indicated by a report presented by Schrenck-Notzing on a case of inversion improved by hypnotism. The patient, a twenty-eight-year-old functionary whose whole family was neurotic, was so overcome by guilt for having consorted with male prostitutes that he sought the doctor's help. Schrenck-Notzing subjected him to forty-five hypnotic sessions through the spring and summer of 1889. The man had previously admired women intellectually but was now encouraged to dream of their physical attractions. After the seventh session the doctor 'ordered' him to have a 'sexual union' with a woman and it was successfully accomplished, but when the suggestion sessions were halted the old temptations resurfaced. The patient was made to experience horror when he succumbed. To clinch his recovery the doctor orchestrated a dramatic confrontation. 'To finally put to the proof the equilibrium which was more and more re-establishing itself, the patient of his own accord, had intercourse with a woman in the presence of his [male] seducer with whom he immediately broke.'[42] The doctor apparently had no qualms in using a prostitute as a therapeutic device. He also cheerfully envisaged – should the patient fall again – recommencing the therapy.

Cases such as this revealed the apparent contradiction in the thinking of doctors who, while stating that a patient did not have the power to free him or herself from a perversion, still talked of 'cures'. Hypnotism and suggestion therapies were employed by a number of sexologists.[43] Hormonal treatments were recommended by the Spanish doctor Gregorio Marañon, who believed men to be catabolic and women anabolic.[44] The notion that therapists could deal with the sexual deviants who posed the police such difficulties had an obvious appeal. What the doctors failed to establish were either the criteria employed to measure the patient's 'voluntary' participation in such schemes or the success of the rehabilitation. Little evidence ever appeared to prove that any of the therapies worked.

Homosexuals

Even though most of the early sexologists did not set out to legitimate the practices of the deviant, this was often an unintended consequence of their efforts. Simply cataloguing sexual practices and asserting what was the norm led some to resist newly imposed boundaries. Doctors who advanced the notion that homosexuality was a congenital, not an acquired condition, freed some from the guilt that they had once felt for not being able to resist 'temptations'. Many had been looking for just such an argument. Serge Paul noted that as early as the 1890s patients were citing the Marquis de Sade, Jean-Jacques Rousseau and Sacher-Masoch in their defence. The works of Zola, Baudelaire and Dostoevsky were similarly plundered by patients looking for justifications of their desires and actions.

Doctors turned to their own purposes the information they received and attempted to fit each patient to a stereotype, but the collecting and publishing of case histories, even when done for 'forensic' reasons, gave voice to the sexual minorities. Deviants were eager to thrust their stories on doctors. The two groups had a curious symbiotic relationship. Individuals relied on doctors to help analyse their problems but they also strove to present their own view. Though they had to admit to being 'sick' to be heard, their accounts were obviously active, self-justifying and introspective. Their narratives tended to follow the familiar romantic script popularized by the modern novel in which the heroic effort of being true to oneself was ultimately rewarded. In adolescence a self-discovery took place, enormous bravery was demonstrated in violating family and community expectations, attempts at normal, heterosexual relations were made but proved disastrous, and finally the individual came to terms with his or her passion. By unconsciously exploiting the common literary convention of the individual's heroic struggle for self-fulfilment such patients normalized their purportedly 'abnormal' lives.

Pierrette's life story, with which this chapter was introduced, followed the pattern of many of the first-person accounts left by male deviants. He was fortunate to find a sympathetic doctor. Vachet declared that Freud had stripped sexual immorality of its nineteenth-century sacrilegious aura and claimed, as did a number of French commentators, that in the inter-war period perversions were not only talked about, but flaunted with a certain *snobisme*.[45] Vachet noted researchers' new interest in hormones as the possible basis of perversions, but inclined towards the Freudians' stress on the importance of infantile associations and experiences.[46] He presented Pierrette's unique autobiographical account of the life of a transvestite and potential trans-sexual as an example of one individual's resolution of a psychological conflict. Vachet followed Pierre Janet in arguing that instability, depression and bizarre behaviour were manifested by the individual plagued by psychological uncertainty. His or her depression was lifted once the taboo was broken. In this case the young man had turned his source of humiliation – his feminine characteristics – into a source of pride. Vachet noted that the sex change Pierrette dreamed of had already been carried out in Austria. Professor Halban of Vienna offered an operation for men marked by *féminisme*.[47] Vachet believed that moral direction was better than surgery, not because an operation was irremediable but because it was insufficient. Since the trans-sexual's problem was rooted in the nervous system it was accessible to psychotherapy which would discipline, transform and sublimate the deviant's desires so that they posed no danger to the community.

Psychiatrists, psychoanalysts and sexologists unintentionally played important roles in the emergence of new sexual identities. But the sexually experimental did not simply wait for doctors to discover them. Certainly in places like New York, Paris and Berlin active homosexual subcultures existed that were largely indifferent to what sexologists said.[48] Essentialists have argued that there have always been homosexuals. Social constructionists respond that this is an ahistorical assertion; though certain acts associated with homosexuality such as sodomy have been found throughout history, a homosexual identity and self-consciousness was new to the turn of the century.[49] There is a good deal of evidence to support the notion that trial accounts, medical records and works of fiction provided many homosexuals –as they did to an even greater extent for heterosexuals – with a sense that they were not the only ones with their particular penchant, a vocabulary to describe their feelings and role models they might emulate.

The very trials employed to repress homosexuality served to publicize it and give it definition. One result of Oscar Wilde's 1895 court appearance was that the role of the effeminate dandy, traditionally adopted by the ambitious womanizer, became associated with inversion.[50] Some homosexuals felt it necessary to combat such effeminacy. In Germany Adolf Brand and Benedict Friedlander created in 1902 the Committee of the Other which promulgated the older Greek notion that the best men were attracted to other males. A similar plea that homosexuals prove their masculinity was contained in a 1927 English autobiographical account authored by 'Anomaly'. The writer asserted his desire to face his condition with courage, discretion and 'scrupulous regard for morality and for the requirements of the law'.[51] He felt that to reach a respectable English audience he had to assure them that the homosexual, should he fail either to cure or to sublimate his passion, could be counted on to remain chaste.

André Gide in *Corydon* (1924) provided the most famous interwar literary defence of homosexuality. Gide, like many children, had been an avid masturbator. If he did not stop, the family doctor warned the boy when he was only eight, he would be castrated. It was hardly surprising that he was henceforth cautious in revealing his sexual predilections. He remained a virgin until he was twenty-four when he married a cousin; the marriage was never consummated.[52] To his relief, Gide found his homosexual desires obliquely described in the writings of Marcel Proust and Oscar Wilde, whose company he sought out. They both warned him not to write in the first person about same-sex passions but from the 1920s onwards Gide began to insist on his homosexuality. In post-war France the homophobic asserted that homosexuality was an emasculating German vice which threatened the nation with depopulation. Even some homosexuals accepted the Freudian notion that they were narcissists stuck at an early stage of the maturation process. Though Proust tried to naturalize homosexuality, many readers of his *The Cities of the Plain* believed it confirmed current medical notions on the sickliness of vice. In *Corydon* Gide responded to such beliefs by an idealized depiction of the sexual mores of ancient Greece. Clearly hostile to the *fin-de-siècle* medicalization of deviancy, he defended male homosexuality by falling back on the classic notion of a perfect world that once existed of martial and virile men in which women were respected and protected. According to his account, virile homosexuals had actually revered motherhood. Though they had a passion for boys, that in no way prevented them from marrying and raising children. Such masculine men were not to be confused with morally inferior, effeminate 'inverts'. John Addington Symonds had earlier, in *A Problem in Modern Ethics* (1883), employed the same tactic of asking why, if modern Europeans so highly esteemed ancient Greek culture, they did not accept the ancients' liberal views on sexuality. Gide's study in some ways appeared anachronistic. He appealed to notions of martial valour and ignored the problems of the exploitation of youth.[53] His restricted notion of what constituted healthy masculinity and femininity resulted in occasional homophobic and misogynistic musings.[54] He was, of course, searching for arguments that a hostile audience might accept. The work is so stilted that it is easy to forget that Gide, in broaching such a tabooed issue, was courageously risking his reputation as a writer. Even after his many novels won for him in 1947 the Nobel Prize for literature and his entry into the Academie française, he was to declare that he still considered *Corydon* his most important work.

Few read *Corydon* but everyone knew the plays and films of Noël Coward. One of the ironies of the inter-war period is that Coward, whose homosexual inclinations were not widely known, popularized the 'slick and satiny' style of masculinity that many heterosexuals warmly if unwittingly embraced. Homosexuals naturally appreciated the chance to emulate such a role model, but Coward, whose brilliance as a comic satirist could be compared to Oscar Wilde's, took great care to avoid any open avowal which would endanger his career. Only recently has the further irony been noted that Coward's androgynous self-fashioning, which many straight males found so beguiling, was in part his tribute to the stylish lesbians in his social circle.[55]

Unhealthy Women

Radclyffe Hall's *The Well of Loneliness* (1928) provided a defence of lesbianism that was in some ways comparable to Gide's account of male homosexuality. Taking the moral high ground, she argued that if some women were drawn sexually to other women it was due, not to their decadence, but to God's mysterious dictates. She presented her hero Stephen, a boyish young woman, as only discovering the 'truth' about her confused sexual longings in her father's hidden copy of Krafft-Ebing. Hall's portrayal of the self-lacerating, female invert, who did not want to 'become' a lesbian but found she was born one, makes for gloomy reading today; in its time it was a sensation.[56]

To place Hall's work in context it has to be recalled that, though the sex experts tended to label any independent-minded woman as 'unfeminine', they said relatively little about lesbianism. Even those therapists who were critical of conventional morality and sympathetic to their patients aimed at adjusting them to fit the norms of society. The normalizing efforts of the sexologists was made especially apparent in their treatment of gender. They assumed the 'naturalness' of the aggressive male and the passive female. Failure to meet such norms was taken as a sign of a psychic disturbance. Nordau claimed that the psychological stigmata of male homosexuals was their emotionalism and incapacity for action.[57] The masochist was described by Emile Laurent as a man who was subservient to a woman and 'no longer a man in the psychological sense of the word; he is a humiliated being, be it in a simple state of sexual servitude, or in that it extends to pathological forms of perversion'.[58] A man who gave oral sex to a woman was, asserted Dimitry Stefanowsky, a 'passivist' dominated by a *femme sadiste* and ran the risk of ultimately becoming a homosexual fellator.[59] Even the gentle Havelock Ellis legitimated notions of male violence and sexual conquest.

Since the sexologists were almost all men it was hardly surprising that the failure of male arousal associated with so many of the perversions appeared to them to pose the most serious sexual problem. Although there was no shortage of misogynist doctors who portrayed lesbianism in the darkest of hues, female deviance received far less attention than did the male perversions. Doctors asserted that the male sex drive was focused; the female's was diffused and so women could abstain more easily than men.[60] According to Forel, women had restrained sexual appetites and were naturally monogamous and passive. Women's emotions, asserted Charles Féré, did not last as long as men's and they were thus less prone to suicide.[61]

Because women's sexual relations were not regarded as important as men's, Western culture long tolerated much of what in hindsight might be regarded as lesbian behaviour.[62] The nineteenth-century world assumed that women should be bound by ties of emotion and affection. Young women's hugs, kisses and sharing of beds were not proscribed. Their emotional relationships with each other, doctors assumed, would serve as an apprenticeship for their mature sexual relationships with men. Indeed, whatever women might do together could not, in the eyes of some doctors, be ever regarded as sexual.[63] Unlike male homosexuality, female vice at least did not, argued pronatalists, prevent childbirth. Lesbianism was not criminalized and accordingly did not attract the attention of legal reformers. Many did not even understand what lesbianism was. Maud Allan's famous 'Cult of the Clitoris' trial in 1918 revealed the fact that even educated men's sexual knowledge was abysmally low. When one witness spoke of lesbians being addicted to improper activities that provided pleasure but 'did nothing to help the race' and of kisses that could produce an 'orgasm', Judge Darling was frankly puzzled.

> *Judge*: What is the word you used?
> *Spencer*: I am quoting from [the German writer] Bloch.
> *Judge*: Repeat the word you used.
> *Spencer*: Orgasm.
> *Counsel*: Some unnatural vice?
> *Spencer*: No, it is a function of the body.[64]

Few French judges were so naïve. On the continent, sensationalist writers had long exploited the notion of lesbianism being one of the symptoms of a decadent society. Baudelaire originally planned giving *Fleurs du mal* the title *Les Lesbiennes*. The lesbian characters in such works as Rachilde's *Monsieur Venus* (1884) and Zola's *Nana* (1880) were presented as women who drank, smoked and dressed in men's clothing. Novelists tended in the main to exploit lesbian themes merely as a way of portraying upper-class debauchery. Investigators of prostitution such as Lombroso and Martineau asserted that lesbians could also be found in brothels and servants' quarters. The occupants of bordellos were led on, claimed the doctors, from sexual excesses to disgust with men and finally to same-sex passions.[65] Both male writers of fiction and compilers of medical reports, though they spoke of girls being seduced by women, preferred to dwell on the comforting notion that men were responsible for turning passive women into lesbians. The fantasy of the man awakening the woman to sensations she would otherwise be ignorant of clearly served the purpose of reasserting notions of male assertiveness and female passivity. Men accordingly found such pornographic portrayals of lesbianism titillating rather than threatening.[66]

With the twentieth-century stress on companionate marriage the censorious began to regard with suspicion same-sex crushes and infatuations. Teachers took increasing care to ensure that school and college girls did not have 'unhealthy' relationships.[67] Nevertheless, some progressive doctors still argued that female physical relationships did not have to be regarded as necessarily dangerous as they were most likely to be simply manifestations of a passing phase. W. F. Robie cited the account given to him by a twenty-four-year-old woman which included such lesbian experiences. At the age of sixteen or seventeen her room-mate had 'assumed the active role and practiced lesbianism with her on two occasions'.[68] It had no lasting repercussions. Robie then quoted a thirty-one-year-old woman who provided a detailed account of her same-sex experiences. At the age of twenty-two she had moved in with a thirty-year-old woman whom she soon discovered was attracted to her.

> When sleeping together this woman began to hug and kiss her and assumed the role of the man, making the movements of intercourse until, in a few moments, the orgasm occurred. The first time this produced no effect on the younger woman, though she thought it natural enough and what women usually did when they slept together. This act was repeated on several occasions, there being mutual excitement after the first time and mutual orgasm on two occasions. About this time the significance of this was made plain to her by an older woman, who told her something about lesbianism, after reading a newspaper account of the shooting of a young woman by her female lover. This caused her to shun sleeping with this woman.[69]

They remained friends, however, and these experiences, according to Robie, had no apparent impact on the younger woman's subsequent emotional well-being. Indeed, Robie stressed the point that she and her husband had a remarkably successful sex life. 'She has two to three orgasms now at each connection and he withdraws to avoid children. This is by mutual agreement.'[70]

Ellis similarly regarded male homosexuality as biologically determined and therefore irreversible, while he believed that some lesbians were not hereditary types, but rather predisposed to seduction. 'Innocent women' risked being seduced, agreed the Swiss sexologist Forel, due to their being impressionable and only vaguely aware of lesbianism's sexual nature.[71] In France as well liberal physicians continued to view lesbianism indulgently in the years immediately after the First World War, arguing that, with the lack of young men, it was understandable that women would seek comfort where they could get it.[72] They were not degenerates; they simply lacked a healthy option.

There were, of course, doctors who roundly condemned lesbianism. When the healthy woman was supposedly 'passionless', American doctors lumped together prostitutes, lesbians and nymphomaniacs as being 'hypersexual'.[73] Female same-sex relationships were, such experts asserted, linked to masturbation, masculine pastimes and a large clitoris.[74] In the inter-war period such dark portraits of lesbianism proliferated and the toleration of women's love for women waned. In 1927 Edouard Bournet's play on lesbianism, *The Captive*, was forced to close in New York. At the same time Mae West's *The Drag* was shut down and she was arrested as a 'public nuisance'.[75] A denigration of intimate female relationships was one of the unanticipated consequences of the sex reformers' exaltation of the heterosexual passions. According to Marie Stopes, lesbianism attracted the 'independent' type of woman. It unfitted women for a 'real union'. She believed some were born lesbians; others drifted into the vice. Women, according to her, could only 'play' with each other; they could never have a real relationship.[76] Falling back on her curious physiological preoccupations, Stopes argued that the lesbian embrace could literally never provide what women 'needed'.

> Lesbian love, as the alternative is NOT a real equivalent and merely soothes perhaps and satisfies no more than surface nervous excitement. It does not, and by its nature it can never supply the actual physiological nourishment, the chemical molecules produced by the accessory glandular systems of the male. These are supplied to the woman's system when the normal act of union is experienced and the man's secretions are deposited in her body together with the semen.[77]

Even Stella Browne, one of the more active and radical members of the British Sexological Society, argued that if a woman did not have a male lover by twenty-five she would be 'under-vitalised and sexually deficient' and that such sex segregation could lead on to 'artificial' lesbianism.[78]

Those sexologists who eroticized male power, on the one hand, and women's passivity, on the other, sought to shore up existing gender norms.[79] German sexologists like Krafft-Ebing had first popularized the notion that the key symptom of lesbianism was gender inversion. In the twentieth century experts tended to drop the notion that a male homosexual would necessarily appear effeminate but they clung to the idea that a 'real' lesbian – as opposed to the seduced innocent –

would appear masculine. The lesbian's active pursuit of pleasure was taken as proof of her masculine state of mind.

Lesbianism

Appearing in this context, Radclyffe Hall's defence of lesbianism created a sensation. She presented her tall, broad-shouldered, horse-loving character finally discovering in her father's copy of Krafft-Ebing the reason why she felt so 'queer'.

> 'You knew! All the time you knew this thing, but because of your pity you wouldn't tell me. Oh, Father – and there are so many of us – thousands of miserable, unwanted people, who have no right to love, no right to compassion because they're maimed, hideously maimed and ugly – God's cruel; He let us get flawed in the making.'[80]

The importance of Hall, who would be popularly known for having crystallized the image of the 'mannish lesbian', lay in her relentlessly countering the claim that women were seduced into same-sex relationships. In taking up Krafft-Ebing's notion that lesbianism was biologically determined, she appeared to be presenting individual women as tragic victims of fate; nevertheless, the strength of her argument was that it exploded the notion that lesbianism should or could be either punished or prevented.

Little had been written heretofore on the subject of the normality of lesbianism. In France Dr Laupts had pondered the possibility in the 1890s of lesbians and homosexuals forming families.[81] Edward Carpenter was perhaps thinking of lesbians when he referred to 'female neuters' who would not have children but fired with 'social enthusiasm' would turn their maternal instincts to serve the community.[82] Hall's success lay in crafting a novel in which the reader necessarily sympathized with the high-minded heroine at war with an unfeeling society. James Douglas, editor of the *Sunday Express,* immediately recognized Hall's stratagem and attacked the novel as part of 'the plague' of sexual inversion, arguing that it would be better to give a young person poison.[83] An English judge agreed, condemning the book as obscene and ordering it to be destroyed.

In 1922 Victor Marguerite had scandalized French society in depicting in *La Garçonne* the chief character's lesbian relationship. Hall's moralism and discretion were tailored to win over a more restrained British readership. All she said of her chief character's passion for Mary was 'and that night they were not divided.'[84] More importantly, the novel ended with Stephen giving up her love. This was a cunning move. Hall herself led a happy, productive life but in presenting lesbianism in the tragic guise of an innate deviancy, she challenged the world to be compassionate. Leslie D. Weatherhead, a Christian activist, responded by declaring that *The Well of Loneliness* was a beautiful book with nothing morbid or unhealthy about it.[85] This was from a man who castigated masturbation and premarital sex. Freudians were not taken in by Hall's tactic. 'Any girl with the usual homosexual tendencies of adolescence', claimed an American invest-igator, 'may be led to believe that she is condemned and dedicated to a life of homosexuality reading such pseudo-scientific hocus-pocus [i.e. *The Well*] . . . homosexuality in women, as in men, is an acquired neurosis.'[86] Critics charged that, despite Hall's avowals, the novel pro-vided a portrayal of lesbianism that many would find seductive. They thus tried to explain away the appeal of such works. In 1915, after reading *The Intermediate Sex*, a woman contacted Edward Carpenter to say that 'it has lately dawned on me that I myself belong to that class and I write to ask if there is any way of getting in touch with others of the same temperament.' Over 5,000 women wrote similar letters to Hall after the publication of *The Well of Loneliness*.[87]

A good deal is known about Hall and the aristocratic and artistic lesbian Parisian world of Colette, Renée Vivien, Natalie Clifford Barney and Gertrude Stein.[88] Historians are only beginning to gather informa-tion about the mass of ordinary women drawn in the inter-war years by same-sex feelings. In the United States the notes containing songs and poems, which guards caught female prisoners passing to each other, provide glimpses of a lower-class lesbian culture.

> You can take my tie
> You can take my collar
> But I'll jazz you
> 'Till you holler

Observers noted that such women were particularly attracted to songs that could imply gender confusion.

> Mamma's got something sho' gonna surprise you
> Mamma's got something gonna hypnotize you
> Mamma's got something I know you want.[89]

Such cheeky sentiments were miles apart from the guarded portrayal of the passions provided by Hall. A similar earthiness was reflected in the accounts given by the lesbians who participated in George

Henry's New York sex variant study which began in 1935.[90] According to one woman a distinct lesbian culture existed in the metropolis.

> The 'gay girls' are pretty much divided into two groups – 'them that do
> and them that don't' . . . In this enlightened age, it's a pretty backward
> number who pretends she doesn't know what it's all about . . . The soft
> babes dream of being 'taken,' and the tough ones dream of doing that
> little thing for them. Almost without exception, the female homo can
> recall the emotional highlight of her youth with vivid clarity. There was
> an overfond mama demanding constant attention or service, or a nurse
> or a governess who was seductive at bath or bedtime, or an angel of a
> teacher who loved the adulation and gifts of the younger girl. All of
> them can remember loving some female or other with varying degrees
> of intensity up to an including an absolute state of idolatry.[91]

In the bars the 'bitches', she reported, were hard to spot but the overt lesbian sported short hair, played down her breasts and walked with a strut or swagger. With slacks and short hair coming into fashion they were not as easily detected so had to try harder to stand out.[92] But other participants refuted the stereotypes of the femme and butch roles.

The study revealed a series of competing narratives. The doctors took a pathological approach. Robert Latou Dickinson, for example, sought to explain deviancy by investigating the lesbian body, especially the genitals.[93] The male and female homosexuals who participated in the study defended their lifestyle and disliked sharp categorizations. Radclyffe Hall had sought to turn the sexologists' notion of the congenital lesbian to the purposes of reform. The participants in Henry's study were suspicious of doctors, but had a desire to make their voices heard and to advance knowledge. Though lesbians had a limited success in telling their own stories, most informed observers in Paris, New York and Berlin could not by the 1930s ignore the existence of such a female sexual subculture.

Punishments

At the beginning of the century sexologists such as Ellis and Hirschfeld necessarily spoke out against laws that subjected irresponsible or ill deviants to criminal prosecution. In Britain, the Labouchère amendment to the Criminal Law Amendment Act of 1885 made acts of 'gross indecency' between adult males a crime punishable by up to two years in prison. It was under this law that Oscar Wilde, London's most brilliant dramatist, was imprisoned in 1895.[94] The 1898 Vagrancy Act, which included whipping as punishment for male prostitution, pimping, cross-dressing, indecent exposure and selling obscene pictures, remained in force until 1948.[95] In 1935, for example, the charges levied by the police of England and Wales included 3,176 for prostitution, 1,674 for indecent exposure and 840 for indecency with males and 'unnatural' offences.[96] The fact that some prisoners had been arrested as many as two hundred times for the same offence conclusively proved the futility of locking up the compulsive.

In most Western nations lobby groups emerged to campaign for the liberalization of the laws pertaining to sex crimes. The British Society for the Study of Sex Psychology, founded in 1913, began to lobby for law reform in the 1920s.[97] It called for 'New Galileos' who would determine a humane way of dealing with issues such as prostitution, venereal disease and homosexuality. It demanded social rather than moral analysis, honesty instead of ignorance.[98] The society produced pamphlets arguing for the decriminalization of homosexuality, stressing the notion that the practice was involuntary and not due to sexual excesses.[99] Society members included writers like George Bernard Shaw, doctors like Havelock Ellis, feminists like Stella Browne, criminologists like George Ives and psychoanalysts like Ernest Jones. As many homosexuals were members of the society, it made a concerted effort to prove itself a disinterested investigative organization.[100] It enjoyed occasional successes as in 1931 when it lobbied the government to provide Austin Hull, a transvestite convicted of having committed gross indecencies, with therapy. In practical terms the society accomplished relatively little but its very existence signified that enlightened members of the community were taking a serious interest in the sexual minorities.

In France, although those under thirteen were protected and homosexual 'cruising' was suppressed, it was not until 6 August 1942 that the Vichy government made it a crime for a man to have sex with a male minor under the age of twenty-one. As a result of this relative tolerance no sex reform movement emerged in France. The *Association d'Études Sexologiques*, which was established in 1931 with Dr Edouard Toulouse as president and Dr Jean Dalsace as secretary, was a distinctly conservative organization that sought to win the support of the authorities by promising that its investigations would improve the quality of the population.[101]

Weimar Germany harboured the world's most active sex reform organizations. Magnus Hirschfeld founded in 1919 the Berlin Institute for Sexual Science which was both a centre for sex research and a counselling office providing practical information on such issues as contraception and abortion. Such was its success that it received Prussian state funding. Under the auspices of Hirschfeld's Society for Sexology and Eugenics the first international congress dealing with sexuality was held in 1921. Albert Moll headed a rival International Society for Sex Research which sponsored its own congresses in 1926 in Berlin and 1930 in London. As a result of the 1928 Copenhagen Congress, a World League for Sexual Reform was created. Though the Germans dominated the organization, its supporters represented a who's who of the progressive world, including Hannah Stone and W. J. Robinson of the United States, Magnus Hirschfeld and Helene Stöcker of Germany, George Bernard Shaw and John and Dora Russell of Britain, and Madeleine Pelletier and Victor Marguerite of France.[102]

Conclusion

The challenges facing the sex doctors were many; their practical accomplishments should not be exaggerated. They employed a medical vocabulary that, until at least the 1940s, was foreign to most readers. Even the terms 'homosexual' and 'heterosexual' were not widely employed. In popular parlance the homosexual continued to be disparagingly referred to as the 'fairy,' 'tante' or 'pédé'. The very fact that the sexologists discussed tabooed subjects made them appear suspect to many. Havelock Ellis, who was responsible for introducing to the English-speaking world the ideas of Moll, Hirschfeld, Freud and Forel, saw his book *Sexual Inversion* prosecuted as 'lewd and obscene'. Even doctors were affronted by sexual discussions. The *British Medical Journal*, in noting the translation into English of Krafft-Ebing's work, commented that 'There are many morally disgusting subjects which have to be studied by the doctor and by the jurist, but the less such subjects are brought before the public the better.'[103] An 1919 editorial in an English tabloid went so far as to make the bizarre claim that perversions were caused by reading continental sexology texts:

> practically all that is filthy and degrading can be directly traced to the pernicious teaching of the Teuton criminal. The use of noxious drugs and the horrible practices of the unsexed were introduced to this country from Berlin and Vienna, and it is time that the professors of unnatural practices were plainly told that England is no place for them.[104]

Sexology countered such suspicions by promising to provide new forms of therapy that would assure the smooth running of society. Edouard Toulouse reflected the conservative side of sexology in his insistence that science would provide order, discipline and direction.[105] The debate over the perversions took place against the alarming backdrop of a host of social transformations – declining fertility, emerging feminism, the rise of white-collar work – that appeared to blur the sex roles. Sexology, in promising to establish order and stability, responded to the claims of those who, like Serge Paul, declared that civilization needed boundaries.[106]

The sex doctors saw themselves more as humanitarians than as disciplinarians. They boasted that they helped turn the response of society faced with the pervert from one of disgust to one of compassion. They set out, in the words of Havelock Ellis, 'to save patients much persecution and the police much bewilderment'.[107] Their chief argument was that certain sexual practices once regarded as sins and then as crimes had been revealed to be symptoms of an illness. They were particularly effective in pointing out the problems of simple repression. Yet, in insisting that therapy should replace imprisonment, many doctors revealed themselves to be less liberal than they imagined themselves to be. Their interest in hormonal research, for example, reflected an obvious desire to re-establish the notion of a biological basis for sexual differences.

The sexologists and psychiatrists did not, of course, speak with one voice. The more radical countered that it was wrong to talk of cures. Harold Picton, in a 1923 pamphlet written for the British Society for the Study of Sex Psychology, attacked the desire to 'treat' deviants and noted that sexual standards varied.[108] Norman Haire, an Australian gynaecologist active in British sex reform circles, pointed out that as France had no law on incest or homosexuality and Britain did not criminalize lesbianism or contraception it was difficult to make wide claims about what constituted 'unnatural' acts.[109] René Guyon was of the opinion that one did not have to argue that homosexuality was congenital in order to defend it. Some cases were simply a matter of taste and like any sex act should be permitted as long as the liberty and free consent of one's partner was respected. Guyon attacked the very notion of therapeutic intervention and asked why even Freud fell back on such imprecise and unscientific terms as the 'normal,' 'abnormal' and the 'reasonable man'.[110]

In the following short chapter, Sigmund Freud's work is finally dealt with in some detail. He cannot be lumped in with the writers of marriage manuals or the sexologists or the sex reformers yet his influential ideas can be detected casting a shadow across many of their inter-war discussions. He was the most adventuresome of sexual theorists and at the same time a man who could not free himself from the cultural preoccupations of his age.

6

'Frigidity': Sigmund Freud, Psychoanalysis and Gender

The famous Professor Halban of Vienna who, Vachet had noted, had performed sex change operations on men had also performed sexual surgery on women. His efforts in this area were praised by Marie Bonaparte in a 1932 paper which she presented on the problem of frigidity. Freud, she pointed out, had demonstrated that normal women gave up the clitoris as their chief source of sexual pleasure and moved on to experience the mature vaginal orgasm. Unfortunately, therapists found that for many women the clitoris remained regrettably eroticized. The psychoanalytically enlightened had to recognize this lag as a sign of women's infantilism if not their bisexuality. Bonaparte conceded that for some the problem was due to the fact that their clitoris was too far from the vagina. The answer to such a *fixation clitoridienne*, she suggested, was surgical intervention to cut and move the clitoris to a more suitable locale so that the excitement it engendered would aid rather than detract from genital penetration. Bonaparte concluded her amazing essay, which came complete with disturbing photographs of the procedure, by hailing the modern surgeon's ability to aid the psychoanalyst.[1]

This story of the peculiar enthusiasm of one of Freud's most devoted followers is worth telling because many historians are of the opinion that what was most original about Freud was his break with the eugenic project to reinscribe social and moral perversions on the body itself and his more modern attempt to read variations in desire as largely individual and psychological. The truth was, however, that Freud, whose insights had to be taken into account by every serious sexual investigator of the twentieth century, never made as clean a break with biology as is so often believed. Sigmund Freud (1856–1939), in providing accounts of his patients' problems, was to prove himself a master story-teller, but the most important myth that he propagated was that his approach to sexuality was unique and unprecedented. It is true that the first generation of sex doctors were tainted by their association with the policing of the perversions. Freud made therapy increasingly acceptable by extending it to include respectable neurotics and was the only sex expert of the early twentieth century whose work would continue to draw adherents after the Second World War. He was in many ways strikingly original but it would be an exaggeration to regard him, as many of his adherents did, as a revolutionary. The real interest of psychoanalysis resided in the fact that it drew on both contemporary sexological investigations and many of the common sexual preoccupations of the early twentieth century.

Freud did differ from the sexologists. He did not just provide sexology with yet another framework to study perversion; his most lasting contribution was to make normal sexuality an object of scientific investigation. In past generations, if one's sex life was not all that one might have wished, the failing could be dismissed as only another of life's many minor disappointments. In the early twentieth century, as increasing numbers of commentators claimed that any normal person had to experience sensual bliss, the pursuit of sexual satisfaction took on an unprecedented importance. 'Sexual love', Freud asserted, 'is undoubtedly one of the chief things in life, and the union of mental and bodily satisfaction in the enjoyment of love is one of its culminating peaks. Apart from a few queer fanatics, all the world knows this and conducts its life accordingly; science alone is too delicate to admit it.'[2] Such an evolution was understandable given the fact that with modernization public life was becoming more bureaucratized and the division of labour was making work less fulfilling. The middle classes, able to separate work and family, similarly split their public and private worlds. They increasingly compensated for the humdrum routinization of their professional lives by embracing the romantic notion that only in the private realm was their authentic self fully revealed. Accordingly, a successful sex and family life on which one's identity was based and confirmed became, so the sex experts claimed, the new criteria of status and well-being.

Such an assertion meant that sexual fiascos now had to be viewed as serious problems. To whom could the despondent turn? Ironically, patients looked for help to those doctors – the 'anxiety-makers' some would call them – who had done the most to problematize sexuality in the first place. 'Psychology is the disease of which it claims to be the cure', joked the Viennese satirist Karl Kraus.[3] The self-respecting enlightened members of the middle class relied less on the help of the untutored churchman or sympathetic family member; they felt they needed the counselling of qualified medical experts who employed the language of positivistic science and advanced observable and verifiable findings. A host of professional helpers responded to the demand – the most famous ultimately being Freud and his disciples – in supplying an anxious population of consumers with a variety of services to construct, maintain and repair their identity.[4]

Freud, by explaining that all neuroses had a sexual origin, appeared to give order to a disorderly world. Christians had, of course, long maintained that Adam and Eve's sin led to the world's sufferings. Freud adopted a non-metaphysical approach to provide a modern, natural and scientific explanation of human unhappiness. A generation of researchers were talking about sexual problems; Freud's originality lay in erecting an entire explanation of civilization based on the centrality of sex.[5] He moved from first believing that adult neuroses were due to the memories of actual assaults individuals had experienced as children to the idea of infantile sexual fantasy. The 'unconscious', where such thoughts were spawned, he set out to map. His message, as spread by generations of therapists, centred on the notion that infantile sexuality existed, that the neuroses were caused by sexual repression, and that the sexual drives influenced all of human history. Most readers had only a shaky understanding of the scenario that held that the id demanded gratification, the ego judiciously regulated the promptings of the unconscious, and the super-ego internalized the restraints of society. What the public understood Freud to argue was that if the sexual drives were frustrated illness would result.

It says something of the spirit of the times that Freud's *Interpretation of Dreams* appeared in English in 1913, the same year as D. H. Lawrence's *Sons and Lovers*. Both played up notions of Oedipal attractions and the struggle between the physical and cerebral. Freud's work, initially limited to an academic readership, was only popularized following the war.[6] He liked to portray himself as a rebel and his disciples presented him as a resolute opponent of the Victorian double standard. Newspapers warned their readers to beware the psychoanalyst who, they claimed, defended primitive, instinctual and biological drives and went so far as to preach sexual liberation, permissiveness and decadence. 'The unwholesomeness of morbid introspection has always been recognised by healthy-minded men and women, and we hope that parents and all who have control of the young will set their faces sternly against experiments which, in the name of science, may ruin a generation.'[7]

But to understand Freud's success it has to be appreciated that, though he cast the discussion of sexuality in a new light, he was far from being a sexual revolutionary. He was no supporter of sexual 'experimentation' and firmly believed that 'something in the nature of the sexual instinct itself is unfavourable to the realization of complete satisfaction'.[8] He views on birth control made this clear. While Marie Stopes and Margaret Sanger were convinced that access to contraception would revolutionize marital relationships, a gloomy pessimism pervaded Freud's entire discussion of attempts to limit family size. In ' "Civilized" Sexual Morality', frequently cited by the Freudian left as his most radical work, he painted the following black picture of married life, based, it should be noted, on the premise that there was no effective way of controlling fertility:

> This brings us to the question whether intercourse in legal marriage can offer full compensation for the restriction imposed before marriage. There is such an abundance of material supporting a reply in the negative that we can give only the briefest summary of it. It must above all be borne in mind that our cultural sexual morality restricts sexual intercourse even in marriage itself, since it imposes on married couples the necessity of contenting themselves, as a rule, with a very few procreative acts. As a consequence of this consideration, satisfying sexual intercourse in marriage takes place only for a few years; and we must subtract from this, of course, the intervals of abstention necessitated by regard for the wife's health. After these three, four or five years, the marriage becomes a failure in so far as it has promised the satisfaction of sexual needs. For all devices hitherto invented for preventing contraception impair sexual enjoyment, hurt the fine sensibilities of both partners and even actually cause illness. Fear of the consequences of sexual intercourse first brings the married couple's physical affection to an end; and then in a remoter result, it usually puts a stop as well to the mental sympathy between them, which should have been the successor to their original passionate love. The spiritual disillusionment and bodily deprivation to which most marriages are thus doomed puts both partners back in the state they were in before their marriage, except for being the poorer by the loss of an illusion, and they must once more have recourse to their fortitude in mastering and deflecting their sexual instinct.[9]

Freud was clearly exaggerating and presenting a portrait perhaps of his own marriage, but not that of society as a whole.[10]

At the turn of the century Freud was very much aware of the desire of the middle class to limit births but considered all attempts to prevent conception as potentially hazardous. He was interested in Wilhelm Fliess's theories of periodicity as it might lead to the discovery of a rhythm method of birth control, but Fliess, a man who believed that there was a special connection between the genitals and the nose and that accordingly nosebleeds were a vicarious form of menstruation and cocaine a cause of miscarriages, could hardly be accepted as a pioneer birth controller.[11] Yet Freud seriously believed Fliess was on to something. 'I still look to you', he wrote to Fliess 'as the Messiah who will solve the problem I have indicated by an improvement in technique.'[12] Freud, like most early twentieth-century doctors, appeared to view 'artificial' forms of contraception with disfavour. Yet Freud was, as he himself so many times declared, not a 'respectable' doctor but one dealing with the tabooed subject of sex. Havelock Ellis would, in 1906, go so far as to state that the changing opinions of the advanced medical world had led 'to the assertion, now perhaps without exception, by all medical authorities on matters of sex that the use of methods of preventing conception is under certain circumstances urgently necessary and quite harmless'.[13] In claiming that 'all medical authorities' were of this opinion Ellis was being far too sanguine but he could list as defenders of the use of the condom such well-known contemporaries as Kisch, Forel, Krafft-Ebing, Moll, Schrenck-Notzing, Löwenfeld and Furbringer.[14] Moreover, the German-speaking world was unique inasmuch as here the economic and medical arguments in favour of birth control were supplemented by those of feminists such as Gisela Streitberg, Helene Stöcker, Elizabeth Zanzinger, Oda Olberg and Camilla Jellinek who went so far as to defend abortion.[15] In short, Freud as a well-read continental could not help but be aware of the writings of a host of progressive commentators in which it was declared that contraception was harmless. Freud disagreed with these sex radicals and his arguments must therefore be viewed as based not on an ignorance of the issues but on differing values and beliefs.

Freud's belief in the dangers of contraception might well have been exaggerated given the fact that his knowledge of birth control practices was based in part on the peculiar problems posed by his clients. Their accounts of the anxieties engendered by coitus interruptus could only reinforce any prejudices he might have already harboured against such tactics. Freud's preoccupation with birth control coincided with his personal concerns at the dramatic growth of his own family.[16] In classic fashion, Freud, the poor young medical man, fearful of the burdens of wife and children, was engaged at the age of twenty-six but postponed marriage until thirty. And after the wedding in 1886 the babies began to arrive. In 1887 a girl was born, in 1889 the first son, in 1891 the third. Six children in nine years – the very years in which he was writing that the discovery of a reliable method of contraception would be a godsend but at the moment none was effective. His own solution was to give up sexual relations with his wife. Ernest Jones discreetly noted, 'the more passionate side of married life subsided earlier with him than it does with many men.'[17] Freud was more open; he wrote to Fliess in 1897: 'Sexual excitation is of no more use to a person like me.'[18] He even discussed the ending of his sex life with Emma Jung for in 1911 she reminded him of a conversation they had had: 'You told me about your family. You said then that your marriage had long been "amortized," now there was nothing to do except – die.'[19]

Freud's fame, of course, was not based on his discussion of contraception. His notoriety stemmed from his assertion that the 'nervous complaints' which appeared to plague the bourgeoisie of the *fin de siècle* were due to self-destructive repressions of unconscious sexual desires. The caricatured portrait of Freud that the media popularized was of some sort of sex-crazed Viennese professor, intent on violating every taboo. A 1922 London meeting on 'Religion and Psychoanalysis' heard a Dr Orchard assert that the science was 'dogmatic and obsessed with sex', and that Freud's teachings gave 'unbridled licence to free sex-expression'.[20] As the discussion of his views on contraception indicated, this was certainly not true. His writings, if anything, turned to new notions of the unconscious to reinvigorate the old idea that males and females were dramatically different sexual beings.

Gender

Freud was at his subversive best when he stated that heterosexuality, far from being a self-evident fact, was as difficult to explain as homosexuality.[21] He seemed to be setting out for himself the ambitious agenda of problematizing that which most contemporaries took for granted. His fellow medical scientists analysed abnormal sexual behaviour; his self-declared goal was to provide an explanation of 'normal' sexuality. He began his enterprise on the familiar ground of abnormal sexuality with a devastating critique of the degeneracy theories that his colleagues had advanced over the previous several decades to explain homosexuality. Taking an anthropological rather than a pathological approach, he pointed out that in some cultures same-sex relationships were almost an institution. And in modern Europe 'inversion', Freud noted, was not rare; indeed, the number of homosexuals was 'very considerable'.[22] It was therefore wrong to regard sexual inversion as being somatic; it had to be an acquired rather than an innate trait.

Freud's key insight lay in his distinguishing between the sexual aim (what one does) and the sexual object (with whom one does it). Yet Freud still accepted the idea that normal development should result in genital heterosexuality.[23] He considered perverts, inasmuch as they had became stalled or side-tracked at some stage of sexual development, as immature or 'sick'. Freud felt that if a man's perversion replaced his normal sexual aim and object he should be regarded as suffering from a pathological condition.[24] Freud's interest in homosexuality was based on his belief that studying inversion was a way of better understanding heterosexuality. Such an investigation revealed that the linkages of sexual instinct and sexual object were not as tightly bonded as usually thought. Freud showed the complexity and composite nature of the perversions and claimed to be able to reverse the process and deconstruct the sexual history not only of the pervert and the neurotic but also of the normal. Analysing perverse behaviour, Freud pointed out, 'gives us a hint that perhaps the sexual instinct itself may be no simple thing, but put together from components which have come apart again in the perversions'.[25] On the one hand, he continued to define perversions in a traditional way as those acts that delayed the 'final sexual aim' but on the other argued that the normal was built on the perverse.[26] In suggesting that only a blurred line separated the two, he advanced his most important insight: the fragility of that which had heretofore been regarded as indissoluble, the bonding of the object and the aim of sexual instinct.

Freud, having got off to such a promising start, appeared poised to revolutionize the understanding of gender, and particularly of masculinity because he repeatedly acknowledged that his work focused on male sexual development. In disturbed families, he claimed, the males would be perverts, while the women, 'true to the tendency of their sex to repression, are negative perverts, that is, hysterics'.[27] Sexual attraction, he wrote in 1905, 'can best be studied in men. That of women – partly owing to the stunting effect of civilised conditions and partly owing to their conventional secretiveness and insincerity – is still veiled in an impenetrable obscurity.' And as late as 1926 Freud was still admitting: 'We know less about the sexual life of little girls than of boys. But we need not feel ashamed of this distinction; after all, the sexual life of adult women is a "dark continent" for psychology.'[28]

As feminists later complained, Freud based his understanding of both sexes on the examination of male patients.[29] He presented the phallus as the only genital worth noticing. The penis was so important not because of the pleasure it could give, according to Freud, but because of 'its organic significance for the propagation of the species'.[30] It represented a victory of the needs of the race over those of the individual. He credited women with 'penis envy'. He asserted that men found women's genitals disgusting. 'Probably no male human being is spared the fright of castration at the sight of a female genital.'[31] This revulsion was hardly surprising as he was sure that men's conviction that women did not have a penis led 'them to an enduringly low opinion of the other sex'.[32]

On one level, no thinker was more male-centred than Freud. But because femininity was, according to him, something that women had to construct, he presented it as problematical and stressed the complexity of its development. The masculinity of the male he took as a given, and male gender was accordingly rendered invisible or transparent while women's sexuality was necessarily misrepresented when forced to fit the procrustean bed of Freud's male-centred theories. When, for example, he asserted that the highest sexual pleasure was attained by the 'discharge of the sexual substances', he made it only too clear that he took the mechanics of male sexual pleasure as the norm.[33] But more important than Freud's apparent ignorance of female physiology was his discounting of women's psyche. He spoke in an old-fashioned way of maleness being 'activity' and femaleness 'passivity'; of a 'brake' necessarily being put on young women's sexuality while young men's libido had to be released; of women stoically accepting the prohibitions on sexual activity that men happily broke.[34]

Freud tried on some occasions to distance himself from his male contemporaries' low view of women, but on others provided abundant evidence that he shared such opinions. He claimed that women were not as highly developed as men, equating the child to the 'average uncultivated woman in whom the same polymorphously perverse disposition persists. Under ordinary conditions she may remain normal sexually, but if she is led on by a clever seducer she will find every sort of perversion to her taste, and will retain them as part of her own sexual activities.'[35] Yet such women had a role to play. In the 'civilized world' more than one man found – although, Freud insisted, not the well-educated like himself – that the respect in which they held 'well-brought up women' was sexually inhibiting. Accordingly such a man, said Freud, would only develop 'full potency when he is with a debased sexual object'.[36] Freud concluded that even 'good' women, having a less highly developed super-ego than men, were less ethical and rational. 'We must not allow ourselves to be deflected from such conclusions', he warned his colleagues, 'by the denials of the feminists, who are anxious to force us to regard the two sexes as completely equal in position and worth.'[37]

Freud's portrayal of women was grossly flawed. But what did he have to say about masculinity? What one discovers is that Freud was very vague as to what exactly it was that made a normal man 'manly'. Indeed, what was most striking in Freud's use of the term 'masculinity' was that he almost always used it in a negative or backhanded fashion. 'Masculinity' was, according to Freud, something that a normal woman should *not* have; that a lesbian certainly would have; and that a male homosexual, despite expectations, might have. Freud insisted on describing the clitoris as the female penis. Therefore he attributed a 'wholly masculine character' to little girls who masturbated.[38] To become a woman a girl would have to discard her 'infantile masculinity', her 'masculinity complex'.[39] Adopting a sort of Orwellian 'doublethink', Freud made the paradoxical claim that 'masturbation, at all events of the clitoris, is a masculine activity and that the elimination of clitoral sexuality is a necessary precondition for the development of femininity'.[40] 'Masculine' women, according to Freud, continued to be motivated by the envy and bitterness which they first felt when, as little girls, they realized that they lacked their brother's sign of masculinity. 'Behind this envy for the penis, there comes to light the woman's hostile bitterness against the man, which never completely disappears in the relations between the sexes, and which is clearly indicated in the strivings and in the literary productions of "emancipated" women.'[41] An independent woman necessarily could not be a feminine woman.

The question of the flawed, independent female naturally led Freud on to the subject of lesbianism. Freud asserted that lesbians exhibited 'masculine characteristics, both physical and mental'.[42] That is to say, though he discounted the idea that the male homosexual was innately perverse, in the case of women inverts Freud followed popular opinion in claiming to detect a linkage between their sexuality and the rest of their mental qualities. Given the unnaturalness of those females addicted to same-sex relationships, the perceptive observer, Freud implied, could not help but detect the stigmata of their guilt.

Freud regarded male inversion simply as an acquired 'deviation' in respect of the 'appropriate' sexual object. He credited some male homosexuals turning back towards their own sex after an unfortunate experience with women. More importantly, Freud attributed to homosexuals a horror and depreciation of women which in turn he claimed had been caused by their discovery that women did not have a penis.[43] Yet Freud observed that homosexual males were not necessarily effeminate. 'In men the most complete mental masculinity can be combined with inversion.'[44] They can, he asserted, 'retain the mental quality of masculinity'.[45] Freud felt no need to explain what he meant by 'mental masculinity' knowing that his readers would take it as shorthand for 'rationality'. The concepts of 'masculinity' and 'femininity' in Freud's hands were thus turned to peculiar purposes. Freud asserted more than once that 'anatomy is destiny', but in the case of women he obviously did not believe it.[46] For men the pleasures of the penis were central from the beginning to the end of their journey towards heterosexual maturity. Their sexual development was, he wrote, 'the more straightforward and the more understandable, while that of the females actually enters upon a kind of involution'.[47] Girls found their greatest pleasure in the clitoris but, Freud sternly warned, they had to give it up and turn to the vagina when the 'pursuit of pleasure comes under the sway of the reproductive function'.[48]

Nineteenth-century doctors knew that the vagina had few nerve endings and therefore could not become a prime pleasure centre. Freud was in fact the first medical man to assert that women experienced two orgasms, the clitoral and the vaginal. But in turning to a contorted simile, in which he likened the clitoris to 'pine shavings [which] can be kindled to set a log of harder wood on fire', Freud gave away just how improbable he feared his argument would sound to female readers. Freud was forced by the logic of his explanation of the 'masculine' nature of clitoral pleasure to make this bizarre declaration. For Freud, female 'normal' sex had to be reproductive and therefore vaginal. To justify the necessity of vaginal penetration, he was inevitably led on to argue that the female who abandoned the perverse 'masculine' joys of the clitoris would, via the vagina, be compensated with a higher, more 'feminine' sort of sexual pleasure.

Freud was attacked for saying many things, but never in his lifetime for the notion of this unlikely migration of a woman's pleasure centre from her clitoris to her vagina. By a remarkable sleight of hand, which his otherwise critical male medical contemporaries failed to detect, Freud claimed that he had discovered that which he had invented – the vaginal orgasm. He downplayed old categories of female pleasure and created new ones, thereby launching a revolution that was soon internalized. Why was this argument so readily accepted and so quickly made part of medical orthodoxy? Part of the answer must be that Freud's unlikely scenario spoke to the needs of contemporaries concerned both by faltering fertility rates and women's attempt to free themselves from dependence on males.

Tom Laqueur has stated that Freud's importance was that he revealed that male and female roles were created by socialization and so too was vaginal female pleasure.[49] Laqueur is right on the second score; several generations of women were led to believe that if they failed to have vaginal orgasms they were in some vital way inadequate or, as Freud put it, 'crippled'.[50] Freud, though he was being prescriptive when he claimed to be descriptive, did reveal how the powers of socialization could impact on notions of femininity. But Freud did not show men's sexuality being so radically socialized and left the notion of normal masculinity unexamined. Although Freud was later attacked by feminists for focusing primarily on male sexual development, the truth is that he worked harder and more imaginatively to provide an explanation for 'normal' female sexuality while leaving male sexuality unproblematized. Freud rarely described normal men as being masculine because to do so would be redundant. He took it as a given that a normal man was 'manly'.[51] Disciples like Alfred Adler followed him in calling for *la protestation virile* – the old sexual dichotomies were to be reintroduced. Though Freud claimed to be deconstructing the opposition between deviant and normal sexuality, in fact he rendered invisible the gendering of normal males. He did not, as he claimed, mark out the 'royal road' that would lead to an understanding of the gendered natured of twentieth-century sexuality.

Freud's popularity among doctors – compared to sex reformers like Ellis and Hirschfeld at least – was due to the fact that he attempted to restrict his investigations to the established medical world. Psychoanalysis was a form of therapy for a patient who by definition was suffering from an ailment.[52] If Freud was eventually to enjoy a greater prestige than his contemporaries it was due both to his analytical gifts and his brilliance as a story-teller. There was a certain irony in that Freud, who spoke so eloquently of the discontents created by civilization, proposed to treat the former rather than envisage changing the latter. Sexual problems – the result of changing economic and social relationships – helped give rise to a science which asserted the primacy of individual rather than social change. Like so many of his contemporaries, Freud was given to displacing social fears on to sexuality. And yet there was enormous subversive potential in Freud's pertinent observation – one he did not take sufficiently to heart himself – that to know what a culture insisted was marginal or deviant was to know what was in fact central. Negation and acknowledgement went together.

Psychologizing Sex

Freud's ideas were to be turned to a variety of purposes. They reinvigorated misogyny. His disciples attributed homosexuality to the boy frightened by the mother into fleeing women; and lesbianism to the girl being driven away from men by a cold, distant father. Not surprisingly feminists, since they threatened gender boundaries, were frequently accused by doctors of harbouring lesbian tendencies. Some psychoanalysts went so far as to attack all emancipated women as frigid or lesbian or man-haters, addicted to enemas and afraid of penises. Such commentators, though purportedly discussing the female perversions, were clearly most preoccupied by waning male power.

They appear to have sought – by their extreme valorization of passive femininity and their condemnation of aggressive hysterics, nymphomaniacs and lesbians – to compensate for a feared decline in the male sexual drive.[53]

Such views were popularized by inter-war misogynists like Ludovici, Teutsch and Wieth-Knudsen. Antony Ludovici, in his psychoanalytically inspired, *Man: an Indictment* (1927), asserted that, due to the growth of maudlin attitudes, man had fallen to the station of the subordinate of woman. The rising rate of male impotency he attributed to the growth of feminism.[54] All this was unnatural because women were naturally inferior. They were infantile by nature and dragged further down by the toll of childbirth. Ludovici wanted to keep them in that state. The woman, he asserted, was man's 'beloved parasite'.[55] He claimed that feminism, by defending the woman's right to control her body, 'masculinized' her. Such a woman was not functioning properly.[56] In *The Choice of a Mate* (1935) he went on to claim that feminists had long legs and boyish figures and were obviously masculine.[57] His advice was that a man should avoid marrying a genius and seek out a 'doe-like' creature. His own wife was a Girton girl but he assured his readers that she had forgotten everything she had learnt there.[58] In France Robert Teutsch followed a similar line, asserting in *Le Féminisme* (1934) that normal women were rendered irrational by their menses four days a month. Those females masculinized as a result of feminism he attacked as *les frigides*. The giving of the vote in the United States had, he argued, accomplished nothing and in any event Europeans could never be like the Americans.[59] K. A. Wieth-Knudsen, professor of political economy at Trondheim, agreed in condemning feminism for perverting maternity. European women, he grumbled, were well treated yet insisted on complaining of their lot.[60] The authors of *Frigidity in Women* (1936) declared that if women would only 'entrust' themselves to men frigidity would be vanquished and along with it the 'ridiculous manifestations of the woman's movement'.[61] Such writers were responding to a perceived decline in male authority by equating the feminist, the lesbian and the woman seeking to control her fertility as symbols of a decadent, sterile age.[62]

But psychoanalysis was also turned to more constructive purposes. Karen Horney attempted to employ Freud's thought to produce a more positive portrayal of female sexuality.[63] Psychoanalysts and sex reformers used his notions in asking for humane treatment of the deviant. Jacques Lacan, who following the Second World War created in France his own school of psychoanalysis, first gained notoriety by his 1933 analysis of the famous Papin affair in which two servants had cut to pieces their mistress and her daughter.[64] In England Ernest Jones, Freud's biographer, was convinced that psychoanalytic therapy led to many improvements. Grace Pailthorpe called for the therapeutic treatment of all criminals who, she believed, were 'without exception in some way "psychopathic"'.[65] Pailthorpe, a researcher who examined women prisoners in London's Holloway Prison, noted that it was ludicrous to speak of perverts making a 'free choice'. Their histories revealed unconscious motivation. Pailthorpe probably won few converts to her Freudian interpretations – she believed that one woman stole a purse because it represented a womb and another bit chunks out of apples because she was thinking of her mother's breast – but she effectively pointed out the financial cost of existing incarceration policies.[66] Edward Glover concurred that citizens had a right to be protected, but that society in turn should be tolerant of the childlike behaviour of the 'backward' and give every sexual offender the chance of getting treatment.[67]

Psychoanalysis was to flourish most in the affluent, optimistic culture of the United States where therapists popularized the idea that it was possible by 'adjustment' to reconcile the apparently irreconcilable demands of culture and instinct. 'The Americans always pursue that which they don't have', Karl Kraus joked, 'antiques and inner life.'[68] W. F. Robie accepted the value of Freud's cathartic method and believed that sexual traumas underlay much, if not all, hysteria; he was not, however, convinced that such traumas always occurred before puberty and were necessarily subconscious or that abreaction or suggestion cures always worked.[69] He felt confident that he could speed up marital therapy by simply advising husbands on how to perform more successfully in bed. He similarly tried to disabuse women of their sexual fears. He reported that as soon as he told Mrs L., a thirty-six-year-old patient who suffered from depression, that masturbation was not injurious her anxiety disappeared.[70] Similarly, Robie assured a Miss N. that her problems were caused by unsatisfied natural sexual cravings. This thirty-six-year-old woman felt that her life had been wasted. She had flirted with men and allowed kissing that resulted in voluptuous sensations. One lover threw her over. She had run after a married man and made herself a 'damned fool'. She now found herself so excited and yet depressed that she had had to give up her job. She was haunted by the notion that she was good only as long as she did not masturbate or have sex. Robie reassured her that her desires were natural and she still might marry. His understanding and a prescription of potassium bromide, he told his readers, returned her in three months' time to full health.[71]

Conclusion

The stories told by the sex experts, the sexologists and the psycho-analysts could be employed either to erode or reinforce traditional sexual boundaries. But both conservatives and radicals agreed that the findings of sexual science had helped to chip away at the solidity of the idea that reproductive heterosexuality was a natural given.[72] Freud led a variety of researchers who pointed to evidence that suggested that the supposedly fundamental, unalterable reproductive instinct was the result of a variety of psychic combinations and developmental processes. The experts were swinging round to the view that hetero-sexuality was a fragile construct, which without the support of expert counselling or sex education might topple over into the perversions. Such discussions in the inter-war period were limited to the enlightened portions of the middle classes but the confused notion that 'healthy' sexuality was being further undermined by the morbid speculations of activists and academics became a commonplace. These fears were quickly exploited. Mussolini and Hitler proved themselves master propagandists in asserting that only an authoritarian regime could counter the threats which sexual degeneracy posed to traditional values and family forms. When the Nazis came to power Freud's books were burnt in Berlin. Driven from Vienna by the most exteme adherents of biological politics, Freud spent the last year of his life in London.

7

'Compulsory Heterosexuality': Eugenicists, Fascists and Nazis

In 1910 Henry H. Goddard, an American psychologist in charge of the Vineland, New Jersey, Training School for Feeble-minded Boys and Girls, had the family lineage of one of his charges investigated by an assistant. She reported that the inmate was descended from the tainted stock produced in one wretched hovel.

> For a quarter of a century this hut existed as a hotbed of vice, the resort of the debauched youth of the neighborhood, and from its walls has come a race of degenerates which out of a total of four hundred and eighty descendants, numbers in almshouse cases, in keepers of houses of prostitution, in inmates of reformatories and institutions for the feeble-minded, in criminals of various sorts and in feeble-minded not under state protection, 143 souls![1]

Historians have demonstrated that the investigator manufactured much of this damning family tree evidence and that, in his book on Vineland, Goddard doctored the photos of the inmates of his institution to make sure they looked sufficiently depraved.[2] Nevertheless, until at least the 1940s a sizeable portion of the public in the Western democracies fell back on studies such as Goddard's to support the contention – today associated with the Nazis – that the uncontrolled reproduction of misfits endangered the larger community.

Because the Nazi persecution of men suspected of homosexuality and women of abortion represented the twentieth century's most dramatic demonstration of the explosive power of sexual panics, the temptation is to regard Germany's descent into biological politics as unique. The Nazi regime came to power in April 1933 with the avowed policy of purging Germany of the contamination of sexual degeneration. In May Ernst Röhm's storm-troopers destroyed Magnus Hirschfeld's Institute of Sex Research, burning 10,000 of the books harboured by what the Brown Shirts labelled this institute of 'dirt and filth'. Ultimately, Hitler's state would castrate sex offenders, send thousands of homosexuals to the concentration camps and pass laws making abortion punishable by death. His government took its first official step in the policing of sexuality in July 1933 with the Law on Preventing Hereditarily Ill Progeny, which allowed doctors to sterilize those deemed to be unfit to reproduce. With hindsight it is easy to see that in undertaking such a policy Germany was embracing an ideology in which racial and sexual panics were intimately intertwined. But in the early 1930s few imagined that the Nazis' population programme would lead on to euthanasia and eventually the extermination of non-Aryans. Sterilization was regarded by many in the West as a humane, rational way of preventing the reproduction of the 'problem class'.[3] Placing the Nazi activities in the context of the sexual and eugenic preoccupations of neighbouring states makes it clear that both fears of shifting gender and class relations and backlashes against them abounded throughout the Western world in the inter-war period.

Eugenics

Historians who first chronicled the activities of the birth controllers, marriage experts, sex educators and sexologists tended to accept uncritically their liberatory claims. A key preoccupation of the preceding chapters has been to demonstrate that, in fact, those who sought to re-make sexuality often advanced complex narratives. Simply by defining what they considered to be a good and healthy sex life led them to conjure up a picture of one that was bad and unhealthy. Such writers almost inevitably contrasted the social benefits which the reproduction of the 'fit' would assure with the costs that would be entailed by the reproduction of the 'unfit', degenerate and members of social problem groups. Eugenicists across the Western world exploited such purported dangers to call for the sterilization of the feeble-minded; the leaders of Nazi Germany ultimately used them to justify euthanasia and racial purification programmes.

Eugenics, the science of the production of fine offspring, was the brainchild of the Englishman Francis Galton (1822–1911). Whereas many of the followers of Charles Darwin, his cousin, believed that the process of natural selection led to the inevitable improvement of the race, Galton raised the alarm at the turn of the century that the struggle for survival was being reversed inasmuch as contraception was employed primarily by the better off. The fact that the lower classes had larger families than the upper was taken by such pessimists as

worrying evidence of the survival of the 'unfit', those who according to the biological determinists had come into the world with their
'mainspring broken' and should have disappeared. Following Galton,
the eugenicists collected and published family pedigrees to demonstrate that like produced like. On the one hand, their hope was that
via a policy of 'positive eugenics', such as child allowances, the state
would reward and encourage the reproduction of the healthy. On the
other, the plotting of families plagued by feeble-mindedness, poverty
and criminality was used by the eugenicists to convince the public
of the legitimacy of employing forms of 'negative eugenics' – such as
detention or sterilization – to restrict the reproduction of the unhealthy.
Accordingly, the English Eugenics Education Society successfully pushed
for the 1913 Mental Deficiency Act in the hope that the institutionaliza-
tion of the mentally unfit would limit their fertility.

The English eugenicists were at first opposed to the birth controllers, but in the 1920s began to close ranks with them. Havelock
Ellis noted that contraception allowed 'selection in reproduction'.[4]
Dr C. P. Blacker agreed that since the fit already limited family size
dysgenic consequences could only be avoided if the 'drunken unem-
ployables' were cajoled into following their lead. In a special 1923
issue of the *Practitioner*, which for the first time dealt openly with contraception, Lady Florence E. Barrett concurred. 'To attempt to lower
the number of the efficient while the inefficient multiply', she wrote,
'spells disaster in the future.'[5]

Marie Stopes's social preoccupations were made clear in *Birth Control News* which was filled with columns on the racial and national
necessity of birth control. Stopes was as concerned to raise the fertility of the upper classes as to lower that of the working classes. She
accepted, as did Margaret Sanger who soon dropped her ties with
the American left, the eugenic argument that the struggle for survival
was being reversed with the 'unfit' now outbreeding the fit and the
country threatened by 'race suicide' and degeneration.[6] Birth control
offered a way of improving the lives of the unskilled and the ignorant
and of limiting their numbers. The working woman had to be taught
birth control, Stopes asserted, because 'such knowledge is not only
essential to her private well-being, but essential to her in the fulfilment of her duties as a citizen.'[7] 'Birth control', agreed Sanger, 'is
essentially an education for women.'[8]

Stopes criss-crossed England during the 1920s lecturing to labouring
audiences. Her goal was to make available to them rational methods
of fertility control employed by the wealthy and well-educated. It
would, she believed, not only improve their lives; it would also ease
the load of the middle class, weighed down as it was in her words

by 'crushing' taxes. 'Contraception is obviously indicated', she wrote, 'rather than the saddling of the community with children of a very doubtful racial value.'[9] Surprisingly enough, the grassroots defenders of birth control tended to be American radicals or British Labour Party supporters who simply ignored Stopes and Sanger's ludicrously elitist outbursts. 'Soon', Stopes prophesied, 'the only class callously and carelessly allowing themselves to hand on bodily defect will be the morons of various grades, sometimes called the "social problem group".'[10] For the careless, the haphazard and the mentally deficient who refused to employ birth-control devices made available to them she envisaged the more stringent measure of sterilization. Her repeated references to 'the thriftless, unmanageable, and the appallingly prolific' and to 'the hopelessly rotten and racially diseased' made it more than apparent that she had little sympathy for the life of the lower classes.[11]

A sense of the self-righteousness of those attracted by eugenic ideas in the English-speaking world was perhaps best provided by the works of Antony Ludovici who paraded his distaste for the 'botched' and the degenerate.[12] Ludovici went so far as to outrage even the members of the British Society of Sex Psychology by defending incest on the grounds that it was an acknowledged form of breeding fit stock.[13] Christianity, which opposed such notions, he claimed, inculcated morbid and decrepit values that exalted the soul over the body. He argued that all the great races were inbred and cited in support German authorities, English geneticists such as Reginald Ruggles-Gates and F. A. E. Crew, and Paul Popenoe, the American defender of the sterilization of the feeble-minded.[14] Ludovici held what he called 'extreme' random breeding to be responsible for insanity and feeble-mindedness. Society had to prevent unhealthy choices being made by requiring at the very least premarital examinations. A misalliance was a eugenic 'crime'.[15] On the continent the Swiss physician Auguste Forel had earlier asked that those suffering from tuberculosis, rickets and haemophilia avoid reproducing, and called for the elimination of criminals, lunatics, alcoholics and drug addicts by sterilization.[16] In the 1930s Edouard Toulouse and the *Société de Sexologie* continued to propagate such views in France.[17]

Many in England agreed that the country should not be 'swamped by imbeciles' but worried that sexual surgery was too drastic a measure.[18] The English eugenicists' campaign for 'voluntary' sterilization of the feeble-minded ultimately proved unsuccessful.[19] Similarly in Catholic Europe, because of the opposition of the Vatican to any form of fertility limitation and the continuing popularity of the Lamarckian belief in environmental forces, eugenicists made limited headway. It was the United States which undertook the world's most aggressive programme to limit the reproduction of the unfit. In 1896 Connecticut decreed that no imbecile, epileptic or feeble-minded person could marry if the wife were under forty-five. By 1914 many states in the North had followed suit. Because the fertility of blacks and immigrants was played up by the media as posing WASPs with the prospect of 'race suicide', the eugenic lobby in America enjoyed unparalleled success. Eugenic concerns led to the funding of serious sex research thanks to John D. Rockefeller who established the American Social Hygiene Association in 1913 and its research arm, the Bureau of Social Hygiene.[20] Eugenic preoccupations likewise underpinned both the federal government's placing of restrictions on immigration and more than twenty states' sterilization legislation.

In 1907 Indiana passed the world's first law allowing for the sterilization of the feeble-minded. California went furthest in putting such ideas into practice, and by the end of the 1930s had carried out operations on over 20,000 patients.[21] In Canada, Alberta adopted a similar programme in 1928 and was followed by British Columbia in 1933.[22] The Catholic church succeeded in countering eugenic legislation in southern Europe, but most of the nations of Protestant Europe – with the notable exception of Britain – adopted sterilization programmes.[23] Women, members of ethnic minorities and the poor were those most likely to be subjected to such operations. In the inter-war world many in Europe and North America recognized the gains to be made by exploiting the apparent linkages between population politics, female emancipation, fertility differentials and ethnic hatreds. Germany was a special case, but there, as elsewhere, sexual panics were employed by politicians, professionals and business leaders to deflect attention away from the social problems caused by the structural flaws of an inequitable economic system.

Weimar Germany

In Germany the sudden demobilization and return of millions of soldiers following the First World War necessarily led to instability and rising social tensions. Conservative commentators pathologized Germany's problems, attributing the nation's remarkably high rates of post-war illegitimacy and venereal disease to moral laxity. Their obvious intent in scapegoating sexuality was to cloak the incompetence and inequities of the Kaiser's recently toppled regime. Right-wing groups opposed to the new Weimar Republic particularly sought to exploit the sexual uncertainties of demobilized men returning home.[24] The myth of the Reich having been 'stabbed in the back' by traitors was paralleled by the notion that women had betrayed their absent spouses. German films in the 1920s and 1930s continued to employ women characters, such as Lulu in *Pandora's Box*, as representatives of the seductive, dangerous side of amoral modern life.[25] In reality, the lives of women in traditional occupations – domestics and farm workers – were largely unchanged. But with their short skirts and bobbed hair the new generation of young office employees, though representing a structural shift in the economy towards the service sector more than anything else, appeared to be the epitome of the 'new woman'. The notion of the sex-mad 'new woman' – very much a male projection – was played up by the press and the popular media. Conservatives took reports of female promiscuity at face value, raising the spectre of the nation sliding into the permissive world of Russian sexual liberation personified by the Soviet feminist and Bolshevik Alexandra Kollontai.

More frightening was Germany's own Helene Stöcker, the leader of the small but vociferous League for the Protection of Motherhood and Sex Reform, who dared to lead the life of a liberated woman. Because she lived unmarried with a man and described women's sexual urges as natural as hunger she was regarded by many as a wild-eyed radical.[26] Like Ellen Key, the Swedish feminist, her defence of unmarried mothers was thought to be a defence of 'free love'. The main feminist movements avoided sex issues and the enormous Catholic and Evangelical groups continued to hold maternity central to a woman's life.[27] In imperial Germany the pronatalists had described pregnancy as the 'woman's active service' and most women's groups continued to believe that a woman's place was in the home.[28] Those alarmed by any perceived declines in traditional family forms inevitably attributed them to the corrosive influence of female autonomy.[29]

Nevertheless, by the 1920s German sexual practices were changing: employment of birth control was widespread, and the number of abortions by 1930 was estimated in the hundreds of thousands. Fertility rates which had briefly risen after the war plummeted in Germany as elsewhere with the onset of the 1929 Depression. All commentators felt obliged to rally in their own way to the defence of the family. The parties of the right, castigating the socialists for defending 'sexual Bolshevism', presented themselves as the best qualified to oppose depopulation. They repeated *ad nauseam* that declining birth rates proved that the body politic was ravaged by degenerative forces. They held that the self-centredness of women – not economic pressures – was responsible for high divorce and low fertility rates. They sought to create a sense of moral crisis in referring to purported 'epidemics' of abortion, venereal disease, illegitimacy and homosexuality. They exploited the idea of a 'sterile Berlin' open to an invasion of prolific

Slavs. Numerous moral leagues, arguing that private actions had national consequences, emerged to defend 'National Vitality' and to work towards 'Regeneration'.[30]

Weimar politicians on the left, now including women members of the Reichstag, responded to the population problem by pushing for positive welfare measures of family allowances and paid maternity leave. The republic thus gave some evidence of a commitment to egalitarianism in turning away from the imperial regime's pronatalism and in seeking to assist motherhood by providing better antenatal care, obstetrics and midwifery. The Law for the Protection of Mothers of 16 July 1927 guaranteed women three-quarters of their wages for four weeks before and six weeks after delivery. Germany led the world in such maternal welfare measures and pronatal incentives.[31] The socialists and communists, doctors and feminists, clergy and sex reformers who plunged into the discussions of maternity, sexuality, contraception and abortion often had contradictory preoccupations but agreed on the necessity of protecting the population, reducing the abortion rate and defending the family. Their goals were far from radical. Just as corporate leaders were increasingly recognizing the advantages of bureaucratizing industry, so too a similar enthusiasm for rationalization and efficiency was shared by many of the public figures who participated in the Weimar discussion of sexuality.

These discussions were not immune to foreign influences. From the west came Hollywood movies which spread new youthful fashions and explicit representations of sexuality throughout Europe.[32] Conservative Germans consequently regarded America as the home of sex, sodomy, birth control, crime, materialism and family and racial disharmony. Margaret Sanger did in fact help to popularize birth control in Germany by lecturing and providing funds, but it was a two-way exchange; she had earlier smuggled German diaphragms and contraceptive creams into the United States via Canada.[33] From the east Weimar Germany received news of the new sexual codes being elaborated in the USSR where in 1920 abortion, though still not a 'right', was legalized.[34] Accordingly, the German Communist Party, advancing the Bolshevik model, moved into sex reform in 1928 with the intent of broadening its base of popular support.

Among German progressives modernity was increasingly equated with the rational discussion of sexuality. Germany witnessed the remarkable growth of a variety of sex reform organizations. The nation's network of birth control and sexual advice clinics, sparked by the pioneering work of propagandists like Max Hodann and Magnus Hirschfeld, was unrivalled in Europe. The first sexual advice centre opened in Berlin in 1919; by 1930 the municipal government was sponsoring a dozen marriage guidance centres. The German left initially found the individualism of the birth controllers' message somewhat of a problem and preferred to regard family limitation as an economic necessity rather than a woman's right. Similarly, it hoped that reason rather than eroticism would prevail in the discussion of sexual issues. Women won some space in which to exercise their fertility rights, but the left never succeeded in completely accepting the significance of gender. Nevertheless, all the leftist parties saw the need to grapple with sex issues if only to attract a working-class audience and usurp lay sex reformers. The German Socialist Party (SPD) and the German Communist Party (KPD) went far farther than the other political parties of Western Europe in defending women's right to control their own bodies. Birth control and marriage clinics represented to the left a social good which favoured the improved quality – if diminished quantity – of the population.

Germany was unique, despite occasional police harassment, in having genuinely grassroots birth control movements in the larger cities. Altogether the sex reform leagues had over 150,000 members with supporters ranging from commercial businesses to communists. The National League for Birth Control and Sexual Hygiene founded in 1928 boasted over 10,000 supporters. By the 1920s it was so obvious that the birth rate could not be artificially sustained that one commentator jibed that the idea of outlawing contraceptives was akin to that of 'banning pistols in order to prevent suicide'.[35] Private businesses made huge profits producing condoms and other rubber goods. By 1932, 1,600 condom-vending machines were in operation across Germany.[36]

The national campaign against venereal disease played an important part in spreading the use of condoms. Birth control, once tabooed, was regarded increasingly as a form of responsible sex by those who argued that, in addition to preventing unwanted conceptions, it could stave off the threats to health and prosperity posed by VD, TB, alcoholism and inherited diseases. The stress on family values helped advance the defence of birth control even among those alarmed by falling fertility rates. Churchmen – except for Catholics – grudgingly felt that they had to accept barrier methods of contraception as tools of social hygiene if only to combat the ravages of venereal disease. Left-wing physicians provided many of the clinic services and slowly medicalized the birth control organizations. Doctors' support was particularly crucial in making birth control legitimate. It was they who advanced the social hygiene argument that the Protestant clergy slowly accepted.

Many doctors defended contraception on the grounds that it was better than abortion. And high female suicide, maternal mortality and

morbidity rates eventually forced on German society a reappraisal of
its harsh anti-abortion law. Paragraph 218 prohibited all abortions that
were not medically indicated. The year 1925 saw the peak in abortion
prosecutions with 7,193 of the 8,402 charged being convicted.[37] In
1927 the government, under pressure from the left, restricted prosecutions, but the communists pressed on with their campaign for
reform of the law. Pope Pius XI responded in 1930 with his encyclical
Casti Connubi (On Christian Marriage), condemning all methods of
fertility control and the morals of the 'new woman'. The pope's assault,
along with the arrest of two doctors implicated in abortions in 1931,
sparked widespread protests against paragraph 218 highlighted by a
'self-denunciation campaign' in which doctors who secretly serviced
women were urged to go public. A law that created 800,000 women
criminals a year could not, its opponents asserted, be just.[38] The German pro-abortionist movement succeeded in organizing monster rallies
and winning the support of such celebrities as Albert Einstein, Fritz
Lang, Kurt Tucholsky and Bertolt Brecht. Abortion reform – advanced
as a welfare proposal essential to the well-being of the working class
– promised to benefit not only women, in decreasing legal penalties,
but also the leftist political parties in increasing their clientele, doctors
in allowing them to usurp the roles previously occupied by lay practitioners, and finally the state which increased its surveillance of female
sexuality.[39] Even if some entered the fray with ulterior motives, there
was no country in the Western world where abortion was so openly
defended.

The new respectability enjoyed by fertility control entailed certain
costs. Sex reforms were institutionalized in the form of sex, marriage,
prenatal and birth control clinics supported by municipal governments and health insurance companies. Doctors replaced lawyers
in setting government population policy and, while sympathetic to
women, necessarily medicalized fertility control. When doctors took
over lay organizations they not only made them more hierarchical;
they also shifted the focus from traditional forms of contraception to
more scientific types that necessarily increased the profession's power.
Fertility control (including abortion) was medicalized but, as was
proved in the case of the use of IUDs, not necessarily made any safer.

The Weimar Republic's range of birth-control services and maternal legislation offered women the obvious advantages of better health
and emancipation from the constraints of biology. But many staffing
such clinics assumed a eugenic view of motherhood. The medicalization of services was increasingly accompanied by arguments in favour
of selective breeding. The government used marriage counselling
centres to promote responsible marriages and kept eugenic files on

their clients. Doctors took on board a eugenic language that referred to 'fit' and 'unfit' mothers. Should 'asocials', they asked, be allowed to reproduce? Some physicians were led on to suggest sterilization, which was cheap and foolproof, for those not competent to employ contraception.[40] They targeted the epileptic, alcoholic, tubercular and criminal. In theory, prior to 1933 sterilization was illegal but such operations were carried out in large numbers. As the doctors' language revolved around the 'degeneration' of the unfit as opposed to the healthy working class, the left did not protest. Indeed, many leftists openly hoped by investigation and counselling to prevent 'irresponsible sex'. German feminists were also attracted by the notion that eugenics would raise the status of women and ensure the birth of healthy children.

Among the major German political formations a consensus emerged in favour of a positive eugenics and defence of traditional family forms. The Weimar constitution explicitly referred to the necessity of maintaining the 'purity of the family'. The doctors, clergy and politicians of Weimar Germany, as much as they might differ, overwhelmingly believed in the primacy of the patriarchal family, eugenic health and accordingly in the necessity of subordinating women's freedom to the needs of the community. Eugenic concerns warranted the surveillance by doctors and social workers of those labelled 'careless and negligent' and underpinned the increased use by the state of powers that could curtail individual liberties.

Some leftists, concerned that the 'sexual misery' of the working class was due to poor housing and lack of privacy, sketched out more radical visions of sexuality and comradeship. The communist sex/political organization, the Unity League for Proletarian Sexual Reform, defended sexual desire, attacked bourgeois marriage, defended prostitutes, demanded sex education and attributed deviancy to capitalism. In warning of the Nazi threat of the surveillance of sexuality and in its criticism of petty bourgeois morality it followed the line popularized by Wilhelm Reich in Vienna.[41] Reich, who moved to Berlin in 1930, if not 'mad' as some of his contemporaries believed, was certainly eccentric and not as central to German sexual politics as he later claimed.[42] The most remarkable efforts to revolutionize morality were made by socialists and feminists like Adele Schreiber and Max Hodann. Hodann, a well-known 'sex-doctor' and political activist, castigated van de Velde as the best known of the 'salvage experts' of bourgeois marriages, but while declaring monogamy a disaster was not clear himself on what might replace it.[43] Hodann's real importance lay in the matter of fact fashion in which he advised a huge clientele through his writings and counselling on the legitimacy of seeking sexual pleasure.

The years 1928–33 witnessed the height of the reform movement linking doctors, workers and intellectuals. Germans such as Hirschfeld placed themselves at the forefront of the international sex reform organizations. Berlin, harbouring Europe's most lively and visible homosexual and lesbian communities, drew the attention of avant-garde writers and artists such as W. H. Auden and Christopher Isherwood. All of these successes the conservatives regarded as symbols of the nation's decadence. The progressives in fact reached only a small percentage of the population and their radicalism would be used as an excuse by many members of the bourgeoisie to throw themselves into the arms of the Nazis.

Fascist Italy

The Nazis' attempt to turn the sexual clock back followed a trajectory laid out in advance by the Italian fascists. Mussolini and his followers in the early 1920s presented themselves as vigorous opponents to any change in gender relations. Exploiting pre-existing currents of misogyny, the fascists nationalized sexuality, placing enormous stress on their adulation of virility and their disdain for the effeminate. The Black Shirts appealed to young middle-class men in portraying the liberals as impotent and themselves as ardent, passionate and youthful. A real man, the fascists asserted, was the potent, prolific heterosexual. Accordingly, the regime taxed bachelors and in 1931 criminalized homosexual acts. Mussolini in his youth had supported free love and neo-Malthusianism but once in power insisted that men prove their manhood by marrying and fathering large families. Bologna's mayor proved his loyalty in calling on men not to use coitus interruptus: 'Screw and leave it in! Orders of the Party!'[44] The party's official line was: 'Society today despises deserters, pimps, homosexuals, thieves. Those who do not perform their duty to the nation must be put in the same category. We must despise them. We must make the bachelors and those who desert the nuptial bed ashamed of their potential powers to have children.'[45]

Mussolini in his early years flaunted his affairs and mistresses. After 1926 the fascists became increasingly bourgeois, attacking pornography, prostitution and even comic books suspected of over-exciting boys.[46] The state employed censorship to counter sex education. It informed Italian women that their job was to produce babies. Misogyny was state sanctioned, yet many women were susceptible to fascist notions of a female mission.[47] There were some 'new women' in Milan and Rome, but few were allowed to venture into the public arena and the peasants in the south lived life much as they had always done. Fascism was contradictory inasmuch as it wanted women to be both modern and traditional. Italian woman, though mobilized, gained little as a result of either the war or fascism. Like the French they did not receive the vote, and after 1925 had to give up their suffrage activities. Few in southern Europe questioned motherhood as part of the core identity of womanhood. A young woman like Hildegart Rodriguez who defended birth control in Spain was regarded by the respectable as debauched.[48]

The fascists propounded the argument that the more prolific the state the healthier it was, whereas a stunted sex drive revealed itself in tuberculosis, alcoholism and low fertility. Mussolini followed up on these odd notions and, as part of his plan for national reconstruction, called for an increase in population.[49] In fact, Italy unlike most of Europe already had a high fertility rate. At the end of the 1920s when the United Kingdom had 56.43 births annually for every 1,000 women, Italy had 95.35.[50] Foreign observers believed Italy was over-populated and noted that its high fertility was accompanied by a high mortality rate. The fascists drive for population growth signified their preference for the quantity rather than the quality of the population.[51]

The Italian neo-Malthusian movement, begun in 1913 by the revolutionary syndicalist Luigi Berta and momentarily supported by the young Mussolini, was necessarily condemned by the fascists as anti-patriotic.[52] After 1926 birth control, described as a 'leprosy', was outlawed as a crime against the state although condoms continued to be produced because men needed them for protection from venereal diseases.[53] The fascists countered abortion by the draconian 1930 and 1941 laws against all 'antidemographic' acts.[54] Corrado Gini led Italian demographers in lamenting Italy's slow population growth, but aside from putting in place some minor maternalist policies the fascists accomplished little. A National Agency for Maternity and Infancy oversaw the provision of tax relief and subsidies to large families but fertility fell in Italy as everywhere else in Europe. In practical terms it seemed to make little sense to push pronatalist policies in an over-populated country. In political terms, however, the fascists found their policy paid dividends. The Romans pacified the masses with 'bread and circuses'; the fascists offered them 'fornication and *figli* [sons]'.[55] The fascists successfully used the 'battle for births' both as a simple diversion and as a tactic to normalize and moralize society by shoring up normal gender relationships.

By the 1929 Lateran Accords, the Catholic church, which had its own moral agenda based on dogma and tradition, and the fascist state united to defend traditional family forms. In much of northern Europe religious justifications of motherhood declined and were replaced by eugenic arguments in the early twentieth century. Eugenics was not very strong in Italy and even Corrado Gini, its leading advocate, was, like other Latin eugenicists, interested in welfare programmes to raise the birth rate rather than the sterilization and negative eugenics policies of Protestant Europe.[56] Similarly, it would be only after 1936 that the Italian fascists would begin to take on board some aspects of the racism and anti-semitism so dear to the Nazis.

The Nazis

The Nazis had from the start promised to purge Germany of sexual decadence. In *Mein Kampf* (1923) Adolf Hitler asserted that Aryans were 'men' and the Jews were not, that those tainted by venereal disease should not be allowed to reproduce, that early marriages were needed to combat prostitution, that birth control was a danger because it limited genetic choice and led to degeneration, that the sexual excitation proffered by films, plays, paintings and posters undermined the morals of youth, and that young men had to be rendered hard by gymnastics and sport.[57] Hitler and his followers were not simply conservative prudes. Their stance on sexuality was necessarily ambiguous. They, like the Italian fascists, initially gained notoriety by posing as the enemy of stuffy bourgeois moralism and as the representatives of youthful radicalism. In the long run, however, Hitler recognized that if he were to win over the business and military elites he would have to purge his movement of its less respectable elements.

Hitler first exploited the fears of alienated veterans in advancing a comforting message that stressed the importance of virility and male bonding. The fledgling Nazi Party sought the support of young men by parading its contempt for the feminine and by striving for a reinvigorated masculinity. The Nazis promised to produce through sport and fitness an energized and virile male body that would be a force of order rather than disorder. The German nudist movement was in the same years claiming to restore health and discipline through the freeing of the body from bourgeois constraints.[58] Statues of naked male youths representing the *Volk* were likewise common in Nazi publications. The question of exactly what the *Männerbund* or community of men's relationship to the traditional family would be was never fully resolved. Hitler was himself very much aware of the danger of it toppling over into homosexuality.[59]

Hitler long depended on the support of Ernst Röhm, the homosexual leader of the Brown Shirts. Röhm and his friends actually flaunted their homosexuality as a way of attacking bourgeois morality. The public was thus faced with the glaring contradiction that, while the Nazis attacked pornography and nude sunbathing, Röhm continued to hold a powerful position as head of the SA. When, because of the army's fear of the SA as a rival, he became too much of a political liability, Hitler had him killed in the 'Night of the Long Knives'. Hitler made homosexuality a political issue by asserting that the June 1934 purge of Röhm and his associates was the only fate worthy of such 'disgusting apes'. Party officials thereafter used homosexual charges to intimidate church and army opponents.

Hitler attempted to cloak the contradictions inherent to his brand of sexual politics by focusing his movement's hatred on the dangerous 'other'. Communists, Jews and homosexuals were homogenized by the Nazis as the enemy. A confidential Gestapo report noted:

> It is especially important to demonstrate the connections between the Jewish-Marxist spirit and the signs of decay so present under the previous system in the areas of sexual science (sex reform efforts, such as Magnus Hirschfeld's Institute, the campaign against paragraph 218, Communist workers sexual journals, plus modern art and pedagogy).[60]

Hirschfeld, who fortunately had left Germany in 1930, died in Nice in 1935. The Nazis destroyed his institute and liquidated the sex reform leagues.[61] They declared that a sex war of sorts was being fought in which homosexual men and aborting women were the enemy.

The Nazi stress on virility required them to present themselves as enemies of effeminate and emasculated degenerates. In 1935 the regime broadened the scope of article 175.[62] To be prosecuted it was no longer necessary for a homosexual to be caught in the act. Homosexuality was regarded by the Nazis as a crime against the race inasmuch as it rendered men impotent. The law was not extended to lesbians since it was held that even deviant women could still have children.[63] A special centre was established by the Nazis to root out abortion and homosexuality and the police were sent out to raid homosexual clubs. Under the Third Reich, the pre-1933 medical literature was used to argue that homosexuals were 'sick', either because of an inborn pathology or an evil choice they had made.[64] Although the authorities believed that homosexuals, unlike Jews and gypsies, could be re-educated, approximately ten thousand were sent to the concentration camps where, wearing pink triangles, they were consigned to the bottom of the inmate hierarchy. Heinrich Himmler, head of the SS, the most extreme enemy of homosexuals, called for the execution or the 'snuffing out' of the life of such unworthy culprits.[65]

The Nazis took some time to work out the contradictions of their views on the family. Italian fascists tended to make relatively simple appeals to traditional forms of patriarchy. Hitler at first lauded the primacy of the male community but eventually swung round to defend traditional morality. Accordingly, he stressed his intent to re-establish natural gender roles. Fatherhood was glorified and women's independence denigrated. 'In the ideology of National Socialism there is no room for the political woman . . . (Our) movement places woman in her natural sphere of the family and stresses her duties as wife and mother.'[66] The Nazis violently opposed woman's emancipation which, declared Hitler, was part of a Jewish plot. The mother, who sacrificed herself for the family became the Nazis' symbol of true womanhood. The regime worked to popularize new female aesthetic standards.[67] Though worried that female athletes might harbour lesbian sentiments, the Third Reich supported women's sports.[68] And in countering the boyish flapper or the blonde Hollywood starlet, Nazis and fascists sought to popularize the image of the healthy maternal figure.

The communists had warned women of the Nazi threat of institutionalized misogyny: 'They want to make you into willing breeding machines. They want you to become men's servants and maids.'[69] Like the fascists, the Nazi regime sought to impose 'compulsory heterosexuality.'[70] They closed birth control and venereal disease clinics and shut down the municipal marriage counselling centres. The Nazis called on women to join in the 'battle of births'. To support the cult of motherhood the regime provided child allowances and offered marriage loans in the hope of lowering the age of marriage and thus combating prostitution. Though companies were, for prophylactic purposes, still permitted to produce condoms, a 1941 law forbade the importation of contraceptives.[71] Divorce was made easier in hopes that remarriage and new births would result.[72] Aryan maternity homes were established and racially desirable children rounded up. Hitler even mused about allowing every German man to have two wives.

Hitler's regime regarded abortion legislation as a weapon to be used in the ongoing racial conflict. Under the Nazis the Weimar abortion law was again rigidly enforced. An Aryan woman who aborted was committing a crime against her race. Therapeutic terminations accordingly dropped in Germany from 44,000 in 1932 to 4,131 in

1937.[73] Under the pressure of war the abortion of German women was in 1943 made punishable by death. A similar law had already been passed in Vichy France by Marshal Pétain. To keep the race pure, however, Aryan women raped by aliens were allowed to abort. And to eliminate inferior stock the state targeted Jews, gypsies, prostitutes, slave labourers and non-Aryans for forced abortions. One hundred thousand compulsory abortions were ultimately carried out. With the same intent of restricting the reproduction of inferior races, the Germans raised the age of marriage in occupied Poland to twenty-eight for men and twenty-five for women.

German birth and marriage rates did rise after 1933, but the Nazis took credit for the sort of demographic resurgence that was noted in many other countries emerging from the depths of the Great Depression. The Nazis were not as pronatalist as they pretended to be; indeed, their policies were in practice clearly anti-natalist.[74] They lauded the value of big, healthy families but actually offered small baby bonuses. They first told women to get out of the labour market and return home, but after 1939 ordered them to stay put. They exiled 200,000 Jewish women and subjected 100,000 captives to forced abortions. They had sex offenders castrated.[75] Hitler spoke of the centrality of the family but in fact the needs of the state constantly over rode it.

The Nazis advanced a hodgepodge of ideas drawn from early twentieth-century discussions on the need to protect the race and family from degeneration and outsiders. They were not, as was seen above, unique in using 'race' as a criterion. Indeed, the Nazis took over much of the progressive biomedical model elaborated in Weimar Germany. In Nazi Germany negative eugenics finally triumphed, but it was more than a simple evolution.[76] In Weimar Germany discussions of 'eugenics' were more rhetorical than real. Underlying much of the enthusiasm for the more rational control of sexuality was the eugenic notion, accepted even by Catholics, of making welfare more efficient by assuring hereditary health. By the late 1920s the Society for Racial Hygiene was envisaging forced sterilizations and even the killing of the severely disabled. The Nazis put such plans for the restriction of the reproduction of the feeble-minded into practice. The 1933 Law for the Prevention of Hereditarily Diseased Offspring followed the United States model.[77] But the German legislation could be used for political purposes; any opponent of the regime risked being declared retarded and subject to surgical intervention. The Nazis, in ultimately sterilizing 400,000 Germans, thus turned to their own purposes the shift begun under the Weimar Republic from reproductive hygiene to racial hygiene. German racism in the 1930s was unique inasmuch as it was institutionalized and moved from theory to practice. The ambitions of the regime can be gauged from Frick's estimate that 20 per cent of Germans were 'unfit'.

The Nazis launched campaigns of massive state intervention with the intention of reconstituting motherhood, eugenics and sexuality. Sterilizations led on to euthanasia and euthanasia to the final solution of genocide.[78] Jews, communists and women were targeted by the Aryanization programmes. At first Aryan husbands were pressured by the state to divorce Jewish wives. Then the 1935 Nuremberg Law for the Protection of German Blood and Honour allowed for 'Heredity Health Courts' to make decisions on the termination of 'Lives unworthy of life'. Finally, in the concentration camps the sexual and racial enemies of the regime were liquidated.

Conclusion

A review of the Nazi treatment of sexuality reveals a number of ironies. First, what was striking about their stress on natural sex roles was that it represented in its most chilling form a general movement of ideas. The Nazis invented very little. They appropriated and pushed to their logical conclusions the commonplace anti-libertarian views of the early twentieth century. Nor were the Nazis alone in harbouring fears of a mixing of the races. One might recall that in the United States the spectre of black men raping white women led to waves of lynchings which resulted in over 3,800 victims between 1889 and 1940. In fact, only about one-quarter of the vigilante episodes were actually connected to sexual activities and no white male was so punished for raping a black woman. As late as 1939, 64 per cent of whites surveyed agreed that lynching was necessary to protect white women.[79] Because of their tolerance of lynching – described as 'folk pornography' – progressive Europeans long regarded Americans as uncivilized.[80] Yet fears of race-mixing were pervasive. In England the eminent biologist Reginald Ruggles-Gates in *Heredity in Man* (1929) attacked miscegenation which he likened to 'making up a machine with spare parts'.[81] Antony Ludovici defended the notion that the beautiful were the healthy and lamented the current 'uglification of humanity'.[82] In Vichy France, the Nazis' collaborators prided themselves on their defence of the family and the race.[83] In every Western state there were politicians so preoccupied by threats to the race that they felt radical measures of repression were required. The Nazis went furthest in their remedies.

The second irony was that, by a process of social amnesia, the fact that the Nazi programme was motivated by such generalized fears was quickly forgotten. Indeed, a range of sex issues that the Nazis had exploited became implicated in the Cold War struggle. Abortion and homosexuality remained criminalized after 1945. Since homosexuality was a crime in Anglo-Saxon countries, the history of Nazi persecution of sexual minority groups was ignored.[84] In Germany itself, article 175 criminalizing homosexuality was kept on the books until the 1960s. The term 'homosexual' in the hysterical Cold War climate came to mean the potential communist pawn. Abortion also continued to be treated as a crime.[85] The term 'abortion' was employed as a code word for a changing social reality; it meant the new, emancipated, frivolous woman. Eugenic sterilization, which was carried out in Canada and the United States until the 1970s, was not considered too serious a problem though commentators chided the Nazis for being 'excessive'. But the child allowance programme – a rare progressive form of family legislation which the Germans had employed in the 1930s – was ended by the allies since the Americans regarded it as socialistic in nature.

The third irony was the hostility encountered in the West by the most resolute opponents of the Nazis. European sexology was destroyed by the war and would re-emerge in the 1950s as an American discipline.[86] To the German sex reformers in exile, many of whom were Jews and communists, America seemed conservative and philistine. If they were to move into respectable organizations like Planned Parenthood they had to drop their radicalism; the Rockefeller Foundation would not support purported subversives. But a German birth controller like Hans Marmsen, who worked right through the Nazi period, opposed abortion and was involved in the sterilization programme, though he avoided joining the party, was the sort of respectable professional the Americans turned to in re-establishing birth control services in post-war West Germany.[87]

The final irony was the way in which sexual stories continued to be employed by those who sought to smear their opponents. The Nazis had used charges of sexual deviancy as a brush with which to tar their victims. Following the war, sex continued to be used as a dirty word wielded by the victors to tarnish the reputations of the defeated. The Nazis had attacked their opponents as degenerates; the allies in turn castigated Hitler and his followers as sexual deviants.[88] Did Hitler have one or two testicles? Was he impotent? Did he have syphilis? Was his father illegitimate? These were the sort of inconsequential questions that scholars seriously pondered in their search for an explanation of the Nazi horrors. Critical theorists such as Wilhelm Reich and Walter Adorno spoke more generally of the success of fascism being due to the effeminate or emasculated 'authoritarian personality' seeking order and discipline. Arthur Schlesinger Jr claimed in 1949 that all totalitarian states had a tendency to 'pervert politics' into 'something secret and furtive like homosexuality in a boys' school'.[89] By such reasonings, commentators consciously sought to shore up the normalizing of sexual behaviour. These writers, in maintaining that those who did not have 'normal' sex lives posed a possible danger to society, chose to forget that this was the same message Adolf Hitler had propounded.

8

'Surveying Sex': From Alfred C. Kinsey to Hugh Hefner

The twenty years or so that separated the ending of the Second World War from the outbreak of the 'sexual revolution' of the 1960s was marked by a swirl of conflicting cultural currents. On the one hand, social scientists announced the discovery of momentous shifts in sexual behaviour and, on the other, rival observers strenuously attempted to deny the reality of such changing sexual mores. Marriage counsellors, psychologists and sex surveyors emerged to provide accounts of such new characters as the 'smothering mom', the divorcee, the play-boy and the teenage delinquent. A host of sex experts in the 1950s particularly sought to compensate for what they assumed had been the war's corrosive impact on notions of masculinity and femininity by exaggerating 'traditional' gender divisions. Sociologists such as Talcott Parsons, for example, argued that only by men and women fulfilling radically different, gender-specific roles could family happi-ness and stability be assured. Alfred Kinsey, associated in the public mind with the blurring of such identities, found himself castigated by conservatives as a subversive and possibly a communist dupe. Never-theless, he was to enjoy enormous influence by presenting himself not as a sex revolutionary, but as a detached and objective observer of sexual behaviour. Because of the Western world's faith in powers of reason and science, Kinsey's findings were by the end of the 1950s being hailed and exploited by opponents of the sexual status quo who ranged from Hugh Hefner of *Playboy* magazine to the first adherents of America's gay rights movement.

Kinsey

Kinsey's name was, in the post-Second World War world, a by-word for scandalous sexual revelations.[1] Although he was regarded by many as an academic voyeur, those who actually purchased and read his 1948 best-seller *Sexual Behavior in the Human Male* discovered a middle-aged Indiana University professor of entomology fired with a compulsion for collecting enormous reams of data. Having turned his attention from the study of gall wasps to the subject of human sexuality, he produced a blizzard of charts and graphs to hammer home the reality of his amazing discoveries. Kinsey noted that insects – his first love – offered wide variations; the wing length of some species could vary up to eighteen times. When he came to look at humans he was dazzled by an even more staggering diversity. He interviewed one man who had ejaculated only once in thirty years and another who had thirty orgasms every week. That the two men's sexual activities differed by a ratio of 45,000 to 1 was remarkable, yet for Kinsey what was even more striking was the fact that the two individuals were otherwise unexceptional; certainly neither could be consider 'abnormal'. Yet generations of self-important but innumerate observers, Kinsey complained, not only fell back on such meaningless terms as 'normal' or abnormal', they had terrorized patients with loaded words like 'infantile, frigid, sexually under-developed, under-active, excessively active, over-developed, over-sexed, hypersexual, or sexually over-active'.[2]

Kinsey claimed that it had been the Indiana University students' demand for a marriage hygiene course that had led him to turn somewhat reluctantly to the study of human sexuality; in reality, he leapt at the opportunity to expose the extent of sexual ignorance in America.[3] As a biologist Kinsey refused to categorize any biological act as 'abnormal', a term coined by philosophers and priests. Unfortunately, their moralizing tradition, he argued, had been carried on by Freud's followers; the psychoanalysts' concept of sublimation was simply a new way of calling for sexual abstinence.[4] Kinsey wryly noted that what such experts called 'abnormal' behaviour was found in 60–75 per cent of the population. Psychologists by only seeing self-selected samples of neurotics had been led to believe in the pathological nature of certain sexual acts. In contrast, Kinsey boasted of the objectivity of his in-depth survey of tens of thousands of healthy college students, church-goers and club members which non-judgementally set out to report on the variety of sexual acts ordinary white Americans engaged in.[5]

Kinsey's work grew out of a tradition of American sex research based on the collection of extensive case studies in which researchers tended to focus increasingly on action, rather than on emotion. Such an approach had both advantages and disadvantages. Lewis Terman, who assumed that normal sex could only be heterosexual coition and showed a disinterest in foreplay, magnified the significance of intercourse and drew rigid boundaries between normal and abnormal behaviour.[6] In response, Kinsey wondered why sex should be equated only with heterosexual coitus. Why not simply ask informants the more basic questions of how the biological process of 'sexual release' was achieved? When Kinsey did ask men about their sexual 'outlets' he found that over the course of their lives 'true heterosexual intercourse' occupied only fourth place; masturbation, wet dreams and heterosexual petting preceded it. Masturbation, Kinsey concluded, was ubiquitous and, though psychiatrists were still reluctant to admit it, harmless. So, too, was the homosexual sex play which 60 per cent of his subjects recalled having as boys. Once males began their sex lives they never stopped; Freud's notion of a latency period was, Kinsey insisted, incorrect. Indeed, the male's sex drive peaked in the late teen years, the very time when adult society was making its most strenuous efforts to enforce abstinence on youth. Perhaps attempting to play on anti-feminist sentiment, he noted the cruel irony that older women, whose sex drives were only about one-fifth of young men's, were the very ones preaching repressive forms of sex education and leading the campaigns against juvenile delinquency.[7] It was futile for society to attempt to prevent sex. Armies and prisons had failed to impose such restraints; what hopes had civil society?

In any event, Kinsey insisted that sex was not debasing. To the old claim that those who gave in to their sexual urges were mental and moral misfits he responded that, on the contrary, his data revealed that the most sexually active were among those who were most pro-fessionally successful. Countering the nineteenth-century notion of a 'seminal economy' that held that one had a limited reserve of sexual energy that should not be squandered, Kinsey declared that sexual activity was a sign of health. In a hymn to virility he claimed that those males who had the earliest sexual experiences went on to become the most 'alert, energetic, vivacious, spontaneous, physically active, socially extrovert, and/or aggressive individuals in the popula-tion'.[8] Those who were late to start their sex life were handicapped.

Kinsey's most sensational findings pertained to homosexuality.[9] Just as he replaced one notion of sexual intercourse with the idea of a variety of sexual releases, he similarly attacked the narrowness of the concepts of 'homosexuality', 'heterosexuality' and 'bisexuality'. If, in trying to sort out subjects, one began with such a limited number of predetermined categories, the research findings were anticipated in advance. Kinsey abandoned such stereotypes and simply asked his male subjects if they had by any means ever climaxed with another male. Thirty-seven per cent stated that they had. Kinsey, though initially surprised, concluded that this was probably an under-estimation. He was not asserting that over a third of the population was 'homo-sexual'; what he advanced was the notion of a sexual continuum along a scale from '0' for the individual who had never had a homo-sexual experience (about 50 per cent of the male population) to '6' for men who throughout their whole life had only had same-sex relationships (about 4 per cent). The remaining 45 per cent had experienced both forms of sexual release at least once in their lives.[10] Kinsey critiqued Ellis and Hirschfeld for seeking to isolate a 'Third Sex' that was exclusively homosexual, preferring to assert more generally that homo-sexuality was an 'expression of capacities that are basic in the human animal'.[11] Many of America's best-adjusted men – if their sex lives were revealed – would, Kinsey declared, be categorized under exist-ing laws, moral codes and psychiatric teachings as perverts. Was this too alarming a prospect to contemplate? He offered one faint ray of hope. If society ceased to ostracize and persecute the sexually experimental, the number driven to homosexual exclusivity might be lessened. At present, America's restrictive moral code, in labelling some men as deviant, limited them to 'perverse' forms of behaviour.[12]

Kinsey's 1953 report on *Sexual Behavior in the Human Female* created another sensation.[13] Here his predecessors included Katherine Bement Davis who, with Rockefeller support, had gathered data on the sex lives of 2,200 American women, which revealed in the late 1920s high rates of female masturbation and use of contraceptives.[14] Perhaps the most important finding of Kinsey's study, based on nearly 8,000 subjects, was his rediscovery of the importance of the clitoris for female pleasure. He was accordingly led on to defend masturbation against the psychoanalysts who insisted that women needed training in 'vaginal response'.[15] A 1949 English text had typically stated that a man seeking to arouse a woman should know how to locate the clitoris – described prosaically as 'the size of a split pea' – but then went on to declare that compared to the clitorally induced climax the vaginal orgasm had 'a richer, deeper and finer quality'.[16] Kinsey retorted that the vaginal orgasm was a myth and the claim that masturbation had a harmful impact on coitus simply was not true; indeed, it had a bene-ficial effect. In his sample only half of the women who had not had an orgasm prior to marriage had them regularly after marriage, three times less than those who had had a premarital orgasm. He came to the same optimistic conclusions regarding the beneficial effects of premarital petting.[17] Pleasure was a learned response, and one's educa-tion could never begin too soon. What about actual intercourse? Fifteen years previously Dorothy Dunbar Bromley and F. H. Britten revealed that 25 per cent of American women had intercourse at least once before marriage.[18] Kinsey's data indicated that now only about 50 per cent of brides were virgins. He again asserted that women's emotional capacities were improved by experience, which was indicated by the positive correlation between coital orgasms before and after marriage.[19] He conceded that he might have stumbled upon a self-selected sample of over-responsive females, but thought not.[20]

Kinsey's comments on lesbianism were as shocking as those he made about homosexuality. Terman had found that women were more likely than men (8 per cent as opposed to 5 per cent) to report same-sex feelings, and he cited Katherine Bement Davis's finding that one-fifth of the unmarried reported overt same-sex practices and G. V. Hamilton's 1929 study that 26 per cent of wives admitted to a homosexual episode.[21] Kinsey found that 28 per cent of his female sample had had sexual contact with another female, somewhat less than the rate of male same-sex behaviour.[22] He was impressed by homosexual contacts which he found were 'highly effective' in bringing women to orgasm. The fact that the higher the educational level the higher the incidence of such affairs Kinsey attributed to middle-class parents' success in protecting college girls from heterosexual contacts.[23] He scoffed at the common belief found in many authors, including Ellis, Freud and Terman, that lesbians would appear masculinized. He was equally amused that some experts insisted that those with homosexual tendencies should not marry in an attempt to cure themselves, while others said that they should as 'women have more fluid minds and sometimes do respond more or less normally when sexually awakened'.[24] Kinsey caustically pointed out that the law neither forced nor forbid anyone to marry.

The Post-war Family

Despite the enormous sales enjoyed by Kinsey's books, his sensational findings led conservative newspapers and politicians promoting Cold War hysteria to besmirch his name. Though few took seriously the idea that he harboured communist sympathies, he was castigated in Congress and such was his notoriety that the Rockefeller Foundation eventually had to terminate his funding.[25] His assertions were all the more startling, given the fact that they were made in the decades hailed by many with hindsight as the 'golden age of the family'. This was a culture in which a triumphant America informed the world via films and later television shows such as *Ozzie and Harriet* and *Leave it to Beaver* that traditional gender norms were sacrosanct. The optimism and self-assurance of those who made such pronouncements on sexual normality – citizens of a country in which it appeared everyone could now anticipate sharing in the familial suburban pleasures of house, car and kitchen appliances – seemed well grounded. Europe took longer to recover from the ravages of war but there, too, by the 1953 coronation of Queen Elizabeth – her family a decorous model of respectability – life also seemed to have returned to 'normal'.

Despite Kinsey's troubling assertions, Western gender norms in the 1950s appeared more solid than ever. Divorce rates were low and marriage rates high. Families were not large but there were more families with children than ever before. Such findings provided good reasons for North Americans in particular to feel optimistic. Those who had survived both a Depression and a world war assumed that in an age of relative affluence social and sexual conflicts were relics of the past. Ironically such heightened expectations of family well-being soon gave rise to nagging anxieties. The 1950s proved to be a time of transition, not of calm. At home sexual pessimists bemoaned the growth of suburbanization, white-collar work and youth culture to which prosperity had given rise. When they turned their eyes outward they saw in communism, the Cold War and the atom bomb, a variety of forces that they feared would overwhelm their society where evidence suggested sexuality sapped moral vigour. In the post-war world many feared that declining fertility and rising divorce rates were symptoms of the erosion of family values. These problems were in turn traced back by a new generation of experts to the old notion that men women and young people were failing to fulfil their prescribed age and gender roles.

Would fertility drop to dangerously low levels? During the war the American and Commonwealth armies provided their troops with condoms to protect them from disease and some expressed concern that their use would spread in peacetime.[26] One British doctor asserted that 'contraceptives, like high explosives, are immensely powerful and far reaching in their effect.' Allowing earlier marriages, she hoped, could reduce promiscuity, abortions and venereal disease, but she worried that they would also lead to the spoilt child of the small, dysgenic family.[27] The pessimistic predicted that cheap contraceptives would ultimately result in a drop in the white population and flaccid societies lacking vitality, hope, enterprise and adventure.[28] The post-war democracies, though preoccupied by the need for a population policy and essentially pronatalist, at least did not want to be seen as sharing the fascist regimes' hostility to contraception. In Germany, however, the churches' role in the Nazi period was covered up and priests continued self-righteously to preached pronatalism well into the 1950s.[29]

In Britain family planning was supported as part of the National Health Service. Curiously, a blossoming of clinics occurred just as fertility rates rose. This post-war 'baby boom' was a surprise, though it was more of a 'boomlet' on the continent, and in Britain, North America and Australia birth rates remained high through the 1950s and into the 1960s. In England the birth rate rose from 15.8 per 1,000 in 1931 to a peak of 20.5 in 1947 and then declined in the 1950s; in the United States it was up to 24.5 in 1951. The three-child family once again displaced the two-child family as the norm. Old class fertility differentials were largely eradicated; fertility tended now to follow a 'U' curve with the lower and upper classes having only a slightly higher family size than the middle classes.

The 'baby boom' seemed in England at least to prove wrong the conservative argument enunciated in the 1930s that family size necessarily declined as responsibility for health, education and care of the elderly was assumed by the state. The resurgence of natality was made possible by improvements in wages during the prosperous post-war decades. Marriage rates rose as high as they could go and the big church wedding came back into fashion. Women married earlier and had their children sooner. Age of marriage dropped. 'In 1931 only 7 per cent of English males 15–24 years of age were married. In 1951, the proportion was 12.5 per cent and by 1957 it was 14.9 per cent.'[30] Many couples consciously compensated for the sacrifices they or their parents had made during the Depression and the war. Some were just less vigilant in their contraceptive practices.[31] In America the Depression had spurred on the establishment of birth control clinics but they still provided limited services and no new contraceptives appeared on the market. Most people depended on friends or acquaintances for information on birth control, not on doctors who claimed there was little demand. Coitus interruptus was still widely employed and 'accidents' happened. Indeed, a British study noted that on occasion 'withdrawal becomes a weapon [of the husband], designed in intentional misuse to bring about conception and ensure a wife's fidelity.'[32]

Divorce

Moralists were equally concerned that the relaxing of morality occasioned by the war would spill over into increased adultery once the troops returned home.[33] Extra-marital affairs were in theory still taken very seriously in the 1950s. In the United States the ten northeastern states treated them as crimes punishable by prison terms, though such laws were rarely enforced. Psychologists attacked adultery as a sign of immaturity.[34] In Kinsey's view the appeal of such affairs was simply a search for pleasure. He found that the working-class male tended to have extra-marital affairs early in life, the upper classes in middle age. Working-class women 'expected' their men to 'step out'.[35] An English researcher found, not surprisingly, that for their part unhappily married women frequently wanted an extra-marital fling.[36] Those who suffered as a result of affairs, Kinsey claimed, did so primarily because society put such high value on fidelity and social conformity. Premarital experience did not, as moralists assumed, lead to a greater number of extra-marital liaisons. Both those who did and did not experience premarital coitus had identical rates of adultery.[37] Whatever moralists might say, the general public regarded such escapades with a high degree of tolerance, if not envy.

Most commentators insisted that the danger of adultery was that it led to divorce.[38] In Canada the divorce rate peaked in 1947, having tripled since 1941.[39] In the United States the rate doubled immediately after the war and in England, where it was much lower, it increased five-fold. Sixty thousand divorces were granted there in 1947 but both the English and American rates declined into the 1950s. Kinsey was one of the few to argue that adultery did not inevitably harm marriage. He found that only about a fifth of those women who had affairs and divorced believed that adultery was the prime motivating factor.[40] Men, however, were twice as likely as women to blame divorce on a wife's affair. In a country such as England, where a divorce could not be attained unless adultery had been committed, the dissolution of marriage was necessarily sexualized. The British public relied on divorce reports for *risqué* reading as they inevitably contained accounts of weekend sea-side trysts being interrupted by seedy hotel detectives. The 1923 Matrimonial Causes Act held that a husband's adultery could, like a wife's, be sufficient grounds for divorce, but it still did not permit a couple to agree to a divorce. 'Whenever I explain certain sections of the law my clients conclude that I must be mad or drunk', noted a solicitor who went on to point out: 'If you violently knock your wife about every night the ordinary person will conclude that you have not much affection for her; but the law requires you to prove it by sleeping with another woman.'[41] The Church of England actually protested in 1935 that some people were only 'pretending' to commit adultery.[42] But both spouses could not be adulterers; the law insisted that there had to be both a guilty and an innocent partner. In 1937 cruelty and desertion were added to the statute but a 'matrimonial fault' continued to be required until divorce reform came to Britain in 1969. The intent was to remove moral blame by ending the notion of 'matrimonial offence'. Such reforms, which finally brought British law into line with that of most American states, gave heightened importance to the quality of the marital relationship, on the one hand, while on the other they recognized that though sex was supposed to be restricted to marriage, 'love' permitted exceptions.

Sex in marriage was spoken of far more openly in the 1950s, especially by the professionals providing marriage counselling who assumed the task of ensuring that couples did not even envisage separation. They assumed that the dashing of men's and women's growing expectation that love and sensual pleasure would be provided by marriage largely explained the turn towards divorce.[43] Married life accordingly had to be made more appealing, especially if it were to face up to the additional disruptions that had been caused by the war. Even Catholic clerics came to accept the importance of sexual compatibility. The Vatican, which held secularization responsible for undermining family life, accepted marriage counselling because it promised to strengthen the couple. In France spouses turned to Catholic agencies such as the *Association du Mariage Chrétien*, though the church's continued hostility to contraception alienated many believers.[44] In Protestant countries there was a perceived need for new experts on family matters now that traditional confidants – family members, pastors, neighbours – were less available and doctors and lawyers ill prepared to offer advice.[45]

Those attracted to marriage counselling came from a variety of backgrounds but in the main emerged out of the old social hygiene movement. In the United States the Marriage Council first won the support of eugenicists and progressives because of the fear of the impact that the Depression was having on families. They included Paul Popenoe, an admirer of Hitler and an apologist of the Nazi eugenic programme in the 1930s, and the nation's best-known advocate of the sterilization of the feeble-minded. Indeed, the propaganda pieces that he produced at the Human Betterment Foundation of Pasadena, California were widely cited by eugenicists in Canada and Europe.[46] Popenoe established in 1930 the American Institute of Family Relations in Los Angeles, inspired in part by the German marriage advice bureaux, as the country's first research and counselling centre on marriage and parenthood.[47] As eugenics fell into disrepute, he increasingly identified himself as an expert in marriage counselling.[48] His basic hereditarian concerns were unchanged. In a 1947 article, entitled 'First Aid for the Family', he asserted:

At the bottom of society there is always a rotten layer that is a source of trouble and expense, but the social and biological decay that is most dangerous is that which begins at the top. Among the 'social elite' and the climbers the birth rate has been falling and marriage has been deteriorating for a couple of centuries.[49]

Popenoe presented a gloomy picture of American suburban life with wives, devoted to bridge and movies, abandoning their motherly responsibilities. What was required, according to him, were large families because each additional child reduced the chance of a marital break up.[50] Divorce was not an answer; it was a symptom of one's failure to be an adult; sexual maladjustments simply needed to be straightened out. The criticism of family life voiced by radicals only caused further confusion as did the works of film-makers and novelists who harped on unhappiness. Central to Popenoe's view of family stability was the necessity for a clear separation of the sexes The blurring of gender roles – which he attributed to uppity women – caused most family problems. 'Unfortunately, the trend of education during the last generation has been unfavourable because the dominance of a doctrinaire feminist point of view has led to a depreciation of the difference between the sexes and frequently to ignoring them or denying them altogether.'[51]

Similar eugenic preoccupations coloured the works of Lewis Terman who moved from IQ research to work on an 'orgasm prediction scale'. Seeking to do for sexuality what Binet had done for intelligence, he also created a scale for masculinity and femininity based on traditional gender stereotypes.[52] Why, pondered Terman, were 33 per cent of wives according to his criteria sexually 'inadequate'? Feminists such as Stopes had blamed clumsy husbands. Terman, taking the depressed, conformist nature of women as a given, concluded that the wife's personality was to blame, which, in turn, he believed had a genetic basis.[53] Sexual compatibility, he happily noted, was in any event not always crucial to family stability.

Eugenicists did not monopolize marriage counselling.[54] More progressive individuals such as Abraham and Hannah Stone moved into the field from the less reputable world of family planning. Emily Mudd, a Quaker who had established the first birth control clinic in Philadelphia in 1927, founded the American Association of Marriage Counsellors. Similar religious preoccupations coloured the views of the National Marriage Guidance Council in England which, beginning in 1938, produced such texts as *How to Treat a Young Wife*.[55] In part its work was a response to radicals such as Bertrand Russell who had called the very purpose of marriage – for those without children – into question.[56] The council accepted birth control for the married but opposed premarital sex. Churchmen once used children as way of legitimating their policing of the family; now that contraception permitted one to be married and not have children, Christians increasingly saw the necessity of discussing non-procreative sex.[57]

If a marriage were threatened by an outsider some experts were still suggesting in the 1940s that the husband threaten the lover with violence and the wife with the loss of her children.[58] The more advanced hoped that such coercive scenarios could be avoided altogether if the importance of sex in marriage were recognized. In *Modern Marriage*, E. F. Griffith noted that sexual incompatibility was the root of most marriage problems.[59] David Mace, Britain's chief advocate of marriage guidance, described marital disharmony as a 'disease'.[60] Such reformers hoped, by improving sex, to restrict it to the marriage bed. The happy couple would then recognize the strengths and freely embrace the old values of chastity and fidelity. This scenario held that women had to find marital sex pleasurable and Emily Mudd accordingly provided advice on how the husband should 'court' his wife.[61] Similarly, Mace set sexual harmony as the goal, envisaging the re-educating of the husband to end the wife's frustration.[62] To counter husbands from straying, wives for their part were enjoined to make themselves more responsive and attractive.

For some women the news that they had to experience sexual pleasure simply meant that they were burdened with yet another duty to fulfil. Woodside and Slater's British study, which provided a more intimate view of married life than Kinsey's dry tabulations, was revealing. They found that couples assumed that there were *standards* of sexual activity and so responded to many questions with the answer 'just normal'. Couples tended to have sex twice a week, the man being proud to say that he was not a 'beast' or a 'maniac', the woman – who frequently had no great expectations of pleasure – commenting that her spouse did not 'bother me much' or was 'thoughtful'. Thirty per cent of the women found sex distasteful.[63] A later English study produced much the same results. Eustace Chesser found that women did not need orgasm to claim sexual satisfaction. Only 24 per cent said that they always had orgasm, yet 43 per cent insisted they had 'a lot' of sexual satisfaction. Ten per cent said they 'rarely' had orgasm, yet only 5 per cent declared that they had no sexual satisfaction.[64]

Such findings seemed to support Kinsey's view that marriage counsellors would have limited success since they propagated 'the sort of intellectual eroticism which the upper level esteem', such as foreplay and mutual orgasm, but which was foreign to the lower classes.[65] He found, for example, that 90 per cent of the well-educated had intercourse in the nude as opposed to only 43 per cent of those who had not gone beyond grade school. The college-educated were more likely than those less advantaged to engaged in deep kissing, petting and oral sex.[66] Middle-class youths tended to pet and refrain from intercourse;

working-class youths did the opposite. Marriage manuals, he argued, were of little use since they did not recognize that such behaviour patterns were set in early life. Yet Kinsey seemed to have exceptionally low expectations of males' ability to be re-educated, particularly when it came to prolonging intercourse.[67] Three-quarters of his male sample took only two minutes to complete coition, which he sanguinely regarded as unexceptional, given that chimpanzees took only ten to twenty seconds. His women readers were presumably not impressed by such reasoning. 'Unhappiness' was a concept Kinsey had difficulty coming to terms with but one which the marriage counsellors, for all their faults, acknowledged. Marriage counselling was both a symptom of a shifting morality and a response to it. Counsellors, though opposed to the dissolution of marriage, were by their increased stress on the quality of married life unintentionally providing arguments that could be employed to justify a spouse seeking happiness in a new, outside relationship.

Psychology

Psychologists also offered explanations for family unhappiness that were more accessible than the cold statistics advanced by Kinsey. They were also far more optimistic about 'curing' people of their sexual ills. The gist of their approach was summed up in an article entitled 'Making Normal People' that appeared in an 1954 issue of *Marriage and Family Living*. 'A boy's nervous breakdown may be due to the major sociopathy of the war or Momism', the author speculated, 'and the Momism may be the direct result of Pop's wrong vocational choice or his connubial ineptness.'[68] Here, in a nutshell, were the chief concerns of the supporters of the crude psychoanalysis that enjoyed enormous popularity in the 1950s: the need for husbands, wives and children to learn to adjust to their natural roles.[69] In the inter-war years psychoanalysis had percolated out from the haunts of Greenwich Village radicals and bohemians to the mid-west so that by the 1940s the vocabulary it had popularized made it possible for Americans to discuss once tabooed sexual issues. In its therapeutic guise psychoanalysis dominated the treatment of sexual issues in the United States from the 1920s, with therapists assuming the role of the nation's moral guardians.

Psychology's first task was to woo women back to femininity. Fears of sexual anarchy were dealt with in the 1950s by public expressions of exaggerated fidelity to traditional norms, especially when it came to women's sexuality. Psychologists advanced the notion of a more democratic family, a partnership but one in which roles were clearly differentiated.[70] What was the woman's natural role in the 1950s? Her actual options were changing radically but cultural norms were still repressive. Women were clearly supposed to be married. Governments linked social benefits to sexual morality; in Canada as in Britain benefits were cut off from women living with men to whom they were not married. And married women were supposed to be at home. Millions of women, called by the state during the war to enter munitions factories while their children were cared for in crèches, soon found their jobs and child-care facilities gone. The British government recognized that women could not be forced to quit their jobs yet its failure to provide cheap day-care penalized working mothers.

Women were bombarded by pronatalist propaganda and, for lack of any other option, many were won over by the appeal of domesticity and femininity subsequently dubbed the 'feminine mystique'. Even Sanger's American Birth Control League, seeking to disassociate itself from the disturbing notion of individual women's rights and to exploit familial sentiment, was rechristened the Planned Parenthood Federation of America.[71] Enormous pressure was placed on women to become perfect mothers. The work of psychologists like John Bowlby on the importance of the child's attachment to the mother simply added to busy women's guilt.

If a woman did devote herself to motherhood she might be labelled a smothering mother responsible for turning her son into a homosexual. In many ways this critique was simply a carry-over of interwar musings of conservatives like Hermann Keyserling with his attack on the unstable emotional woman, and the matriarchialism purportedly unique to America which rendered men dependent.[72] The word 'momism' was actually coined by Philip Wylie, author of *Generation of Vipers* (1942), to castigate the dominating woman who, though relegated to suburbia, still succeeded in emotionally crippling her son.[73] The not so subtle message that the male had to subdue the independent female was captured in innumerable movies in which Clark Gable or Cary Grant finally resorted to a good spanking to bring the self-centred heroine to her senses.

The injunction of psychologists and marriage counsellors that women also had to be good sex partners caught them in yet another double bind. Expectations had once been low. As late as 1930 Dr Howard Kelley, professor of gynaecology at Johns Hopkins University, had denied the notion that women sought pleasure in intercourse: 'their participation is but a matter of complaisance'.[74] Now expectations were high and, though Kinsey noted that a third or more of women did not regularly achieve orgasm, by the 1950s the woman who failed to climax risked being labelled 'frigid'. A wife needed sexual experience to be good in bed, but women who had sex before marriage reported being looked down upon by their husbands.[75] Freudians, of course, stressed the woman's need not to be just pleasured but to have the correct form of pleasure – the vaginal orgasm.

The flip side of 'momism' was the weak father figure personified by the emasculated males in television serials such as *Leave it to Beaver* and *Father Knows Best*. With more women in the workforce, talk of a collapse of the 'breadwinner' ethic and rumours of rising numbers of men deserting their families, post-war America experienced a 'crisis in masculinity'. The loss of male authority and the rise of the dominating mother was advanced as a root cause of juvenile delinquency in such films as James Dean's *Rebel Without a Cause*. The old notion that a man proved his 'maturity' by simply marrying and having children now seemed to lack bite.[76] Accordingly, new reasons were sought to justify male superiority. At the literary level, a variety of commentators from Norman Mailer and Ernest Hemingway in the United States to the 'Angry Young Men' in Britain expressed the feeling that men had to fight to prove themselves in an increasingly suburbanized, affluent, female-oriented world. Hardboiled novelists like Raymond Chandler delighted in killing off their female characters.[77] Similarly, the 'bitch' heroines in best-sellers such as *Gone with the Wind* and *Forever Amber* were always punished. In America, Europeans noted with surprise, portrayals of violence against women were permitted while sex was censored.

Other men preferred flight to fight. Even the members of the Beat generation, who seemed to attack most aspects of the American way of life, produced in Jack Kerouac's *On the Road* (1957) a classic portrayal of male escapism.[78] At the level of the mass media, Hugh Hefner's *Playboy*, which first appeared in 1953, represented yet another variant of the beleaguered male's backlash. Previous men's magazines such as *Outdoor Life* and *True* had sought escape in the great outdoors. Hefner, exploiting the pin-up genre popularized during the war, offered his bachelor readership an escape at home or in the penthouse via a fantasy of sexual consumerism. With a peculiar American earnestness, he produced a 'philosophy' to dignify his undertaking. Critics regarded him as simply the producer of masturbatory pornography seeking, by a compulsive harping on the female form, to reassure his readership that though it had shed many of the accoutrements of old-fashioned forms of masculinity it was no less virile. Like so many other male 'rebels' of his generation, he was sensitive to the charge that any departure from traditional norms of manliness might be seen as a slide towards homosexuality.

Teenagers

Given such concerns, the tough lower-class male sex symbols of the 1950s, such as Marlon Brando in *The Wild Ones* or the singer Elvis Presley, were regarded by their male elders with some ambivalence. Lack of respect for father figures was lamented but reassuring heterosexual physicality was applauded. Much of this revolt against male sexual decorum was accompanied by a strong anti-homosexual bias. Rock and roll did bridge for some, however, class and race divides and permitted an outlet for young women's expression of sexual yearnings.[79] When the insolence of such idols was aped by the young, many parents, having suffered through the Depression, were angered and puzzled that their children, growing up in the affluent 1950s, were not more content. Those who bemoaned the 'decline of the family' forgot that children in previous centuries had been sent out early in life into domestic service or apprenticeships. In the post-war world they stayed in school and lived at home until their late teens and married in their early twenties. Fears of a 'generation gap' and 'juvenile delinquency' became staple topics for magazine writers, but a longer experience of dependency could only be expected to result in the emergence of new and occasionally disturbing forms of youth culture. Generations once succeeded each other; now they overlapped. For young people the reality was that the 1950s saw the end of patriarchalism. In England and Germany the courtship and marriage patterns of the working and middle classes were becoming similar. Age of puberty and menarche dropped four months per decade. Boys were now fully grown by seventeen, not twenty-three, as had been the case in 1900. Working-class youths, dating at thirteen or fourteen, had earlier sexual experiences than their social superiors.[80] Sexual high jinks was one way in which young people could achieve emotional independence from their parents. Increased premarital sexual activity, plotted by Kinsey and permitted in part by a rise in contraceptive use, usually led on to marriage. It could hardly be called an 'emancipation'.[81]

Young women's wayward behaviour was much more closely scrutinized than young men's since it was equated in the public mind with promiscuity. In Britain in 1938–9, 30 per cent of brides arrived at the altar pregnant and one-seventh of all children were born as a result of extra-marital intercourse.[82] The war was believed to have brought a further disruption and sexual licence; the number of illegitimate births jumped in the years immediately following the peace.[83] Kinsey's suggestion that those alarmed by the 130,000 out-of-wedlock births that took place each year in the United States should make

some effort to see that contraceptives were made more readily available was ignored.

In the 1950s the single, sexualized girl was regarded as posing the
greatest threat to gender norms and family stability.[84] Female sexuality was likened to a bomb that was about to go off; it was no accident
that the bikini bathing suit was named after the Pacific atoll where
atomic testing took place. Young women were racked by conflicting
sexual fears and desires. Despite sex education much remained mysterious. Liz Heron recalled that as a girl she demanded to know from
the boys what was meant by the word 'FUCK' which they had indus-
triously chalked on the school wall. Their puzzling explanation was
that it was 'how Teddy Boys say goodnight to their girlfriends'.[85]
American teenagers appeared more knowing. Their sexual norms were
increasingly established by magazines such as *Seventeen* (established
in 1944 to exploit the youth market), *True Romance* and *True Confessions* and the reports of mass polling agencies.[86] Girls puzzled over
the wisdom of kissing on a first date or when to accept petting. They
were caught in a double bind; they had to be both 'good' and sexy.
They learned to act sexually mature while insisting that they were not.

Girls found that they had to be instrumental to win popularity
because what was important was not what actually happened but
what people would say. The judgement of peers was crucial. 'Before
the war', argues Beth Bailey, 'American youth prized promiscuous
popularity, demonstrating competitive success through the number
and variety of dates they commanded. After the war, youth turned to
"going steady," saying that the system provided a measure of security
and escape from the pressures of the post-war world.'[87] English girls,
Sheila Rowbotham notes in contrast, did not experience the 'orderly
dating' depicted in American movies, yet in both nations adults still
placed the onus on the woman to control the sexual behaviour of the
male.[88] In the late 1950s a young woman who sported a tight skirt and
black stockings had reason to fear being labelled a 'slut'. Rape, she
was warned by psychoanalysts, was often due to the provocation,
albeit unconscious, of the woman.

In the sex education books, such as Evelyn Duvall's *Love for Teenagers* produced by the Association for Family Living, girls were told
that they were responsible for controlling petting.[89] The 'good' girl
was the one who most forcibly resisted sexual overtures. The difficulty of obtaining diamonds, one expert pertinently noted, was what
made them precious.[90] Abstention seemed to Kinsey a curious preparation for an active married sex life; his data revealed that women's
premarital sexual experiences increased the chances of their sexual
pleasures once married. Nevertheless, youth continued to be lectured

on the evils of masturbation and homosexuality, the unreliability of contraception, and the murderous effects of abortion. 'The truth was', stated one writer, recalling the sexual anxieties that educators had successfully drilled into many American teens, 'I feared sperm almost as much as I feared communists.'[91] Words that teenagers actually employed, like 'screw' and 'come', were carefully avoided by school counsellors. Kinsey's findings that 50 per cent of women had premarital sex was simply passed over in silence.

The confusion that many teens experienced was exacerbated by the conflicting messages they received. A society that purportedly respected the demure female was the same one in which the military had encouraged the use of female pin-ups during the war to boost morale.[92] Betty Grable's legs and Jane Russell's bust were two of the most familiar icons of the 1950s. The American media were unembarrassed by their fixation on the pneumatic attractions of perfect 36–24–36 beauty-contest winners. And in the same years that American psychiatrists were attempting to oppose the 'sexual freedom' of girls, big business was commercializing sex in films and advertising on an unprecedented scale. Teenagers were particularly targeted. The sex life of youth was made a public issue by corporate America's insistence on selling to young girls lipstick and high heels, girdles and training bras, Kotex and Tampax. Menstruation was even made the subject of a Walt Disney educational cartoon viewed by an estimated 93 million American women.[93] Hollywood made millions producing films all about 'sex' in which physical sex – thanks to the censoring of the Hays code – was never actually portrayed. Commercialized sexuality was exported round the world. Light sex comedies were welcomed even in Catholic Italy because the church and the Christian Democrats were far more frightened by the social criticism of Italian neo-realist films.[94]

In the United States necking and petting, dating and playing the field, going steady and being pinned finally won some legitimacy, but 'going all the way' remained taboo. Predictably sexuality became a site for resistance and contestation.[95] Indulging in sex was for some young women the most obvious form of rebellion; they sought sex not so much for pleasure as for knowledge and power.[96] 'When American schoolgirls blossom out, millions strong, in their brothers' shirts, over skin tight dungarees with a copper-riveted clitoris on the fly', noted one psychoanalytically oriented observer, 'it is not in response to any epidemic urge for comfort. It is because they want the status that goes with the pants.'[97] Their high expectations in turn often led to the disappointments chronicled in a rash of coming of age novels written a generation later. At the time, few disappointed by their first sexual encounter dared to ask: 'Is that all there is?' Popular Freudianism, such as that of Helene Deutsch, supported the notion that the normal woman would first discover herself incomplete (the castration complex), then shift her affections from her mother to father (the Oedipus complex) and finally move on to mature womanhood. Her failure to develop and ultimately enjoy vaginal orgasm would be taken as a symptom of either frigidity or latent lesbianism.

A middle-class parent's greatest fear was to discover that a daughter was pregnant. 'We will tell them all that Jane is dead' was the first thought of one white American father who intended to hide the family's shame from friends and family.[98] Teen pregnancies were nothing new; but it was not supposed to happen in suburbia. Race was particularly central to the discussion of illegitimacy in the United States. White legislators regarded the single motherhood of blacks – irresponsible and over-sexed – as 'normal'. It was assumed that they would make do. They were denied adoption services while young white women were pressured to give up their babies. The assumption was that the white woman's marriageability, if not her virginity, could be restored. Successful re-socialization would be signalled by her repentance and realistic acceptance of the passive female role.

As if a pubescent teenager was not enough of a problem, parents were warned by psychologists that even young children were exposed to new forms of sexual victimization. Frederic Wertham, a New York psychiatrist, won instant notoriety when in his *Seduction of the Innocent* (1953) he attacked comic books for being the root cause of juvenile delinquency.[99] Dime novels and 'penny dreadfuls' had been blamed by judges at the turn of the century for promoting crime. American comic books, which emerged with their super-heroes in the 1930s, were castigated for raising sexual appetites. Wertham claimed that comic books spread unhealthy and cruel notions. 'Sex maniacs' could be produced by a reading of illustrations that portrayed bare-chested men and women exposing their 'headlights' engaging in sado-masochistic play. He went so far as to claim that Superman was a fascist and Batman and Robin obviously a homosexual couple. The latter's life in the Bat cave was 'like a wish dream of two homosexuals living together'.[100] Wonder Woman he labelled a lesbian. 'For boys, Wonder Woman is a frightening image. For girls she is a morbid ideal.'[101] Wertham's claims that a reading of comics led to masturbation, psychological problems, delinquency and prostitution by both sexes was taken seriously by the Senate Judiciary Committee. A panicked industry immediately promised self-policing through the Comic Book Authority. The portrayal of sex, violence and even sweat was curbed, and the number of comic titles dropped from

650 in 1954 (when the Authority was established) to 250 by 1956.[102] The British, who as a result of war had witnessed an invasion of 'American-style' sex and violence comics, launched their own campaign in the late 1940s to protect 'innocents' which resulted in the Children and Young Persons (Harmful Publications) Act of 1955.[103] Though Tory MPs associated deviancy with communism, the British Communist Party was in fact actively opposed to horror comics because of their American content. On both sides of the Atlantic the comic book panic was a symptom of parents' feeling that they were losing control of their children to the media. It was comforting to believe that if it were not for the incitement of such literature children's sexual delinquency would end. Such media bashing was an episodic phenomenon. In the 1950s the print media was critiqued for being a contributing cause of divorce, delinquency and extra-marital affairs. Television would be the culprit in the 1980s.

Communists and Homosexuals

Fears of the 'seduction' of youth was not a new phenomenon but it was an especially charged notion in the climate of the Cold War. The Korean War of 1953–4, the Russian suppression of the Hungarian revolution in 1956, the launching of Sputnik in 1957, and the execution of the Rosenbergs in 1958 all helped to maintain the West's siege mentality. The flight of the British spies Guy Burgess and Donald Maclean to the Soviet Union and the defections of American soldiers in Korea were regarded as evidence of the communists' diabolical skills of brainwashing and seduction. It was in this context that Senator Joe McCarthy, recognizing the political dividends that could be accrued by exploiting a moral panic linking homosexuality and communism, launched in 1950 his witch hunt for 'security risks'.[104] As a response to the panic, Harry Hay and others organized in Los Angeles the Matachine Society, America's first openly gay organization.

The crackdown on homosexuality was all the more traumatic inasmuch as it followed the war years in which an American gay world – the term 'gay' was used in the 1940s for both men and women – had begun to coalesce as a result of the uprooting of civilian life. Conscription forced many to confront their own sexuality. Those 'marching to a different drummer' included actors Tyrone Power and Rock Hudson, essayist Gore Vidal, and novelist John Cheever. Curiously enough, life in the military, a macho culture in which 'cocksucker' was the ultimate insult, allowed some gays a way of declaring themselves.[105] Same-sex contacts and the establishment of friendships were facilitated by canteens, clubs and YMCA hotels. Gay bars emerged, not just in San Francisco and New York but in San José and Kansas City. In the barracks, homosexual buffoonery, dedication to one's buddy and even emotional entanglements could be explained away by officers as simply due to deprivation, or ignored by comrades according to the code of 'live and let live'. Drag routines, with the inevitable Carmen Miranda female impersonators whose sexual preferences were open to interpretation, were standard fare when entertaining the troops. Women in the WACs, though not allowed the same frivolity, were permitted more open displays of same-sex affection, and in motor pools located a supportive milieu in which working-class lesbian slang references to 'butch', 'dyke', 'lady' and 'girl' were popularized.[106] But tolerance could turn as quickly to harassment. Homosexuals always risked being discharged as undesirables. As the war progressed the military high command sought to tighten screening, employing psychiatrists and clergy to extort confessions from troublemakers.[107] The abnormal family – with dominant mother and absent father – was responsible, claimed the experts, for producing homosexuals.[108] Hundreds of men were confined to 'queer stockades'. Many more slipped through the net and returned home with a new sense of sexual self-consciousness.

Most of what the general public knew about homosexuality came from court reports. Over 4,000 homosexuals were discharged from the American military between 1947 and 1950. Senator McCarthy then turned on the civil service, leading the Republicans in accusing President Harry Truman of sheltering perverts. In 1950 the Senate authorized formal investigation of those whose 'degraded' and 'immoral' activities made them unreliable. The premise was that homosexuals were seductive and themselves in danger of being blackmailed. Under President Dwight D. Eisenhower more than sixty civil servants a month were fired. The military and civil service purge of 'security risks' was followed by police crackdowns in the major American cities. The problem of homosexuality was in the meantime 'rediscovered' by doctors. In 1952 the American Psychiatric Association developed the *Diagnostic and Statistical Manual of Mental Disorders* (DSM-1) that declared homosexuality a sociopathic personality disorder.[109] Fears of homosexuality also underlay the post-war panic over sexual psychopaths. This spectre of perverts was played up by J. Edgar Hoover, chief of the FBI, and between 1947 and 1955 twenty-one states passed laws targeting deviants, the supposed purpose being to better protect women and children. The preoccupation with 'sick' perverts deflected attention from the fact that assaults on women were usually carried out by male friends or family members.[110]

Persecution of homosexuals was not limited to the United States. In Canada the pulp novel *Women's Barracks* was prosecuted in 1952 as a lesbian obscenity.[111] The Royal Canadian Mounted police had by 1960 opened files on over 9,000 suspected gays and designed a 'fruit machine' to detect civil servants with homoerotic preferences.[112] In West Germany between 1953 and 1965, 38,000 men were found guilty of homosexual offences.[113] The law they had violated, article 175, had been employed by the Nazis, but in 1957 the Federal Constitutional Court, arguing that the statute ensured the stability of the family and hence that of the state, refused to overturn it. In Britain in the 1950s male homosexual offences rose five-fold, chiefly due to police zeal. Britain was less paranoid about the spectre of homosexuality than the United States and the surge in numbers arrested proved an embarrassment, especially when prominent individuals such as Lord Montagu of Beaulieu, the actor John Gielgud and *Daily Mail* writer Peter Wildeblood appeared in court. Reformers asked why the law sought to restrict the actions of consenting adults. Even those who felt homosexuals deserved 'treatment' pointed out that the existing legislation was cruel and unworkable.[114] Though the Conservative government did not wish to appear lax, it was obvious that existing policing arrangements were not working. The result was the establishment in 1957 of the Wolfenden Committee which had as its mandate the revision of the laws pertaining to homosexuality and prostitution. The 1950s ended with closeted homosexuals gaining in confidence yet more aware than ever before of the dangers of 'coming out'.

Conclusion

The election in 1960 of the inveterate womanizer John F. Kennedy as President of the United States has often been taken as symbolizing the end of a sexually oppressive decade. But just as some have argued that the '1960s' did not begin until about 1965, so too it could be claimed that the most important critique of the sexual morality of the 1950s was Kinsey's study of male sexuality which appeared before the decade did – in 1948. Moreover, at an individual level throughout the 1950s youths, women and homosexuals resisted as best they could the dictates of the defenders of the sexual status quo. They were not fighting some monolith. The elites were themselves divided on how best to respond to the increasing evidence that massive shifts in sexual behaviour were occurring. The beginning of the relaxing of restraints that are usually associated with the 'swinging sixties' can be traced back to the business and political establishments' search in the

1950s for more pragmatic and efficient means by which to manage sexual problems. Though the reform of the law on homosexuality in England was not to occur until 1967, the very fact that the Wolfenden Committee had been established in 1957 revealed that many in positions of authority recognized that existing methods of repression were counter-productive.[115] Criminalizing forms of consenting adult sexual behaviour kept up the pretence of moral protection but incurred heavy costs, including police corruption and blackmail.[116] The same argument was made to support the reform of the law on prostitution, though the result of the United Kingdom's 1959 Street Offences Act was to drive women off the streets and into the hands of pimps.[117]

Contraception was for pragmatic reasons at last openly welcomed by Western governments in the mid-1950s. Though they lauded the domestic 'baby boom', they regarded the rapid population growth of the Third World as a threat to the global social order. The Rockefellers, financial supporters of the Population Council, were only the best-known corporate leaders concerned that Asia, Africa and South America, impoverished through over-population, would fall to the communists. Eugenic preoccupations also re-emerged in the 1950s in studies warning that the white nations could be submerged by the yellow and the black.[118] Once fertility was seen as posing 'real' dangers, doctors and bureaucrats could finally rationalize turning their full energies to tackling the problem.[119] Women's use of contraceptives was increasingly hailed not as selfishness, but as a sign of responsible parenting.

Yet another force leading to a bending of the sexual codes was the pressure exerted by advertisers and movie-makers in pursuit of the huge profits that they realized could be made by exploiting young peoples' interest in the erotic. Restless youths, including now those millions drawn from the working-class, represented an increasingly large part of the consumer market. The success of *Playboy* magazine dramatically demonstrated to corporate America that producing pornography was not a subversive undertaking, but a sound business venture. In a free market it became increasingly difficult to justify even the suppression of novels once labelled as obscene because of their explicit sexual passages, such as D. H. Lawrence's *Lady Chatterley's Lover* or William Burroughs's *The Naked Lunch*.[120]

The exact impact that Kinsey's work had in this process is difficult to pin down. He was credited with demystifying sexuality. One historian has observed of Kinsey and his followers that 'the matter of factness and neutrality of scientific discourse – its apparent lack of a moral agenda – contributed to its triumph and endurance'.[121] Yet his message was not as radical as some imagined. He said, in effect, that 'what is, is right'. Humans were driven by certain animal appetites that would inevitably express themselves. He advanced a liberal maxim, which could be traced back to John Stuart Mill, that whatever did not impact negatively on others should be allowed. Kinsey's findings were in many ways obviously subversive but he made it clear that his intent was to maintain existing social and sexual hierarchies. Men, he believed, had more active and therefore better sex lives than women. Single males had four times as much sex as single females. Married women did not find intercourse as pleasurable as married men. After having reviewed the physiological, psychological and hormonal causes of such disparities, Kinsey concluded that they were more due to women's early socialization than to either men's animality or incompetence. Women accordingly had to learn to be more like men.[122]

Similarly, working-class men had to be taught to be more like middle-class men. The latter, Kinsey argued, having a sophistication and understanding which the lower classes lacked, enjoyed the healthiest sex lives. His stress on 'social level' suggested a remnant of eugenic thinking. Kinsey would be most remembered, however, for having revealed the high level of American men's homosexual experiences. He finessed such findings by providing the reassuring argument that the fact that a man had had such an experience did not mean he was a homosexual. The primacy of male heterosexuality emerged from Kinsey's report largely unscathed. Indeed, Kinsey pushed an assimilationist model, suggesting that in the more liberal environment he envisaged even the small percentage of 'exclusive homosexuals' might be reduced. Whether or not he actually believed this is a moot point. The importance of the assimilationist story which Kinsey told was that it was both progressive for its time and yet reassuring. Knowing that feminists and homosexuals drew strength from many of his findings, Kinsey, who died in 1956, would no doubt have been surprised to know that only a few decades later many of the opponents of the sexual status quo would reject his notion of assimilation and move on to embrace 'identity politics'.[123]

9

'Sexual Revolution?': the Pill, Permissiveness and Politics

In the course of his closely observed if fictional depiction of one man's adulterous entanglements in a small New England town, John Updike provided in *Couples* (1968) a passage that would be forever associated with the moral climate of the 1960s. 'They deftly undressed, she him, he her. When he worried about contraception, she laughed. Didn't Angela [his wife] use Enovid yet? *Welcome*, she said, *to the post-pill paradise.*'[1]

Perhaps the most popular cultural myth of the latter half of the twentieth century is that the 1960s witnessed a 'sexual revolution'. The baby boomers – so their children assume – were able to give free vent to their appetites for sex, drugs and rock and roll. Especially sex. The advent of the contraceptive pill at long last promised to make penetrative sex worry free. Middle-class male youths could finally give up heavy petting as their source of orgasmic pleasure. Young women no longer had a reason for saying 'no'. But in the same decades that saw the appearance of the permissive Cosmo girl and the popularization of the pill sex experts downgraded coitus and highlighted the importance of clitoral stimulation. Intercourse was likened by Germaine Greer, with her inimitable gift for the *bon mot*, to a man masturbating in a woman's vagina. And Greer was pro-sex! Some of her more radical sisters in the 'second wave' of feminism that burst on the scene in the late 1960s declared that heterosexual intercourse – now categorized as a means employed by men to oppress women – had to be avoided altogether. The heady stories told by sexual liberationists were increasingly countered by more sober accounts of feminists' consciousness raising and homosexuals' tales of 'coming out'. The gay and lesbian liberation movements, in critiquing the male, heterosexist assumptions of those lauding the 'joy of sex', thus began to shift the focus of the sexual debates. If the 1960s and 1970s are still to be labelled years of 'sexual revolution' it is in the sense that the period witnessed, not one simple liberation, but the emergence and clash of a variety of new sexual scripts.

The Pill

The sexual revolution of the 1960s was popularly perceived as a generational conflict. Youth was, as ever, eager to distance itself from its elders but they were initially inspired by women and men such as Alfred Kinsey, Alex Comfort, Herbert Marcuse and Simone de Beauvoir who had already been actively involved in the sex debate for decades. Perhaps the century's most important sexual innovation – the invention of the contraceptive pill – was due to the birth controller Margaret Sanger who had been born in 1879. Although she had largely abandoned the public spotlight in the late 1930s, Sanger continued to pursue the search for a foolproof contraceptive that like vaccination would pre-emptively protect a patient's health. Her desire was to make life simpler for women, to distance the sex act as much as possible from the process of contraception, and to lower efficiently the fertility of the unfit. She had faith in medical science ultimately providing such a breakthrough. Early hormonal research, carried out in Austria by Dr Haberlandt thanks to Rockefeller money, proved that ovulation in animals could be prevented by injections of oestrogen.[2] Experimental work on steroid interference was also pursued by Dr B. P. Wiesner at Edinburgh in the 1920s, similarly supported by American funds.[3] In the United States itself Gregory Pincus began work in the late 1930s on synthetic hormones at the Worcester Foundation for Experimental Biology. He discovered that, since the hypothalamus and the hypophysis controlled ovulation, the process could be blocked if these organs' activities were simulated by a drug. The original intent of such investigations was not to produce a better contraceptive, but Sanger, to whom Pincus was introduced in 1950, recognized the practical possibilities of his work. She in turn recruited Katherine McCormick, a wealthy, active feminist and long-time birth control supporter, as financial angel of his studies. By 1951 Pincus proved that progesterone inhibited ovulation and began a search for a synthetic hormone. John Rock was asked to test the new drug on women in Boston; extensive clinical trials were undertaken in Puerto Rico in 1956. Rock, a devout Catholic and Harvard gynaecologist who had earlier opposed contraception but was now alarmed by the threat of over-population, declared that the pill was a 'natural' contraceptive that Catholics could in good conscience employ. In 1960 the Food and Drug Administration allowed the sale of a Searle synthetic anovulent as an oral contraceptive pill; other American drug companies soon produced similar products. In 1961 the pill began to be sold in Britain.

Neither Rock nor Sanger intended to launch a sexual revolution. They were preoccupied by the need to preserve stable family values and world order. They believed that the oral contraceptive could help ensure such stability. The appearance of the contraceptive pill – not a conversion to feminist, neo-Malthusian or eugenic arguments – brought the medical profession onside in favour of birth control. Biochemical and hormonal contraception appealed to doctors' idea of 'real' medical science and complemented their view of the necessity of scientific experts managing births. Their desire to sanitize reproduction was made clear in embryology texts; the metaphors employed to describe conception and development had once been drawn from common, earthy domestic activities (sowing, baking and fermenting), but now doctors spurned such lowly associations and drew their metaphors from the science of engineering. They appeared to be more comfortable – given their references to 'pelvic floors', 'follicle walls', 'cervical canals', 'storage and transport of ovum' – when regarding the uterus as a construction site rather than a human organ. Similarly, doctors who were still embarrassed to fiddle with messy cream or floppy rubber contraptions were happy to distribute a pill, a product of scientific research, a 'preventive medicine' that was simply prescribed.[4]

Sanger was convinced that her tactic of building coalitions – in particular by turning to doctors for support – though regarded by some as a sell-out of the birth control movement's radical and feminist past, had proved successful. Only in this way could the men who controlled the powerful foundations that funded scientific research be interested in questions that initially lacked glamour. Politicians and social scientists were more motivated by threats of 'population explosions' than by women's demands for reproductive autonomy.[5] The provision by the state or philanthropic organizations of contraceptives represented not so much sexual liberation as a more finely tuned form of social control. Sexuality was 'bureaucratized' by birth control clinics in which counsellors found themselves frequently torn between the competing ideologies of feminism and family planning.[6]

Proponents of birth control in France, where it was still illegal, advanced the argument that doctors should be 'freed' from a restrictive law, that contraception promised a way of ending the blight of botched abortions, and that married couples who, thanks to reliable contraceptives, were not continuously preoccupied by fears of unwanted pregnancies, would have a better sex life and accordingly more stable relationships.[7] These were certainly not the arguments of sex radicals. In *La Contraception au service de l'amour*, for example, Dr Weille-Hallé simply provided basic instructions on a range of contraceptives such as diaphragms, stressing that conscientious contraceptive use was like 'brushing teeth' in that it was a habit that aided romance.[8]

In 1961 the first *Centre de Planning Familial* in France was established in Grenoble by Doctor Henri Fabre; the second was shortly afterwards set up in Paris. As a way of getting round the law against contraceptive 'propaganda', in order to obtain information one had to become a member of the organization. Although having a relatively small clientele, the establishment of these clinics made possible the collection of reliable data on French sexual and contraceptive practices. Pierre Simon, preoccupied by family planning concerns and the belief that if ignorance were conquered sexuality could be a force for social cohesion, exploited such findings to provide the first scientific reports on a range of French sexual practices.[9]

A clear sign of the growing public tolerance of birth control was given when in the 1965 presidential election François Mitterrand, the cautious socialist candidate, came out in favour of relaxing the law on contraceptives; he was opposed by Gaullist nationalists like Michel Debré. General de Gaulle himself had spoken grandly of France one day having a hundred million citizens. But even the pronatalist nationalist right was divided on the wisdom of opposing the distribution of contraceptive information which was so clearly desired by the majority of the population. The argument that the availability of contraceptives would bring down the worrying abortion rate clearly impressed the undecided. De Gaulle himself dropped his opposition and contraception was finally decriminalized in December 1967 under a bill sponsored by the Gaullist deputy Lucien Neuwirth.[10]

In the more relaxed moral climate of the 1960s the Catholic church found it increasingly difficult to reconcile its proclaimed sensitivity to the needs of its youthful adherents while maintaining its traditional avowals of hostility to contraception.[11] The church made it known that it tolerated the rhythm method and took it as a given that a family would want only a 'reasonable' number of children. The arrival of the birth control pill in the 1960s offered yet another way out; some Catholics claimed that its chief function was to regularize the ovulation cycle and that it only indirectly prevented births. Pope Paul VI attempted to end the church's ambiguous position by his 1968 encyclical, *Humanae Vitae*, which vigorously condemned all 'artificial' forms of contraception, but many priests simply chose to ignore the teachings of the Vatican. Similarly, American Catholics, reassured by John Rock and accustomed to almost a decade's use of the pill, were largely indifferent to the pope's views.[12] It should be recalled, however, that through the 1960s the pill was employed by only a minority of women in North America. In Europe withdrawal would long remain an important form of contraception; in France in the 1970s, for example, 18 per cent of French couples still relied on coitus interruptus.[13] In 1970 only 6 per cent of French women were on the pill; 1974 reforms allowed it to be distributed to minors and by 1975 the number of French women employing it had jumped to 25 per cent.

Many asserted that with the advent of the pill women finally controlled their fertility and no longer had to rely on the man being 'careful'. The appearance of *Prudence and the Pill*, a British film starring David Niven that exploited the comic possibilities of a husband replacing his wife's birth control pills with aspirins, showed how acceptable the discussion of contraception had become by 1968. Although women employing the pill experienced a variety of disturbing side-effects, most welcomed a contraceptive that was apparently completely effective and free of what were now regarded as the depressingly unromantic preparations of earlier methods of contraception. Men were naturally delighted to be relieved once and for all of any responsibility for birth control. Both doctors and patients embraced the idea of the pill as a panacea. In point of fact, it was not all that superior to barrier methods of protection that were methodically employed. Like any other contraceptive, the pill could be forgotten or misused. 'Effectiveness' still depended on conscientious employment.

Family Change

Although the mass distribution of the pill and the IUD and the liberalization of abortion did not take place until the late 1960s, journalists and scholars chose to hold the new technologies responsible for the beginning of another rapid drop in fertility that began in the mid-1960s. By 1975 the English birth rate was down to 12.2 per 1,000, below the lowest point previously reached in 1933.[14] The media bewailed the increased numbers of 'childless women', ignoring the fact that although family size had declined the percentage of women bearing children had actually increased. In America, 20 per cent of women born in the 1901–10 cohort were childless, as opposed to only 7.3 per cent of the 1931–5 cohort. In Britain in 1921, 83 per cent of women married by the age of forty-five; in the 1960s, 96 per cent.[15] Basic family norms were maintained though their meanings shifted.[16] The twentieth century witnessed a transition from a world in which it was common for some people to have large families, while others never married or reproduced, to a world in which almost everyone married and had a small family. Indeed, the continual barrage of propaganda launched by sexologists, doctors and educators in favour of efficient sexuality, motherhood and child-rearing, begun in the early 1900s and still showing no signs of letting up, had successfully implanted the notion that a woman who did not reproduce was somehow incomplete. Sanger and Stopes would have been pleased to see that a highly effective means of birth control, in place of undermining the ideology of motherhood, had become its essential prop.

Births were clustered together so that by her late twenties the average woman was free of childbearing. With longer life expectancy, it meant that she would live for another fifty or so years after her last delivery whereas her nineteenth-century counterpart spent most of her life bearing or rearing offspring. Most women after the Second World War accordingly expected both to marry and to have a career. From the 1960s onwards the mass production of cheap clothing and foodstuffs undermined the rationale of full-time housework. Women worked outside the home because they wanted to. Their demands for control of their reproduction assured the provision of the oral contraceptive and the eventual liberalization of the abortion law. These in turn provided women with a greater freedom to pursue career and educational opportunities. In Britain only 10 per cent of mothers were employed in 1900 as opposed to 50 per cent in 1976. The fact that a woman worked was no longer a badge of the family's working-class status. British social scientists in the 1970s hailed the rise of the 'symmetrical family' as the last remnants of working-class traditions of separate male and female sexual cultures appeared to have been eradicated.[17] Class and ethnic demographic differentials did not disappear, but a general pattern of small family size became true of all groups. The old joke that the family was reduced in size to fit Ford's four-seater car seemed not that far off the mark. Perhaps the most dramatic symbol of this 'homogenization of experience' was the control of menstruation that resulted from the taking of oral contraceptives. Every user now had a strict twenty-eight-day cycle.

From the 1960s onwards both marriage and divorce rates rose. Princess Margaret's 1978 divorce was only the first of many that would indicate that the British royals were no more immune than any other family to dysfunctional relationships. In the 1950s Kinsey had determined that a quarter of women would have a least one extra-marital affair; a 1973 survey put the figure at 40 per cent. Polls revealed that the public was increasingly tolerant of such adventures. The media played up reports of 'open marriages', 'swinging couples' and 'group sex' as incriminating evidence of women's moral decline but such experimentation could also be interpreted as extreme attempts to sustain monotonous marital bonds.[18] With longer life expectancy, marriages that once lasted less than thirty years now could reach at least forty-five years. Only in the 1970s in a country such as Britain did divorce 'compensate' for the decline in spousal deaths as a cause of family break up.[19] In the nineteenth century, the single-parent family was due to widowhood; in the twentieth it was due to divorce. Though the number of English divorces doubled between 1969 and 1973 (climbing from 51,000 to 118,000) the rate was far lower than that in the United States. About 40 per cent of those divorced had married before the age of twenty. In France a new divorce law was put in place in 1975. Even Italy introduced legislation which proponents claimed would end spousal murder or 'divorce Italian style'. Spain's 1981 divorce law was hailed by some as the most important manifestation of its newly democratized regime. The point repeatedly reiterated by divorce reformers, like Leo Abse in Britain, was that the availability of a liberal form of divorce would not lead to promiscuity; rather it would end disastrous marriages and allow the establishment of healthy ones.

In the 1960s the maintenance of antiquated laws reflecting the preoccupations of the prudish became the butt of the 'sick' sexual humour of American comics like Mort Sahl and Lenny Bruce. 'In New York', Bruce pointed out, 'it's illegal – "seemingly sexual intercourse with a chicken." That's the literal. Now, could you even fantasize that? Doing it to a chicken? They're too short.'[20] Using the more serious argument of the right of free expression, liberals pressed for the revamping of censorship and obscenity laws. The United States Court of Appeal in 1960 pronounced D. H. Lawrence's *Lady Chatterley's Lover* not obscene. William Burroughs's *The Naked Lunch*, Henry Miller's *Sexus* and Vladimir Nabokov's *Lolita* were soon allowed to be sold. In 1973 the Supreme Court ruled that 'community standards' would henceforth determine what was pornographic, not the old standard of redeeming social value. Female nudity began to appear in serious films such as Ingmar Bergman's *Silence* (1963). *I am Curious Yellow* (1967) crystallized Sweden's reputation for sexual liberalism and a segment of the country's film industry ultimately moved on into hard core pornography.[21] In the United States Larry Flynt's *Hustler* magazine, begun in 1974, published photographs of female genitalia which even *Playboy* and *Penthouse* found offensive. Flynt to his surprise would eventually find some defenders who argued that in taking to its logical extremes the violation of sexual taboos he was actually subverting heterosexual desire.[22] Such publications faced legal prosecution but in the mid-1960s conservative campaigners such as Mary Whitehouse who attacked the 'filth' allowed on British television seemed distinctly old-fashioned. It was predictable that a woman should lead such a movement. The attack on censorship, though defended on libertarian grounds, was made by men and primarily addressed male sexual needs.

Youth Culture

We now know that few public figures were more driven by their sexual needs than John Fitzgerald Kennedy. In 1960, however, the election of Kennedy – at forty-three years of age the youngest president in American history – was taken to symbolize the emergence of a new generation of liberal politicians who had set as their governments' goals modernization and efficiency. Lyndon Johnson in the United States and Harold Wilson in Britain followed this script, presenting themselves as champions of individual freedoms and pragmatic realism. They defended progressive legal and legislative reforms on the premise that antiquated law codes had to be revamped to keep pace with changing social realities. As regards the laws pertaining to sexuality, this meant in essence separating morality and criminality. In the memorable words of Pierre Trudeau, the prime minister of Canada who introduced legislation in 1969 that reformed the laws dealing with homosexuality, abortion, divorce and birth control, 'the state has no place in the bedrooms of the nation.'[23] For a time many believed that state surveillance of sexual practices had indeed been brought to an end. Another important but unstated purpose of such reforms was to respond to the public's suspicion that the elites hypocritically violated the very sexual codes which they sought to impose on the working class and the young. To the delight of many in June 1963, John Profumo, the British Minister of War – or, as Peter Sellers joked, the 'Minister of Whore' – was revealed by the press to have been sharing the favours of Christine Keeler, a purported 'call-girl', with a Soviet agent. The public clearly enjoyed seeing someone hoist with his own petard. No one mentioned that, despite the media's constantly playing up the threat of traitorous homosexual spies, the greatest post-war sex and security scandal was a result of excessive heterosexual desires.

The press normally took little interest in the sex lives of the middle-aged. Social observers were far more preoccupied by the rise in the number of young people having sex before marriage. In the United Kingdom in 1974 by the age of eighteen 65 per cent of boys and

47 per cent of girls had had sex. The gap between the sexes was closing.[24] Although the sale of the birth control pill was initially restricted to the married, many commentators began to talk of the chemical contraceptives being responsible for this new 'sexual revolution'.[25] If 'sexual freedom' was a consequence of the pill, it certainly was not the intention of its creators. Only a tiny percentage of the American population was willing to assert in the early 1960s that premarital sex was 'right'. Once the pill was available, however, youths took advantage of the liberty it purportedly provided.[26] In the public mind the pill was probably more important for the 'freedom' it represented than for what it actually accomplished. Most premarital sex still led on to marriage which is why progressives, such as Eustace Chesser in *Unmarried Love* (1965), began to give the issue a fair hearing.[27] Nevertheless sex, once only legitimated as a romantic rite if it led to coupling, was increasingly accepted as a pleasure in itself. Accordingly, when the age of marriage, having dropped to an all-time low in the 1960s, began to rise again in the 1970s, sex was not postponed. 'Shacking up', once associated with the lower classes, now became a tactic of college students. Cohabitation in the early 1970s in a sense simply replaced the earlier marriages of the 1950s. In France in 1968–9, 17 per cent of those who married had lived together; by 1977, 44 per cent.[28] Those who defended the new morality, which blurred the line between marriage and non-marriage, were echoing in an unconscious fashion the argument made in the 1920s by progressives such as Bertrand Russell and Ben Lindsey that marriage was only necessary once children arrived on the scene.

If the 1960s witnessed a widening of the generation gap it was partly fuelled by the sheer increase in the number of young people coming of age – the 'baby boomers'. Between 1960 and 1970 those in the eighteen to twenty-four year age cohort in the United States increased by 53 per cent.[29] A sense of the apparent inability of the generations to communicate was captured in Mike Nichols's 1967 smash hit *The Graduate*, a rare American portrayal of the seduction of a young man by an older woman. This film, hailed by many as the quintessential 1960s' movie, is particularly interesting inasmuch as it focused solely on the hero's sexual self-absorption. Viewing it today provides no sense that the civil rights, anti-Vietnam and feminist movements were about to peak. The film thus serves as a helpful reminder that many male youths in the 1960s were simply egged on to become more hedonistic and narcissistic, but not to question political or gender norms. Male ideals changed very little in a purported age of sexual revolution. Hollywood in the 1960s was still producing John Wayne epics, whereas European directors such as François Truffaut and

Federico Fellini were providing more nuanced portrayals of masculinity. In the 1950s rock-and-roll world, the male rebel adopted the pose of the 'greaser'; in the 1960s the androgynous, long-haired look, which appeared effeminate to an older generation, was exploited by musicians such as Roger Daltry and Jim Morrison. The musical *Hair* both spoofed and captured the importance that such stylistic signalling held for the young. Some artists such as Andy Warhol sought to blur gender lines in film; the English painter David Hockney did not hide his homosexuality. Nevertheless, a strong anti-homosexual bias was obvious in much of the male push for sexual liberation. If The Rolling Stones appeared in drag it was a sign of their confidence in their heterosexuality. They would be best known for misogynistic songs crafted to support their bad boy persona such as 'Under my Thumb' and 'Brown Sugar'. Despite appearances, the playboy spy hero of the James Bond films, with his compliant female companions like 'Pussy Galore', differed little from the rock star and his groupies. To judge by the injunctions of the commercial media the young man's greatest ambition – whatever his hair length – was to be a successful philanderer. Marriage or 'settling down' was therefore represented as forced domestication which women and respectable society sought to impose on men. In countless films, such as Karel Reisz's *Saturday Night and Sunday Morning* (1960), the comforting notion was propagated that women were ultimately responsible for hindering the rebelliousness of males.

All the evidence suggests that in fact young women were changing their sexual behaviour far more dramatically than young men. Between 1965 and 1975 young women found themselves catapulted from a world in which flat-chested teenagers were expected to wear girdles and training bras to one in which the bra-less look was *de rigueur*. While the young men of the 1960s sported long hair, the young women bared their thighs in mini skirts. The big-busted female icons of the 1950s, such as Monroe and Russell, were displaced by the skinny, little-girl look of Twiggy. The British pop culture world of Carnaby Street and Mary Quant produced skimpy clothes for 'chicks' and 'dolly birds' which, while claiming to 'free' them, accentuated their vulnerability. The female body was made even more accessible in 1970–1 when the topless fad began at St-Tropez, France.[30]

A popular explanation for the sexualization of American girls is that The Beatles, who toured the United States for the first time in 1964, made sex look unthreatening and fun. The pill made it possible. It was not quite that simple. The fact that a book like *Ann Landers Talks to Teenagers about Sex* (1963) sold so well indicates that the public recognized that youthful female sexual behaviour had already begun to shift. More American women were in college – by the late 1970s there were almost as many female as male students – and under increased pressure to 'lose' their virginity.[31] The daughters of 1950s' mothers – those who came of age in the 1960s and 1970s – were planning on marriage but not intent on becoming full-time, stay-at-home child-minders. The freedom which school and employment offered them in an affluent decade allowed time for experimentation before marriage. Such female curiosity was imaginable because the 1950s whore/virgin dichotomy was under attack. Permissiveness, a host of commentators argued, actually allowed more equitable relationships. Helen Gurley Brown, in *Sex and the Single Girl* (1962), asserted that as the young woman was expected for some time to be financially independent it followed that she should be sexually independent. As editor after 1964 of *Cosmopolitan* she spread the word, once unthinkable in a woman's magazine, that 'nice girls' did it. Even in films the adventuresome woman no longer had to meet a tragic end. Actresses Julie Christie in *Billy Liar* (1965) and Jeanne Moreau in *Jules et Jim* (1961) personified attractive, sexually liberated females lumbered with ineffectual men.

In the new 'singles culture' popularized by magazines such as *Cosmopolitan* freedom was equated with sexual pleasure; now the young woman who did not like sex was increasingly regarded as deviant. The pill, she was told, meant that contraception was no longer related to the sex act; penicillin had ended fears of venereal disease. Statistics revealed that the rate of premarital intercourse, which had risen in the 1920s and then plateaued, rose again in the 1960s. Women's behaviour changed more than men's: between the 1950s and the 1980s, female rates of pre- and extra-marital sex went up, while male rates shifted only slightly. By 1975 *Redbook*'s survey asserted that 90 per cent of women engaged in premarital sex.[32] Erica Jong's *Fear of Flying* (1973) used the form of the picaresque novel to immortalize the liberated woman's desire for a 'zipless fuck'. The book was regarded at the time as a celebratory depiction of sex free of all ulterior motives or power games.[33] The media dubbed this closing of the gender gap in sexual relations a 'revolution'.

The Joys of Sex?

Women were having more sex, but was it the sort of sex that they wanted? A generation of experts thought not. Kinsey had noted that up to 50 per cent of women did not find sex pleasurable. He had also rediscovered the clitoral orgasm which had been 'lost' or denied by

the psychoanalysts. In his words, the vagina was 'of minimum importance in contributing to the erotic responses of the female'.[34] Indeed,
he was of the opinion that the vagina, like the breasts, did more to
arouse the male than the female. At the same time, he insisted that if
women received the right sort of tactile stimulation they would be
just as orgasmic as men. He suggested that couples work out their
'sexual adjustments in marriage' and he included chapters dealing
with the physiological, psychological and hormonal factors in sexual
response and orgasm. Robert Latou Dickinson, another American researcher, to understand what occurred during orgasm, employed an
electrical vibrator and a penis-shaped glass tube to view the changes
taking place in a masturbating woman.[35] The 'heirs' of Kinsey and
Dickinson were Masters and Johnson.

William H. Masters and Virginia E. Johnson in *Human Sexual Response* (1966) provided a scientific justification for the demand for
sexual pleasure that women were already voicing.[36] Masters, who
began his observation of orgasms in 1954 at George Washington
University in St Louis, created the new field of sex therapy. In the late
1950s he married Virginia Johnson and they became a husband and
wife team. At first they mainly saw men worried by impotence or
premature ejaculation; but in the 1960s their patients were women
seeking orgasm. When their research work was initially reported, the
public felt an unease upon hearing that sex was being subjected
to laboratory experimentation and – with miniature cameras inside
plastic penises – observation. But Masters and Johnson were extremely
shrewd in reporting their work to the media in a palatable fashion.
They always appeared in white lab coats to exploit the medical mystique and distance themselves from sex radicals. Most importantly,
they presented themselves as a therapy team dealing with the 'marriage problems' of both husband and wife. Men were reassured that
penis size was not important. Women were told that prescriptions
that worked for their spouses did not necessarily work for them. The
therapists declared their commitment to proving that women could
experience the same pleasure as men. Indeed, they demonstrated that
women could have multiple orgasms. And they shifted the focus from
Kinsey's concern for the quantity of sex to the quality of the orgasm.
They did not, like Kinsey, focus attention simply on the clitoris but
noted the importance of stimulating the entire mons area. By teaching
techniques of orgasmotherapy, starting with an education in masturbation, they claimed it was possible to ignore cultural conditioning and
to circumvent the psychoanalytic preoccupation with the psyche that
might demand years of treatment. In reporting remarkably high success
rates, they laid the basis for a whole new profession of caregivers.[37]

Masters and Johnson's emphasis on the purely physical aspects of sex – all a woman had to do was to learn the 'squeeze technique' – appears stultifying in hindsight, but in the late 1960s was considered by many to be a major advance.[38]

The new orthodoxy that simple penetration no longer promised female satisfaction led to an explosion of self-help sex books from David Reuben's *Everything You Wanted to Know about Sex but Were Afraid to Ask* to *The Sensuous Woman* by 'J', which sold nine million copies. Perhaps the best known, Alex Comfort's *The Joy of Sex,* appeared in 1972, a cookbook-style of sex manual that lauded every form of sexual pleasure while critiquing the anxiety-makers. As a man who had begun his career as a philosophical anarchist, Comfort held that non-repressive sexuality was a correlate of social justice; that is, both personal and political liberation were linked.[39] Yet a fairly traditional agenda could be detected in a book that placed the 'missionary position' under 'main course' and 'bisexuality' and 'transvestism' under 'problems'. Comfort did prove his radical credentials, however, by also treating 'doctors' in the 'problems' section.

The most important non-medical sex researcher was Shere Hite whose first book, *The Hite Report on Female Sexuality* (1976), dwelt on women's unhappiness with males' failure to respond or reciprocate. Her confidantes reported that masturbation or clitoral stimulation was essential and most women did not achieve orgasm by vaginal penetration.[40] Nevertheless, they felt guilty for not performing adequately. Men had had their sexual revolution, Hite concluded, but women were only beginning theirs. She particularly stressed the importance of tenderness and emotion that was lost in the sex therapists' approach. Women had to help each other. In such manuals as *Our Bodies Ourselves* women were instructed to rediscover their own bodies. In the United States some self-help groups provided speculums so women could view their cervixes. Quoting one author who reported that '"there are several groups of women who get together in New York City and on their dining room tables or couches look at changes in the cervix"', Nora Ephron wryly noted, 'it is hard not to long for the days when an evening with the girls meant bridge.'[41] Nevertheless, Ephron went on to acknowledge that such acts were a healthy manifestation of women's dissatisfaction with most doctors' lack of interest in female sexual unhappiness.

The result of this spate of writings, reports and surveys was that varieties of 'deviant' sexual pleasure were increasingly mainstreamed. In America, by 1975, 85–90 per cent of women had tried fellatio. Men were more reluctant to reciprocate. The point was that both sexes wanted oral gratification and the realization began to dawn that this meant that the long-sought-for simultaneous orgasm might not be possible. Separate but equal sexual worlds would be the best one could hope for. The popularity of oral sex also led to a blurring of the line separating heterosexual and homosexual pleasure. The increased attention which sex manuals such as Comfort's gave to anal sex and sado-masochism as legitimate forms of pleasure provided another link to the world of homosexuality. It should have come as no surprise when Nancy Friday revealed that many heterosexuals reported having had homosexual fantasies.[42] Liberated heterosexual sex, with the decline of genital sexuality and rise of extended foreplay, was beginning to appear no less 'perverse' than queer sex.[43]

Make Love, Not War

This upturn in sexual experimentation is only fully understandable if placed in its political context. The producers of films and magazines found it profitable to portray sex as a form of youth rebellion. A variety of radical political movements, though hostile to capitalism, also embraced the notion that sexual and political liberation were intertwined. The first thought of more than one college student who lived through the Cuban missile crisis of October 1962 was to wonder how a nuclear holocaust would affect his or her sex life. The notion that 'the personal is the political' was voiced on campuses everywhere. Young people were more cosmopolitan. For North Americans, England was both the sexually permissive 'swinging London' captured in Michelangelo Antonioni's film *Blow-up* (1968) and the annual Campaign for Nuclear Disarmament marches to Aldermaston that began in 1960. For Europeans, the United States was music, flower power and drugs in San Francisco or Woodstock and political protests. The civil rights sit-ins and 'freedom rides' which inspired a generation in the early 1960s led on to the anti-Vietnam War demonstrations after 1964. In France students had been earlier involved from 1958 to 1962 in the campaign for the freeing of Algeria. European universities had made even fewer concessions than their American counterparts to changing social mores and accordingly disruptions in France began in 1966 at Nanterre over the prohibition of male and female students being in each other's rooms. This proved to be a run-up to the May 1968 'events' in which Paris was paralysed by students protesting at first the government's authoritarian educational policies and ultimately the very nature of the bourgeois state.

Brandishing such slogans as 'make love, not war' student protesters critiqued bourgeois morality. Underground newspapers such as *It* and

Oz in London and the *Berkeley Barb* in California printed outrageous sexual manifestos. The 'old left' had resolutely avoided sex issues; the 'new left' of the 1960s embraced them. Leftist students, enthused by the notion that authentic selfhood was found in free sexuality, sought to combine Marx and Freud.[44] They found that decades earlier Wilhelm Reich and Herbert Marcuse had done just that in critiquing the totalitarian nature of Western sexual morality. Marcuse in *Eros and Civilization* (1955) had argued that capitalism was motivated by the 'performance principle'. Only by employing surplus repression which in effect desexualized the body could capitalism make the body available for productive labour. In *One Dimensional Man* (1964) Marcuse seemed to suggest that the 'pervert' who fought against the resulting 'genital tyranny' was therefore some sort of political rebel.[45] Marcuse was not simply a sexual libertarian. He was concerned that if the radical restructuring of society did not take place sex could be turned to purposes of repressive tolerance. Many of his young readers who pondered the dialectics of liberation probably missed the nuance. 'There was a lot of this belief', recalled one participant, 'that if you took off your knickers you'd smash the state.'[46]

Given their belief that capitalism was the cause of sexism, men in the new left began to propound a free love morality. Men would not be as possessive but more communitarian in their relationships. The basic premise, however, was the old one of men seeking greater access to women. The slogan 'Girls say yes to guys who say no!' was unembarrassedly employed by the Students for a Democratic Society to support draft resistance. Similarly, in the civil rights movement inter-racial affairs were presented by black men to white women as the way in which they could attack the racist state.[47] Women's sense of being sexually exploited was confirmed by Stokely Carmichael's famous response to the question of what role women played in the Student Non-violent Coordinating Committee: 'The position of women in SNCC', he replied, 'is prone.' In response to such jibes women within the American new left began to analyse the pleasures and dangers of sexuality. They were both excited by and resentful of this new world in which there were fewer clear rules and commitments. Some recognized that advances were being made. 'Women were having more sex that was not procreational, and claiming the right to it as well as paying a lower social and emotional cost'.[48] But not all were ready to abandon themselves. They wanted to say yes to sex and no to sexism. They saw the need both to defend the woman's right to sexual pleasure and to condemn male promiscuity. The result was that by 1967 feminists began to split off from the new left to create their own movement.

The Women's Movement

'Second-wave' feminism, like so many other new creations of the 1960s, had its roots in the 1950s. The notion that if a woman were to become more than simply the 'other' she would have to be sexually and economically independent – first made by Simone de Beauvoir in *The Second Sex* which appeared in its English translation in 1952 – was rediscovered in the 1960s. Her new readers were struck by her insightful analysis of the objectification of women. They were similarly impressed by Betty Friedan's point that in an age of pop psychology the middle-class woman who expressed her unhappiness with the sexual status quo would be likely to be described as suffering from penis envy. Friedan's *Feminine Mystique* (1963), an analysis of the stultifying impact of 1950s American suburban life, became an immediate classic. In 1966 she went on to launch the National Organization of Women (NOW) so that professional women could lobby for an end to sexual discrimination. Friedan's brand of liberal feminism viewed both genders as controlled by mystiques. Younger women who assembled in the consciousness-raising groups which suddenly blossomed across North America placed more stress on subjective experiences and direct political action. They gained their first notoriety by protesting the 1968 Miss America pageant at Atlantic City. The press was more taken with the notion that bras were burnt than with the fact that the commodification of women was critiqued, but feminism was now newsworthy. By the early 1970s even the readers of staid women's magazines were being exposed to the feminist message. *Ms* magazine in New York, edited by Gloria Steinem who had first gained attention by her exposé of the working conditions of bunny hostesses in Hefner's Playboy clubs, and *Spare Rib* in London soon provided the movement with their own mouthpieces.

What the feminists' view of sexual pleasure should be was a central theme in such publications. Women discovered in consciousness-raising groups that they were not alone in faking orgasms or in finding that their partners asked them to be honest but were unhappy when they were. It was in this context that the concerns of sexologists and feminists met. Feminists in the main followed Kinsey and turned against Freud.[49] They eagerly concurred on the oppressive nature of the 'myth of the vaginal orgasm'.[50] They were similarly dismissive of Marxist men who informed them that slogans such as 'smash monogamy' were really pointless since the family was no longer capitalism's main instrument of control.[51] Kate Millet's *Sexual Politics* (1970) attacked the misogyny of male culture, arguing that only free sex could lead to healthy relationships.[52] Shulamith Firestone advanced the notion that sexual dichotomy was the basis of sex, class and racial domination. In a very American fashion she envisaged technology ending at least one form of oppression: artificial reproduction, she predicted, would free women from the burden of birthing.[53] Others were far less sanguine, especially when in 1970 a United States Senate Subcommittee began to report on the dangers of the pill. Women, some realized, had gained more effective methods of birth control only at the price of assuming full responsibility for the inconveniences and risks involved. No one wanted to have to rely again on coitus interruptus, but the argument could be made that, as unsatisfactory as it might have been, it at least required a high level of male involvement. The second wave of feminists were in effect asking the question – which Stopes and Sanger, had they been alive, might well have regarded as some perverse throwback to the Victorian age – whether it was possible that women, in being given high-tech contraceptives, were losing control of their own bodies.[54]

The abortion struggle – the main feminist campaign of the 1970s – reinforced such concerns. The pill was no sooner in mass circulation than the tragic rash of deformities in the early 1960s caused by Thalidomide (a sedative employed by pregnant women) sparked public fears about the side-effects of all biochemicals. But the Thalidomide disaster also provided ammunition for reformers advancing the 'quality of life' argument to justify abortion. Abortion was not, as many assumed, the last resort of the seduced and abandoned. In France, for example, a 1947 study revealed that 73 per cent of those who aborted were married women. Paris harboured fourteen illegal clinics and each department had at least one.[55] As many of the proponents of contraception had argued that the availability of birth control would end the blight of botched operations, it proved more difficult to move on immediately to reform the abortion law. The success of the next campaign depended on the impetus of the feminist movement. Although 1955 legislation permitted French doctors to provide therapeutic abortions, illegal operations could be punished by up to five years in prison. There is no way of knowing the exact numbers of abortions that were carried out in France in the two decades following the Second World War, but authorities estimated they ranged between 250,000 and 850,000 per year. In 1969 *Planning Familial* started the *Association Nationale pour l'Étude de l'Avortement* and the issue was further pursued by *Mouvement de Libération des Femmes* in the 1970s.

The groundswell of support in favour of reform of the abortion law grew. Doctors expressed their concern that, although the numbers were far smaller than they had been in the 1930s, women continued to die as a result of back-street quacks. Lawyers complained that the vast number of criminal operations made a mockery of the law. Abortion lobbying groups protested that the existing legislation ignored the World Health Organization's definition of 'health' which included 'physical, mental and social well-being'. Abortion laws were accordingly reformed across the Western world in the late 1960s and early 1970s.[56] Eastern bloc nations, with the apparent desire to have more direct power to enforce population policy, tended to permit abortion, while restricting access to contraception. In East Germany abortion was available but even there the government enforced restrictions in the 1950s and 1960s. Repression proved impossible and the communists reformed their abortion laws in 1972 much in the same way as did the Western states.[57]

In France public awareness of the issue was dramatically raised when, on 5 April 1971, 343 prominent French women, including Simone de Beauvoir, Catherine Deneuve, Marguerite Duras, Gisèle Halimi, Jeanne Moreau, Bulle Ogier and Françoise Sagan, proclaimed in a *Nouvel observateur* article that they had aborted.[58] To defend them, Gisèle Halimi created a pro-abortionist movement entitled 'Choisir' which won the support of feminists, doctors and members of the Communist Party. In 1972, Halimi made an impassioned call for law reform while successfully turning to account the Bobigny trial of a sixteen-year-old woman whose abortion had been denounced to the police by the very man who had impregnated her.[59] The public was clearly sympathetic; prosecutions ceased. In 1973 Valéry Giscard d'Estaing, the recently elected French president who had earlier expressed his support for reform of the abortion law, created a *Secrétariat d'État de la Condition Féminine* under Françoise Giroud and entrusted Simone Veil, the minister of health, with the task of hammering out the necessary legislation.[60]

The year 1973 also saw the landmark *Roe* v. *Wade* decision in which the United States Supreme Court held that a woman's 'right of privacy' overrode existing state laws against early abortion. The relaxing of the law led to a decline in maternal mortality and morbidity associated with criminal abortion. Though abortion was liberalized the control of the process was kept firmly in the hands of the medical profession whose freedom and discretion in implementing policy were confirmed. A woman's 'right' to control her body was not recognized. Abortions continued to be treated as services requiring the close policing and surveillance of doctors; the women who sought them (in North America, increasingly younger, unmarried women) did not cease being stigmatized and demeaned. Abortion, when it began to be treated in films such as *A Taste of Honey* (1961) and *Alfie* (1966), always had to be portrayed as a tragedy.[61]

Feminism and Lesbianism

The abortion issue was only one of the problematic sides of sexuality that feminists began to explore. Rape was another. Nancy Friday, in *My Secret Garden* (1973), had discussed women's rape fantasies in the context of forms of stimulation that abetted heterosexual pleasure. A far more serious approach to the subject was made by Susan Brownmiller who, in *Against our Will* (1975), argued that all men had throughout history employed rape to keep all women in a state of fear. Sexual assault, she claimed, was not an 'abnormal' act but a symptom of male dominance.[62] In the United States rape had a particular resonance since Southern racists – who with impunity assaulted black women – had long argued that the protection of white women justified the lynching of black men.[63] Leftist males were accordingly outraged to find feminists accusing them, simply because of their gender, of being implicated in such assaults. Pornography also drove a wedge between progressive men and feminists. In the United States the film *Deep Throat* (1972), hailed by *Screw* magazine as the first pornographic film that had a plot, made 30 million dollars. Its success proved that pornography had become part of mainstream culture. Though the story was a pure male fantasy – Linda Lovelace having her clitoris in her throat could only be pleasured by giving blow jobs – the film was the first of its sort to which men took their wives and girlfriends. In France, *The Story of O*, another fictional account of a woman who learns to love her role as a sex slave, when it first appeared in the 1950s enjoyed only a cult following. In 1975, however, it was produced as a film and portions were serialized by the popular magazine *L'Express*. Such public acceptance of pornography drove women's groups in both North America and Europe into the larger analysis of sexism.

The feminist preoccupation with pornography was a response to many women's fear of the sexualization and vulnerability that they felt had been produced by the 1960s. The notion that images played a powerful role in eliciting violence was spelled out in the title of Robin Morgan's classic article 'Theory and Practice: Pornography and Rape'.[64] Pornography told people that women loved being the victims of men and that cruelty and violence were normal. In eroticizing subordination, pornography victimized all women and empowered all men. Those holding such views played up the idea that women had a special, less animalistic nature than men. Morgan's hope was that the pornography issue would broaden feminism inasmuch as it transcended class and race barriers. In fact, the subject split the feminist movement. Liberal and socialist feminists were not only irritated by the moral self-righteousness and essentialism of the most strident anti-pornographers, they pointed out that Doris Day movies were just as degrading to women but no one spoke of censoring them.

Those who did grapple with the issues of rape, wife-battering, pornography and incest were increasingly sceptical of the advances made during the sexual revolution. Many leftist men regarded themselves as feminists but were increasingly viewed by radical feminists with suspicion. If men were not the enemy who were? As early as 1969 the supporters of radical feminism began to portray all men as oppressors inasmuch as all men benefited from the exploitation of women. Radical feminists created the terms 'sexism' and 'sexual politics' which raised the shocking notion of a power struggle existing in every family as in every other area of social life.[65] Some began to view sex itself as a poison pawn, an instrument that primarily served male needs. Separatist feminists regarded all sex as tainted by male violence and misogyny. And did not the rediscovery of the clitoris mean that men were dispensable?[66] It seemed logical enough for some to move on to embrace – for political as well as for personal reasons – lesbianism.

The general public knew remarkably little about lesbianism in the 1960s. The popular film *The Killing of Sister George* (1968), though considered daring, simply reinforced the old notion that women given to same-sex passions were doomed to lives of hysteria and sadness. In England it was only in 1971 that the first serious academic study was devoted to the subject.[67] In America 'lesbian feminism' had already emerged as a response to sexism.[68] Initially, feminists were skittish about lesbianism, fearing that it was just another way of putting women into bed. Nevertheless, the direction in which radical feminism would move was revealed in Valerie Solanas's SCUM (Society for Cutting Up Men) *Manifesto* written in 1967. A woman who only received the avid attention of the press after she shot and nearly killed Andy Warhol in June 1968, Solanas argued that women had to free themselves not just of men but of sex.[69] By the 1970s, Ti-Grace Atkinson was arguing that 'feminism is the theory, lesbianism is the practice'.[70] In France Monique Wittig imagined a utopia of 'lesbian peoples'.[71] The metaphor of the 'nation' appeared in Jill Johnson's *Lesbian Nation* (1973), which argued that men were the enemy, heterosexuality symbolized women's defeat and it followed that lesbianism was the only way to end women's exploitation. Kate Millet, who had only a few years earlier defended the heterosexual woman's desires for a liberated sexuality, now came out as a lesbian.[72] Adrienne Rich in her discussion of 'compulsory heterosexuality' advanced the idea that until patriarchy ended women could not make a free choice.[73] Heterosexuality she believed was neither normal nor innate; a woman's 'frigidity' was not a fault but a form of resistance. She went on, employing the concept of a 'lesbian continuum', to propound the romantic notion that all women were lesbians to the extent that they supported each other in friendship and comradeship. Rich would similarly argue that all women were mothers and that it was necessary to break down the barrier that patriarchy used to separate childbearers from the childless.[74]

Betty Friedan believed that lesbians in the feminist movement – she labelled them 'the lavender menace' – threatened the chances of moderate organizations such as NOW to build political coalitions. They perversely confirmed the argument, long made by conservatives, that all feminists were man-hating lesbians. Second-wave feminism had begun by denying the importance of gender and demanding 'equal rights'. The emergence of 'cultural feminism' resulted in a more inward-looking ideology that stressed female difference. Some women felt they had to choose between feminism and lesbianism. On the one hand, liberal feminists like Friedan revealed their homophobia, while on the other there were lesbians who derided abortion and child care as 'straight' women's issues and made heterosexual women feel inadequate or gullible. Heterosexual feminists were naturally angered to be informed by separatist feminists that they were 'fucking with the oppressor'. Lesbians who remained in the feminist movement continued to advance a political agenda. To the disappointment of activists like Atkinson, there were others who revealed themselves – like heterosexuals – to be primarily preoccupied by the pursuit of sexual pleasure. For them, lifestyle soon replaced politics.[75]

The soul searching of middle-class, self-proclaimed lesbian feminists was of scant importance to working-class women who were already living the life.[76] They had more practical problems to contend with. In the 1950s anti-homosexual panics had focused on the danger of 'lesbian moms'. Doctors offered psychological interpretations and a range of therapies for deviant women whom they believed to be sexually immature and sado-masochistic. Yet in the same years that produced the image of the 'lesbian sicko' spaces were being colonized by lesbians. Tabloids provided information on bars, clubs and resorts patronized by homosexual women. Lesbian pulp fiction, playing up the image of seductive butches and innocent victims, was also available. The butch–femme roles, which crystallized among working-class women, were regarded by observers as an aping of heterosexual mores.[77] Such roles did provide some reassuring structure and were necessarily rigid in order to withstand the repression of the 1950s. Some believed only butches were 'true lesbians'. Yet in many cases the butch image was adopted for the aggressive purposes of violating gender standards; the woman who claimed it did not necessarily harbour any desire to be a man. Moreover, women might switch roles from butch to femme.

Middle-class lesbians were initially put off by the stereotyped culture of bar butches and street dykes. And the middle-class activists were themselves split. The older generation in America were represented by the Daughters of Bilitis who from the 1950s quietly lobbied on behalf of lesbians just as the Mattachine Society discreetly worked for gay men. The younger 'lesbian feminists' were far more radical. They sought to bridge class and race divides. They reclaimed butch–femme roles and sado-masochism, believing that female desire could be both unleashed and purified. A sense of how far their self-confidence had grown could be gained by comparing Radclyffe Hall, who sought acceptance for the deviant in respectable society and despised the notion of a lesbian 'scene', with the women of the 1970s who embraced the notion of a separate 'lesbian nation'. *The Well of Loneliness* (1928) ended tragically; in Rita Mae Brown's *Rubyfruit Jungle* (1973) the spunky lesbian heroine triumphed.

Gay Rights

The politicization of male homosexuality – because it had in most Western nations been subject to decades of criminal prosecution – necessarily followed a different trajectory from that of lesbianism. The repression of homosexuals was severest between the 1930s and the 1950s. The notion of the 'closet' was a creation of these times when sexual minorities were forced to lead a subterranean life.[78] The assaults and discrimination that homosexuals faced meant that it was crucial for them to be able to 'pass' as heterosexuals in public. The feeling of oppression led some to the view that they shared a minority status with women. In a sense this mirrored the arguments of the homophobic who sought to keep other men in line by threatening them with the effeminate labels of 'sissy', 'pansy' and 'fairy'.

Between 1945 and the mid-1960s in the United States, where both major political parties concurred on the threat of subversives and need for surveillance, homosexuals were regarded as both sexually and politically unreliable. A film like *The Manchurian Candidate* (1962) played on the idea of the communists' ability to employ 'brainwashing' to infiltrate the country with sexual and political saboteurs. Even when Cold War fears declined and an era of *détente* began, suspicions of homosexual 'conspiracies' remained. Gays were accused of controlling the worlds of film and fashion. *Life* magazine protested in

June 1964 that homosexuals were 'flaunting' themselves. In the same year, Walter Jenkins, Lyndon Johnson's chief of staff, was arrested in a YMCA rest room.[79] The post-war medical consensus was that such self-destructive actions proved that homosexuality was not a crime but a disease. This implied that a cure was possible. But general practitioners were ill qualified to deal with the issue; many continued to confuse homosexuality with paedophilia. The 'experts' had equally blinkered views. Psychoanalysts, convinced that homosexuality was due to the neurotic patient having a weak father and aggressive mother, subjected clients to countless sessions in inculcating such views. Endocrinologists employed dangerous hormonal treatments. They could blunt the homosexual's sex drive; they could not eliminate the direction of the passion.[80] The crudest responses were made in Denmark and Norway where homosexual patients were castrated. In Britain aversion therapy was employed. One form consisted of inducing men to vomit every time they viewed pictures of male nudes.[81] The obvious, though rarely noted, irony was that the very doctors who referred to homosexuals as 'sick' employed therapies that purposely made healthy men ill.

Kinsey opened up the topic of homosexuality by revealing how extensive same-sex sexual practices were. Subsequent investigations demonstrated that attempts at both curing and punishing homosexuals did not work. Moreover, the stigmatization of homosexuality, asserted investigators like Michael Schofield, led to an epidemic of anti-social acts including lying, promiscuity, alcoholism, suicide, police corruption and blackmail. Bizarrely enough, if a homosexual fell into the clutches of the law he was punished for consorting with other men by being sent to an all-male institution. Like Kinsey, Schofield concluded that the 'containment' of homosexuality could be best accomplished by dismantling the laws that isolated it.[82] Increasing numbers of medical and legal experts argued that to take into account changing realities, to protect health and to prevent the law from falling into disrepute it had to be reformed in areas pertaining to prostitution, abortion and contraception. The same argument was employed for those insisting on the decriminalization of homosexuality.[83]

In The Netherlands homosexuality had been decriminalized immediately after the war and in 1946 a counselling and support organization known as COC emerged. These events were reported in England where the process of decriminalization was launched in 1957 with the publication of the report of the Wolfenden Committee on Homosexuality and Prostitution. Wolfenden did not so much call for the acceptance of homosexuality as argue that private, consensual, non-violent acts should not concern the police. His assumption was that homosexuality was a medical rather than a criminal problem. Those pressing for reform included Lord Attlee, Bertrand Russell and A. J. Ayer.[84] By the 1960s homosexual characters began to be sympathetically portrayed in such films as *A Taste of Honey* (1961). In *Victim* (1961) Dirk Bogarde courageously risked his reputation as a matinee idol by playing the role of a homosexual victimized by blackmailers. Once the Labour Party achieved a comfortable majority in 1966 it passed the Sexual Offences Act (1968) which put into place the reforms called for by Wolfenden a decade earlier. The decriminalization of homosexuality between consenting adults in private was a modest step. The act did not pertain to Scotland or Northern Ireland, members of the armed forces or the merchant marine.[85] The age of consent for homosexual males was set at twenty-one, whereas for heterosexual women it was sixteen. A 1969 Dutch report showed that young men had no need for special protection; nevertheless, in England prosecutions for gross indecency with males between sixteen and twenty-one actually increased after 1968.[86] The goal of the British legislation was improved social management and discipline, not sexual liberation. Much of the stigma of homosexuality remained. Jeremy Thorpe, leader of the Liberal Party, had his career destroyed in 1976 when news seeped out of an alleged relationship with a younger man.

In post-war France conservative doctors – who condemned homosexuals as lazy and unproductive and likened them to Nazis and Arabs in their preference for male company – appealed not to science but to common prejudice.[87] Nevertheless, well-known homosexuals such as the actor Jean Marais and the playwright Jean Cocteau enjoyed the benefits of an informal legal immunity. The less well-placed faced fines and prison terms of up to three years.[88] Despite the North American discoveries made by the man French homosexuals referred to as 'Saint Kinsey', the French government maintained the laws passed by the Vichy government. Indeed, in 1960 the Mirguet ordinance against 'indecent behaviour' extended the surveillance of acts that might be construed as inciting debauchery.[89] The police periodically swooped down on steam baths, and the courts condemned three to four hundred men each year throughout the 1960s.[90]

The May 1968 'events' sparked the revolution of *les pédés*. French feminists took the lead in launching sexual protests; gay men followed. The *Front Homosexuel d'Action Révolutionnaire* of Guy Hocquenghem appeared. Jean-Louis Bory and others set out to demolish the myths of the misogyny and effeminacy of gays that heterosexuals had spun. Leftist intellectuals such as Daniel Guérin came out. In employing terms like '*gai*' and 'coming out', the French revealed the extent to which sexual issues in the late twentieth century were Americanized.

Opinion polls revealed that sympathy for homosexuals was growing; although the public still thought that they suffered from some sort of illness, it was regarded as a private matter. Police harassment continued into the 1970s. Only in 1982 after the Socialists came to power was the French law on homosexuality finally reformed with the age of consent set for males, as for females, at fifteen.

In the United States the members of the Mattachine Action Committee of Harry Hay had struggled for years for 'acceptance' and a simple end to discrimination. Middle-class homosexuals avoided publicity, hoping that a low profile and the slow education of the public would bring understanding.[91] But just as the women's liberation movement broke with the liberal feminists, so too in the late 1960s the gay rights movement broke with older homosexual lobbying groups and adopted a more radical, assertive notion of 'gay liberation'.[92] In so doing its members were inspired by the civil rights and anti-Vietnam War movements in which many had participated. And, like the feminists, they too found the American new left initially hostile and homophobic. Gays were attracted to pro-feminist men's groups yet some feminists also viewed them with suspicion. There was an irony in this inasmuch as a common conservative charge was that feminism, in producing aggressive women, had led the 'weakest' men to topple over into homosexuality.

The four-day Stonewall riots enjoy the legendary status of having launched the gay liberation movement. They began in June 1969 with a police raid on a Greenwich Village gay bar. The story goes that for the first time patrons refused to put up with police harassment and fought back. In fact, San Francisco had been the site of similar confrontations since the mid-1960s.[93] Nevertheless, the Stonewall riots – because of where and when they occurred – detonated an explosion of gay self-assertiveness. Men's consciousness was raised. Liberation groups sprang up across America and then around the world. Thousands of men, from Vancouver to London, 'came out of the closet'.

As opposed to the quiet lobbying of earlier homosexual groups, gays stressed action and employed sit-ins and demonstrations to demand changes. 'Gay pride' marches quickly became an annual ritual. Whereas discretion had once been lauded, by the 1970s gays held that secrecy was dangerous. To substantiate such claims they could point to enquiries on gay life in Germany and America that revealed the therapeutic importance of coming out. Statistics suggested that candour cut the suicide rate in half.[94] The love that dared not speak its name soon became, its supporters joked, a neurosis that would not shut up. It was a sign of the times that scientific meetings became the scenes of political demonstrations by gays protesting against the notion that homosexuality was a sickness. Under such pressure the American Psychiatric Association in 1973 removed homosexuality from its *Diagnostic and Statistical Manual of Mental Disorders*.[95] Gay rights activists also confronted churches and professional groups. Their success in forging alliances with liberal lawyers and clergy led fifteen states by 1976 to dismantle their anti-sodomy laws. Larger cities and university towns passed civil rights codes. The extent of change should not be exaggerated. Unlike European nations, each American state had its own set of laws and many which remained on the books – pertaining to age of consent, sodomy, indecency and fornication – could be used to police homosexual activity.

Gays, like African-Americans, Chicanos and women, portrayed themselves as struggling against an oppressor. Like other liberation movements they moved on to assert an 'ethnic' identity. The term 'gay' was taken to mean a specific identity as opposed to 'homosexual' which referred simply to sexual behaviour. 'I find my identity as a gay man as basic as any other identity I can lay claim to', Michael Denneny asserted. 'Being gay is a more elemental aspect of who I am than my profession, my class, or my race.'[96] Many gays no longer strived for simple integration; they insisted on the recognition of their special needs. Such a lauding of 'identity politics' was taken furthest in the United States. White American homosexuals no doubt embraced this new tribalism because they were less entangled than their European counterparts in class, religious or ethnic cultures.[97] Many of those who once attacked identity labelling ended up employing it. Concrete demonstrations of such identity politics were offered by the emergence of homosexual neighbourhoods and communities. San Francisco became the Mecca of homosexuals around the world, but every major Western city had gay clubs, bars and bathhouses providing commercialized proof of gays' existence.[98] The 1970s witnessed an unprecedented opening up of private and public spaces for gays which in turn became the foci of resistance against police harassment.

The gay sexual ideal was of a liberal, fun-loving, romantic, non-possessive, partnership.[99] Homosexuals prided themselves on having more egalitarian relationships than straights. Whereas once gay men sought 'trade' they now sought equals – other gay men. Public pick-up places were abandoned for private clubs. Increasingly, the goal was not casual sex but longer-term relationships. The stereotypes of 'fairy' and 'queen' which had once been embraced were beginning to be discarded. The stereotypes and the 'gay clones' that replaced them were subjected to self-parody by the American pop band Village People. Experimental and casual sex certainly did not disappear. American men had scores of partners they met in bars, baths and clubs. The 'tops' and 'bottoms' who played out sado-masochistic fantasies no doubt often deconstructed, spoofed and caricatured straight sex, but that did not mean that their own relationships were free of oppression and power.

The great victory of gays and lesbians was in winning visibility. In 1965 the average person could not name a single well-known homosexual; by the end of the 1970s it was impossible to ignore the gay movement. Almost every political party and profession had gay sections or groups. In Britain in 1977 the first lesbian MP and in 1980 the first gay MP declared themselves. Michel Foucault, the French philosopher, who popularized the notion that doctors had created the 'homosexual' in the late nineteenth century for the purposes of control and surveillance, regarded such apparent advances with caution.[100] He had been drawn to the sexual underworld because of its refusal to accept authority and defended gay sado-masochism in part because it violated bourgeois norms.[101] At the same time he was suspicious of gays who harped on identity and feared gay pride could result in ghettoization. He opposed all binary notions and warned his readers that they always had to combat the delusion of having arrived at the 'truth'.

Conclusion

By the 1980s the general public, whether it liked it or not, had been familiarized with a series of new sexual stories about gender inequality, premarital sex, abortion and 'coming out'. Western society by and large accepted the fact that contraception, abortion, common law marriages, premarital sex and homosexuality seemed here to stay. In a country like Italy, where femininity had long been equated with maternity, amazing transformations had taken place in the space of three generations. Women moved from relying on natural methods of fertility limitation, to coitus interruptus, to the pill.[102] In North America in the same short period of time many of those who once feared the 'truth' getting out that they were lesbians or homosexuals now proudly flaunted their identity. Such changes signified both a degree of liberation and the acceptance of new modes of regulation. They were neither the cause nor effect of any major dislocation in the capitalist world. The new sexual stories were in part tellable because the unprecedented prosperity of the West in the 1960s and early 1970s undermined much traditional censoriousness. The question was whether such sexual advances could be maintained in an age of economic restraint.

10

'Backlash': AIDS and the Sexual Counter-revolution

In November 1991 Magic Johnson, the thirty-two-year-old American basketball star, informed the press that he had tested HIV-positive. Some expressed disbelief; others, according to *Time* magazine, 'were sobered at the thought that if even the most enchanted and mobile of bodies was vulnerable, it could, as Johnson pointed out, "happen to anybody".'[1] If the 1960s are thought of as a time when hedonistic youth embraced a myth of sexual liberation, the last two decades of the twentieth century are associated with conservatives successfully crafting a series of cautionary tales aimed at inculcating abstinence. The temptation is to divide time neatly up into either liberal or conservative epochs, but it has to be resisted if one's intent is to gain a better understanding of the complex shifts which occurred in beliefs and behaviour. The 1960s were not all that great; the 1990s were not all that bad. At the end of the millennium the media's exploitation of those telling stories of being HIV-positive or 'survivors of sexual abuse' or 'in recovery' certainly guaranteed that the darker side of sexuality received unprecedented attention. The purported purpose of such presentations might have been to shore up traditional standards, but they made available to the public a greater range of sexual scripts. Ordinary men and women were not indifferent to the complexities of sexuality. Why so many public observers insisted on speaking in some simplistic way of sexual losses and gains requires analysis.

Time magazine happily declared in 1984 that the sexual revolution was over. AIDS and its accompanying homophobia did not begin – but were intimately linked in the public mind with – the 'big chill'. A host of other issues were also taken by observers as signs of a sexual backlash: the rise of the Christian right and its attacks on day care, affirmative action and sex education, the recruitment of feminists into the anti-pornography crusade, the emergence of the men's movement and the accompanying onslaught on non-traditional family forms, and the growing viciousness of anti-abortion zealots which climaxed in their bombing of women's clinics and the killing of doctors.[2]

An economic downturn provided the backdrop to the shift towards conservative moralizing. The affluent, optimistic 1960s and early 1970s were displaced by a new age of pessimism, restraint and cut-backs. The faltering of the economy signalled the final end of the long post-war boom and a drop in real wages. In this uncertain climate the political right managed to convince the electorate that it had the requisite know-how to respond to the crisis. Its leaders took it as a given that economic retrenchment entailed a return to conservative moral standards. In the United Kingdom Margaret Thatcher, first elected as Prime Minister in 1979, campaigned on family values, as did Ronald Reagan in his 1980 presidential bid. Each wanted government out of the boardrooms but back in the bedrooms of their nations.

Both the conservatives and their opponents agreed that there was a 'backlash', but such rhetorical stridency masked the complexity of the sexual politics and practices of the last decades of the twentieth century. There was first the obvious problem that the politicians who exploited the notion of a return to traditional sexual standards were hardly moral paragons themselves. Several of Thatcher's closest advisers, including Cecil Parkinson in 1983 and Jeffrey Archer in 1986, were caught in compromising sexual liaisons. Ronald Reagan was an even more curious crusader for family values: a divorced Hollywood actor whose two children lived the sorts of lives he attacked as decadent. The truth was that most politicians and ordinary people declared themselves opposed to 'too much' change but accepted experimentation by people whom they knew. Even many of the adults who opposed youthful permissiveness with appeals to the dictates of 'nature' or scripture preferred to forget their own indiscretions. When television evangelists such as Jimmy Swaggart were caught with prostitutes they simply asked for forgiveness and returned to their moralizing crusades.

Moreover, different nations were in these decades going through different stages of sexual change. While Britain and the United States were supposedly experiencing a sexual counter-revolution, some European countries were just beginning the transition that more 'advanced' nations had begun decades earlier. In Russia, where in the early 1990s a mere 3 per cent of women were on the pill, modern forms of contraception were only beginning to challenge abortion as the chief fertility control method.[3] In Spain, where Franco had long maintained sexual repression, abortion was legalized and punk styles and topless beaches were accepted only in the mid-1980s – less than a decade after the dictator's death.

In the West one witnessed a complex process of advances and retreats. The use of the term 'backlash' was mystifying inasmuch at it assumed a false polarity, suggesting that clear-cut victories were once made and then suddenly lost. The reality was less simple. The newly invigorated right appeared to be on the march, but at the same time the general public's views were in some areas becoming more liberal; for example, levels of support for abortion and a tolerance of homosexuality generally rose. The response pollsters received depended on what questions were asked. Surveys in Europe and North America repeatedly revealed both the public's opposition *in the abstract* to abortion and its acceptance of the notion that there were a number of scenarios in which a woman had a clear right to abort. On a host of similar sexual issues the public was split in its own mind. A more sexually pluralistic age was emerging in which the classic man and woman in the street found themselves discussing, if not approving, everything from test tube babies, trans-sexuals, bisexuals and child abuse to incest, sado-masochism and 'lipstick lesbians'.

AIDS

AIDS clearly cast an ominous shadow over almost every aspect of late twentieth-century sexuality. When penicillin appeared in the 1940s many believed that sexually transmitted diseases would soon be a thing of the past. The wonder drug seemed to cure syphilis with miraculous ease and rates of infection soon plummeted. Gonorrhoea still posed serious problems and herpes, when it appeared in the early 1980s, was first hailed as at worst a 'killer' and at best a blight that would drive the promiscuous back to monogamy. With the advent of AIDS the whole range of such sexually transmitted diseases came to be regarded as little more than irritants. Whether in fact AIDS itself should have been classified as a sexually transmitted disease is debatable since it is not spread simply by sexual means. Nor is it in itself a death-dealing disease; it simply incapacitates the immune system which allows the entry of opportunistic infections. Though the original rumours of the 'gay plague' emerged in 1981, the Center for Disease Control in Atlanta determined that in fact the first North American case appeared much earlier.[4] The general public was swept up in the AIDS hysteria when, following the death of the 1950s film star Rock Hudson, *Life* magazine devoted its August 1985 cover story to the AIDS crisis. The disease had already claimed 11,000 victims in the United States alone.

The medical scientists who first detected the syndrome labelled it Gay Related Immune Deficiency (GRID) and the sexual side of AIDS was never to be lost. It was soon established that AIDS (the acquired immune deficiency syndrome) spread as a result of HIV (the human immune deficiency virus). News of AIDS initially seemed to confirm moralists' warnings. Promiscuity was targeted by the press which delighted in reporting that some of the early AIDS patients had on average a thousand sexual partners. Even some gays wondered if straights were right, that homosexuals were being punished for their trespasses. Public fear quickly climbed and by 1986 a panic had set in. Patrick Buchanan, Nixon's former speech writer, declared that the sexual revolution was devouring its children; AIDS was nature's vengeance on those who had tried to violate its laws.

In the public mind AIDS was not simply transmitted, it was 'caused' by sex. The Christian right in the United States regarded the syndrome as God's punishment of dangerous and guilty sinners; it bewailed the 'gay disease', while attacking the sex education and birth control programmes that might alleviate it. Homophobia was let loose. Conservatives were never to give up the pleasing notion that there was some sort of poetic justice in a virus transmitted by body fluids exterminating the sexually experimental. When the internationally known gay designer Gianni Versace was killed in 1997 the media immediately attributed his murder to a male prostitute turned serial killer seeking revenge for having been infected by his clients with AIDS. The story was proved false but eerily echoed the way in which Jack the Ripper's killing of prostitutes a century earlier had been similarly attributed to a man driven mad by syphilis. The sexually deviant, both accounts clearly implied, 'deserved' such retribution.

By 1987 the press announced that heterosexuals were also at risk. Victims were doubling every month though a new drug, AZT, was now available. The discovery of haemophiliacs who fell ill due to contaminated blood supplies raised the issue of 'innocent' victims of the plague. The sympathy which victims deserved was apportioned according to their class, age, race and sexual orientation. In Europe the panic exacerbated a hostility to all immigrants. In North America the first targets of the press were the dangers posed by gays, intravenous drug users and young, poor black males. Next came black women castigated as the mothers of AIDS babies and as threats (as prostitutes) to white men. Health agencies and the media largely ignored lesbians. Everywhere governments saw as their chief concern the protection of white heterosexual youth.

The danger of the spread of the disease into the heterosexual world finally sparked serious state involvement in prevention and detection.

For the most part governments manifested a failure of nerve. Their initial reluctance to provide information or protection alternated with bouts of panic. In the United States the Bush administration was afraid of appearing to condone the sexual activity of the young even if not responding meant placing them at risk of death.[5] Administrators believed that their first duty was to stop young people from experimenting and force them to feel embarrassed by sex. The government embraced the comforting notion that it was possible to split the 'good' from the 'bad', to prevent the former from being seduced or lured into the tempting sexual activities of the latter.

Though Europe watched America and had time to prepare itself for the AIDS onslaught, neither Thatcherite Britain nor Socialist France did much better.[6] Indeed, instead of showing any sympathy to the gay community, Thatcher's government passed section 28 of the Local Government Act of 1988 aimed at preventing local authorities from 'promoting' homosexuality in any way.[7] France was the European nation with the highest number of victims. An IFOP (*Institut Français d'Opinion Publique*) poll in 1986 of the children of the 1960s found that 54 per cent accepted gays, though 95 per cent said that AIDS did not affect their own behaviour.[8] Youth felt invulnerable. A 1987 poll revealed a marked decline in public support; 38 per cent of respondents now believed gays spread AIDS and 50 per cent agreed that the disease was a punishment for a dangerous way of life.[9] Respectable French publications hailed a purported return to chastity and fidelity while neo-fascists like Le Pen openly attacked the '*sidaïque*' (SIDA being the French acronym for AIDS).[10] In West Germany *Der Spiegel* carried its first report of AIDS under the title 'Terror from Abroad'.[11] The enemy was the 'other' – the addicts, immigrants and haemophiliacs – and it followed that those who felt themselves besieged immediately thought of quarantines and forcible testing. The Netherlands and Scandinavia provided rare examples of doctors and gay community activists actually cooperating. For the most part public commentators contrasted 'normal' behaviour with the 'risk-taking' of gays. The not-so-subtle message was that society needed to be protected as much from the deviant as from the disease.

The horror of AIDS and the lobbying by well-connected white gay males finally convinced states of the necessity of dealing with sex issues with an unprecedented candour. As AIDS crossed over, heterosexuals began to empathize if not identify with gays. By 1988 popular support for gays in France began to rise again and 15 per cent of heterosexuals now stated that they were changing their own sexual behaviour.[12] In the United States public support for gays climbed and even George Bush, a Republican president, signed the Federal Hate

Crime Statistics Act which offered homosexuals some legal protection. The term 'safe sex' entered the popular vocabulary. Europeans grappled explicitly with the problem of popularizing prophylactics. American posters at first would not venture beyond showing a man holding a sock with the motto 'Putting on a condom is just as simple.' Governments were led to consider even making condoms available in jails and prisons; it took the AIDS crisis to force a broaching of the tabooed subject of male rape. The disease also re-ignited the discussion of prostitution, an age-old problem complicated in the late twentieth century by sex tourism and international prostitution rings. Nearly all the South American transvestite prostitutes of Paris, the French were alarmed to discover, were HIV-positive.

Gays

Some have argued that the full hedonistic lifestyle of the 1960s sexual revolution was probably only practised in the gay male subculture. AIDS hit just when the gay movement was enjoying its greatest visibility. By 1990 its victims included such luminaries as dancer Rudi Nureyev, actor Brad Davis, jazz musician Miles Davis and dramatist Tony Kushner whose *Angels in America* provided a classic portrayal of the tragic consequences of the plague. With the cross-over of AIDS, public sympathy for gays among heterosexuals increased. The 1993 success of the Hollywood film *Philadelphia* starring Tom Hanks was taken as a sign of heterosexual culture opening its arms to gays. Red ribbons were seen everywhere but what was actually occurring, some homosexual activists complained, was a 'de-gaying' of AIDS. The media wildly exaggerated the dangers it posed middle-class heterosexuals. Magic Johnson was presented as an example that 'AIDS can happen to anyone.' In fact, he was handsome, rich and heterosexual – precisely *not* the sort of person at risk. Randy Shilts pointed out that as always social barriers protected the well-off from the fate awaiting the marginal. The media insisted on focusing on the sexually acquired form of AIDS while it slighted the social and economic factors that might have helped to destroy an individual's immune system. And even the sexual side of AIDS was only discussed in such a way as to present a bleak and cautionary portrayal of homosexuality. The mass media quailed at the thought of pondering the pleasures of deviant sex.

Nevertheless, the publicity produced by AIDS led to a slowly increasing public acceptance of homosexuality. In France, for example, where the gay movement was relatively weak, full decriminalization of homosexuality having only occurred in 1982, AIDS made the French aware of the centrality of homosexuals in their culture.[13] Reiser, the nation's most brilliant cartoonist, spoofed the 'cancer gay' that took his life.[14] Cyril Collard, in his novels and films about gay and bisexual victims, attracted before his early death a large, youthful audience.[15] Jean-Paul Aron, historian and intellectual, was the first important French public figure to provide a personal account of one man's struggle with the disease. Chiding his old friend Michel Foucault for shamefully never having revealed his own illness, Aron confessed that, until he had AIDS, he too never thought of himself as a homosexual.[16]

In the United States and Britain the gay movements revealed remarkable strength. They countered government agencies' emphasis on individual responsibility and 'risky behaviour' by stressing the importance of the community's response. The term 'person with AIDS' was employed by the movement to valorize the individual and counter the disempowering label of 'victim'. Straight society, gays pointed out, wanted homosexuals to feel guilty but it was that very society that had produced the sexual furtiveness which pushed some homosexuals into a world of anonymous, dangerous sex. It was true that in the past secrecy had often added to the mystique of homosexuality. Now the notion propounded by activists was that health was best preserved by a self-confident – not shameful and guilt-ridden – gay youth. 'Safer sex' was to be an essential part of the gay identity. 'Buddies' would take care of each other. That meant that mundane issues such as housing, employment and diet also had to be on the agenda. London by 1997 had an HIV-positive club and its own edition of the US magazine *Poz*.[17] Of course, under the pressure of the disaster some gays became apolitical. Others, such as the members of ACT UP, were radicalized. In response to the United States army's continuing to expel over a thousand gays and lesbians a year, radicals took up the tactic of 'outing' closeted gays working for the government. The first victim was the Pentagon's television spokesperson during the 1991 Gulf War. The increased self-confidence and political strength of gays explained in part the interest taken in them by Bill Clinton in his 1992 presidential election bid.

The havoc caused by AIDS having given rise to a nostalgia for family life, an important segment of the gay community increasingly embraced domesticity. The 1990s saw them demanding the right to marry, have children and a regular family life. Denmark in 1989, Norway in 1993 and Sweden in 1994 sanctioned same-sex unions. In 1995 the mayor of St-Nazaire, France, provided a gay couple with a *certificat de concubinage*. By 1996 the socialist-controlled *arrondissements* of Paris followed suit.[18] In reaction, in 1996 the United States House of Representatives proposed a Defence of Marriage Bill which strictly defined marriage as the union of one man and one woman, but in Canada in the same year same-sex couples won the right to receive spousal support.[19] The proponents of gay marriage defended it on the conservative grounds of offering social stability. Because of their suspicion of its 'mainstreaming' implications and the fact that marriage was already desacralized, few gays took advantage of such options.

Queers

The issue of the cross-over of AIDS necessarily focused attention on bisexuality. Charlotte Wolff had produced the first full-length study of bisexuality in England in 1977. Some of the men she surveyed reported from 300 to 3,000 sexual exploits; no woman admitted to more than 20.[20] One problem complicating the community response to AIDS was that many such bisexual men did not regard themselves as gay.[21] In fact, bisexuals – whom doctors had lumped in with gays – along with transvestites, trans-sexuals and sado-masochists were in the 1990s demanding their own recognition.[22] Gays were split on the issue of trans-sexualism, suspicious that those seeking surgery were simply trying to conform to straight conventions.[23] Some feminists were similarly hostile to both transvestites and trans-sexuals, regarding them as little more than insulting parodies of the feminine.[24] Bisexuality had a greater success, with a parading of 'gender blending' being exploited by performing artists such as Madonna and David Bowie.[25]

In the 1990s the more radical gay groups such as Queer Nation took up the term 'queer' – once used as a pejorative – and embraced it as a badge to describe the entire range of sexual minority groups. Some lesbians resented the emergence of the term 'queer', regarding it as a means employed by men to reabsorb lesbians into a culture dominated by gay males.[26] Lesbians, often shut out of patriarchal gay groups where contempt for women was at times paraded, tended also to be hostile to the cross-generational sex and promiscuity defended by some gays.[27] Dealing in their own way with homophobia, lesbians created clubs, courses and support groups. Some lesbian theorists purposely ignored contraception and abortion as heterosexual problems yet many saw themselves as having more in common – as in issues pertaining to rape – with straight women than with homosexual men.[28] The lives of lesbians were controlled not so much by criminal laws as by statutes pertaining to child custody, taxes, health, immigration and pensions. At the same time, they were themselves divided over a range of issues including censorship, prostitution, intergenerational sex, pornography and trans-sexuality. In the 1990s a younger generation of 'lipstick lesbians' toppled the dowdy 1970s lesbian notion that women had to avoid the feminine trap. Instead, some young women followed Madonna's idea of exploiting femininity, not for men, but for other women. One could be both chic and butch was the message conveyed by the appearance of Canadian singer k. d. lang on the cover of *Vanity Fair*. Few could have predicted a decade earlier that the 'coming out' on national television of comedian Ellen Degeneris in 1997 would be enthusiastically applauded by a large segment of the American public.

As lesbians tended to have more stable and equitable partnerships than gays, it followed that they were not as enthusiastic as gay men in calling for a lowering of the age of consent. Lesbians also were in the main hostile to the genetic explanations of homosexuality that in the 1990s many gays found attractive. The biological basis of homosexuality had been looked for a century earlier by Ellis and Krafft-Ebing. In contrast, Kinsey had asserted that there was no difference between gays and heterosexuals. His message, which valorized assimilation, was liberating in the 1950s but forty years later an important part of the gay community swung back towards the essentialist argument and took up the idea that sexual orientation was not a 'choice'. The biological determinist view surfaced in the work of Dean Hamer who claimed to have found a DNA marker for gayness on the X chromosome.[29] Simon LeVay, having studied the brains of men who died of AIDS, asserted that the 'gay brain' had certain peculiarities.[30] The British press was even reporting in 1998 the discovery of 'gay fingerprints'. Researchers who brandished such biological arguments hoped to confound conservatives who insisted that gays had made bad 'choices', but those who were attracted to genetic explanations ignored the dangers posed by a return to hereditarian notions. The truth was that socio-biological explanations were still stigmatizing.[31]

The rediscovery in the 1990s of the role eugenics had played in the not so distant past served as a reminder of the dangers of linking sex and science. One woman's successful 1995 law suit against the Alberta government for her wrongful sterilization led to both a cash award of $750,000 and a dredging up of the history of eugenics in Canada.[32] Americans recalled that in the United States over 50,000 individuals had been sterilized under similar legislation.[33] Sweden only learned in 1997 of the fact that 60,000 of its citizens had been similarly operated on between 1935 and 1976.[34] Less draconian laws had been in force in Denmark, Norway and Finland. Forcible sterilization was still practised in Switzerland.[35] In Australia in 1997 the press reported that since 1992 over 1,000 mentally handicapped women and girls had been sterilized without court permission.[36] These practices revealed how far states, equipped with genetic rationales, would go in the policing of the sexuality of the marginal. When intelligence was believed to be inherited, the 'feeble-minded' had been targets of such legislation. If people came to believe that there was such thing as a gay gene, asked the cautious, might not homosexuals face a similar fate?

Backlash

There were many moralists willing to embrace almost any form of repression to counter homosexuality. Gays, the Christian right asserted, had risen from 'cesspools' to assault children. AIDS provided conservatives with another excuse for ostracizing the deviant, but there were more profound reasons for their anger and moral indignation. They represented groups that once had power and now had lost status. This backlash was primarily led by men – indeed, a 'men's movement' emerged in the United States to counter feminism. Masculinity once seemed clear, unquestionable and natural.[37] The current crisis, such groups asserted, had been primarily caused by women unilaterally redefining themselves. American men had in fact been organizing since the early 1970s when George Gilder claimed in *Sexual Suicide* (1973) that drugs, crime and violence were a result of disrupted gender roles. If things did not change, he had pessimistically predicted, a 'genocide' of males would result. The first men's association was begun by Richard Doyle who in 1976 produced *The Rape of the Male*. Modern men, such spokespersons claimed, felt isolated, powerless and angry. Even *Playboy* and *Esquire* joined the fray, asserting that men had had enough of the emasculating sensitivity induced by bleeding heart liberals.[38]

Divorce and child custody were the central preoccupations of such groups. Books with titles such as *Fatherless America* and *Life without Father* exploited the fear that a new morality was undermining the family.[39] The struggle focused on the rise of single-parent families and the fact that gays and lesbians were seeking to have their marriages recognized.[40] David Popenoe emerged as the leading defender of the new 'familialism'. Picking up where his eugenicist father had left off, Popenoe argued that what was needed was a 'lifelong, sexually exclusive, heterosexual, monogamous marriage, based on affection and companionship, in which there is a sharp division of labour (separate spheres) with the female as full-time housewife and the male as primary provider and ultimate authority'.[41]

The charge that black families were a tragic example of gender inversion was responded to by Louis Farrakhan's Nation of Islam Million Man March of 1995 which saw an army of African-American men converge on Washington, DC to pledge to be better fathers and husbands. Even many in the black community opposed to his conservative view of the family responded to the call. Two years after this unprecedented success, almost as many white male 'Promise Keepers' assembled on the Washington Mall. Composed overwhelmingly of Republican Protestants, they declared the number one problem facing society was 'sexual sin' which could only be conquered if men reasserted their power within the family.[42] The brain-child of a University of Colorado football coach, the Promise Keepers emerged out of the Christian evangelical churches.[43] These supporters of the religious right were morbidly preoccupied with sexuality. They presented themselves – living in an age of moral decline when adultery was epidemic and most men had enormous difficulty in controlling their hormones – as valiantly fighting for sexual purity. The sceptical detected a pornographic voyeurism in the sweaty delight with which the Promise Keepers lovingly dissected sexual sins. One observer likened the rapt attention which thousands of excited men gave to a Promise Keeper's explicit depiction of a virgin's wedding night to an 'evangelical gang bang'.

The *Roe* v. *Wade* decision of 1973 which recognized the constitutional right of abortion was the spark that led to the emergence of the Christian right. Opposition to abortion linked conservative Catholics and evangelicals.[44] Conservatives regarded it as a moral wrong, not as a symptom of general shifts in social attitudes and medical practices.[45] Their obvious targets were the working women who had 'failed' as mothers, yet right-wing women interpreted the 1973 decision as a sign of male irresponsibility. The ensuing struggle among women frequently pitted educated supporters of choice against pro-life housewives.[46] The Right to Life movement succeeded via the 1977 Hyde Amendment to cut federal funding of abortions. In Britain the Society for the Protection of Unborn Children exerted similar pressure. By the 1980s many American states were insisting on parental and spousal notification for abortions. In the 1990s pro-choice forces were winning the rhetorical battle, but the debate made little difference. Pro-life forces so physically intimidated physicians that 83 per cent of American counties did not have a single abortion provider. The pro-life and pro-choice forces were locked in a perversely sustaining symbiotic relationship which looked as though it would go on for decades. Both groups quickly realized that to mobilize supporters it

was useful to play up the threats posed by their opponents. Commentators noted that a victory for one side inevitably led to some waning
of vigilance by the winners and a re-dedication to the struggle by the
losers, but such references to the 'two sides' in the debate privileged
the power of the Christian right; the clear majority of Americans supported choice.

In Europe the situation was not much different. In June of 1995
when conservative Jacques Chirac was elected president of the Fifth
French Republic, his newly appointed prime minister took advantage
of the tradition of the giving of an amnesty for minor offences to
pardon the squads of violent anti-abortionist commandos who in the
previous year had stepped up their intimidating assaults on clinics
and hospitals. Although the leaders of such raids, including churchmen and former military officers, had repeatedly been tried and found
guilty of intimidating behaviour, the courts had never until 1995 given
them more than suspended sentences. Women's groups, supported
by trade unionists, the *Ligue des Droits de l'Homme* and *SOS-Racisme*
succeeded within a few days in exerting sufficient pressure both in
the streets and in the press to force the government to backtrack and
finally drop the idea of including the commandos in the proposed
amnesty.[47] The brief skirmish reminded many complacent onlookers
that French women's struggle for their reproductive freedom was far
from over.[48] Yet access to abortion in France was not as threatened as
in post-communist Poland or re-united Germany, and France, unlike
Canada and the United States, did not have 'right to life' zealots shooting doctors and bombing clinics.

The American commentator Pat Buchanan asserted that pro-choice
forces represented a scourge worse than that posed by the 'Evil Empire'
of communism.[49] Evangelist Jerry Falwell contrasted what he called
'God terms' (mother, childbirth) to 'devil terms' (lesbianism, communism, abortion). Accordingly, in the spring of 1996, each of the leading
Republican contenders for the party's presidential nomination asserted
that he was pro-life. It is difficult not to believe that such rhetoric
drove some on to violence. In the United States pro-life forces began
with the picketing and vandalism of offices and doctors' homes and
proceeded to the bombing of clinics. The murder of American doctors
and clinic receptionists by anti-abortionists in Massachusetts and Florida
was followed in November 1994 by the first shootings of Canadian
doctors.[50] The twenty-fifth anniversary of the *Roe* v. *Wade* decision in
January 1998 was marked by the bombing of an Alabama abortion
clinic resulting in yet another death.

Pro-choice activists had hopes that if abortions could be simply
carried out in a doctor's office the attacks on clinics and hospitals

would be ended. Such an option appeared to be offered by RU 486 or mifepristone – the French 'abortion pill' – which was first developed in the 1970s, widely used in Europe and China in the 1980s, and brought to the attention of North Americans in the 1990s. Since threats of boycotts prevented the drug's French manufacturer Roussel-Uclaf from distributing it in North America, the Clinton administration in 1994 prevailed upon the firm to relinquish its US rights to a non-governmental organization. Approval for use of the drug in the United States was given in 1996.[51] Yet pessimists concluded that, given the poisonous climate of opinion, even the impact of RU 486, which would largely eliminate the need for abortion clinics, might be minimal.

Feminism and Pornography

Abortion had been the great feminist victory of the 1970s. In the 1980s and 1990s the movement sought to make heard the voices of victims of abuse, of marital rape and wife-battering.[52] At the same time it called for new restrictions on male sexual behaviour. Its most telling revelation was that the home was a dangerous place for women. Previous generations of feminists had protested against the exploitation of prostitutes, women on the street; now the concern was increasingly with marital rape and wife-beating in the home. In Sweden marital rape was recognized as early as 1965; in Britain only in 1991. Progress was even slower in the United States, which went some way in explaining why women expressed so much glee in 1993 on hearing the news that John Bobbitt's wife had lopped off his penis.[53]

Feminist lobbying led to the reform of laws on rape, making it easier for victims to come forward. Rape and sexual assault rates appeared to rise; feminists argued that sexual violence was not, as the right suggested, necessarily increasing, but was now simply more likely to be reported. Previously, evidence of actual violence was required to prove rape; but with law reform a woman did not have to demonstrate physical resistance. American researchers, in popularizing the notion of 'date rape', went on to attack the myth that the sexual aggressor was always the 'stranger'.[54] North America also produced the vaguer concept of 'sexual harassment' which conservatives derided as 'political correctness' run amok. The 1991 trial of William Kennedy Smith proved that, despite such changes, convictions for sexual assault were still not easily obtained.[55]

Feminists were also in the late 1980s turning their attention to the seriousness of incest and child abuse.[56] Judges learnt to their discomfort that should they simply attribute a man's incestuous crime to his 'frigid' wife or seductive daughter, they were likely to be attacked in the press. Cases of the 'recovered memory' of 'survivors' of sexual abuse were more problematic. American talk-show hosts loved to play up the tales of women 'in recovery' and accounts of infants preyed on by satanic cults. In response, defenders of the 'false memory syndrome' used occasional high-profile cases based on unsubstantiated charges to debunk every report of child abuse as the product of feminist or psychotherapeutic suggestion.[57] Impossible to dismiss were the public revelations in the 1980s and 1990s of the boys who had been preyed on for years by paedophile priests in orphanages and schools from Newfoundland to Ireland.[58] Reports of sexual abuse which decades earlier would have been discounted out of hand were now followed up. The United States government passed the Federal Child Abuse Act in 1984.[59] States which refused to provide the expensive social services which would protect the health and well-being of children were only too willing to court popularity on the cheap by castigating sexual abusers.

Conservative politicians were also opposed to pornography. Feminists were divided on the subject. All agreed that the last decades of the twentieth century had witnessed a proliferation of sex shops and 'X'-rated films; the question was what to do about them. The approach of the feminist opponents of pornography who garnered most of the media's attention was spelled out in Robin Morgan's classic assertion: 'Pornography is the theory, and rape is the practice.'[60] This claim appeared to be substantiated when Linda Lovelace (Linda Marchiano) the star of *Deep Throat*, which when it first appeared had been hailed as a product of a more relaxed sexual environment, asserted in her autobiography that she had been abducted, tortured and exploited by a gang of pornographers.[61] Pornography, its opponents argued, was an instrument of male control which in eroticizing violence lied about and debased women. Sexually abused children ended up in the industry as exploited and passive actresses. The films they were forced to participate in goaded their viewers on to precipitate a further cycle of sexual violence. It appeared obvious that pornography had a desensitizing impact, and that it condoned or elicited violence; it was very difficult, however, actually to prove it. Nevertheless, those who advanced such arguments succeeded in having a 1985 Canadian Special Committee on Pornography and Prostitution recommend the criminalization of violent and sexually explicit material.[62] In the United States the 1986 Meese Commission report asserted that even non-violent pornography was harmful.[63]

The anti-pornography lobby consisted of strange bedfellows. In North America it included leaders of the Christian right and radical feminists. A number of the most vocal of the latter group took an increasingly pathological view of sexuality.[64] Adrienne Rich attacked gay men as the epitome of anonymous, promiscuous male sexuality. Andrea Dworkin asserted that sex was used by men to control women. For Catharine MacKinnon the representation of any subordination of women was pornographic.[65] In England Shelia Jeffreys, claiming that women who were drawn to S/M were motivated by self-hatred, went on to denigrate those dazzled by what she called the 'fetishes' of choice and freedom.

Moderates within the feminist camp were worried by the essentialism which appeared to permeate the anti-pornographers' arguments that women were inherently spiritual and men animalistic.[66] This smacked of the old notion of woman as victim, who necessarily had to be afraid of sexuality. Seeing how censorship could be turned against them, lesbians and social constructionist feminists opposed the criminalization of sexually explicit representations. Accordingly, in the 1980s, the so-called 'pornography wars' erupted with groups such as Feminists Against Censorship insisting that both the pleasures and dangers, the complexity and contradictions of sexuality had to debated.[67] They attacked the simplistic analyses of their opponents and their unconvincing data which purportedly proved the harmfulness of pornography. Serious research suggested that such linkages were difficult to make.[68] The best one could say was that pornography likely led to self-abuse, not necessarily to the abuse of others.

Moderate members of the women's movement protested that the feminist supporters of censorship seemed to think pornography was sexism rather than a product of a sexist society. A host of mainstream discourses produced representations of women that were just as debasing as those found in pornography yet no one called for them to be banned. Indeed, some pointed out that the female characters in porn films were far less likely to be represented as suffering than their counterparts in legitimate Hollywood films. And did pornography depict men in control? Almost every porn film climaxed with a depiction of the blow job, thereby pandering to men's curious insistence on seeing the 'money shot'. Feminist media critics concluded that such sad attempts to capture the 'truth' of pleasure spoke to men's insecurities, not their power.[69]

The anti-pornography faction, drawing its examples from marginalized hard-core porn, which represented a tiny percentage of the industry's output, called for laws, its critics noted, that would censor almost any portrayal of women. Gloria Steinem tried to distinguish between the erotic and the pornographic in order to distance feminists from the conservative defenders of censorship. Younger feminists, with a post-modernist interest in language, changing meanings and interpretation, asked why only the conservatives' reading of films and books should be accepted. Feminist artists and intellectuals – noting that fantasy was not to be confused with reality – warned against giving more power to state agencies. The more daring spoke of the need for alternative sexual images and some went on to defend female pornography which promised to problematize normality, depict powerful females, and subvert the male gaze.[70]

The common assumption was that pornography was gendered: that it was produced by men for other men, but in the 1990s women began producing it. Female agency was introduced as women, particularly lesbians, began to discuss sexuality directly in public. Those who produced their own explicit sexual representations pointed out that the same image would, depending on its audience, be viewed differently. Pat Califa, a self-proclaimed 'kinky dyke', poured ridicule on the moral panics over 'kiddie porn' and 'missing children' which she claimed were orchestrated for repressive purposes by the police and conservative feminists.[71] Such critics pointed out that dildos and leathers were produced by capitalism yet could be turned to subversive purposes. The classic example of such 'in your face' attempts to use pornography against sexism was the work of Annie Sprinkle, an ex-prostitute, who in her World Wide Web 'Public Cervix Announcements' pushed exhibitionism to the point of exposing her genitals.[72]

Youth

It is difficult to determine what impact the sexual ideologues had on youth. Adults, impressed by the butch or androgynous styles adopted by so many younger heterosexual women, had the impression that gender roles were being blurred. Similarly, the pony tails and earrings that were once the sole province of gays became common male accoutrements. But, like the fashions for body piercing and tattoos that mushroomed in the 1990s, such fads ceased to have much subversive resonance. Feminists lamented the fact that, despite their appeals to young women to be more independent, the traditional heterosexual romantic scripts still had immense power to shape desires. In particular, the 'beauty myth', which held that physical attractiveness was a women's chief capital, was as powerful as ever.[73] Several generations of North American girls had been brought up playing with the 'Barbie doll' which critics condemned as the icon of 1990s femininity – sexy but sexless, anorexic but driven by consumption.[74] Dieting was to the twentieth century what corseting had been to the nineteenth century. It was hardly surprising that some young women dreamt of aping the 'super models' – the real-life demonstrations of the triumph of the hyper-feminine – by turning to plastic surgery and body sculpting.

Conservatives were more disappointed than progressives by youth's imperviousness to moral injunctions. The Christian right, asserting that the sexual revolution was over, pushed abstinence programmes and tried to induce teens to take pledges of virginity. In fact, adolescents had sexual encounters at ever younger ages. In France, a 1984 poll revealed that by their late teens the majority of young people had had sex. Girls were said to be 'deflowered' and the boys '*déniaisé*' (taught a thing or two); 68 per cent of the boys and 50 per cent of girls had enjoyed the experience.[75] In the United States about half of women had sex before college, the percentage having increased in the 1970s and 1980s and then plateaued in the late 1980s at 60–70 per cent.[76] In Britain in the mid-1990s, seventeen was the average age of first intercourse. Parents generally acknowledged what was happening. Throughout most of the Western world the old disparities that once separated the timing and sexual practices of males and females, of the working and middle classes, were eroded.[77]

Why did youth have sex? Young people increasingly rejected the 'new morality' of the 1960s that had called for affection and permissiveness. Now in a world dominated by a fun culture and a private ethic it was permissible just to feel good. Sex was less furtive yet less idealized. Girls now phoned to ask boys out. Young women were no longer expected to postpone sex until they were married or even in steady relationships. Indeed, the British press played up the notion of English girls completing their education by going on 'bonking' vacations. It was not a question of if, but how well the sex act would be done. Accordingly, glossy girls' magazines were filled with stories of how to seduce men and have more orgasms.

Youths were less likely to declare themselves 'carried away' by sex, having more pragmatic concerns centred on careers and studies. First intercourse usually happened on the spur of the moment, sparked more by curiosity than romance. It was increasingly approached as a learning process.[78] Sex was used to garner self-esteem, pleasure, popularity and security. Boys candidly admitted to being simply 'curious' Girls tended to say that they did it because they were 'in love'. They too wanted the experience; if they said they were 'in love' it was because that was the term necessary to justify their having sex. Girls had an increasing number of sexual partners though still not as many as boys. A boy who was promiscuous was admiringly called a 'bit of a lad'; a girl who aped his behaviour still ran the danger of being labelled a slut, slag or tart.[79]

Love was not necessary to justify intimacy yet most young people sought steady relationships and commitments. One night stands were rare. Girls wanted affection. Madonna's popularity was interpreted by some as a manifestation of a form of safe sex – women could look sexy but did not have to deliver. The appeal of the late 1990s 'Girl Power' groups was purportedly due to their delivering a similar message. Surveys showed that, in fact, girls felt that they did have to deliver. Sex was used by them to prove themselves independent women, to rescue or shore up relationships. Foreplay often gave them the greater pleasure but they had to move on to penetration. They were far more likely than boys to be disappointed. 'It was awful and terrible', one recalled, 'I was trembling. Every time he saw me he wanted to have sex. I hated it, but I still did it – about five or six times.'[80] Girls saw themselves as seeking love and regarded the boys as wanting 'only sex', the 'Perfect 10' or the 'babe'.

The pill both allowed sexual freedom and hid the evidence of its being exercised, yet it tended not to be used by the young. First intercourse was often unprotected. An American study found that one-third of teens did not use birth control the first time and one-fifth never used it. A British survey published in 1994 revealed that 30 per cent of sexually active teenage women never used contraceptives.[81] Those who did mainly relied on the male condom and withdrawal. Many simply did not think of using contraceptives. Some were forgetful or drunk or afraid of spoiling the romance. Some just did not bother. That girls might now ponder the question of whether they should demand that the boy use a condom did demonstrate that some progress had been made. The popular magazines and medical literature said that girls should. AIDS activists popularized the slogan 'No glove, no love' (in Quebec 'Sans condom, c'est non!') and increasingly the condom was used, not to protect the woman from pregnancy, but both partners from disease. Yet many girls ran the risk of believing 'it' would not happen to them; they would be lucky. They confessed to being too embarrassed by the doctor or druggist to buy contraceptives and to thinking that to insist on them would cheapen the relationship, making sex appear too planned. Girls worried that their appearing to know too much about contraceptives would imply that they were tramps or that they suspected their partner of being promiscuous; by such a self-exploiting logic their *not* using protection was presented by them as a token of trust. The more stable the relationship the more regular the young woman's contraceptive use tended to be.

Some researchers gave credence to the notion of an 'epidemic' of teenage pregnancies in claiming that contraceptive use did not rise as fast as sexual activity.[82] The United States in the 1980s had on average one million illegitimate pregnancies and 400,000 abortions a year. By the age of eighteen 10 per cent of white and 25 per cent of black women were mothers. Four-tenths of white and nine-tenths of non-white births in the age cohort fifteen to nineteen years were to unmarried women.[83] Such unwed mothers were the ones most at risk in the community of entering lives of chronic poverty.[84] Investigators asserted that a solution would be a new contraceptive suitable for the 'sporadic and spontaneous' sex life of the average teen.[85] The Reagan administration, while bewailing adolescent motherhood, knowingly exaggerated the dangers of the pill in order to keep it out of the hands of the young. Nevertheless, from 1950 onwards the birth rate of fifteen- to nineteen-year-olds declined as did the overall rate of pregnancy which had peaked in 1957. Canada's teenage pregnancy rate was less than half that of the United States, but there, too, despite conservative lamentations about promiscuous youth, a dramatic decline took place between 1974 and 1992, the number dropping from 57,000 to 38,000.[86]

Unexpected and unwanted pregnancies still posed major problems. The conservatives who played up the idea of their nations being swamped by an 'epidemic' of teen pregnancies were the very ones most likely to oppose abortion. Who were having abortions? The majority were increasingly young, unmarried women. For example, in Canada in 1975 more than 31 per cent of patients had been married but in 1994 only 21 per cent.[87] Opponents of abortion, in trying to make young people ashamed of their sexuality, encouraged the very ignorance that most likely put them at risk of an unwanted pregnancy.[88] Studies revealed that the more positive the young were about their sexuality the more likely they were to use contraception. Investigators did not find evidence to substantiate the claim that easy access to abortion services undermined contraceptive use. A good percentage of young women were understandably ambivalent about terminating a pregnancy. They tended not to tell their parents but seek reassurance from girlfriends. In the end, the overwhelming majority – despite the gloomy warnings of moralists – were happy with their decision.[89]

The young woman who went through with her pregnancy and decided to raise her child on her own could then expect to be attacked by conservatives as a single parent. The purported immorality of single parenthood was brought to the attention of the American public in 1992 when vice-presidential candidate Daniel Quayle castigated the television character 'Murphy Brown'. Quayle's ineptitude quickly made him a figure of fun but conservatives would not abandon an issue that appeared to jeopardize the traditional family structure. The religious right went on to suggest 'bridefare' programmes under which those who married would be rewarded and those who did not would be penalized. President Clinton tried to play the role of moralist by including in his 1996 welfare bill provisions to encourage abstinence. The government promised it would pay twenty million dollars in annual bonuses to each of the five states that recorded the sharpest reductions in illegitimate births from 1999 to 2002.[90]

Coupling

Those entering the marriage market in the 1980s and 1990s had to contemplate talking to a sex partner about such issues as the use of condoms or the need to be HIV tested.[91] Claiming that AIDS proved the dangers of promiscuity, the media asserted that the last decades of the twentieth century would see a return to traditional values and a strengthening of marriage. It was a sign of the times when in 1985 a book entitled *How to Make Love to the Same Person for the Rest of your Life and Still Love It* became a best-seller in America.[92] Coupling, cocooning and romance were declared to be in vogue. It was difficult, however, to detect any sharp change in sexual practices. Rates of premarital sex continued to edge upward. In the 1950s a man who slept with a 'nice girl' was expected to follow the 'china shop morality': 'you break it, you buy it.' In the 1980s and 1990s casual sex for women found greater acceptance. Whereas it used to be the case that for 50 per cent of French women their first sexual partner would be the man they would marry, by the 1990s it was only true for 10 per cent.

Anal sex continued to be practised by only a small minority of heterosexuals. Oral sex, in part because of the fear of AIDS, increased in popularity among the young, preceding or even replacing vaginal penetration.[93] A French survey found that 50 per cent of women born between 1922 and 1936 tried fellatio, and 90 per cent of those born between 1960 and 1969.[94] A character in *Clerks*, a film supposedly reflecting youthful North American mores, argued that a girl who gave a blow job could still consider herself a virgin. The tabloid exposés of President Clinton's liaison with a young White House staffer reported that he took a similarly benign view of the practice. Its rising popularity (or reportage) was remarkable; in the 1950s Kinsey had found it being employed by only small numbers of the middle class. The law had not kept pace with changing mores; in the 1990s in many American states as well as in the District of Columbia oral sex was still a crime.

AIDS not only contributed to people's experimenting with non-penetrative forms of sex. Though marriage rates declined in the last decades of the twentieth century, French historian Michelle Perrot predicted that AIDS would reanimate notions of coupling and mono-gamy.[95] Numerous magazines, in exploiting the old notion of the plight of the spinster, appeared to attempt to stampede women into marriage. A 1986 *Newsweek* story, in attributing the lack of suitable male partners to the number of gays in New York, contained the famous line that a forty-year-old woman had a better chance of being killed by a terrorist than getting married.[96] The fall in marriage rates was not restricted to the United States. In France marriages peaked in 1972 (417,000) and declined through the 1980s to 1986 (266,000).[97] Sixty per cent of those who did marry first lived together. The percentage of couples in common-law relationships climbed from 6.2 per cent to 12.4 per cent between 1986 and 1996. French researchers noted that the more educated a woman was the less likely she was to marry. Christine Delphy, arguing that cohabitation required a lower emotional investment, concluded that such women recognized the inegalitarian nature of marriage.[98] Cohabitation increasingly included having chil-dren. The percentage of French babies born out of wedlock in France rose from 3 per cent in 1975 to 33 per cent in 1996.[99] In England and Wales 28 per cent of all births in 1990 were extra-marital.[100]

For many, cohabitation simply preceded marriage. The couple-oriented culture and the notion of romantic love that infused it were still extremely powerful and mystifying especially for young women. Sex was regarded as playing a central role in assuring marital harmony. The family was increasingly viewed as a fragile entity dependent on the sexual satisfaction of both partners and sex was positively evalu-ated by the public if it held the family together. Women once wanted orgasms; now counsellors and therapists were saying that they had to have them. For some couples sex became work. One Englishman confessed: 'There's a lot of pressure to be good – to make the woman come. If the woman makes the first move then the pressure is worse. You know, give her five orgasms or something. Thank God for oral sex, that's all I can say.'[101] The general public slowly accepted that simple penetration was not all that women needed. Pornography and experimentation were used to rejuvenate relationships.[102] Some regarded the turning of women to kinky sex and body piercing as perhaps the most striking phenomena of the 1990s. The ruminative began to wonder if there was anything entitled to be called 'authentic sex'.

Members of all sexual persuasions shared a belief in the democratization of sexuality that manifested itself in the conscious, calculated pursuit of shared orgasms.[103] The anxious turned to professional experts such as psychoanalysts and therapists for help. Social and gender inequalities and differences tended to be papered over by such experts. Those setting the norms revealed a lowered level of tolerance for the sexually dysfunctional. American investigators turned low sex drive into a disease, Inhibited Sexual Desire (ISD). The message of the therapists was that it was now all right to be a member of a sexual minority; what was essential was that one functioned efficiently.[104] Sexologists attempted to programme spontaneity, stressing the need to learn to masturbate so one could learn in turn how to be a good partner. At the other end of the spectrum sexologists produced the 'sexual addiction' syndrome, pathologizing the notion that there could never be enough sex. 'Addicts' were provided by the therapists with their own twelve-step recovery programme.[105]

Given that women's right to be sexual outside of marriage was still not achieved, one could not claim that the double standard had disappeared. When surveys were undertaken of how the French would protect themselves from AIDS, men said they would use a condom, women said they would be faithful to one partner.[106] In public, monogamy was still the norm, even if it was serial. Promiscuity was publicly condemned, though more by women than by men. Such moralism was especially strong in the United States. The French press discreetly ignored President Mitterrand's illegitimate child, but in 1988 Gary Hart had to end his campaign for the White House when the media exposed his extra-marital affair. Prudes were shocked in 1992, however, when Bill Clinton weathered a similar attack and went on to win the presidency. Those who believed that the rash of divorces and adulterous revelations that hit the British royal family in the 1990s would lead to its demise were similarly disappointed. The high level of divorce rates in the Western world was generally attributed to sexual problems, though experts cited a host of other issues, in particular financial worries. A cynical French observer simply attributed increased female adultery to the rise in the number of women having a second car. In the United States the number of divorces increased continuously hrough the 1960s and 1970s and then plateaued through the 1980s at just under 2.4 million per year, declining slightly in the 1990s. A similar trajectory was followed by the marriage rate.

Marriage meant constant use of contraception. French polls revealed that in the 1990s younger women took contraception for granted. They simply did not realize what a difference it had made to the lives of previous generations.[107] Family size at the beginning of this century varied inversely to class position – the upper classes having the smallest families and the lower the largest. There were also wide variations in family size. In the late nineteenth century families of four were as common as families of ten children. By the 1990s there was little variation; the vast majority of those who did have children had one or two. By the 1980s about 90 per cent of married couples in most Western countries were employing some means of contraception. A mid-1990s British survey of women's contraceptive practices found that 28.8 per cent used the pill, 25.9 per cent the condom, 23.6 per cent sterilization and 6.7 per cent the IUD.[108] The married, concerned by the increased incidences of cancer and blood clotting associated with the oral contraceptive, had shifted away from using it, but young women continued to find the effectiveness and convenience of the lower dose pill irresistible. A 1996 study, compiled from about 90 per cent of all the world-wide epidemiological research, concluded that birth control pills did not increase the long-term risk of breast cancer, but still noted concerns about their use by women who smoked, had high blood pressure or were diabetic.[109]

AIDS revived the use of condoms. To the annoyance of Queen Elizabeth, a Norwegian condom company ran an advertisement in 1995 consisting of a picture of Princess Diana dressed in white and the caption: 'It's hard to see on the outside whether someone has had casual sex with casual partners. It happens in the best of families. One can never be too careful.'[110] The protection which sheaths offered against transmission of the AIDS virus dramatically increased their popularity among the single.[111] Even a female condom was introduced to the North American market in 1988. Someone remarked at the time that the pill gave women the right to say yes to sex; AIDS gave them the right to say no. Researchers found that the use of the condom, as a means to protect oneself from disease as opposed to preventing pregnancy, increased. In the United States the percentage of women using birth control whose partners used condoms grew from 12 per cent in 1982 to 18 per cent in 1990.

New Reproductive Technologies

In 1978 the English researchers Drs Patrick Steptoe and Robert Edwards announced to the world that they had managed the birth of Elizabeth Brown, the first 'test-tube' baby. The demand for such reproductive technologies was fuelled at least in part by increased numbers of women in the last decades of the twentieth century putting off childbearing. Children tended, until the 1970s, to be born early in a marriage; by the 1990s they were being postponed. While the number of women having babies in their teens and twenties dropped, those in their thirties soared.[112] For example, the proportion of first births for Canadian women in their thirties increased from 18.5 per cent to 28.5 per cent between 1974 and 1992. Middle-class women increasingly postponed childbearing to complete their education and establish a career. Wanting more information about their pregnancies and fearing the birth of a disabled child, they naturally welcomed the new testing techniques offered by doctors. Those who found that they were infertile and chose not to adopt (which was made more difficult as the supply of babies was restricted by more teenage mothers either aborting or keeping their infants) turned to infertility clinics for assistance. By the mid-1980s it was becoming an accepted notion that even the unmarried woman might purposefully seek a conception to round out her life.

Western culture had long been preoccupied by infertility. In the 1930s English doctors castigated much childlessness as intentional and selfish, a cause of discord and divorce. Their first inclination was to blame the bad habits of men and the bad health of women. Doctors did recognize, however, that sterility was relatively common; flu and overwork could cause temporary sterility. Long-term problems could be caused by infections, mumps, and tube blockage due to abortion. Doctors read secondary sexual characteristics – voice, beard, muscles, penis, as well as assertiveness – as indicators of male potency and offered a range of rejuvenation therapies.[113] In 1939 Edward Griffith recommended artificial insemination using the husband's semen and a buffering solution.[114] A 1941 English text advised its readers on how couples could practice artificial insemination themselves by placing a semen-soaked wad of cotton in the woman's vagina.[115] A case of adultery in which a Canadian husband reported that his wife had been artificially inseminated came to light as early as 1921.[116]

The United States had a particularly high rate of infertility; between the 1920s and the 1950s over 20 per cent of white women under forty were childless. The rate was cut in half in the 1960s.[117] Ironically, medical scientists like Gregory Pincus and John Rock, though best known for their pioneering work on the oral contraceptive pill, began their research in the 1940s with the goal of employing hormones to cure infertility. The medical profession was publicly opposed to birth control through much of the twentieth century; in the 1990s its attitude towards embryonic research was more 'liberal' than the general public's. High-tech artificial reproduction was a medicalized process that served to demonstrate in the most dramatic fashion doctors' power of giving nature a helping hand.[118]

France had its first test-tube baby – *ces enfants qu'on fabrique* – in 1982.[119] Were women to be better off in this world of 'brave new babies'? Margaret Atwood in her 1985 novel *The Handmaid's Tale* thought not, and provided a bleak view of an advanced society in which women were reduced to the role of 'reproductive vessels'. Nevertheless, *in vitro* fertility clinics sprang up everywhere. They had low success rates and high prices. Their activities raised a host of issues concerning the ethics of carrying out research on, and later disposing of, surplus eggs and embryos. Did such clinics endanger the health of resulting children? Did they turn women into breeding machines? Feminists such as Toronto sociologist Margrit Eichler were concerned that, since the profit motive largely determined the research agenda, poor women were doomed to be exploited as 'surrogate mothers', while being themselves denied access to expensive fertility-enhancing procedures. They also worried that the new medical technologies were shifting the attention of doctors from the mother to the fetus as patient. In the 1980s and 1990s court orders were sought by governments and individuals to intervene on behalf of the fetus against the mother in everything from attempts to block abortions to charges filed against mothers for injuries suffered in the womb.[120] What such actions signified was the desire to abstract reproduction, to isolate the mother, suggesting that her fertility choices were not a product of her social, cultural and sexual needs.

The new reproductive technologies, like the old, had both their advantages and disadvantages.[121] It was a question of who would control them and to what ends they would be turned. Artificial insemination allowed lesbians to conceive without the direct involvement of men.[122] Women who devoted their twenties and thirties to careers, and then turned their minds to childbearing only to find themselves infertile, now had the option of seeking medical assistance. The media thrived on the conundrums posed by the new technologies: did a sixty-year-old woman have the 'right' to be pregnant; could a widow demand to be inseminated by her dead husband's sperm; should thousands of frozen embryos be allowed to perish because the law governing their use set limits on their storage? What most observers ignored was the racialized nature of a medical system that served mainly white, middle-class women and the fact that the search for the treatment of infertility was chiefly due to the rise and media manipulation of pronatalist sentiment, not to the much ballyhooed breakthroughs in technology.[123]

Conclusion

The successful cloning of a sheep in 1997 was heralded by many as a frightening portent of an increasingly homogenized world in which sex would no longer be necessary for human reproduction, a world in which everyone would look and act the same. Yet the approach of the millennium appeared also to be heralding a pluralistic age which offered a greater variety of sexual scripts, though clearly a few hegemonic ones. The panic over AIDS had been first seized upon by the moralists in the hope of forcing a 'return' to one rigid model of sexual behaviour. They asserted that the fate of the syndrome's victims served as a warning to others of what happened when the forces of pollution and contamination were let loose.[124] Such attempts to inculcate shame convinced few besides the already converted. Instead, the AIDS crisis and the 'safe-sex' message provided a context in which a variety of new sexual scenarios were explored. Among gays and lesbians there were some who sought to have their rights to marriage and children sanctioned by the state. Others attempted to work out long-term yet non-monogamous relationships free of the possessiveness of heterosexual coupling. And still others parodied or 'performed' straight sex, some lesbians even employing rubber phalluses that undercut the older feminist idea that penetration was a male-imposed desire.[125] For its part the heterosexual public revealed a growing curiosity about the lifestyles of queers, as popularized by commercial artists who appropriated and purveyed aspects of black, Latin and homosexual culture.[126] Non-penetrative sexual practices were increasingly employed by straights. Observers suggested that the growing popularity of common-law relationships, in which partners sought to be open about such issues as the domestic division of labour and sexual reciprocity, provided evidence of a search by heterosexuals for something like the assumed equality of gay couples. The media particularly attributed the appearance of the 'new man' – sensitive, anti-sexist, confused, cosmopolitan – to the influence of gays and feminists.[127] The cross-over in AIDS was thus paralleled by a cross-over of sexual scripts. The new *fin de siècle* was for the sexually adventurous the best of times and the worst of times.

Conclusion

In the late twentieth century everyone told sexual stories, even the conservatives who claimed in the same breath that there was too much talk about sex. In 1997 the *Wall Street Journal* protested the fact that American universities offered courses on the history of sexuality and then went on at length to describe what it called a 'Syllabus for Sickos'.[1] Careers could be made in crafting such indignant attacks on purported sexual laxity. In May of 1998 the American wire services noted that the woman responsible for improving Paula Jones's image (the secretary who had accused President Clinton of sexual harassment) was moving on to head a conservative women's group that was seeking to have other states adopt California's chemical-castration law for repeat child molesters.[2]

This study has analysed 'stories' told about sexuality by both conservatives and radicals, by both experts and ordinary men and women. Historians who have examined the history of sexuality in the twentieth century have also produced their 'stories'. The most common theme in the first accounts was of 'change' or progress. Given Western culture's premise that change is good, early investigators were prone to label any lack of movement in beliefs or behaviour as a 'lag'. When change appeared to take place rapidly, as in the 1960s, it was dubbed a 'revolution'; when it was impeded, as in the 1980s, it was construed as a 'backlash'. But what did one mean by such terms? How was change measured? Critics have asked if there actually were any significant shifts in sexual practices. After all, romance, monogamy, family and coupling were in the 1990s – as they were in the 1890s – still central to Western culture. Indeed, a larger percentage of the population than ever before was embracing such norms.

Perhaps the most popular current 'story' told of Western sexuality is that the main twentieth-century change has been the erosion of the class and gender differences that were so glaringly evident in

Victorian times. Michael Anderson argued a decade ago that a 'homogenization of experience' could be documented with the emergence of the modern life-cycle.[3] He noted that the enormous class differentials that once set off the marriage, fertility and mortality patterns of the upper and middle classes from those of the working classes had been gradually diminished. Evidence of a speeding up and standardization of life-course events was found across the Western world. Young people reached their age of sexual maturity earlier than ever before. Fewer young people postponed sex until after marriage. Once married most women (at least until the 1970s) completed their childbearing by the age of thirty, leaving more than half of their life ahead of them. There emerged in the twentieth century a 'right time' (usually earlier with each generation) to reach sexual maturity, to lose one's virginity, to marry, to have children. Age of menopause was, with an improving standard of living, postponed, thereby increasing women's fecund years, and the expectation grew that women like men would continue to be sexually active long after the age of fifty. National differences eroded along with class differences. The low birth rate of the French in the 1880s had been unique. By the 1980s there was little to choose between the fertility levels of the Western nations, be they Catholic or Protestant. And by the end of the twentieth century all Western nations relied on the same methods to control fertility – the pill and sterilization – whereas earlier there had been marked differences, the French and Italians relying up to the 1950s on coitus interruptus whereas the British, Germans and Americans had turned to condoms and diaphragms.

Perhaps the most striking example of this apparent homogenization of experience was the 1990s campaign waged by gays and lesbians to have the right to marry and to have children. Conservatives, disturbed by the notion that homosexuals might even discreetly exist on the margins of society, were outraged that purported sexual subversives should now seek to couple and raise offspring like the 'normal'. Such mainstreaming led some sociologists by the late 1990s to talk of the 'decline of the closet'. Steven Seidman's younger informants reported hardly knowing what the closet was. Since gay life now had a legitimacy in a large segment of both the straight and gay communities they felt no difficulty in being upfront about their sexual orientation.[4] It was a sign of the times that in June 1998 a group of academics held in New York City a 'Post-Gay' symposium devoted to the analysis of the movement of homosexuals beyond identity politics.

Liberal-minded heterosexuals congratulated themselves that gays were finally following the sexual pattern of monogamy and domesticity set by straights. Some, in contrast, argued that in many ways – as evidenced among heterosexuals by rising rates of oral, anal and other 'perverse' sexual acts, the idealization of egalitarian relationships, and the acceptance of the notion that a child is not necessary to cement a partnership – heterosexuals were following fashions set by the homosexual community. Sex, in the opinion of many, necessarily grew in importance in an age of high divorce and low fertility rates; it was increasingly all that was left to keep couples together.

The notion of gay parenting directs attention to the assertion made by many social commentators that what was 'modern' about twentieth-century sexuality was that sex and reproduction were split. In the Christian world, sex had been only permissible and acceptable if the intent was to procreate. So, for example, masturbation was viewed by some churchmen as worse than rape inasmuch as there was no chance that the former act could result in offspring. In modern culture, so the story goes, sexual pleasure was considered good in itself, and how and why it was obtained was of secondary consideration.[5] Accordingly, the psychiatrists, psychoanalysts, social workers, therapists and educators who presented themselves after the Second World War as the experts in such matters stressed the mental health aspects of sexuality. Sexual norms were increasingly determined by their purported influence on the individual's health and personal growth. One witnessed a progressive shift in how sexual practices were viewed. In the nineteenth century they were judged as a symptom of an individual's moral worth; at the turn of the century they were attributed to a person's biological drives; and in the late twentieth century they were interpreted as reflecting the individual's psychological make-up. Sexuality was increasingly viewed, not as good or bad depending on whether or not it resulted in procreation, but whether or not it served as a means of love and an expression of affection. Accordingly, it came to be argued that love legitimated a range of heretofore tabooed forms of sexual activity within marriage. This was followed by the legitimization of heterosexual acts prior to marriage. By the 1970s this relationship ethic resulted in a growing segment of the public's acceptance of healthy, same-sex relationships.[6]

Such an evolutionary scenario, though helpful, can be deceivingly unilinear and self-congratulatory. First, it can lead to a downplaying of the continued power of the sort of homophobia that underlay the 1993 defeat of President Clinton's attempt to legalize homosexuality in the United States Army. Fear of gays was even used to justify murder. Between 1993 and 1996 the 'homosexual-panic defence' was advanced by the accused in thirteen murder trials in New South Wales.[7] Ironically, the sexual panics focusing on the danger of the 'other' increased in the very century when the processes of modernization and globalization purportedly diminished class, gender and ethnic differences.

Secondly, the liberalizing, homogenizing thesis was based on the assumption that the same motives lay behind the same behaviour; that an action had the same meaning for different participants. Outward similarities all too often cloaked hidden differences. Gender differences have to be taken into account. An obvious expansion of 'coupling' occurred in the twentieth century. But what was a couple? Two individuals in an egalitarian or hierarchical relationship? The factors of race and class also could not be forgotten. Rich and poor, blacks and whites might all have had smaller families, but did they do so for the same reasons and did they have the same experiences? Racial discrimination, class differentiation, state manipulation and commercial exploitation all played crucial roles in shaping sexuality in the past, and all the indications are that they will continue to play such roles in the future.

It was also all too easy to ignore the fact that what standardization there was came at certain costs. Lifelong bachelorhood had a place in the nineteenth century. In the twentieth century, as marriage rates increased, unmarried men in their thirties could have their heterosexuality questioned. As sex experts vaunted performance in bed, married women who did not climax as readily as their spouses ran the risk of having doctors declare them 'frigid'. With the spread of contraception the majority with small families began to talk disparagingly of the minority with many children as 'breeding like rabbits'. With new norms of sexual performance established, the phrase 'sex as work' emerged. Since at least the time of Aldous Huxley's *Brave New World* (1932) warnings were raised against sex addiction or the banalization of passion, what André Béjin refers to as 'programmed spontaneity'. Graham Heath and Christopher Lasch, in noting that researchers, businessmen and sex reformers all directly benefited from changing standards, added their voices to those lamenting the emergence of a new sexual orthodoxy, with new pressures to conform to the 'unrestricted pursuit of sexual gratification'.[8] That men as well as women felt subjected to such forces explained in part the huge demand in America for Viagra, hailed in 1998 as the first pill to cure impotence. Some older men were now so convinced of the importance of penetrative sex that they filed suits to force insurance companies to pay for the drug on the grounds that an erection was a 'medical necessity'.[9]

The chief weakness of the homogenizing thesis, however, is that it shored up the belief, so popular and pervasive in Western culture, that sex now took place in a private realm – the bed being hailed as the one place at least where everyone was autonomous and equal. Cultural historians, aware of the insights offered by feminist scholarship, could not accept such a notion that social pressures and popular beliefs could be as easily shed as one's clothes. How could it be asserted that women, who were still so lacking in power outside the bedroom, had suddenly became the equals of men once within it? Women's right to be sexual outside marriage might have been proclaimed but the double standard still existed. There is little doubt that a new rhetoric of romantic love blossomed in the twentieth century; the question is whether it was as 'liberating' as is so often assumed or chiefly served to disguise and mystify existing disparities in power relationships. The idea that one had moved from the 'bad old days', when sexuality was restricted by demands made by family, religion, society and economy, to a modern culture in which desire was based on freedom and affection, fed into the tendency to assume some 'civilizing process' by which sexual liberalism had percolated through society with the final production of common enlightened values. The stories analysed in this account reveal that the reality was more complex.

What of the future? The Internet has been exploited by everyone from pornographers and paedophiles looking for trade, to infertility clinics trawling for egg donors, to the lonely and the hopeful seeking 'love bytes'.[10] Calls for censorship of the Internet reflect the general feeling that the traditional ways of managing and classifying sexual and reproductive practices by reference to 'nature' are increasingly difficult. Few celebrate the loss of the natural – some queer activists are the exception. Most people lament the notion that nature no longer provides a solid basis upon which the organization of sexuality can be built. Queer activism and the Christian right are opposite responses to the commonly felt experience of the loss of the natural, with queer activists wanting to celebrate post-natural sex and the right wanting to legislate into existence 'normal sex' – which, if it were natural, would not need the support of the law.[11] But this 'death of nature' theme is hardly new; it cropped up in almost all of the early twentieth-century debates reviewed in this study and will no doubt be carried on into the next millennium.

The starting premise of the study was that sex was not a natural act. It was continuously shaped and regulated. Stories played a key role in constructing sexuality in the twentieth century and one can be confident that in the twenty-first century Western culture will still not have finished with accounts of its panics and pleasures.

Notes

Introduction

1　See Ken Plummer, *Telling Sexual Stories: Power, Change and Social Worlds* (Routledge, London, 1995).

2　The term entered the English vocabulary via a 1892 translation of Richard von Krafft-Ebing; see Joseph Bristow, *Sexuality* (Routledge, London, 1996).

3　Ian Hacking, 'Making Up People', in *Reconstructing Individualism: Authority, Individuality and the Self in Western Thought*, eds T. C. Heller, Morton Sosna and David Wellbery (Stanford University Press, Stanford, 1986), pp. 222–36; Jeffrey Weeks, 'Questions of Identity', in *The Cultural Construction of Sexuality*, ed. Pat Caplan (Tavistock, New York, 1987), pp. 31–51.

4　Leonore Tiefer, *Sex is Not a Natural Act and Other Essays* (Westview Press, Boulder, Colo., 1995).

5　This study could be compared to the following three types of work. First, studies such as Carolyn J. Dean, *Sexuality and Modern Western Culture* (Twayne, New York, 1996) that particularly employ gender difference as a way of investigating sexuality. Secondly, studies that place sexuality in the social and political context of a particular nation-state, such as John d'Emilio and Estelle B. Freedman, *Intimate Matters: a History of Sexuality in America* (Harper and Row, New York, 1988); Gary Kinsman, *The Regulation of Desire: Sexuality in Canada* (Black Rose Press, Montreal, 1987); for Britain, Jeffrey Weeks, *Sex, Politics and Society: the Regulation of Sexuality since 1800* (Longman, London, 1981) and Lesley Hall, *Hidden Anxieties: Male Sexuality, 1900–1950* (Polity Press, Cambridge, 1995); for France, Antony Copley, *Sexual Moralities in France: New Ideas on the Family, Divorce and Homosexuality* (Routledge, London, 1989) and Mary Louise Roberts, *Civilization without Sexes: Reconstructing Gender in Postwar France, 1917–1927* (University of Chicago Press, Chicago, 1994). Thirdly, books that focus on the sexual sciences, including Paul Robinson, *The Modernization of Sex: Havelock Ellis, Alfred Kinsey, William Masters and Virginia Johnson* (Cornell University Press, Ithaca, 1989); Janice M.

Irvine, *Disorders of Desire: Sex and Gender in Modern American Sexology* (Temple University Press, Philadelphia, 1990); Lawrence Birken, *Consuming Desire: Sexual Science and the Emergence of a Culture of Abundance* (Cornell University Press, Ithaca, 1988); Vern Bullough, *Science in the Bedroom* (Basic Books, New York, 1994); Roy Porter and Lesley Hall, *The Facts of Life: the Creation of Sexual Knowledge in Britain, 1650–1950* (Yale University Press, New Haven, Conn., 1995).

6   Michel Foucault, *The History of Sexuality* (Allen Lane, London, 1979), vol. 1: *An Introduction.*

7   Margaret Sanger, *An Autobiography* (Norton, New York, 1938), p. 92.

8   See June Rose, *Marie Stopes and the Sexual Revolution* (Faber and Faber, London, 1992), pp. 76–8; Ellen Chesler, *Woman of Valor: Margaret Sanger and the Birth Control Movement in America* (Simon and Schuster, New York, 1992); James H. Jones, *Alfred C. Kinsey: a Public/Private Life* (Norton, New York, 1997), pp. 273–6.

9   Jean-Paul Sartre, *Nausea*, trans. Robert Baldick (Penguin, Harmondsworth, 1965), p. 61.

Chapter 1 'The Cult of the Clitoris': Sexual Panics and the First World War

1   John Russell Stephens, *The Censorship of English Dramas: 1824–1901* (Cambridge University Press, Cambridge, 1980), p. 112.

2   *Verbatim Report of the Trial of Noel Pemberton Billing, MP on a Charge of Criminal Libel Before Mr Justice Darling* (Vigilante Office, London, 1918); Michael Kettle, *Salome's Last Veil: the Libel Case of the Century* (Granada Publishing, London, 1977); Felix Cherniavsky, *The Salome Dancer: the Life and Times of Maud Allan* (McClelland and Stewart, Toronto, 1991).

3   Home Office 144/1498 364780.

4   Kettle, *Salome's Last Veil*, p. 114.

5   Ibid., p. 117; and for the argument that the trial was a laughable attack on the defenders of Wilde, see Claude Cahun, 'La "Salome" d'Oscar Wilde: le procès Billing et les 47,000 pervertis du "Livre Noir" ', *Mercure de France*, July 1918, pp. 69–78.

6   One symptom would be an old misogynist like Belfort Bax lamenting the decline of male clubs and complaining that now men were being forced to regard their wives as intellectual companions. Ernest Belfort Bax, *Reminiscences and Reflections of a Mid and Late Victorian* (Allen and Unwin, London, 1918), pp. 64–6, 174, 197–201.

7   Richard Wall and Jay Winter (eds), *The Upheaval of War: Family, Work and Welfare in Europe, 1914–1918* (Cambridge University Press, Cambridge, 1988).

8   Richard A. Voeltz, 'The Antidote to "Khaki Fever"? The Expansion of the British Girl Guides During the First World War', *Journal of Contemporary*

History, 27 (1992), pp. 627–38; Angela Woollacott, ' "Khaki Fever" and its Control: Gender, Class, Age and Sexual Morality on the British Homefront in the First World War', *Journal of Contemporary History*, 29 (1994), p. 332; Philippa Levine, ' "Walking the Streets in a Way No Decent Woman Should": Women Police in World War One', *Journal of Modern History*, 66 (1994), p. 45.

9   *History of the Great War*, (HMSO, London, 1921), vol. 2, p. 121; for similar findings for the Second World War, see J. W. Tice, 'Venereal Disease in the Royal Canadian Airforce', *Canadian Journal of Public Health*, 37 (1946), pp. 45–56.

10   Richard Bessel, *Germany after the First World War* (Clarendon Press, Oxford, 1993), p. 231.

11   Dr Magnus Hirschfeld, *The Sexual History of the World War* (Cadillac Publishing, New York, 1941), p. 38.

12   Marek Kohn, *Dope Girls: the Birth of the British Drug Underground* (Lawrence and Wishart, London, 1992).

13   Hirschfeld, *Sexual History of the World War*, p. 233.

14   Barbara Tchayykovsky, 'The Problem of Babies', *The Shield*, July 1915, p. 53.

15   Dr Paul Rabier, *La Loi du mâle à propos de l'enfant du barbare* (Vigot, Paris, 1915); Ruth Harris, 'The "Child of the Barbarian": Rape, Race and Nationalism in France during the First World War', *Past and Present*, 141 (1993), pp. 170–206.

16   James Morgan Read, *Atrocity Propaganda, 1914–1919* (Yale University Press, New Haven, 1941), pp. 214–15.

17   Jurgen Reulecke, 'Mannerbund versus the family: middle-class youth movements and the family in Germany in the period of the First World War', in *The Upheaval of War: Family, Work and Welfare in Europe, 1914–1918*, eds Richard Wall and Jay Winter (Cambridge University Press, Cambridge, 1988), pp. 443–4.

18   Michael C. C. Adams, *The Great Adventure: Male Desire and the Coming of World War One* (University of Indiana Press, Bloomington, 1990); George Mosse, *Fallen Soldiers: Reshaping the Memory of the World Wars* (Oxford University Press, New York, 1990), pp. 48, 165–66; Jay Winter, *Sites of Memory, Sites of Mourning: the Great War in European Cultural History* (Cambridge University Press, Cambridge, 1995).

19   Dr Paul Voivenel, 'A propos de Sacher-Masoch: les allemands et le marquis de Sade', *Progrès médical*, 17 February 1917, p. 6; Nicoletta F. Gullace, 'Sexual Violence and Family Honor: British Propaganda and International Law During the First World War', *American Historical Review*, 102 (1997), pp. 714–47.

20   Cate Haste, *Keep the Home Fires Burning: Propaganda in the First World War* (Allen Lane, London, 1977), pp. 84–6; John Horn and Alan Kramer, 'German "Atrocities" and Franco-German Opinion, 1914: the Evidence of German Soldiers' Diaries', *Journal of Modern History*, 66 (1994), pp. 1–33.

21 C. Courouve, 'L'Uranisme entre la France et l'Angleterre', in *André Gide et l'Angleterre*, ed. Patrick Collard (Birkbeck College, London, 1986), p. 101.

22 Andre Leri, *Shell Shock: Commotional and Emotional Aspects* (University of London Press, London, 1919), p. 118; Millais Culpin, *Psychoneuroses of War and Peace* (Cambridge University Press, Cambridge, 1920); Norman Fenton, *Shell Shock and its Aftermath* (Kimpton, London, 1926).

23 For the argument that new therapies, such as suggestion under hypnosis, would be the quickest way whereby the shell-shocked could be cured and sent back to the lines, see M. D. Eder, *War-Shock: the Psychoneuroses in War Psychology and Treatment* (Heinemann, London, 1917), pp. 128–33; see also Eric J. Leed, *No Man's Land: Combat and Identity in World War One* (Cambridge University Press, Cambridge, 1979), pp. 163ff.

24 The best known portrayals of anal eroticism occur in Erich Maria Remarque's 1928 classic *All Quiet on the Western Front*.

25 Klaus Theweleit, *Male Fantasies*, trans. Stephen Conway (Polity Press, Cambridge, 1987), vol. 1: *Women, Floods, Bodies, History*.

26 Hirschfeld, *Sexual History of the World War*, p. 134.

27 Ibid., p. 124.

28 E. E. Southard, *Shell-Shock and other Neuropsychiatric Problems* (Leonard, Boston, 1919), p. 257.

29 Lord Alfred Douglas, *The Rossiad* (Dawson, London, 1916), p. 15.

30 *Morning Post*, 6 June 1918.

31 Alain Corbin, *Women for Hire: Prostitution and Sexuality in France after 1850* (Harvard University Press, Cambridge, Mass., 1990).

32 Joanna Bourke, *Dismembering the Male: Men's Bodies, Britain and the Great War* (Reaktion Books, London, 1996), p. 161.

33 Richard Davenport Hines, *Sex, Death and Punishment: Attitudes to Sex and Sexuality in Britain since the Renaissance* (Collins, London, 1990), p. 228; see also Frank Mort, *Dangerous Sexualities: Medico-Moral Politics in England since 1830* (Routledge and Kegan Paul, London, 1987).

34 M. T. Connelly, *The Response to Prostitution in the Progressive Era* (University of North Carolina Press, Chapel Hill, 1980).

35 Allen M. Brandt, *No Magic Bullet: a Social History of Venereal Disease in the United States since 1880* (Oxford University Press, New York, 1985), pp. 52–96, 106; see also Jay Cassel, *The Secret Plague: Venereal Disease in Canada, 1836–1939* (Toronto University Press, Toronto, 1987).

36 Walter Heape, *Sex Antagonism* (Constable, London, 1913), pp. 3, 4.

37 Paul Gaultier, *Les Maladies sociales* (Hachette, Paris, 1913).

38 Angus McLaren and Arlene Tigar McLaren, *The Bedroom and the State: the Changing Practices and Politics of Contraception and Abortion in Canada, 1880–1997* (Oxford University Press, Toronto, 1997), p. 15.

39 James F. MacMillan, *Housewife or Harlot: the Place of Women in French Society, 1870–1940* (St Martin's Press, New York, 1981), p. 126.

40 Yet Radclyffe Hall, whose *The Well of Loneliness* (1928) was to be the first lesbian classic, looked back with fondness on the tumultuous war years.

41   Philippa Levine, 'Race, Sex and Colonial Soldiery in World War One', *Journal of Women's History*, 9 (1998), pp. 104–30.

42   John d'Emilio and Estelle B. Freedman, *Intimate Matters: a History of Sexuality in America* (Harper and Row, New York, 1988), p. 186.

43   *The New York Times*, 10 October 1909, part 3, p. 2.

44   Stephane Audoin-Rouzeau, *A travers leurs journaux: 14–18, les combattants des tranchées* (Armand Colin, Paris, 1986).

45   On the homoeroticism of the trenches, see Paul Fussell, *The Great War and Modern Memory* (Oxford University Press, New York, 1975).

46   Bessel, *Germany after the First World War*, p. 229.

47   Bourke, *Dismembering the Male*, p. 160.

48   *The Shield*, April 1914, p. 138.

49   Patricia Stubbs, *Women and Fiction: Feminism and the Novel, 1880–1920* (Barnes and Noble, New York, 1979), p. 55.

50   Laura Engelstein, *The Keys to Happiness: Sex, and the Search for Modernity in Fin-de-Siècle Russia* (Cornell University Press, Ithaca, 1992); Eric Naiman, *Sex in Public: the Incarnation of Early Soviet Ideology* (Princeton University Press, Princeton, NJ, 1997).

51   Fernand J. J. Merckx, *The Bolshevism of Sex: Femininity and Feminism* (Higher Thought Publishing, New York, 1921), pp. 148–93.

52   Raymond Radiguet, *Le Diable au corps* (Grasset, Paris, 1923); Mary Louise Roberts, *Civilization without Sexes: Reconstructing Gender in Postwar France, 1917–1927* (University of Chicago Press, Chicago, 1994), pp. 39–40.

53   Claudia Koonz, *Mothers in the Fatherland: Women, the Family and Nazi Politics* (St Martin's Press, New York, 1987), pp. 25–6.

54   *The Times*, 24 July 1920, p. 7; *Illustrated Police News*, 29 July 1920, p. 4.

55   Roberts, *Civilization without Sexes*, p. 138.

56   Patrick Fridenson (ed.), *1914–1918: L'Autre front* (Les Editions ouvrières, Paris, 1977); Margaret Higonnet et al. (eds), *Behind the Lines: Gender and the Two World Wars* (Yale University, New Haven, Conn., 1987); Françoise Thébaud, *La Femme au temps de la guerre de 14* (Stock, Paris, 1986).

57   Marie-Monique Huss, 'Pronatalism and the Popular Ideology of the Child in Wartime France: the Evidence of the Picture Postcard', in *The Upheaval of War: Family, Work and Welfare in Europe, 1914–1918*, eds Richard Wall and Jay Winter (Cambridge University Press, Cambridge, 1988), pp. 229–68.

58   Paul Weindling, *Health, Race and German Politics between National Unification and Nazism, 1870–1945* (Cambridge University Press, Cambridge, 1989).

59   Klaus Theweleit, *Male Fantasies*, trans. Stephen Conway (Polity Press, Cambridge, 1988), vol. 2: *Male Bodies: Psychoanalyzing the White Terror*.

60   Sandra M. Gilbert and Susan Gubar, *No Man's Land: the Place of the Woman Writer in the Twentieth Century*, vol. 2: *Sexchanges* (Yale University Press, New Haven, Conn., 1989), pp. 258–323; Bourke, *Dismembering the Male*.

61 Adrian Caesar, *Taking it Like a Man: Suffering, Sexuality and the War Poets: Brooke, Sassoon, Owen, Graves* (Manchester University Press, New York, 1993); Graham Dawson, *Soldier Heroes: British Adventure, Empire and the Imaginings of Masculinities* (Routledge, New York, 1994); Fussell, *The Great War and Modern Memory*; Eric Leeds, *No Man's Land: Combat and Identity in World War I* (Cambridge University Press, Cambridge, 1979); Modris Eckstein, *The Rites of Spring: the Great War and the Birth of the Modern Age* (Houghton-Mifflin, Boston, 1989).

62 Rosa Maria Bracco, *Merchants of Hope: British Middlebrow Writers and the First World War, 1919–1939* (Berg, Oxford, 1993); Gilbert and Gubar, *No Man's Land*, pp. 258–323.

63 Ekstein, *Rites of Spring*, p. 292.

64 Stephane Audoine-Rouzeau, *La Guerre des enfants, 1914–1918* (Armand Colin, Paris, 1993).

65 Bourke, *Dismembering the Male*.

66 See A. Maud Royden's introduction to *Downward Paths: an Inquiry into the Causes which Contribute to the Making of the Prostitute* (Bell, London, 1916); George Bernard Shaw, *Mrs Warren's Profession* (Constable, London, 1910), p. 196; Mrs Cecil Chesterton, *In Darkest London* (Stanley Paul, London, 1926).

67 Ruth Rosen, *Lost Sisterhood: Prostitution in America, 1900–1918* (Johns Hopkins University Press, Baltimore, MD, 1982), p. 134; David J. Langum, *Crossing the Line: Legislating Morality and the Mann Act* (Chicago University Press, Chicago, 1994).

68 Francis Champneys, 'Venereal Disease and Prophylaxis', *Nineteenth Century and After*, 82 (July–December 1917), p. 1051.

69 Royal Commission on Venereal Disease in the United Kingdom, *Parliamentary Papers*, 16 (1916).

70 The Venereal Disease Act of 1917 also prevented chemists from providing the diseased with assistance. Edward J. Bristow, *Vice and Vigilance: Purity Movements in Britain since 1700* (Gill and Martin, London, 1977), p. 149; Association for Moral and Social Hygiene, *The State and Sexual Morality* (Allen and Unwin, London, 1920), p. 58.

71 Bourke, *Dismembering the Male*, pp. 156–60.

72 H. R. Murray, 'Science and the White Slave', *Penny Illustrated Paper*, 20 August 1910, p. 269.

73 *The Times*, 23 July 1923, 11b; 4 August 1923 7b; 5 August 1923 7d.

74 Frank Mort, *Dangerous Sexualities: Medico-Moral Politics in England since 1830* (Routledge, London, 1987), pp. 151–88.

75 *The Times*, 5 June 1918.

76 Elisabeth Domansky, 'Militarization and Reproduction in World War One', in *Society, Culture and the State in Germany, 1870–1930*, ed. Geoff Eley (University of Michigan Press, Ann Arbor, 1996), pp. 427–63.

77 Elizabeth Fee, 'Sin versus Science: Venereal Disease in Baltimore in the Twentieth Century', *Journal of the History of Medicine and the Allied Sciences*, 43 (1988), pp. 141–64.

Chapter 2   'Hypersexual Youths':
Premarital Sex and the Sex Educators

1   Fritz Wittels, 'Sadistic Tendencies in Parents', in *The New Generation: the Intimate Problems of Modern Parents and Children*, eds V. F. Calverton and Samuel D. Calverton (Allen and Unwin, London, 1930), pp. 44–5.

2   Howard P. Chudacoff, *How Old Are You? Age Consciousness in American Culture* (Princeton University Press, Princeton, NJ, 1989).

3   Geoffrey Pearson, *Hooliganism: a History of Respectable Fears* (Macmillan, London, 1983); John Gillis, *A World of their own Making: Myth, Ritual and the Quest for Family Values* (Basic Books, New York, 1996).

4   F. Musgrove, *Youth and Social Order* (Routledge and Kegan Paul, London, 1964).

5   Thea Vigne, 'Parents and Children: 1890–1918', *Oral History*, 3 (1975), pp. 8–9; see also Thea Thompson, *Edwardian Childhoods* (Routledge and Kegan Paul, London, 1981).

6   Colin Campbell, *The Romantic Ethic and the Spirit of Modern Consumerism* (Blackwell, Oxford, 1987).

7   See E. H. Hare, 'Masturbatory Insanity: the History of an Idea', *The Journal of Mental Science*, 108 (1962), pp. 1–25; Jean Stengers and Anne van Eck, *Histoire d'une grande peur: la masturbation* (Éditions de l'Université de Bruxelles, Brussels, 1984); Freddy Mortier, Willem Colen and Frank Simon, 'Inner-Scientific Reconstructions in the Discourse on Masturbation (1760–1950)', *Paedagogica Historica*, 30: 3 (1994), pp. 817–48.

8   Leslie D. Weatherhead, *The Mastery of Sex* (Student Christian Movement Press, London, 1931), p. 124.

9   Emma F. Angell Drake, *What a Young Wife Ought to Know* (Briggs, Toronto, 1901), p. 239, cited in Michael Bliss, ' "Pure Books on Avoided Subjects": Pre-Freudian Sexual Ideas in Canada', *Historical Papers* (1970), p. 91.

10 Mary Scharlieb and F. Arthur Sibly, *Youth and Sex: Dangers and Safeguards for Girls and Boys* (Nelson, London, 1919), p. 74.

11 Ibid., p. 99.

12 George Orwell, 'Boys' Weeklies', *Horizon*, 1 (1940), pp. 174–200; Frank Richards, 'A Reply to George Orwell', *Horizon*, 1 (1940), pp. 346–56.

13 *The Boys' Own Annual*, 20 (1897–8), pp. 304, 320; see also pp. 112, 114, 192.

14 Sigmund Freud, *An Autobiographical Study*, trans. James Strachey (Hogarth Press, London, 1948), pp. 42–6; see also Hannah Decker, *Freud in Germany: Revolution and Reaction in Science, 1893–1907* (International Universities Press, New York, 1977), pp. 134ff.; Jeffrey Masson (ed.), *The Complete Letters of Sigmund Freud to Wilhelm Fliess, 1877–1904* (Harvard University Press, Cambridge, Mass., 1985), pp. 41, 43, 57–8, 61, 78–9.

15 James Paget, *Clinical Lectures and Essays* (Longman Green, London, 1875), pp. 268–92.

16 F. R. Sturgis, *Sexual Debility in Man* (Redman, London, 1901), p. 68.

17 Havelock Ellis, 'Perversion in Childhood and Adolescence', in *The New Generation*, eds Calverton and Calverton, p. 535.

18 Dr Caufeynon [Jean Fauconney], *L'Onanisme chez l'homme* (Charles Offenstadt, Paris, 1902), pp. 8, 9, 45, 107; Dr Jaf [Jean Fauconney], *Physiologie du vice* (Charles Offenstadt, Paris, 1904), pp. 8, 205.

19 W. F. Robie, *Rational Sex Ethics: a Physiological and Psychological Study of the Sex Lives of Normal Men and Women* (Richard G. Badger, Boston, 1916), pp. 247, 250.

20 Ibid., p. 47 (case XIX).

21 Ibid., p. 46 (case X).

22 Ibid., p. 36.

23 Ibid., p. 39 (case VII).

24 Ibid., p. 43 (case IX).

25 Ibid., pp. 265–7.

26 For attacks on Robie, see V. F. Calverton, *The Bankruptcy of Marriage* (John Hamilton, London, 1929), p. 156.

27 Robie, *Rational Sex Ethics*, pp. 257, 260.

28 Ibid., pp. 38–9 (case VI).

29 Ibid., p. 64 (case LXII).

30 Karen Dubinsky, *Improper Advances: Rape and Heterosexual Conflict in Ontario, 1880–1929* (University of Chicago Press, Chicago, 1993), p. 55.

31 Robie, *Rational Sex Ethics*, p. 40 (case VII).

32 Lesley Hall, 'Forbidden by God, Despised by Man: Masturbation, Medical Warnings, Moral Panic, and Manhood in Great Britain, 1850–1950', *Journal of the History of Sexuality*, 2 (1992), pp. 69–113.

33 Cyril Bibby, *Sex Education: a Guide for Parents, Teachers and Youth Leaders* (Macmillan, London, 1944), pp. 153–71.

34 Victoria de Grazia, *How Fascism Ruled Women: Italy, 1922–1945* (University of California Press, Berkeley, 1992), p. 57.

35 Maureen Sutton, *We Didn't Know Aught: a Study of Sexuality, Superstition and Death in Women's Lives in Lincolnshire during the 1930s, '40s and '50s* (Paul Watkins, Stanford, 1992), pp. 8, 9, 14, 15.

36 Derek S. Linton, *'Who Has the Youth, Has the Future': the Campaign to Save Young Workers in Imperial Germany* (Cambridge University Press, Cambridge, 1991); Harry Hendrick, *Images of Youth: Age, Class, and the Male Youth Problem, 1880–1920* (Clarendon Press, Oxford, 1990); J. Robert Wegs, *Growing Up Working Class: Continuity and Change among Viennese Youth, 1890–1938* (Penn State University Press, University Park, 1989).

37 Gail Bederman, *Manliness and Civilization: a Cultural History of Gender and Race in the United States, 1880–1917* (University of Chicago Press, Chicago, 1995), pp. 101–10.

38 Émile Pourésy, *La Gangrène pornographique* (Foyer Solidariste, Roubaix, 1908).

39 Annie Stora-Lamarre, *L'Enfer de la IIIe République: censeurs et porno-graphes 1881–1914* (Imago, Paris, 1990), p. 21; Heywood Broun and Margaret Leech, *Anthony Comstock: Roundsman of the Lord* (Albert and Boni, New York, 1927).

40 On the notion that pornography's enemies first saw it as posing religious and political dangers and that the question of its threat to 'decency' was a new nineteenth-century preoccupation, see Lynn Hunt (ed.), *The Invention of Pornography: Obscenity and the Origins of Modernity, 1500–1800* (Zone Books, New York, 1993).

41 Pourésy, *La Gangrène pornographique*, pp. 214–37.

42 Ibid., pp. 293, 419.

43 For Italy, see Gaetano Bonetta, *Corpo e nazione* (F. Angeli, Milan, 1990).

44 Leslie Brewer, *The Good News: Some Sidelights on the Strange Story of Sex Education* (Putnam, London, 1962).

45 On one occasion the senior Proust begged his son – then aged seventeen – to stop masturbating for at least four days. Their argument centred on Marcel's infatuation with a school chum and the father's beliefs about the connection between masturbation and degeneracy. Marcel Proust, *Correspondence avec Daniel Halévy* (Editions de Fallois, Paris, 1992), p. 43. I have to thank Michael Finn for this reference.

46 Paul Good, *Hygiène et morale: étude dédiée aux jeunes gens* (Aberlen, Paris, 1903 [first edn 1898]).

47 Scharlieb and Sibly, *Youth and Sex*, p. 8.

48 Ibid., p. 51.

49 Ibid., p. 60.

50 Ibid., p. 120.

51 Ibid., p. 123. Sibly cited Bernard Hollander, *Hypnotism and Suggestion* (Putnam, London, 1910) as a source of his inspiration.

52 Paula S. Fass, *The Damned and the Beautiful: American Youth in the 1920s* (Oxford University Press, New York, 1977).

53 John Gillis, *Youth and Society: Tradition and Change in European Age Relations, 1770–Present* (Academic Press, New York, 1974).

54 Harry Hendrick, *Images of Youth: Age, Class, and the Male Youth Problem, 1880–1920* (Clarendon Press, Oxford, 1990), p. 105.

55 Joseph F. Kett, *Rites of Passage: Adolescence in America, 1790 to the Present* (Basic Books, New York, 1977).

56 J. B. Keswick, *Woman: her Physical Culture* (L. N. Fowler, Scarborough, 1895), pp. 88–9.

57 Sutton, *We Didn't Know Aught*, pp. 17, 19, 29; Jane Farrell-Beck and Laura Klosterman Kidd, 'The Roles of Health Professionals in the Development and Dissemination of Women's Sanitary Products, 1880–1940', *Journal of the History of Medicine and Allied Sciences*, 51 (1996), pp. 325–52.

58 Auguste Forel, *The Sexual Question*, trans. C. F. Marshall (Medical Art Agency, New York, n.d. [first French edn 1905]), pp. 228–31.

59 Pierre Garnier, *Anomalies sexuelles: apparentes et cachées* (Garnier, Paris, 1889), pp. 490–502.

60   Kevin White, *The First Sexual Revolution: the Emergence of Male Hetero-sexuality in Modern America* (New York University Press, New York, 1993), p. 93.

61   White, *The First Sexual Revolution*, p. 65.

62   Rev. A. Herbert Gray, D. D., *Men, Women and God: a Discussion of Sex Questions from the Christian Point of View* (Student Christian Movement, London, 1924), pp. 106, 118.

63   Katherine Bement Davis, *Factors in the Sex Life of Twenty-two Hundred Women* (Harper and Brothers, New York, 1929), p. 247.

64   Bibby, *Sex Education*, p. 112.

65   Kathy Peiss, *Cheap Amusements: Working Women and Leisure in Turn of the Century New York* (Temple University Press, Philadelphia, 1986).

66   Derek Thompson, 'Courtship and Marriage in Preston between the Wars', *Oral History*, 3 (1975), p. 39.

67   Bruno Wanrooij, 'The American Model in the Moral Education of Fascist Italy', *Ricerche storiche*, 16 (1986), pp. 407–23.

68   Beth Bailey, *From Front Porch to Back Seat: Courtship in Twentieth Century America* (Johns Hopkins University Press, Baltimore, 1988); Karen Lystra, *Searching the Heart: Women, Men and Romantic Love in Nineteenth-Century America* (Oxford University Press, New York, 1989); Ellen K. Rothman, *Hands and Hearts: a History of Courtship in America* (Harvard University Press, Cambridge, Mass., 1987).

69   White, *The First Sexual Revolution*, p. 159.

70   Thomas Mann, 'Marriage in Transition', in *The Book of Marriage*, ed. Hermann Keyserling (Brace and Company, New York, 1926), p. 258.

71   White, *The First Sexual Revolution*, pp. 85, 93, 96.

72   Robie, *Rational Sex Ethics*, p. 57 (case LX).

73   Drs Jaf and Saldo, *Physiologie secrète de l'homme et de la femme* (Denans, Paris, 1908), p. 87.

74   *Illustrated Police News*, 12 January 1919, p. 7; 23 January 1919, p. 4; Marek Kohn, *Dope Girls: the Birth of the British Drug Underground* (Lawrence and Wishart, London, 1992).

75   Lea Jacobs, 'Censorship and the Fallen Woman Cycle', in *Home is Where the Heart Is: Studies in Melodrama and the Woman's Film*, ed. Christine Gledhill (British Film Institute, London, 1987), pp. 100–13. By 1934 the Catholic League of Decency succeeded in having Hollywood limit its portrayal of 'kept women'.

76   Lorine Pruette, 'The Flapper', in *The New Generation: the Intimate Problems of Modern Parents and Children*, eds V. F. Calverton and Samuel D. Calverton (Allen and Unwin, London, 1930), p. 589.

77   Mary Ware Dennett, 'Sex Enlightenment for Civilized Youth', in *Sex in Civilization*, eds V. F. Calverton and S. D. Schmalhausen (Allen and Unwin, London, 1929), p. 99; see also Sheila Jeffreys, *The Spinster and her Enemies: Feminism and Sexuality, 1880–1930* (Pandora, London, 1985). Dennett was an active defender of women's suffrage, the single tax, birth control and twilight sleep.

78 Phyllis Blanchard, 'Sex and the Adolescent Girl', in *Sex in Civilization*, eds Calverton and Schmalhausen, pp. 538–46.
79 Pruette, 'The Flapper', pp. 572–9.
80 Phyllis Blanchard and Carlyn Manasses, *New Girls for Old* (Macaulay, New York, 1930), cited in Pruette, 'The Flapper', p. 583.
81 A 1908 French study stated that few brides were completely ignorant, and warranted the sobriquet *demi-vierges*; Jaf and Saldo, *Physiologie secrète*, p. 104.
82 Pruette, 'The Flapper', pp. 583–7.
83 Dorothy Dunbar Bromley and Florence Haxton Britten, *Youth and Sex: a Study of 1300 College Students* (Harpers, New York, 1938), p. 136.
84 Carolyn Strange, *Toronto's Girl Problem: the Perils and Pleasures of the City, 1880–1930* (University of Toronto Press, Toronto, 1995), p. 205.
85 Meyrick Booth, *Youth and Sex: a Psychological Study* (Allen and Unwin, London, 1936), pp. 22, 24, 40.
86 Ibid., pp. 139, 145.
87 Ibid., pp. 170–1.
88 Ibid., p. 202.
89 Leslie D. Weatherhead, *The Mastery of Sex* (Student Christian Movement Press, London, 1931), p. 42.
90 Ibid., p. 19.
91 Ibid., p. 66.
92 Wegs, *Growing Up Working Class*, p. 118.
93 Dennett, 'Sex Enlightenment', p. 105.
94 Exner did attempt an early quantitative study, *Problems and Principles of Sex Education: a Study of 948 College Men* (Peck and Wells, New York, 1915).
95 Scott Nearing, 'The Child in the Soviet Union', in *The New Generation*, eds Calverton and Schmalhausen, pp. 232–43; see also Floyd Dell, *Love in the Machine Age* (Farrar and Rinehart, New York, 1930).
96 Margaret Mead, *Coming of Age in Samoa* (Morrow, New York, 1928).
97 Margaret Mead, 'Adolescence in Primitive and Modern Society', in *The New Generation*, eds Calverton and Schmalhausen, pp. 179–80.
98 Dr René Allendy, *L'Amour* (Noel, Paris, 1942), pp. 101–2; and see also Henri Fischer, *De l'education sexuelle* (Ollier-Henry, Paris, 1903).
99 Isabel Dingman, 'Your Teenage Daughter', *Chatelaine* (October, 1934), p. 63.
100 Rosa Mayreder, *A Survey of the Woman Problem*, trans. Herman Scheffauer (Heinemann, London, 1913).
101 Atina Grossman, *Reforming Sex: the German Movement for Birth Control and Abortion Reform, 1920–1950* (Oxford University Press, New York, 1995).
102 Linton, *'Who Has the Youth, Has the Future'*, pp. 30–1, 76–7.
103 Cornelie Usborne, *The Politics of the Body in Weimar Germany: Women's Reproductive Rights and Duties* (Macmillan, London, 1992), pp. 80–1.

104   Wegs, *Growing Up Working Class*, p. 133. For the views of the Soviet Union's best-known sex radical, see Alexandra Kollontai, *Love of the Worker Bees* (Virago, London, 1977).

105   George Ryley Scott, *Three Hundred Sex, Marriage and Birth Control Questions Answered* (T. Werner Laurie, London, 1941), p. 28.

106   Ross H. Dalby, C. F., *Young Manhood: a Brochure of Sex Information* (Duckworth, Blenheim, 1943).

107   Bibby, *Sex Education*, p. 99.

108   Martin S. Pernick, *The Black Stork: Eugenics and the Death of 'Defective' Babies in American Medicine and Motion Pictures since 1915* (Oxford University Press, New York, 1996), p. 135.

109   *Simplicissimus*, 2 September 1919.

110   Calverton, *The Bankruptcy of Marriage*.

111   Paula S. Fass, *The Damned and the Beautiful: American Youth in the 1920s* (Oxford University Press, New York, 1977), p. 77.

112   Edward F. Griffith, *Modern Marriage and Birth Control* (London, Gollancz, 1935), pp. 64–5.

113   John d'Emilio and Estelle B. Freedman, *Intimate Matters: a History of Sexuality in America* (Harper and Row, New York, 1988), p. 256.

114   Alfred C. Kinsey, Wardell B. Pomeroy, Clyde E. Martin and Paul H. Gebhard, *Sexual Behavior in the Human Female* (Saunders, Philadelphia, 1953), pp. 242, 268, 298–301. For the view that 'amateur promiscuity' was replacing prostitution, see Gladys Mary Hall, *Prostitution: a Survey and a Challenge* (Williams and Norgate, London, 1933), pp. 91–5.

115   Ginger Frost, *Promises Broken: Courtship, Class and Gender in Victorian England* (University Press of Virginia, Charlottesville, 1995).

116   Paul Thompson, *The Edwardians* (Weidenfeld and Nicolson, London, 1975), p. 71.

117   For an excellent discussion of the cultural, economic and social factors impacting on fertility control decisions, see Simon Szreter, *Fertility, Class and Gender in Britain, 1860–1940* (Cambridge University Press, Cambridge, 1996), pp. 382–440.

118   Kinsey et al., *Sexual Behavior in the Human Female*.

119   Dubinsky, *Improper Advances*, pp. 126–34.

120   Anna Davin, *Growing Up Poor: Home, School and Street in London, 1870–1914* (Rivers Oram Press, London, 1996), pp. 213–14.

121   Elizabeth Lunbeck, ' "A New Generation of Women": Progressive Psychiatrists and the Hypersexual Female', *Feminist Studies*, 13 (1987), pp. 513–39.

122   Ruth Alexander, *The Girl Problem: Female Sexual Delinquency in New York, 1900–1930* (Cornell University Press, Ithaca, 1995); Mary E. Odam, *Delinquent Daughters: Protecting and Policing Adolescent Female Sexuality in the United States, 1885–1920* (University of North Carolina Press, Chapel Hill, 1995).

123   Strange, *Toronto's Girl Problem*, p. 131.

124 Linda Mahood and Barbara Littlewood, 'The "Vicious" Girl and the "Street-Corner" Boy: Sexuality and the Gendered Delinquent in the Scottish Child-saving Movement, 1850–1940', *Journal of the History of Sexuality*, 4 (1994), pp. 549–77.

125 Linda Gordon, *Pitied but not Entitled: Single Mothers and the History of Welfare* (Free Press, New York, 1994).

126 Regina A. Kunzel, *Fallen Women: Problem Girls, Unmarried Mothers and the Professionalization of Social Work, 1890–1945* (Yale University Press, New Haven, Conn., 1993).

127 John Demos and Virginia Demos, 'Adolescence in Historical Perspective', *Journal of Marriage and the Family* (November 1969), pp. 632–8.

Chapter 3 'Selfish Beasts': Marriage Manuals and the Eroticization of Marriage

1 W. F. Robie, *Rational Sex Ethics* (Richard G. Badger, Boston, 1916), p. 90. He used the answers to a questionnaire as the basis for his riveting series of case histories. Robie's work was in turn cited approvingly by other sex reformers such as Marie Stopes.

2 Ibid., p. 106.

3 Ibid., p. 80 (case LXXIV).

4 Ibid., p. 167.

5 Ibid., p. 51 (case XXIV).

6 A twenty-six-year-old mother of two reported having four to five orgasms a week; ibid., p. 52 (case XXV).

7 Ibid., p. 156.

8 Ibid., p. 49 (case XIX).

9 Ibid., pp. 216, 220.

10 Ibid., p. 177.

11 Ibid., p. 15.

12 Thomas Mann, 'Marriage in Transition', in *The Book of Marriage*, ed. Hermann Keyerling (Brace and Company, New York, 1926), p. 258.

13 John Grand-Carteret, *Les Trois formes de l'union sexuelle à travers les ages: mariage, collage et chiennerie* (Mericourt, Paris, 1911); see also Maurice Boigey, *Sylvie ou la physiologie de la femme nouvelle* (Tallandier, Paris, 1933), p. 25.

14 Jean De Bonnefon, *Les Cas de conscience moderne* (Ambert, Paris, 1904), p. 34.

15 Richard Collier, *Masculinity, Law and the Family* (Routledge, London, 1995), p. 247.

16 Elizabeth Blackwell, *Essays in Medical Sociology* (Ernest Bell, London, 1902), pp. 256–93.

17 A. J. Cokkinis, *The Reproduction of Life* (Baillière, Tyndall and Cox, London, 1926), p. v.

18 Emma F. Angell Drake, *What a Young Wife Ought to Know* (Briggs, Toronto, 1901).

19 Paul Goy, *De la pureté rationale* (Maloine, Paris, 1921).

20 Margaret Sanger, *The Pivot of Civilization* (Brentano, New York, 1922), pp. 16–17.

21 Even Catholics were swept up by sexual enthusiasm; see Peter Gardella, *Innocent Ecstasy: How Christianity Gave America an Ethic of Sexual Pleasure* (Oxford University Press, New York, 1985).

22 In Italy until 1919 sharecroppers needed the permission of the landowner to marry. On the custom of trial marriages in Finland and Holland, see Georges Anquetil and Jane de Magny, *L'Amant légitime ou la bourgeoise libertine: code d'amour du XXe siècle basé sur l'égale liberté des deux époux* (Les éditions Georges Anquetil, Paris, 1923), pp. 97–8.

23 As *The Oxford English Dictionary* indicates, in the seventeenth and eighteenth centuries both men and women might be described as 'frigid'. In the twentieth century, sex experts and particularly the psychoanalysts restricted the term to women.

24 Drs Jaf and Saldo, *Physiologie secrète de l'homme et de la femme* (Denans, Paris, 1908), p. 104.

25 Anne-Marie Sohn, *Du Premier baiser à l'alcôve: la sexualité des Français au quotidien (1850–1950)* (Aubier, Paris, 1996), p. 224.

26 Karen Dubinsky, ' "The Pleasure is Exquisite but Violent": the Imaginary Geography of Niagara Falls in the Nineteenth Century', *Journal of Canadian Studies*, 29 (1994), pp. 67–9.

27 John Gillis, *For Better, For Worse: British Marriages, 1600 to the Present* (Oxford University Press, New York, 1985), pp. 189, 296–7.

28 Cited in Marie Stopes, *Marriage in my Time* (Rich and Cowan, London, 1935), p. 72.

29 Ruth Hall, *Passionate Crusader: the Life of Marie Stopes* (Harcourt Brace Jovanovich, New York, 1977).

30 June Rose, *Marie Stopes and the Sexual Revolution* (Faber and Faber, London, 1992), pp. 76–8.

31 Marie Stopes, *Enduring Passion* (McClelland and Stewart, Toronto, 1928). Some found Stopes's romanticism laughable; see Dora Russell, *The Tamarisk Tree* (Elek, London, 1975), p. 168.

32 Stopes, *Marriage in my Time*, p. 57.

33 Stopes, *Enduring Passion*, p. 11.

34 Marie Stopes, *Married Love* (Fifield, London, 1918), pp. 43–4; Stopes, *Marriage in my Time*, p. 64; Stopes, *Enduring Passion*, p. 90; Marie Stopes, *Radiant Motherhood: a Book for Those who are Creating the Future* (Putnam, London, 1920), p. 3.

35 Michael Gordon, 'From an Unfortunate Necessity to a Cult of Mutual Orgasm: Sex in American Marital Education Literature, 1830–1940', in *Studies in the Sociology of Sex*, ed. James M. Heslin (Appleton-Century-Crofts, New York, 1971), pp. 53–77.

36 Angus McLaren, *Reproductive Rituals: the Perception of Fertility in England from the Sixteenth Century to the Nineteenth Century* (Methuen, London, 1984), pp. 19–20.

37   Michel Bourgas, *Le Droit à l'amour pour la femme* (Vigot, Paris, 1919), p. 96.

38   Edward M. Brecher, *The Sex Researchers* (Panther, London, 1972), pp. 106–28.

39   Octave Uzanne noted that the Paris medical faculty, out of a modish fear of microbes, opposed kissing; Octave Uzanne, *Sottisier des moeurs* (Paul, Paris, 1911), p. 65.

40   On the enormous literature devoted to this subject, see Léon Blum, *Du Mariage* (Albin Michel, Paris, 1908); Ellen Key, *Love and Marriage* (Putnam, London, 1911); Havelock Ellis, *The Erotic Rights of Women and the Objects of Marriage* (Beaumont, London, 1918); Alfred H. Tyrer, *The New Sex, Marriage and Birth Control: a Guide Book to Sex Health and a Satisfactory Sex Life in Marriage* (Marriage Welfare Bureau, Toronto, 1943).

41   Ernest R. Groves, *The Marriage Crisis* (Longman Green, London, 1928), pp. 87–8.

42   Ute Frevert, *Women in German History: from Bourgeois Emancipation to Sexual Liberation* (Berg, Oxford, 1989), pp. 132, 134.

43   Carl N. Degler, 'What Ought to Be and What Was: Women's Sexuality in the Nineteenth Century', *American Historical Review*, 79 (1974), p. 1485.

44   Jeanne Deflou, *Le Sexualisme: critique de la préponderance et de la mentalité du sexe fort* (Jules Tallandier, Paris, 1906), p. 301.

45   J. B. Keswick, *Woman: her Physical Culture* (L. N. Fowler, Scarborough, 1895), vol. 1, pp. 87–8.

46   Lesley A. Hall, *Hidden Anxieties: Male Sexuality, 1900–1950* (Polity Press, Cambridge, 1991), p. 104.

47   Lesley A. Hall, 'Changing Perceptions of the Male Conjugal Role in Britain, 1850–1950', in *The Role of the State and Public Opinion in Sexual Attitudes and Demographic Behaviour*, ed. Ad van der Woude (CIDH, Paris, 1990), pp. 462–3.

48   Kenneth Walker, *Marriage: a Book for the Married and the About to be Married* (Secker and Warburg, London, 1951), p. 35.

49   On menstruation, see also George Ryley Scott, *Three Hundred Sex, Marriage and Birth Control Questions Answered* (T. Werner Laurie, London, 1941), p. 75.

50   William Kaye, *When Married Life Gets Dull* (C. Arthur Pearson, London, 1911), pp. 9, 67, 70.

51   Stopes, *Married Love*, p. xi.

52   Ettie Rout, *Safe Marriage: a Return to Sanity* (Heinemann, London, 1922), p. 2.

53   Stopes, *Radiant Motherhood*, p. 15.

54   Anquetil and de Magny, *L'Amant légitime*, p. 38. Anquetil even asserted in *La maîtresse légitime* (Vernet et Earin, Paris, 1923) that France's need for population was so great that polygamy should be legitimized.

55   Bourgas, *Le Droit à l'amour pour la femme*, pp. 109–10; see also Anquetil and de Magny, *L'Amant légitime*, p. 419; Mary Louise Roberts,

Civilization without Sexes: Reconstructing Gender in Postwar France, 1917–1927 (University of Chicago Press, Chicago, 1994), pp. 203–4.

56 Scott, *Three Hundred Sex, Marriage and Birth Control Questions*, p. 8.

57 Stopes, *Enduring Passion*, p. 85.

58 Ibid., p. 39.

59 Theodore van de Velde, *Ideal Marriage: its Physiology and Technique* (Random House, New York, 1957), p. 126; Eustace Chesser, *Love without Fear* (Arrow Books, London, 1966 [first edn 1941]), p. 71.

60 Chesser, *Love without Fear*, pp. 153, 155.

61 Ibid., p. 151.

62 Mary Lynn Stewart, ' "Science is Always Chaste": Sex Education and Sexual Initiation in France, 1880–1930s', *Journal of Contemporary History*, 32 (1997), pp. 381–94.

63 Stopes, *Married Love*, pp. 29–30.

64 B. O. Folwer, 'Prostitution within the Marriage Bond', *Arena*, 13 (1895), pp. 62, 65.

65 Bourgas, *Le Droit à l'amour pour la femme*, p. 98.

66 Van de Velde, *Ideal Marriage*, pp. 223–4.

67 Scott, *Three Hundred Sex, Marriage and Birth Control Questions*, p. 33.

68 Ibid., p. 31

69 Christina Simmons, 'Modern Sexuality and the Myth of Victorian Repression', in *Gender and American History since 1890*, ed. Barbara Melosh (Routledge, London, 1993), pp. 24–7.

70 H. W. Long, *Sane Sex and Sane Sex Living* (Eugenics Publishing Company, New York, 1919, 1937).

71 Keswick, *Woman: her Physical Culture*, vol. 2, p. 68.

72 Ibid., p. 99.

73 Stopes, *Enduring Passion*, p. 90.

74 Stopes, *Marriage in my Time*, p. 64.

75 Stopes, *Enduring Passion*, pp. 45–6.

76 Van de Velde, *Ideal Marriage*, p. 189.

77 Ibid., pp. 223–4.

78 Chesser, *Love without Fear*, p. 39.

79 Bourgas, *Le Droit à l'amour pour la femme*, p. 27.

80 Anquetil and de Magny, *L'Amant légitime*, p. 432.

81 Martine Segalen, *Amours et mariages de l'ancienne France* (Berger-Levrault, Paris, 1981).

82 Scott, *Three Hundred Sex, Marriage and Birth Control Questions*, pp. 76–7.

83 Robie, *Rational Sex Ethics*, p. 114.

84 Scott, *Three Hundred Sex, Marriage and Birth Control Questions*, p. 96.

85 Wilhelm Stekel, 'Frigidity in Mothers', in *The New Generation: the Intimate Problems of Modern Parents and Children*, eds V. F. Calverton and Samuel D. Calverton (Allen and Unwin, London, 1930), pp. 247–60.

86 Antony M. Ludovici, *The Choice of a Mate* (John Lane, London, 1935), pp. 464–5.

87 Ibid., pp. 23–33.

88 Ibid., p. 13.

89 By 1928 this series, which provided advice on a variety of subjects in addition to sexual matters, had 1,200 titles and sales of over 100 million; see Dale M. Herder, 'American Values and Popular Culture in the Twenties: the Little Blue Books', *Historical Papers* (1977), pp. 289–99.

90 Ruth Hall (ed.), *Dear Dr Stopes: Sex in the 1920s* (Penguin, Harmondsworth, 1981).

91 Letter from J. H. to Marie Stopes, 21 November 1934, Marie Stopes Papers, British Museum.

92 Letter from P. G. to Marie Stopes, 23 January 1926, Marie Stopes Papers, British Museum.

93 Yet few college-educated women as yet even knew the word 'orgasm'. See Katherine Bement Davis, *Factors in the Sex Life of Twenty-two Hundred Women* (Harper and Brothers, New York, 1929), p. 111; see also Edouard Brissaud, *Histoire des expressions populaires relatives à l'anatomie, à la physiologie et à la mode* (Mason, Paris, 1892), pp. 64–6, 70, 323.

94 Sohn, *Du Premier baiser à l'alcôve*, p. 84.

95 In France in the early twentieth century only prostitutes spoke of fellatio (*sucer*) and cunnilingus (*faire minette*); Sohn, *Du Premier baiser à l'alcôve*, pp. 30–1.

96 Gillis, *For Better, For Worse*, p. 300.

97 Sohn, *Du Premier baiser à l'alcôve*, p. 108.

98 Letter from I. A. to Marie Stopes, 22 November 1934, Marie Stopes Papers, British Museum.

99 Steven Mintz and Susan Kellogg, *Domestic Revolutions: a Social History of American Family Life* (Free Press, New York, 1988), p. 108.

100 Christopher Lasch, *Haven in a Heartless World: the Family Besieged* (Basic Books, New York, 1977), p. 11.

101 Chesser, *Love without Fear*, p. 11.

102 But the Kinsey data revealed that 80 per cent of American women born prior to 1900 reported achieving orgasm at least once; 86 per cent of the 1900–1909 cohort; 91 per cent of the 1909–1919 cohort; and 93 per cent of the 1920–29 cohort; cited in Degler, 'What Ought to Be', p. 1484.

103 Cited in Walker, *Marriage*, pp. 59, 65.

104 Janet Chance, cited in F. B. Rockstro, *A Plain Talk on Sex Difficulties* (British Sexological Society, London, 1943 [first edn 1934]), p. 55.

105 Walker, *Marriage*, p. 33. By the 1940s one author claimed that the prenuptial breaking of the hymen by the doctor was 'increasing in popularity'. It was useful if the bride dreaded the process or if she planned on employing birth control right away. Advice was given on how the woman could use olive oil and three fingers to deflower herself; Scott, *Three Hundred Sex, Marriage and Birth Control Questions*, p. 91.

106 Walker, *Marriage*, p. 37.

107 Gordon, 'From an Unfortunate Necessity', pp. 53–77.

Chapter 4   'Race Suicide': Birth Control, Abortion and Family Stability

1 W. F. Robie, *Rational Sex Ethics* (Richard G. Badger, Boston, 1916), p. 159.

2 The survey carried out by Dr Celia Duel Mosher (1863–1940) on forty-five women's sex lives at the turn of the century revealed that American middle-class women had access to a range of methods. Some did not employ contraception and some used several methods, the references suggesting that douching was the most popular (16) followed by withdrawal (10), condom (8), rhythm (6) and the cap (4); James Mahood and K. Wenburg, *The Mosher Survey* (Arno Press, New York, 1980).

3 Robie, *Rational Sex Ethics*, pp. 274–5.

4 Ibid., p. 169.

5 Ibid., pp. 213–14.

6 Dorothy Dunbar Bromley, *Birth Control: its Use and Misuse* (Harper, New York, 1934), p. 82.

7 Anton Nyström, *La Vie sexuelle et ses lois* (Vigot frères, Paris, 1910), pp. 229, 257.

8 Margaret Sanger, *An Autobiography* (Norton, New York, 1938); Ellen Chesler, *Woman of Valor: Margaret Sanger and the Birth Control Movement in America* (Simon and Schuster, New York, 1992).

9 Mary Ware Dennett, *Birth Control Laws: Shall We Keep Them, Change Them or Abolish Them?* (Hitchcock, New York, 1926).

10 Ellen Holtzman, 'The Pursuit of Married Love: Women's Attitudes Towards Sexuality and Marriage in Great Britain, 1918–1939', *Journal of Social History*, 16 (1982), pp. 39–52.

11 Marie Stopes, *The First Five Thousand, Being the First Report of the First Birth Control Clinic in the British Empire* (Bale and Danielsson, London, 1925).

12 For the argument that women after giving birth became 'complete' and actually enjoyed better health because of the life energy released during labour, see William Woods Smith, *A Baleful Popular Delusion on the Subject of Motherhood* (Simpkin, Marshall, Hamilton, Kent, London, 1895), pp. 3, 13.

13 Bromley, *Birth Control*, p. xiv.

14 M. R. Higonnet et al. (eds), *Behind the Lines: Gender and the Two World Wars* (Yale University Press, New Haven, Conn., 1987).

15 Havelock Ellis, *Studies in the Psychology of Sex* (Random, New York, 1936 [first edn 1906]), vol. 2, ch. 12.

16 Theodore H. van de Velde, *Ideal Marriage: its Physiology and Technique*, trans. Stella Browne (Random House, New York, 1926). Recent studies arguing that women were 'conscripted' into heterosexuality have curiously slighted the importance of the birth control advocates; see Margaret Jackson, 'Sexual Liberation or Social Control', *Women's Studies International Forum*, 6 (1983), pp. 1–18; Sheila Jeffreys, *The*

Spinster and her Enemies: Feminism and Sexuality, 1880–1930 (Pandora, London, 1985).

17 Margaret Jackson, 'Sexual Liberation or Social Control', pp. 1–18; Robert A. Nye, 'Sex Difference and Male Homosexuality in French Medical Discourse', *Bulletin of the History of Medicine*, 63 (1989), pp. 32–51.

18 Jane Lewis, *The Politics of Motherhood* (Croom Helm, London, 1980), pp. 96–8; Luc Boltanski, *Prime education et morale de classe* (Mouton, Paris, 1969), pp. 57–70.

19 V. A. Zelizer, *Pricing the Priceless Child: the Changing Social Value of Children* (Basic Books, New York, 1985), p. 90.

20 Maureen Sutton, *We Didn't Know Aught: a Study of Sexuality, Superstition and Death in Women's Lives in Lincolnshire During the 1930s, '40s and '50s* (Paul Watkins, Stanford, 1992), p. 53.

21 Marie Stopes, *Enduring Passion* (McClelland and Stewart, Toronto, 1928), p. 28. See also Elizabeth Roberts, 'Working Wives and their Families', in *Population and Society in Britain, 1850–1980*, ed. Theo Baker and Michael Drake (Batsford, London, 1982), pp. 154–55.

22 Linda Gordon, *Woman's Body, Woman's Right: a Social History of Birth Control in America* (Grossman, New York, 1976), p. 324.

23 Lesley A. Hall, ' "Somehow Very Distasteful": Doctors, Men, and Sexual Problems between the Wars', *Journal of Contemporary History*, 20 (1985), pp. 553–74.

24 Diana Gittens, *Fair Sex: Family Size and Structure, 1900–1939* (Hutchinson, London, 1982).

25 Margery Spring Rice, *Working-class Wives: their Health and Conditions* (Penguin, London, 1939).

26 Eduard Bernstein, 'Decline in the Birth-Rate, Nationality, and Civilization', in *Population and Birth Control*, eds Eden Paul and Cedar Paul (Critic and Guide, New York, 1917), p. 164.

27 The Woman's Cooperative Guild declared itself in support of birth control in 1923, and in 1924 a Worker's Birth Control Group was formed after the Labour Party resolved at its annual conference that welfare clinics should provide mothers with contraceptive information. Stopes was dismayed that most feminists avoided the issue through the 1920s. In North America as well only the Depression drove leaders of the woman's movement into open support of family limitation. Lewis, *The Politics of Motherhood*, pp. 197–8; Brian Harrison, *Prudent Revolutionaries: Portraits of Feminists between the Wars* (Clarendon, Oxford, 1987), pp. 63, 78, 110, 282.

28 On coughing, see George Ryley Scott, *Three Hundred Sex, Marriage and Birth Control Questions Answered* (T. Werner Laurie, London, 1941), p. 186.

29 Marie Stopes, *A Letter to Working Mothers* (Mothers' Clinic, London, 1923), p. 6.

30 Margaret Jarman Hagood, *Mothers of the South: Portraiture of White Tenant Farm Women* (University of North Carolina Press, Chapel Hill, 1939), p. 123.

31 Margaret Sanger, *Motherhood in Bondage* (Brentano, New York, 1928), p. 294. Coitus interruptus, several authors claimed, led to nervous breakdowns; see Bernarr MacFadden, *Womanhood and Marriage* (Macmillan, New York, 1922), pp. 147, 153; F. B. Rockstro, *A Plain Talk on Sex Difficulties* (British Sexological Society, London, 1943 [first edn 1934]), p. 78.

32 Marie Stopes, *Married Love* (Fifield, London, 1918), p. 71.

33 Marie Stopes, *Contraception (Birth Control): its Theory, History and Practice* (Bale, London, 1923), p. 70.

34 Sanger, *Motherhood in Bondage*, p. 302. Some American women wrote similar letters to the Children's Bureau in the mistaken belief that it would provide such information; see Molly Ladd-Taylor, *Raising a Baby the Government Way: Mother's Letters to the Chiedren's Bureau, 1915–1932* (Rutgers University Press, New Brunswick, NJ, 1986), pp. 62, 179–83.

35 Sanger, *An Autobiography*, p. 87.

36 Stopes, convinced that she knew more about contraception than any doctor, did not employ physicians but trained nurses and midwives to staff her clinic and was not as vigorous as Sanger in wooing the medical profession. Sanger had, moreover, to compete for leadership of the American birth control movement with Mary Ware Dennett who was opposed to the medical monopoly. American Birth Control League Papers, 110.2, Houghton Library, Harvard University.

37 Sanger, *Motherhood in Bondage*, pp. 294–7.

38 Enid Charles, *The Practice of Birth Control: an Analysis of the Birth Control Experiences of Nine Hundred Women* (William and Norgate, London, 1932), pp. 16, 36, 153.

39 For such assumptions in France, see Anne-Marie Sohn, *Chrysalides: femmes dans la vie privée (XIXe–XXe siècles)* (Publications de la Sorbonne, Paris, 1996), vol. 2, pp. 818–20.

40 Colin Dyer, *Population and Society in Twentieth-century France* (Hodder and Stoughton, London, 1978), pp. 63ff.

41 Karen Offen, 'Depopulation, Nationalism and Feminism in Fin-de-siècle France', *American Historical Review*, 89 (June 1984), pp. 649–51.

42 Mary Louise Roberts, *Civilization without Sexes: Reconstructing Gender in Postwar France, 1917–1927* (University of Chicago Press, Chicago, 1994), pp. 93–121; Françoise Thébaud, 'The Great War', in *A History of Women in the West*, ed. Françoise Thebaud (Cambridge, Mass., Belknap Press, 1994), vol. 5: *Toward a Cultural Identity in the Twentieth Century*, p. 51.

43 Siân Reynolds, *France between the Wars: Gender and Politics* (Routledge, London, 1996), pp. 18–20, 30; see also the special issue of *French Historical Studies*, 19, 3 (1996).

44 Hervé Le Bras, *Marianne et les lapins: l'obsession démographique* (Orban, Paris, 1991); Jay Winter and Michael Teitelbaum, *The Fear of Population Decline* (Academic Press, New York, 1985); Marie-Monique Huss, 'Pronatalism and the Popular Ideology of the Child in Wartime

France: the Evidence of the Picture Postcard', in *The Upheaval of War: Family, Work and Welfare in Europe, 1914–1918*, eds Richard Wall and J. M. Winter (Cambridge, Cambridge University Press, 1989), pp. 329–67.

45 Christane Demeulenaere-Douyère, *Paul Robin (1837–1912): un militant de la liberté et du bonheur* (Publisud, Paris, 1994).

46 Roger-Henri Guerrand et Françis Ronsin, *Le Sexe apprivoisé: Jeanne Humbert et la lutte pour la controle des naissances* (La Découverte, Paris, 1990).

47 Christine Bard (ed.), *Madeleine Pelletier: logique et infortunes d'un combat pour l'égalité* (Côtés-femmes, Paris, 1992); Charles Sowerine and Claude Maignien, *Madeleine Pelletier: une féministe dans l'arène politique* (Les Editions ouvrières, Paris, 1992).

48 William Schneider, *Quality and Quantity: the Quest for Biological Regeneration in Twentieth-century France* (Cambridge University Press, Cambridge, 1990).

49 On ordinary women's struggle to limit fertility, see Françoise Thébaud, *Quand nos grand-mères donnaient la vie: la maternité en France dans l'entre-deux-guerres* (Presses Universitaires de Lyon, Lyon, 1986). On French feminists' avoidance of the issue between the wars, see Christine Bard, *Les filles de Marianne: histoire des feminismes, 1914–1940* (Fayard, Paris, 1995), pp. 366–74.

50 Martine Sevegrand, 'Limiter les naissances: le cas de conscience des Catholiques français (1880–1939)', *XXe siècle: Revue historique*, 30 (1991), pp. 40–54 and 'La méthode Ogino et la morale catholique: une convenance théologique autour de la limitation des naissances (1930–1951)', *Histoire de l'Église de France*, 78 (1992), pp. 77–99.

51 Renée Rousseau, *Les femmes rouges: chronique des années Vermeersch* (Albin Michel, Paris, 1983).

52 F. W. Stella Browne, 'The Right to Abortion', in *Abortion*, eds F. W. Stella Browne, A. M. Ludovici and Harry Roberts (Allen and Unwin, London, 1935), p. 34.

53 Sanger, *Motherhood in Bondage*, p. 410.

54 Alice Jenkins, *Law for the Rich* (London, Skilton, 1960), p. 21.

55 Dr Paul Rabier, *La Loi du mâle à propos de l'enfant du barbare* (Vigot, Paris, 1915).

56 Guerrand and Ronsin, *Le Sex apprivoisé*, pp. 128–9; Sohn, *Chrysalides*, vol. 2, pp. 828–908.

57 Anne-Marie Sohn, *Du Premier baiser à l'alcôve: la sexualité des français au quotidien (1850–1950)* (Aubier, Paris, 1996), pp. 115–19.

58 J. Robert Wegs, *Growing Up Working Class: Continuity and Change among Viennese Youth, 1890–1938* (Pennsylvania State University Press, University Park, 1989), pp. 58–9.

59 Helmut Gruber, 'Sexuality in "Red Vienna": Socialist Party Conceptions and Programs and Working-class Life, 1920–1934', *International Labour and Working-class History*, 31 (1987), pp. 41–4, 57; Atina Grossman, *Reforming Sex: the German Movement for Birth Control and Abortion*

Reform (Oxford University Press, New York, 1995); Cornelie Usborne, *The Politics of the Body in Weimar Germany* (Macmillan, London, 1992).

60 James Woycke, *Birth Control in Germany, 1871–1933* (London, Routledge, 1988), pp. 68–76; Cornelie Usborne, 'Wise Women, Wise Men and Abortion in the Weimar Republic: Gender, Class and Medicine', in *Gender Relations in German History*, eds Lynn Abrams and Elizabeth Harvey (University College London Press, London, 1996), pp. 143ff.

61 Janet Campbell, *Maternal Mortality* (HMSO, London, 1924); *Protection of Motherhood* (HMSO, London, 1927); Barbara Brookes, *Abortion in England, 1900–1967* (Croom Helm, London, 1988), p. 43.

62 Edward F. Griffith, *Modern Marriage and Birth Control* (Gollancz, London, 1935), p. 180.

63 Madeleine Simms and Keith Hindell, *Abortion Law Reformed* (Owen, London, 1971), p. 67.

64 Bernarr MacFadden, *Manhood and Marriage* (Physical Culture Publishing Company, New York, 1916), p. 89; see also his *Womanhood and Marriage* (Physical Culture Publishing Company, New York, 1918), ch. 26.

65 *Canadian Medical Journal*, 29 (1933), p. 445.

66 Frederick J. Taussig, *Abortion: Spontaneous and Induced: Medical and Social Aspects* (Mosby, St Louis, 1936), p. 368.

67 Ellis, *Studies in the Psychology of Sex*, pp. 601–10; Madeleine Simms, 'Midwives and Abortion in the 1930s', *Midwife and Health Visitor*, 10 (1974), pp. 114–16; Nicky Leap and Billie Hunter, *The Midwife's Tale: an Oral History from Handywoman to Professional Midwife* (Scarlett Press, London, 1993), pp. 92–8.

68 Moya Woodside, 'Attitude of Women Abortionists', *The Howard Journal*, 11 (1963), pp. 93–112.

69 Leap and Hunter, *The Midwife's Tale*, p. 98.

70 Madeleine Kerr, *The People of Ship Street* (Routledge, London, 1958), pp. 137, 174.

71 Gruber, 'Sexuality in "Red Vienna"', pp. 37–68.

72 Bromley, *Birth Control: its Use and Misuse*, pp. 3–4.

73 F. W. Stella Browne, 'Women and Birth Control', in *Population and Birth Control*, eds Paul and Paul, p. 254.

74 Alice Jenkins, *Conscript Parenthood: the Problem of Secret Abortions* (Standring, London, 1940); Brookes, *Abortion in England, 1900–1967*, pp. 79–104.

75 John Keown, *Abortion, Doctors and the Law: Some Aspects of the Legal Regulation of Abortion in England from 1803 to 1982* (Cambridge University Press, Cambridge, 1988), pp. 49–108.

76 *Birth Control News*, August 1923, p. 4.

77 Stopes, *A Letter to Working Mothers*, pp. 5, 6, 8.

78 American Birth Control League Papers, 110.5, Houghton Library, Harvard University; Sanger, *An Autobiography*, pp. 88–92, 216, 285, 449; David M. Kennedy, *Birth Control in America: the Career of Margaret Sanger* (Yale University Press, New Haven, Conn., 1970), pp. 16–17.

79 *Birth Control News*, June 1926, p. 2; October 1923, p. 2; May 1924, p. 2; September 1925, p. 1; February 1927, p. 2; May 1928, p. 2.

80 Over three-quarters of the clients of both the US and UK clinics were already employing with a good deal of success the traditional methods of contraception: withdrawal, condom and douche. A study of 10,000 American case histories revealed that in only 4 per cent was the diaphragm used. The author noted that half of the women claimed never to have aborted; the other half reported having had on average two abortions each. Marie E. Kopp, *Birth Control in Practice: Analysis of Ten Thousand Case Histories of the Birth Control Clinical Research Bureau* (McBride, New York, 1934), pp. 55, 109–10, 121–6.

81 Steven Mintz and Susan Kellogg, *Domestic Revolutions: a Social History of American Family Life* (Free Press, New York, 1988), pp. 111–15.

82 R. A. Soloway, *Birth Control and the Population Question in England, 1877–1930* (University of North Carolina Press, Chapel Hill, 1982), p. 277. In the Depression Stopes did describe a simple contraceptive, an oil-soaked sponge; see Marie Stopes, *Preliminary Notes . . . from 10,000 Cases Attending the Pioneer Mothers' Clinic* (Mothers' Clinic for Constructive Birth Control, London, 1930), pp. 12–13.

83 Stopes, *Preliminary Notes*, pp. 20–21.

84 Lewis, *The Politics of Motherhood*, p. 126; Margarete Sandelowski, *Pain, Pleasure, and American Childbirth: from the Twilight Sleep to the Read Method, 1924–1960* (Greenwood Press, Westport, Conn., 1984).

85 Sir James Marchant (ed.), *Medical Views on Birth Control* (Hopkinson, London, 1926), pp. x, 63, 94–5.

86 F. H. Rodin to Anna Kennedy, 29 April 1923, American Birth Control League Papers, Houghton Library, Harvard University.

87 Jo Manton, *Elizabeth Garrett Anderson* (Methuen, London, 1965), p. 284.

88 Griffith, *Modern Marriage and Birth Control*, pp. 61, 79.

89 John Peel, 'Contraception and the Medical Profession', *Population Studies*, 18 (1964), p. 144.

90 The Schlesinger–Rockefeller Family Planning Oral History Project directed by James Reed and deposited at Radcliffe College provides a fascinating account of the development on the margins of respectable medicine from the 1930s onwards of a network of activists such as Alan Guttmacher, Alfred Kinsey, Robert Dickinson and Mary Calderone involved in maternal health, contraception, marriage counselling and sex research.

91 Brookes, *Abortion in England*, p. 2.

92 Robert H. to Marie Stopes, 1 July 1921; Winnifred R. to Marie Stopes, 20 March 1923; Mary W. to Marie Stopes 25 September 1924; A. C. M. to Marie Stopes, 19 January 1933; Stopes Papers, British Library.

93 Leo J. Latz, *The Rhythm of Sterility and Fertility in Women* (Latz Foundation, Chicago, 1932), pp. 60–1. On the rhythm method in France, see Martine Sevegrand, *Les enfants du Bon Dieu: les catholiques français et la procreation au XXe siècle* (Albin Michel, Paris, 1995).

94 For earlier defence of the rhythm method, see Drs Jaf and Saldo, *Physiologie secrète de l'homme et de la femme* (Denans, Paris, 1908).

95 Denyse Baillargeon, *Ménagères au temps de la crise* (Les éditions du remue-ménage, Montreal, 1991), pp. 106–7.

96 Angus McLaren and Arlene Tigar McLaren, *The Bedroom and the State: the Changing Practices and Politics of Contraception and Abortion in Canada, 1880–1997* (Oxford University Press, Toronto, 1997), pp. 116–20.

97 James Reed, *From Private Vice to Public Virtue: a History of the Birth Control Movement in America from 1830 to 1970* (Basic Books, New York, 1978), p. 121.

98 Enid Charles, *The Twilight of Parenthood* (Norton, New York, 1934); Joseph J. Spengler, *France Faces Depopulation* (Duke University Press, Durham, 1938); D. V. Glass, *The Struggle for Population* (Clarendon Press, Oxford, 1936), p. 87; Michael S. Teitelbaum and Jay M. Winter, *The Fear of Population Decline* (Academic Press, New York, 1985), pp. 45–62.

99 Lewis, *The Politics of Motherhood*, p. 199.

100 Nancy Cott, *The Grounding of Modern Feminism* (Basic Books, New York, 1987), p. 165.

101 E. Lewis-Faning, *Report of an Inquiry into Family Limitation and its Influence on Human Fertility during the Past Fifty Years* (HMSO, London, 1949), pp. 8–11; Gittens, *Fair Sex*, p. 162.

102 Ettie Rout, *Safe Marriage: a Return to Sanity* (Heinemann, London, 1922), p. 69.

103 Lesley A. Hall, *Hidden Anxieties: Male Sexuality, 1900–1950* (Polity Press, Cambridge, 1991), p. 92.

104 Griselda Rowntree and Rachel M. Pierce, 'Birth Control in Britain', *Population Studies*, 15 (1961), p. 128.

105 A classic depiction of the white-coated doctor lecturing her patient on the use of the diaphragm was provided in Mary McCarthy's novel *The Group* (Harcourt Brace, New York, 1954), pp. 66–9.

106 Margaret Sanger and Hannah M. Stone (eds), *The Practice of Contraception* (Baillière, London, 1931), pp. 17, 29. In her first pamphlet, *Family Limitation* (1914), written in her radical phase, Sanger had likewise provided recipes for simple astringent douches and cocoa butter pessaries and praised the sponge and condom. In her pursuit of medical legitimation, she later swung her support to the diaphragm.

107 McLaren and McLaren, *The Bedroom and the State*, pp. 92–115.

108 An uncritical account of his life is provided by Doone Williams and Greer Williams, *Every Child a Wanted Child: Clarence James Gamble, M.D. and his Work in the Birth Control Movement* (Countway Library, Boston, 1978); more useful is Reed, *From Private Vice*, pp. 225–77.

109 The new generation of plastic IUDs produced in the 1960s, though more effective than any other contraceptive, were ultimately found to produce similar sorts of infections.

110 V. F. Calverton, *The Bankruptcy of Marriage* (John Hamilton, London, 1929), pp. 128–36.

111 Bromley, *Birth Control: its Use and Misuse*, p. 111.

112 Reed, *From Private Vice*, p. 239.
113 Introduction to Bromley, *Birth Control: its Use and Misuse*, p. xiv.
114 Charles, *The Practice of Birth Control*, pp. 118–19.
115 In the United States 73 per cent of the married women polled approved; see Katherine Bement Davis, *Factors in the Sex Life of Twenty-two Hundred Women*, cited in Bromley, *Birth Control: its Use and Misuse*, pp. 32–3.
116 Mass Observation, *Britain and her Birth-Rate* (John Murray, London, 1945), p. 55.
117 Ibid., p. 58.
118 Ibid., p. 166.

Chapter 5   'Perverts': Mannish Women, Effeminate Men and the Sex Doctors

1 Jeffrey Weeks, 'Questions of Identity', in *The Cultural Construction of Sexuality*, ed. Pat Caplan (Tavistock, New York, 1987), pp. 31–51.
2 Ian Hacking, 'Making People Up', in *Reconstructing Individualism: Autonomy, Individuality and the Self in Western Thought*, eds T. C. Heller, Morton Sosna and David Wellbery (Stanford University Press, Stanford, 1986), p. 228.
3 Alexandre Lacassagne, *Vacher l'éventreur et les crimes sadiques* (Stock, Lyon, 1899), p. 276.
4 Angus McLaren, *The Trials of Masculinity: Policing Gender, 1880–1930* (University of Chicago Press, Chicago, 1997).
5 Pierre Vachet, *La Psychologie du vice. I: Les Travestis* (Editions Grasset, Paris, 1934), p. 30.
6 Ibid., p. 35.
7 Ibid., p. 18.
8 He began masturbating at the age of nine and the number '9' for some reason (Vachet thought possibly because of its shape) came to symbolize for him the male organ.
9 Martin Duberman, *About Time: Exploring the Gay Past* (Meridian, New York, 1991), p. 65.
10 Janice Irvine, *Disorders of Desire, Sex and Gender in Modern American Sexology* (Temple University Press, Philadelphia, 1990).
11 Dr Serge Paul, *Le Vice et l'amour* (Nouvelle librairie medicale, Paris, 1905), pp. 51, 55; see also Lawrence Birken, *Consuming Desire, Sexual Science and the Emergence of a Culture of Abundance, 1871–1914* (Cornell University Press, Ithaca, 1988), pp. 95–6.
12 George M. Beard, *Sexual Neurasthenia* (E. B. Treat, New York, 1884), pp. 106–7.
13 Charles Féré, *Pathologie des émotions* (Alcan, Paris, 1892), p. 434.
14 Ambroise Tardieu, *Etude médico-légale sur les attentats aux moeurs* (J. B. Baillière, Paris, 1858, 2nd edn), pp. 118, 145; see also Louis

Martineau, *Les Déformations vulvaires et anales produites par la masturbation, le saphisme, la défloration et la sodomie* (Vigot frères, Paris, 1905).

15   A. S. Taylor, *The Principles and Practices of Medical Jurisprudence* (J. A. Churchill, London, 1905), vol. 2, p. 368.

16   Benjamin Ball, *La Folie érotique* (Baillière, Paris, 1888), p. 102.

17   Georges Lanteri-Laura, *Lettres des perversions: histoire de leur appropriation médicale* (Masson, Paris, 1979); Robert A. Nye, 'The History of Sexuality in Context: National Sexological Traditions', *Science in Context*, 4 (1991), pp. 387–406; Vernon A. Rosario, *The Erotic Imagination: French Histories of Perversity* (Oxford University Press, New York, 1997).

18   Arnold Davidson, 'Sex and the Emergence of Sexuality', *Critical Inquiry*, 14 (1987), pp. 16–48.

19   Emile Laurent, *Fétichistes et érotomanes* (Vigot frères, Paris, 1903), p. 253.

20   Dr L. R. Dupuy, *The Strangest Voluptousness: the Taste for Lasciviousness* (Medical Library, Paris, 1920); Paul, *Le Vice et l'amour*.

21   Antony Copley, *Sexual Moralities in France, 1780–1980* (Routledge, London, 1989), p. 139.

22   Dr E. Gley, 'Les aberrations de l'instinct sexuel', *Revue philosophique*, 17 (1884), pp. 66–92.

23   Albert Moll, *Die konträre Sexualempfindung* (Fischer, Berlin, 1893).

24   G. Frank Lydston, *The Diseases of Society: the Vice and Crime Problem* (J. B. Lippincott, Philadelphia, 1904).

25   Ibid., p. 309.

26   Ibid., pp. 377–9. William Lea Howard, a Baltimore doctor, claimed to provide in *The Perverts* (Unwin, London, 1902) fictional accounts of sadists, alcoholics and deviants drawn from his own casebooks.

27   Auguste Forel, *La Question sexuelle* (Steinheil, Paris, 1911), p. 260.

28   Ibid., p. 277.

29   Ibid., p. 278; see also Copley, *Sexual Moralities in France*.

30   Jonathan Ned Katz, *The Invention of Heterosexuality* (Penguin, New York, 1995).

31   Forel, *La Question sexuelle*, pp. 273–4.

32   Edward Carpenter, *Intermediate Types among Primitive Folk* (George Allen, London, 1914).

33   A. S. Taylor, *The Principles and Practices of Medical Jurisprudence* (J. A. Churchill, London, 1905), vol. 2, pp. 319–20.

34   John C. Fout, 'Sexual Politics in Wilhelmine Germany: the Male Gender Crisis, Moral Purity, and Homophobia', in *Forbidden History: the State, Society, and the Regulation of Sexuality in Modern Europe*, ed. John Fout (University of Chicago Press, Chicago, 1992), pp. 259–92.

35   Magnus Hirschfeld, *Die Homosexualität des Mannes und des Weibes* (Marcus, Berlin, 1914); see also P. L. Ladame, 'Les Travaux récents des auteurs allemands sur l'homosexualité', *Les Archives de l'anthropologie criminelle*, 28 (1913), pp. 827–61; Charlotte Wolff, *Magnus Hirschfeld: a Portrait of a Pioneer in Sexology* (Quartet Books, London, 1986); Gert Hekma, '"A Female Soul in a Male Body": Sexual Inversion as

Gender Inversion in Nineteenth-century Sexology', in *Third Sex, Third Gender: Beyond Sexual Dimorphism in Culture and History*, ed. Gilbert Herdt (Zone Books, New York, 1994), pp. 213–40; James D. Steakly, 'Per scientiam ad justitiam: Magnus Hirschfeld and the Sexual Politics of Innate Homosexuality', in *Science and Homosexualities*, ed. Vernon A. Rosario (Routledge, New York, 1997), pp. 133–54.

36 The German sex reformers produced a number of 'sex enlightenment films', including Richard Oswald's *Different from the Others*, a sympathetic portrayal of homosexuality.

37 Magnus Hirschfeld, *Die Transvestiten* (Pulvermacher, Berlin, 1910); *Sexualpathologie, Ein Lehrbuch für Ärtze und Studierende* (2 vols, Marcus and E. Webers Verlag, Bonn, 1918); for an English version, see *Sexual Anomalies and Perversions*, ed. Norman Haire (Encyclopaedic Press, London, 1938).

38 See Iwan Bloch *The Sexual Life of our Time* (Allied Book Company, New York, 1930).

39 Arthur Calder-Marshall, *Havelock Ellis* (Rupert Hart Davis, London, 1959); Paul Robinson, *The Modernization of Sex* (Harper and Row, New York, 1976), pp. 42–119; Phyllis Grosskurth, *Havelock Ellis: a Biography* (McClelland and Stewart, Toronto, 1980). Rémy de Gourmount, who advanced a similarly progressive message, had Ellis's work translated into French.

40 See also S. Herbert, *Fundamentals in Sexual Ethics* (Black, London, 1920), p. 135.

41 Havelock Ellis, *Studies in the Psychology of Sex* (Random House, New York, 1936).

42 Albert von Schrenck-Notzing, 'Un cas d'inversion sexuelle amélioré par la suggestion hypnotique', *Premier congrès international de l'hypnotisme expérimental et thérapeutique: comptes-rendus* (Doin, Paris, 1889), pp. 319–23.

43 Forel, *La Question sexuelle*, p. 245.

44 Geraldine M. Scanlon, *La Polemica feminista en la España contemporanea (1868–1974)* (Siglo XXI, Madrid, 1976), pp. 182–8; Gregorio Marañon, *The Climacteric* (Kimpton, London, 1929); Gregorio Marañon, *The Evolution of Sex* (Allen and Unwin, London, 1932).

45 Dr Angelo Hesnard, repeating the crude Freudian notion that homosexuals were effeminate neurotics who suffered from being too close to their mothers, also claimed that in the literary world of 1930s Paris a parading of homosexuality had a certain snob appeal; Dr Angelo Hesnard, *Traité de sexologie normale et pathologique* (Payot, Paris, 1933), p. 638.

46 See Vachet's translation and adaptation of Magnus Hirschfeld, *Perversions sexuelles* (Aldor, Paris, 1931). Vachet, despite being hailed by his editor as 'Le Freud français', opposed too great a stress on early conditioning theory and held that as siblings were often of the same disposition homosexuality was likely to be innate, and possibly hereditary. Therapy accordingly had little chance of success.

47 Vachet, *Les Travestis*, p. 23.

48 George Chauncey, *Gay New York: Gender, Urban Culture and the Making of the Gay Male World 1890–1940* (Basic Books, New York, 1994); Paul Reboux, *Le Nouveau savoir-aimer* (Flammarion, Paris, 1938), pp. 113–23; Christopher Isherwood, *Christopher and his Kind, 1929–1938* (Farrar, Strauss and Giroux, New York, 1976).

49 Jeffrey Weeks, *Sex, Politics and Society: the Regulation of Sexuality since 1800* (Longman, London, 1981).

50 Ed Cohen, *Talk on the Wilde Side: Toward a Genealogy of a Discourse on Male Sexualities* (Routledge, London, 1993), p. 144; Alan Sinfield, *The Wilde Century: Effeminacy, Oscar Wilde and the Queer Movement* (Cassell, London, 1994), pp. 104–18.

51 Anomaly, *The Invert and his Social Adjustment* (Baillière, Tindall and Cox, London, 1927), p. xii.

52 Copley, *Sexual Moralities in France*, pp. 155–80.

53 Martha Hanna, 'Natalism, Homosexuality, and the Controversy over *Corydon*', in *Homosexuality in Modern France*, eds Jeffrey Merrick and Bryant T. Ragan (Oxford University Press, New York, 1996), pp. 202–24.

54 On the notion that Gide wanted to talk about a 'pederast with a pedigree', see Lawrence Schehr, *The Shock of Men: Homosexual Hermeneutics in French Writing* (Stanford University Press, Stanford, 1995), pp. 7–11; Michael Lucey, *Gide's Bent: Sexuality, Politics, Writing* (Oxford University Press, New York, 1995), pp. 68–94.

55 Terry Castle, *Noël Coward and Radclyffe Hall: Kindred Spirits* (Columbia University Press, New York, 1996), pp. 14, 27, 31.

56 Michael Baker, *Our Three Selves: a Life of Radclyffe Hall* (Hamish Hamilton, London, 1985).

57 Nordau cited in L. Roubinovitch, *Hystérie mâle et dégénérescence* (n.p., Paris, 1890), pp. 21–2.

58 Emile Laurent, *Sadisme et masochisme* (Vigot frères, Paris, 1903), p. 256.

59 Dimitry Stefanowsky, 'Le Passivisme', *Archives de l'anthropologie criminelle*, 7 (1892), pp. 294–8.

60 S. Herbert, *Fundamentals in Sexual Ethics* (Black, London, 1920), p. 56.

61 Charles Féré, *Pathologie des émotions* (Alcan, Paris, 1892), pp. 479–80.

62 Lisa J. Lindquist, 'Images of Alice: Gender, Deviancy, and a Love Murder in Memphis', *Journal of the History of Sexuality*, 6 (1995), pp. 30–61.

63 Historians are divided on the question of whether or not only those women who had sex with other women should be called lesbians; see Lillian Faderman, *Surpassing the Love of Men* (The Women's Press, London, 1985).

64 Michael Kettle, *Salome's Last Veil: the Libel Case of the Century* (Granada Publishing, London, 1977), p. 119.

65 Julian Chevalier, *L'Inversion sexuelle* (Storck, Lyon, 1893), p. 232.

66 Jean-Pierre Jacques, *Les Malheurs de Sapho* (Grasset, Paris, 1981), p. 210.

67 Rosemary Auchmuty, 'You're a Dyke, Angela! Elsie J. Oxenham and the Rise and Fall of the Schoolgirl Story', in *Not a Passing Phase:*

Reclaiming Lesbians in History, 1840–1985 (Woman's Press, London, 1989), pp. 119–40.

68 W. F. Robie, *Rational Sex Ethics* (Richard, G. Badger, Boston, 1916), pp. 53–4 (case XXXII).

69 Ibid., p. 58 (case LX).

70 Ibid., p. 61 (case LX).

71 Forel, *La Question sexuelle*, pp. 98–100.

72 Hana, 'Natalism, Homosexuality, and the Controversy over *Corydon*', p. 219. See also the statement that lesbianism was understandable 'in view of present-day conditions, where the surplus of women, and our marriage laws and customs, make it impossible for very large numbers of women to find their natural biological fulfilment'; Laura Hutton, *The Single Woman and her Emotional Problems* (Baillière, Tindall and Cox, London, 1935), p. 104.

73 Carole Groneman, 'Nymphomania: the Historical Construction of Female Sexuality', *Signs*, 19 (1994), pp. 353–7; Lillian Faderman, *Odd Girls and Twilight Lovers: a History of Lesbian Life in Twentieth-century America* (Columbia University Press, New York, 1991).

74 Margaret Gibson, 'Clitoral Corruption: Body Metaphors and American Doctors' Constructions of Female Homosexuality, 1870–1900', in *Science and Homosexualities*, ed. Vernon A. Rosario (Routledge, New York, 1997), pp. 108–32.

75 Emily Wortis Leider, *Becoming Mae West* (Farrar, Strauss and Giroux, New York, 1997), pp. 156–71.

76 Marie Stopes, *Enduring Passion* (McClelland and Stewart, Toronto, 1928), pp. 42–4.

77 Ibid., p. 43. Yet before her marriage Stopes had a brief, passionate relationship with the Canadian doctor, Helen MacMurchy; see their 1909 correspondence in the Stopes Papers, British Library.

78 Stella Browne, *Sexual Variety and Variability among Women* (Beaumont, London, 1915), p. 11; see also Lesley A. Hall, '"I Have Never Met the Normal Woman": Stella Browne and the Politics of Womanhood', *Women's History Review*, 6 (1997), pp. 157–82.

79 Margaret Jackson, *The 'Real' Facts of Life: Feminism and the Politics of Sexuality c.1850–1940* (Taylor and Francis, London, 1994), p. 116.

80 Radclyffe Hall, *The Well of Loneliness* (Virago, London, 1996 [first edn 1928]), p. 207.

81 Dr Laupts, *Perversion and perversités sexuelles* (Carre, Paris, 1896), p. 324.

82 Edward Carpenter, *Love's Coming of Age* (Unwin, London, 1896), p. 68.

83 Vera Brittain, *Radclyffe Hall: a Case of Obscenity?* (Femina, London, 1968), pp. 58–62.

84 Hall, *The Well of Loneliness*, p. 316.

85 Leslie D. Weatherhead, *The Mastery of Sex* (Student Christian Movement Press, London, 1931), p. 201.

86 W. Béran Wolfe cited in Erin G. Carlston, 'Female Homosexuality and the American Medical Community', in *Science and Homosexualities*, ed. Vernon A. Rosario (Routledge, New York, 1997), p. 187.

87 Emily Hamer, *Britannia's Glory: a History of Twentieth-century Lesbians* (Cassell, London, 1996), pp. 15–27, 104–6.

88 Catherine van Casselaer, *Lot's Wife: Lesbian Paris, 1890–1914* (Janus, Liverpool, 1986); Karla Jay, *The Amazon and the Page: Natalie Clifford Barney and Renée Vivien* (Indiana University Press, Bloomington, 1988); Shari Benstock, *Women of the Left Bank: Paris, 1900–1940* (University of Texas Press, Austin, 1986). Colette provided a sympathetic overview in *Ces Plaisirs* (1932) which later appeared as *Le Pur et l'impur* (1941).

89 Julian Carter, 'Normality, Whiteness, Authorship: Evolutionary Sexology and the Primitive Pervert', in *Science and Homosexualities*, ed. Rosario, pp. 169, 170.

90 George W. Henry, *Sex Variants: a Study of Homosexual Patterns* (Paul B. Hoeber, New York, 1941); see also Robert Latou Dickinson and Lura Beam, *The Single Woman: a Study in Sexual Education* (Williams and Norgate, London, 1934), pp. 203ff.

91 Jan Gay, described as a college 'student of social conditions' was probably the author of this account; George W. Henry, *All the Sexes: a Study of Masculinity and Femininity* (Rinehart, New York, 1955), p. 293.

92 On working-class lesbians in the United States from the 1930s to 1950s, see Elizabeth Kennedy and Madeleine Davis, *Boots of Leather, Slippers of Gold: the History of a Lesbian Community* (Routledge, New York, 1993).

93 Jennifer Terry, 'Anxious Slippages between "Us" and "Them": a Brief History of the Scientific Search for Homosexual Bodies', in *Deviant Bodies: Critical Perspectives on Difference in Science and Popular Culture*, eds Jennifer Terry and Jacqueline Urla (Indiana University Press, Bloomington, 1995), pp. 139–48.

94 Cohen, *Talk on the Wilde Side*.

95 Leon Radzinowicz and Roger Hood, *A History of English Criminal Law and its Administration from 1750* (Stevens, London, 1986), vol. 5: *The Emergence of Penal Policy*.

96 E. Roy Calvert and Theodora Calvert, *The Law Breakers* (Routledge, London, 1933), p. 144; *Criminal Statistics: England and Wales 1935* (HMSO, London, 1937), tables iii, vii, xviii.

97 Lesley A. Hall, ' "Disinterested Enthusiasm for Sexual Misconduct", The British Society for the Study of Sex Psychology, 1913–47', *Journal of Contemporary History*, 30 (1995), pp. 665–86; David C. Weigle, 'Psychology and Homosexuality: The British Sexological Society', *Journal of the History of the Behavioral Sciences*, 31 (1995), pp. 137–48.

98 *Policy and Principles*, The British Society for the Study of Sex Psychology, Publication no. 1 (Beaumont, London, 1914).

99 *The Social Problem of Sexual Inversion* [abridged from the German], The British Society for the Study of Sex Psychology, Publication no. 2 (Beaumont, London, 1914).

100 Laurence Housman, *The Relation of Fellow-feeling to Sex*, The British Society for the Study of Sex Psychology, Publication no. 4 (Beaumont,

London, n.d.); Edward Carpenter, *Some Friends of Walt Whitman*, The British Society for the Study of Sex Psychology, Publication no. 13 (Battley, London, 1924).

101 'Le Problème sexologique', *Bulletin de l'association d'études sexologiques*, 1 (1932), pp. 2–5. For scientific investigations Toulouse also headed the Société de sexologie which had its own bulletin.

102 World League for Sexual Reform, *Sexual Reform Congress*, London September 8–14, 1929 (Kegan Paul, Trench, Trubner and Co., London, 1930).

103 *British Medical Journal*, 1 (1893), p. 325, cited in Vern Bullough, 'The Physician and Research into Human Sexual Behavior in Nineteenth-century Germany', *Bulletin of the History of Medicine*, 63 (1989), p. 259.

104 *Illustrated Police News*, 24 April 1919, p. 3.

105 *Bulletin de la société de sexologie*, 1 (May 1932), p. 17.

106 Paul, *Le Vice et l'amour*.

107 Max Hodann, *History of Modern Morals*, trans. Stella Browne (Heinemann, London, 1937), p. 49.

108 Harold Picton, *The Morbid, the Abnormal and the Personal*, The British Society for the Study of Sex Psychology, Publication no. 12 (Beaumont, London, 1923), p. 18.

109 Norman Haire, *Hymen, or the Future of Marriage* (Dutton, New York, 1928).

110 Réné Guyon, *Sex Life and Sex Ethics*, trans. J. C. Flugel and I. Flugel (Bodley Head, London, 1933), p. 271.

Chapter 6 'Frigidity': Sigmund Freud, Psychoanalysis and Gender

1 Marie Bonaparte, 'Les deux frigidités de la femme,' *Bulletin de la société de sexologie*, 1 (May 1932), pp. 161–70.

2 Sigmund Freud, *Standard Edition of the Complete Psychological Works of Sigmund Freud*, ed. James Strachey (Hogarth Press, London, 1953), vol. 12, pp. 169–70, cited in Paul Roazen, *Freud and his Followers* (Knopf, New York, 1975), p. 54.

3 Thomas Szasz, *Karl Kraus and the Soul Doctors* (Louisiana State University Press, Baton Rouge, 1976), p. 4.

4 Peter Berger, 'Towards a Sociological Understanding of Psychoanalysis', *Social Research*, 32 (1965), pp. 26ff.

5 Elisabeth Roudinesco, *Histoire de la psychanalyse en France* (Seuil, Paris, 1986), vol. 1, p. 32.

6 The English psychologist W. H. R. Rivers, in dealing with shell-shock victims, came close to the Freudian notion that a 'symptom covers a spot where a traumatic memory lies buried'; J. A. C. Brown, *Freud and the Post-Freudians* (Cassell, London, 1961), p. 63.

7   *Pall Mall Gazette*, cited in Wallace Martin, '*The New Age' under Orage: Chapters in English Cultural History* (Manchester University Press, Manchester, 1967), p. 274.

8   Freud, 'The Tendency to Debasement in Love', *Standard Edition*, vol. 11, pp. 188–9.

9   Freud, '"Civilized" Sexual Morality', *Standard Edition*, vol. 9, p. 194.

10 For studies in which it is argued that Victorian women enjoyed a more satisfying sex life than believers in the myth of nineteenth-century sexual repression assume, see Carl N. Degler, 'What Ought to Be and What Was: Women's Sexuality in the Nineteenth Century', *American Historical Review*, 79 (1974), pp. 1480–90; Peter Gay, *The Bourgeois Experience: Victoria to Freud* (Oxford University Press, New York, 1984), vol. 1: *Education of the Senses*.

11 Marie Bonaparte, Anna Freud and Ernst Kris, *The Origins of Psychoanalysis* (Basic Books, New York, 1954), pp. 6–7.

12 Freud to Fliess, 10 July 1893, in Bonaparte et al., *Origins of Psychoanalysis*, p. 76.

13 Havelock Ellis, *Studies in the Psychology of Sex* (Random House, New York, 1936), vol. 2, p. 598.

14 Ibid., pp. 598–601.

15 Richard J. Evans, *The Feminists: Women's Emancipation Movement in Europe, America and Australia, 1840–1920* (Barnes and Noble, New York, 1977), pp. 107–8; Ellis, *Studies,* vol. 3, p. 607; Havelock Ellis, *The Task of Social Hygiene* (Constable, London, 1912), p. 89.

16 Roazen, *Freud and his Followers*, pp. 42–52. 'During the period from 1886–1891', Freud complained, 'I did little scientific work and published scarcely anything. I was occupied with establishing myself in my new profession and with assuring my own material existence as well as that of a rapidly increasing family'; *An Autobiographical Study*, trans. James Strachey (Hogarth Press, London, 1948), p. 30.

17 Ernest Jones, *Sigmund Freud: Life and Work* (Hogarth Press, London, 1955), vol. 2, p. 431.

18 Freud to Fleiss, 31 October 1897, in Bonaparte et al., *Origins of Psychoanalysis*, p. 227.

19 Emma Jung to Freud, 6 November 1911, in *The Freud/Jung Letters*, ed. William McGuire (Princeton University Press, Princeton, NJ, 1974), p. 456.

20 Robert Graves, *Goodbye to All That* (Cassell, London, 1957) p. 103.

21 Freud, 'Three Essays on the Theory of Sexuality', *Standard Edition*, vol. 7, p. 144–7. Freud attributed the 'frequency of inversion among the present-day aristocracy' to poor mothering; ibid., p. 230.

22 Ibid., pp. 136, 229.

23 On earlier theorists who elaborate similar developmental theories, see Vern L. Bullough, *Science in the Bedroom: a History of Sex Research* (Basic Books, New York, 1994), pp. 67–7; Frank Sulloway, *Freud: Biologist of the Mind* (Basic Books, New York, 1979).

24 Freud, 'Three Essays on the Theory of Sexuality', *Standard Edition*, vol. 7, p. 161.
25 Ibid., p. 162.
26 Jerome Neu, 'Freud and Perversion', in *The Cambridge Companion to Freud*, ed. Jerome Neu (Cambridge University Press, Cambridge, 1991).
27 Freud 'Three Essays on the Theory of Sexuality', *Standard Edition*, vol. 7, p. 236.
28 Freud, 'The Question of Lay Analysis', *Standard Edition*, vol. 20, p. 179.
29 Sarah Kofman, *L'Enigme de la femme: la femme dans les textes de Freud* (Galilée, Paris, 1980).
30 Freud, 'Anatomical Sex-Distinction', *Standard Edition*, vol. 19, p. 257.
31 Freud, 'Fetishism', *Standard Edition*, vol. 21, p. 154.
32 Freud, 'Three Essays on the Theory of Sexuality', *Standard Edition*, vol. 7, p. 195.
33 Ibid., p. 210.
34 Freud, 'The Tendency to Debasement in Love', *Standard Edition*, vol. 11, p. 187.
35 Freud, 'Three Essays on the Theory of Sexuality', *Standard Edition*, vol. 7, p. 191.
36 Freud, 'The Tendency to Debasement in Love', *Standard Edition*, vol. 11, p. 185.
37 Freud, 'Anatomical Sex-Distinction', *Standard Edition*, vol. 19, p. 258.
38 Freud, 'Three Essays on the Theory of Sexuality', *Standard Edition*, vol. 7, p. 219; 'The Sexual Theories of Children', *Standard Edition*, vol. 9, p. 217.
39 Freud, 'Three Essays on the Theory of Sexuality', *Standard Edition*, vol. 7, p. 235; Freud, 'Dissolution of the Oedipus Complex', *Standard Edition*, vol. 19, p. 178; Freud, 'Female Sexuality', *Standard Edition*, vol. 21, pp. 230, 232.
40 Freud, 'Anatomical Sex-Distinction', *Standard Edition*, vol. 19, p. 255.
41 Freud, 'The Taboo of Virginity', *Standard Edition*, vol. 11, p. 205.
42 Freud, 'Three Essays on the Theory of Sexuality', *Standard Edition*, vol. 7, p. 145.
43 Freud, 'Infantile Genital Organization', *Standard Edition*, vol. 19, p. 144.
44 Freud, 'Three Essays on the Theory of Sexuality', *Standard Edition*, vol. 7, p. 142.
45 Ibid., p. 144.
46 Freud, 'The Tendency to Debasement in Love', *Standard Edition*, vol. 11, p. 189; 'Dissolution of the Oedipus Complex', *Standard Edition*, vol. 19, p. 178.
47 Freud, 'Three Essays on the Theory of Sexuality', *Standard Edition*, vol. 7, p. 207. To become a woman a 'further stage of repression' was necessary; ibid., p. 235.
48 Ibid., p. 197. Even extended foreplay was 'dangerous' inasmuch as preparatory acts deflected from vaginal intercourse; effective restrictions, Freud insisted, were needed for a normal sexual life.
49 Tom Laqueur, *Making Sex: Body and Gender from the Greeks to Freud* (Harvard University Press, Cambridge, Mass., 1990).

50 Freud, 'The Sexual Theories of Children', *Standard Edition*, vol. 9, p. 217.
51 'An instinct for mastery' was one ingredient. The pressures of civilization, in placing particular pressures on men, gave rise to neurosis which some could not withstand. 'The weaker', Freud concluded, 'are succumbing today'; Freud, 'Three Essays on the Theory of Sexuality, *Standard Edition*, vol. 7, p. 188; 'The Tendency to Debasement in Love', *Standard Edition*, vol. 11, p. 190.
52 Sander Gilman, *The Case of Sigmund Freud: Medicine and Identity at the Fin de Siècle* (Johns Hopkins University Press, Baltimore, 1993).
53 On male fears, see Alain Corbin, 'Le "sex en deuil" et l'histoire des femmes au XIXe siècle', in *Le Temps, le désir et l'horreur* (Aubier, Paris, 1991), pp. 91–105.
54 Antony M. Ludovici, *Man: an Indictment* (Constable, London, 1927), pp. 119–36.
55 Ibid., p. 35.
56 Ludovici held that, once a woman was fertile, every period was in effect a wasteful abortion. On eugenic grounds he only supported abortion for the feeble-minded. Antony M. Ludovici, 'The Case against Legalised Abortion', in *Abortion*, eds K. W. Stella Browne, A. M. Ludovici and Harry Roberts (Allen and Unwin, London, 1935), pp. 94–5.
57 Antony M. Ludovici, *The Choice of a Mate* (John Lane, London, 1935), p. 364.
58 Ibid., pp. 411, 436, 469.
59 Robert Teutsch, *Le Féminisme* (Société française d'éditions littéraires et techniques, Paris, 1934), pp. 8, 20, 167.
60 K. A. Wieth-Knudsen, *Le Conflit des sexes dans l'évolution sociale et la question sexuelle*, trans. Dr Brodal (Rivière, Paris, 1931 [orig. 1924]), p. 58; K. A. Wieth-Knudsen, *Natalité et progrès* (Sirey, Paris, 1938 [orig. 1908]), pp. 154–7.
61 Eduard Hitschmann and Edmond Bergler, *Frigidity in Women: its Characteristics and Treatment* (Nervous and Mental Diseases Monographs, New York, 1936), p. 5.
62 Carolyn J. Dean, *The Self and its Pleasures: Bataille, Lacan and the History of the Decentered Subject* (Cornell University Press, Ithaca, 1992), ch. 2.
63 Edith Kurzwel, *Freudians and Feminists* (Westview Press, Boulder, Colo., 1995), pp. 25–7.
64 Jacques Lacan, 'Motifs du crime paranoiaque: le crime des soeurs Papin', *Minotaure*, 3–4 (1933), pp. 25–8; René Allendy, 'Le Crime et les perversions instinctives', *Le Crapouillet*, May 1938, pp. 17–18. The case inspired Jean Genet's play *The Maids* (1947).
65 Grace W. Pailthorpe, *What We Put in Prison and in Preventive and Rescue Homes* (Williams and Norgate, London, 1932), p. 144.
66 Ibid., p. 62. Pailthorpe was inspired by Freud's English popularizers, Ernest Jones and Edward Glover.
67 Edward Glover, *The Social and Legal Aspects of Sexual Abnormality* (ISTD, London, 1947), p. 13.
68 Szasz, *Karl Kraus*, p. 104.

69 W. F. Robie, *Rational Sex Ethics* (Richard G. Badger, Boston, 1916), p. 151.
70 Ibid., p. 164.
71 Ibid., p. 172.
72 Vern Bullough, *Science in the Bedroom* (Basic Books, New York, 1994), pp. 61–92.

Chapter 7 'Compulsory Heterosexuality': Eugenicists, Fascists and Nazis

1 Elizabeth Kite, 'Two Brothers', *The Survey*, 27 (1912), cited in *White Trash: the Eugenic Family Studies, 1877–1919*, ed. Nicole Hahn Rafter (North Eastern University Press, Boston, 1988), p. 76.
2 J. David Smith, *Minds Made Feeble: the Myth and Legacy of the Kallikaks* (Aspen Press, Rockville, Maryland, 1985).
3 Richard A. Soloway in *Demography and Degeneration: Eugenics and the Declining Birthrate in Twentieth-century Britain* (University of North Carolina Press, Chapel Hill, 1990); Pauline M. H. Mazumdar, *Eugenics, Human Genetics and Human Failings: the Eugenics Society, its Sources and its Critics in Britain* (Routledge, London, 1992).
4 Havelock Ellis, *The Task of Social Hygiene* (Constable, London, 1912), pp. 26–32; see also Havelock Ellis, 'Eugenics and St Valentine', *Nineteenth Century and After*, 59 (1906), pp. 779–83; *The Problem of Race Regeneration* (London, Cassell, 1911).
5 C. P. Blacker, *Birth Control and the State: a Plea and Forecast* (Kegan Paul, London, 1926), p. 34; *The Practitioner*, 111 (July 1923), p. 24.
6 Margaret Sanger, *The Pivot of Civilization* (Brentano, New York, 1922), p. 86ff.
7 Marie Stopes, *Radiant Motherhood* (Putnam, London, 1928), p. 207.
8 Sanger, *The Pivot of Civilization*, p. 254.
9 Marie Stopes, *Contraception (Birth Control): its Theory, History and Practice* (Putnam, London, 1923), p. 37.
10 Marie Stopes, *Marriage in my Time* (Rich and Cowan, London, 1935), p. 116.
11 Stopes, *Radiant Motherhood*, p. 116.
12 Antony M. Ludovici, *The Choice of a Mate* (John Lane, London, 1935), p. 25.
13 Ibid., p. 46
14 S. Herbert, *Fundamentals in Sexual Ethics* (Black, London, 1920), pp. 268–71.
15 Ludovici, *The Choice of a Mate*, p. 17.
16 Auguste Forel, *La Question sexuelle* (Steinheil, Paris, 1911); Antoine Wylm, *La Morale sexuelle* (Felix Paris, Alcan, 1907).
17 Anne Carol, *Histoire de l'eugenisme en France: les médecines et la procréation XIXe–XXe siècle* (Seuil, Paris, 1995).
18 H. C. Bibby, *Heredity, Eugenics and Social Progress* (Gollancz, London, 1939).

19 John Macnicol, 'The Voluntary Sterilisation Campaign in Britain, 1918–39', *Journal of the History of Sexuality*, 2 (1992), pp. 422–38.
20 Vern L. Bullogh, 'The Rockefellers and Sex Research', *The Journal of Sex Research*, 21 (1985), pp. 113–25.
21 The policy only ended in the deep South in the 1960s; Edward J. Larson, *Sex, Race and Science: Eugenics in the Deep South* (Johns Hopkins University Press, Baltimore, 1995); Marouf Arif Hassan Jr, *The Rhetoric of Eugenics in Anglo-American Thought* (University of Georgia Press, Athens, 1996).
22 Angus McLaren, *Our own Master Race: Eugenics in Canada, 1885–1945* (Oxford University Press, Toronto, 1990).
23 Gunnar Broberg and Nils Rols-Hansem (eds), *Eugenics and the Welfare State: Sterilization Policy in Denmark, Sweden, Norway and Finland* (Michigan State University Press, East Lansing, 1996).
24 Klaus Theweleit, *Male Fantasies* (Polity Press, Cambridge, 1988), vol. 2: *Male Bodies, Psychoanalyzing the White Terror*.
25 Thomas Elsaesser, 'Lulu and the Meter Man', *Screen*, 24 (1983), pp. 4–36; Patrice Petro, *Joyless Streets: Women and Melodramatic Representation in Weimar Germany* (Princeton University Press, Princeton, NJ, 1989).
26 Amy Hacket, 'Helene Stöcker: Left-Wing Intellectual and Sex Reformer', in *When Biology Became Destiny*, eds Renate Bridenthal, Atina Grossman and Marion Kaplan (Monthly Review Press, New York, 1984), pp. 109–28; Ute Frevert, *Women in German History: from Bourgeois Emancipation to Sexual Liberation* (Berg, Oxford, 1989), p. 191.
27 Nancy Reagin, *A German Woman's Movement: Class and Gender in Hanover, 1880–1933* (University of North Carolina Press, Chapel Hill, 1995).
28 Cornelie Usborne, *The Politics of the Body in Weimar Germany: Women's Reproductive Rights and Duties* (Macmillan, London, 1992), p. 18.
29 The myth was spread that due to war losses marriage rates were down but in fact the percentage of women who married increased in Germany from 34.7 per cent in 1907 to 42.7 per cent in 1933; Atina Grossman, *Reforming Sex: the German Movement for Birth Control and Abortion Reform* (Oxford University Press, New York, 1995), p. 221, n. 30.
30 Paul Weindling, *Health, Race and German Politics between National Unification and Nazism, 1870–1945* (Cambridge University Press, Cambridge, 1989).
31 Grossman, *Reforming Sex*, p. 12.
32 Victoria de Grazia, *How Fascism Ruled Women: Italy, 1922–1945* (University of California Press, Berkeley, 1992), p. 131.
33 Grossman, *Reforming Sex*, pp. 39–41.
34 Abortion, once permitted on economic grounds, was outlawed by the Soviet Union in 1936; Wendy Goldman, 'Women, Abortion and the State, 1917–1936', in *Russia's Women: Resistance, Transformation*, eds Barbara Evans Clement, Barbara Engel and Christine Worobec (University of California Press, Berkeley, 1991).

35 Usborne, *The Politics of the Body*, p. 29.
36 James Woycke, *Birth Control in Germany, 1871–1933* (Routledge, London, 1988), p. 133.
37 Grossman, *Reforming Sex*, p. 247, n. 113.
38 Ibid., p. 83.
39 For the argument that the SPD used class, not feminist, arguments to defend abortion, see Renate Pore, *A Conflict of Interest: Women in German Social Democracy, 1919–1933* (Greenwood Press, Westport, Conn., 1981), pp. 78–80.
40 Grossman, *Reforming Sex*, pp. 71–5.
41 Ibid., pp. 120–3.
42 Reich's theoretical importance lay in his unusual concern for youth, but like others he accepted the medical model of expert sex counsellor; Grossman, *Reforming Sex*, pp. 124–7.
43 Ibid., p. 34.
44 Grazia, *How Fascism Ruled Women*, p. 69; Bruno Wanrooij, *Storia del pudore: la questione sessuale in Italia, 1860–1940* (Marsilio, Venice, 1990).
45 Grazia, *How Fascism Ruled Women*, p. 70.
46 Maria Sophia Quine, *Population Politics in Twentieth-century Europe* (Routledge, London, 1996), p. 47.
47 Grazia, *How Fascism Ruled Women*, pp. 30–6.
48 Mary Nash, 'A Disreputable Sex Reformer: Hildegart, the Red Virgin', in *Wayward Girls and Wicked Women: in Memory of Angela Carter*, ed. Elizabeth Russell (University of Barcelona Press, Barcelona, 1995), pp. 79–86.
49 Carl Ipsen, *Dictating Demography: the Problem of Population in Fascist Italy* (Cambridge University Press, Cambridge, 1996); David G. Horn, *Social Bodies: Science, Reproduction and Italian Modernity* (Princeton University Press, Princeton, NJ, 1994).
50 Quine, *Population Politics*, p. 21.
51 For similar pronatalism in Spain, where abortions had been legalized in republican Catalonia in 1936, but ended with Franco's coming to power, see Mary Nash, 'Pronatalism and Motherhood in Franco's Spain', in *Maternity and Gender Policies: Women and the Rise of the European Welfare States, 1880s–1950s*, eds Gisela Bock and Pat Thane (Routledge, London, 1991), pp. 160–77.
52 Quine, *Population Politics*, pp. 23–5.
53 Grazia, *How Fascism Ruled Women*, p. 55.
54 Denise Detragiache, 'Un Aspect de la politique démographique de l'Italie fasciste: la répression de l'avortement', *Mélanges de l'école française de Rome*, 92 (1980), pp. 691–735.
55 Grazia, *How Fascism Ruled Women*, p. 41.
56 Ipsen, *Dictating Demography*, p. 45.
57 Adolf Hitler, *Mein Kampf* (Librairie critique, Paris, 1930), pp. 224–9.
58 In England nudism was regarded with suspicion though defenders stressed jolly companionship; John Langdon-Davies, *The Future of*

Nakedness (Noel Douglas, London, 1929); An Eye-Witness, *In a Nudist Camp!* (Scottish Protestant League, Glasgow, 1933).

59 George L. Mosse, *Nationalism and Sexuality: Middle-class Morality and Sexual Norms in Modern Europe* (University of Wisconsin Press, Madison, 1985), p. 154.

60 Grossman, *Reforming Sex*, p. 146.

61 Max Hodann, *History of Modern Morals*, trans. Stella Browne (Heinemann, London, 1937), p. 308.

62 Robert G. Moeller, 'The Homosexual Man is a "Man", the Homosexual Woman is a "Woman": Sex, Society and the Law in Post-war West Germany', *Journal of the History of Sexuality*, 4 (1994), pp. 398–404.

63 Claudia Schoppmann, *Days of Masquerade: Life Stories of Lesbians during the Third Reich* (Columbia University Press, New York, 1996).

64 Robert Procter, *Racial Hygiene: Medicine under the Nazis* (Harvard University Press, Cambridge, Mass., 1988), pp. 212–14; Harry Oosterhuis, 'Medicine, Male Bonding and Homosexuality in Nazi Germany', *Journal of Contemporary History*, 32 (1997), pp. 187–205.

65 Mosse, *Nationalism and Sexuality*, pp. 165–8.

66 Erwin J. Haeberle, 'Swastika, Pink Triangle and Yellow Star: the Destruction of Sexology and the Persecution of Homosexuals in Nazi Germany', in *Hidden from History: Reclaiming the Gay and Lesbian Past*, eds Martin B. Duberman, Martha Vicinus and George Chauncey, Jr (New American Library, New York, 1989), p. 372.

67 In Britain, too, journals such as *Health and Strength Annual* and *New Health* carried articles on how to improve the race; see, for example, W. Arbuthnot Lane, 'How to Develop an A1 Race', *New Health*, 2 (1927), pp. 27–8.

68 For an English example of a mixing of eugenic and recreational ideas, see Jill Julius Matthews, 'They Had Such a Lot of Fun: the Women's League of Health and Beauty between the Wars', *History Workshop Journal*, 30 (1990), pp. 22–54.

69 Frevert, *Women in German History*, p. 213.

70 Barbara Spackman, 'Fascist Women and the Rhetoric of Virility', in *Mothers of Invention: Women, Fascism, and Culture*, ed. Robin Pickering-Iazzi (University of Minnesota Press, Minneapolis, 1995), p. 100.

71 Henry P. Davis, Jochen Fleischhacker and Charlotte Höhn, 'Abortion and Eugenics in Nazi Germany', *Population and Development Review*, 14 (1988), pp. 94–8.

72 Frevert, *Women in German History*, pp. 236–7.

73 Grossman, *Reforming Sex*, p. 149.

74 Gisela Bock, 'Antinatalism, Maternity and Paternity in National Socialism Racism', in *Nazism and German Society, 1933–1945*, ed. David F. Crew (Routledge, London, 1994), pp. 110–40.

75 Geoffrey Giles, 'The Most Unkindest Cut of All: Castration, Homosexuality and Nazi Justice', *Journal of Contemporary History*, 27 (1992), pp. 41–61. On the sterilization of sex criminals outside Germany, see Paul H. Gebhard, John H. Gagnon, Wardell B. Pomeroy and Cornelia V.

Christenson, *Sex Offenders: an Analysis of Types* (Harper and Row, New York, 1965); J. Bremer, *Asexualization* (Macmillan, New York, 1959).

76 Grossman, *Reforming Sex*, pp. 69–71.

77 Stefan Kühl, *The Nazi Connection: Eugenics, American Racism, and German National Socialism* (Oxford University Press, New York, 1994); Philip R. Reilly, *The Surgical Solution: a History of Involuntary Sterilisation in the United States* (Johns Hopkins University Press, Baltimore, 1991).

78 Michael Burleigh, *Death and Deliverance: Euthanasia in Germany c.1900–1945* (Cambridge University Press, Cambridge, 1994).

79 John d'Emilio and Estelle B. Freedman, *Intimate Matters: a History of Sexuality in America* (Harper and Row, New York, 1988), pp. 216–18.

80 Gail Bederman, *Manliness and Civilization: a Cultural History of Gender and Race in the United States, 1880–1917* (Chicago University Press, Chicago, 1995), pp. 45–76.

81 Ludovici, *The Choice of a Mate*, p. 140

82 Ibid., p. 165. Oswald Mosley's British Union of Fascists paraded its moralism by insisting that women return to their traditional roles and by attacking the decadence represented by nudist camps and foreign pornography.

83 Francine Muel-Dreyfus, *Vichy et l'éternel féminine* (Seuil, Paris, 1996).

84 Haeberle, 'Swastika, Pink Triangle and Yellow Star', pp. 365–79.

85 In France there were 205 prosecutions of abortionists in 1936 compared with 2,022 in 1947; Muel-Dreyfus, *Vichy et l'éternel féminine*, pp. 319–27.

86 Max Hodann, the most interesting of the Weimar sex reformers, left Germany to participate in the Spanish Civil War. At his death in Sweden in 1946 he was still very much a radical.

87 On Marmsen's *Pro Familia* and Sanger's support for an American-style birth control movement in Germany, see Grossman, *Reforming Sex*, pp. 154, 204–6.

88 Similarly, post-war films and television exploited the titillating myth that Jewish women were continuously raped or forced to serve in brothels; see Sybil Milton, 'Women and the Holocaust: the Case of German and German-Jewish Women', in *When Biology became Destiny*, eds Renate Bridenthal, Atina Grossman and Marion Kaplan (Monthly Review Press, New York, 1984), p. 315.

89 Arthur Schlesinger Jr, *The Vital Center: the Politics of Freedom* (1949), cited in Carolyn Dean, *Sexuality and Modern Western Culture* (Twayne, New York, 1996), p. 60.

Chapter 8 'Surveying Sex': From Alfred C. Kinsey to Hugh Hefner

1 Paul Robinson, *The Modernization of Sex: Havelock Ellis, Alfred Kinsey, William Masters and Virginia Johnson* (Harper and Row, New York,

1976); Cornelia V. Christenson, *Kinsey: a Biography* (Indiana University Press, Bloomington, 1971).

2   Alfred C. Kinsey, Wardell B. Pomeroy and Clyde E. Martin, *Sexual Behavior in the Human Male* (W. B. Saunders, Philadelphia, 1948), p. 199. Kinsey would accept that some acts were either 'rare' or 'common'.

3   For an informative yet relentlessly hostile account of Kinsey, which begins with the premise that he was a masochist and a homosexual, see James H. Jones, *Alfred C. Kinsey: a Public/Private Life* (Norton, New York, 1997).

4   Kinsey et al., *Sexual Behavior in the Human Male*, pp. 206–7.

5   From the start Kinsey was critiqued for being drawn to the over-sexed and for bias in his sampling techniques; see William G. Cochran, Frederick Mosteller and John Tukey, 'Statistical Problems of the Kinsey Report', *Journal of the American Statistical Association*, 48 (1953), pp. 673–716.

6   Lewis M. Terman and Catherine Cox Miles, *Sex and Personality: Studies in Masculinity and Femininity* (McGraw Hill, New York, 1936).

7   Kinsey et al., *Sexual Behavior in the Human Male*, p. 323.

8   Ibid., p. 325.

9   As noted in chapter 5, a rare view of gay culture was provided in George Henry's *Sex Variants* (Paul B. Hoeber, New York, 1941). More than two hundred homosexuals participated in the study which was organized by two members of the gay community, Jan Gay and Thomas Painter. Though Henry imposed a pathological medical model on the personal accounts provided, his study was an advance of sorts because his earlier research, carried out for the Committee for the Study of Sex Variants formed in 1935, began with the premise of a physical predisposition – such as a lesbian pelvis – to homosexuality; Henry L. Minton, 'Community Empowerment and the Medicalization of Homosexuality: Constructing Sexual Identities in the 1930s', *Journal of the History of Sexuality*, 6 (1990), pp. 435–58. See also Robert Latou Dickinson and Lura Beam, *The Single Woman: a Medical Study in Sex Education* (Williams and Wilkins, Baltimore, MD, 1949).

10   Kinsey et al., *Sexual Behavior in the Human Male*, pp. 636–51. The scale, of course, assumed two poles and so was still inherently binary.

11   Ibid., p. 663.

12   Ibid., p. 249.

13   Alfred C. Kinsey, Wardell B. Pomeroy, Clyde E. Martin and Paul H. Gebhard, *Sexual Behavior in the Human Female* (W. B. Saunders, Philadelphia, 1953).

14   Moreover 9.3 per cent of the married reported at least one induced abortion; Katherine Bement Davis, *Factors in the Sex Life of Twenty-two Hundred Women* (Harper and Brothers, New York, 1929), pp. 13–21.

15   Kinsey et al., *Sexual Behavior in the Human Female*, pp. 171–3.

16   Philip M. Bloom, Clifford Allen and H. J. Blackham, *The Grammar of Marriage* (The Ethical Union, London, 1949), pp. 4, 6.

17   Kinsey et al., *Sexual Behavior in the Human Female*, p. 266.

18 Dorothy Dunbar Bromley and F. H. Britten, *Youth and Sex* (Harper, New York, 1938).

19 Of those who did not have an orgasm before marriage, 31–37 per cent did not achieve orgasm in the first year of marriage; Kinsey et al., *Sexual Behavior in the Human Female*, pp. 390–1.

20 Kinsey et al., *Sexual Behavior in the Human Female*, pp. 286, 326–30.

21 Lewis M. Terman, *Psychological Factors in Marital Happiness* (McGraw Hill, New York, 1938), p. 342.

22 Kinsey et al., *Sexual Behavior in the Human Female*, p. 453. Kinsey found that 8–10 per cent of women had homosexual dreams. Men were twice as likely to remember having such dreams probably because they were accompanied by emissions.

23 Ibid., p. 460.

24 Bloom et al., *The Grammar of Marriage*, p. 19.

25 No other country produced anything close to Kinsey's work, though in Britain Mass Observation carried out a 1949 survey – christened the 'Little Kinsey' – that was not published until almost fifty years later; Liz Stanley, *Sex Surveyed, 1949–1994: from Mass Observation's 'Little Kinsey' to the National Survey and the Hite Reports* (Taylor and Francis, London, 1995).

26 George Ryley Scott, *Sex Problems and Dangers in War-Time* (T. Werner-Laurie, London, 1940).

27 Margaret Hadley Jackson, 'Causes and Significance of the Dwindling Family', in *Rebuilding Family Life in the Post War World*, ed. Lord Horder (Oldhams Press, London, 1948), pp. 85, 88.

28 Eva M. Hubback, *Population: Facts and Policies* (Allen and Unwin, London, 1945), p. 19.

29 Atina Grossman, *Reforming Sex: the German Movement for Birth Control and Abortion Reform* (Oxford University Press, New York, 1995), p. 196.

30 John Gillis, *Youth and History: Tradition and Change in European Age Relations, 1770–Present* (Academic Press, New York, 1981), p. 188.

31 Surveys found that a third of the babies born in France between 1959 and 1962 had been undesired; Colin Dyer, *Population and Society* (Hodder and Stoughton, London, 1978), p. 143.

32 Eliot Slater and Moya Woodside, *Patterns of Marriage* (Cassell, London, 1951), p. 198.

33 East and West Germany also had to come to terms with the fact that thousands of women had been raped by the occupying forces; see Norman Naimark, *The Russians in Germany: a History of the Soviet Zone of Occupation, 1945–49* (Belknap Press, Cambridge, 1995), pp. 69–140.

34 See, for example, Erich Fromm, *The Art of Loving* (Harper, New York, 1956).

35 Kinsey et al., *Sexual Behavior in the Human Male*, p. 587.

36 Dr Eustace Chesser, *The Sexual, Marital and Family Relationships of the English Woman* (Hutchinson, London, 1956), p. 517.

37 Kinsey et al., *Sexual Behavior in the Human Female*, p. 428.

38 On adultery and divorce in France, see Anne-Marie Sohn, *Du Premier baiser à l'alcôve: la sexualité des français au quotidien (1850–1950)* (Aubier, Paris, 1996), p. 289.

39 James G. Snell, *In the Shadow of the Law: Divorce in Canada, 1900–1939* (University of Toronto Press, Toronto, 1991); Mona Gleason, 'Psychology and the Construction of the "Normal" Family in Postwar Canada, 1945–60', *Canadian Historical Review*, 78 (1997), p. 454.

40 Kinsey et al., *Sexual Behavior in the Human Female*, pp. 432–6.

41 A. P. Herbert, *Holy Deadlock* (Methuen, London, 1934), pp. 24, 27.

42 Colin S. Gibson, *Dissolving Wedlock* (Routledge, London, 1994), p. 96.

43 On American women's increasingly explicit expressions of sexual disappointment, see Elaine Tyler May, *Great Expectations: Marriage and Divorce in Post-Victorian America* (University of Chicago Press, Chicago, 1980).

44 On responses of Catholic confessors such as Abbé Viollet, see Anne Marie Sohn, 'Catholics between Abstinence and "Appeasement of Lust" (1930–1950)', in *Sexual Cultures*, eds Lesley Hall, Gert Hekma and Franz Eder (Manchester University Press, Manchester, 1999); Martine Sevegrand, *Les Enfants du Bon Dieu: les Catholiques et la procréation au XXème siècle* (A. Michel, Paris, 1995).

45 By 1945, 106 universities in the United States were offering courses on marriage education and family living. College students became in turn the most convenient subjects of those surveying sexual behaviour; Beth L. Bailey, 'Scientific Truth . . . and Love: the Marriage Education Movement in the United States', *Journal of Social History*, 20 (1987), pp. 711–32.

46 E. H. Gosney and Paul Popenoe, *Sterilization for Human Betterment* (Macmillan, New York, 1929).

47 Paul Popenoe, 'Marriage Counselling,' in *Third International Eugenics Congress*, ed. Harry F. Perkins (Williams and Wilkins, Baltimore, MD, 1934), pp. 210–21. *Marriage and Family Living* in its early years carried a number of articles by eugenicists such as Frederick Osborn.

48 During the Second World War he prepared a pamphlet entitled 'Marriage' for the Canadian Legion Educational Services which was distributed to the Canadian armed forces.

49 Paul Popenoe, 'First Aid for the Family', *Maclean's*, 1 May 1947, p. 47.

50 See also Paul Popenoe, *Marriage is What You Make It* (Marriage Publications, New York, 1950); *Divorce – 17 Ways to Avoid It* (Trend, Los Angeles, 1959); *Modern Marriage* (Macmillan, New York, 1927); Terman, *Psychological Factors in Marital Happiness*; Herman Rubin, *Eugenics and Sex Harmony* (Publishers Guild, New York, 1941); Oliver Butterfield, *Marriage and Sexual Harmony* (Emerson Books, New York, 1931).

51 Paul Popenoe, 'Marriage Counselling', p. 216.

52 Terman and Miles, *Sex and Personality*. For low levels of marital happiness, see also Gilbert V. Hamilton, *Research in Marriage* (A. C. Boni, New York, 1929).

53 Terman, *Psychological Factors in Marital Happiness*; L. M. Terman, 'Correlates of Orgasm Adequacy in a Group of 556 Wives', *Journal of Psychology*, 32 (1951), pp. 115–72.

54 Mudd recalled that Popenoe was 'bitter' about being kept out of the National Association of Marriage Counselling; James Reed interview with Emily Hartshorne Mudd, 1974, in the Schlesinger–Rockefeller Oral History Project, Radcliffe College.

55 Jeffrey Weeks, *Sex, Politics and Society: the Regulation of Sexuality since 1800* (Longman, London, 1989), p. 237.

56 Bertrand Russell, *Marriage and Morals* (Liveright, New York, 1929).

57 The Anglican church, in giving in 1930 guarded approval of the use of contraceptives in marriage, had acknowledged that intercourse was one of the legitimate purposes of marriage.

58 Bloom et al., *The Grammar of Marriage*, p. 26.

59 E. F. Griffith, *Modern Marriage* (Gollancz, London, 1934).

60 David R. Mace, *Marriage Counselling* (J. A., Churchill, London, 1948), p. 50; see also David R. Mace, *Does Sex Morality Matter?* (Rich and Cowan, London, 1943).

61 Emily H. Mudd, 'A Case Study in Marriage Counselling', *Marriage and Family Living*, 7 (1945), pp. 52–4.

62 Mace, *Marriage Counselling*, pp. 122–6. The 1952 Royal Commission on Marriage and Divorce called for more marriage guidance.

63 Slater and Woodside, *Patterns of Marriage*, pp. 165–74.

64 Chesser, *Sexual, Marital and Family Relationships*, p. 423.

65 Kinsey et al., *Sexual Behavior in the Human Male*, p. 386.

66 Ibid., pp. 365–9.

67 Ibid., pp. 580–1.

68 Read Bain, 'Making Normal People', *Marriage and Family Living*, 16 (1954), pp. 27–8.

69 Elaine Tyler May, *Homeward Bound: American Families in the Cold War Era* (Basic Books, New York, 1988); Joanne Meyerowitz (ed.), *Not June Clever: Women and Gender in Post War America* (Temple University Press, Philadelphia, 1994).

70 Mona Gleason, 'Psychology and the Construction of the "Normal" Family in Postwar Canada, 1945–60', *Canadian Historical Review*, 78 (1997), pp. 442–77.

71 J. M. Winter, 'The Demographic Consequences of the War', in *War and Social Change*, ed. Harold L. Smith (Manchester University Press, Manchester, 1986), pp. 156–70; Linda Gordon, *Woman's Body, Woman's Right: a Social History of Birth Control in America* (Grossman, New York, 1976), pp. 341–91. Wini Breinis, 'Domineering Mothers in the 1950s: Image and Reality', *Women's Studies International Forum*, 8 (1985), pp. 604–8.

72 Count Hermann Keyserling, *America Set Free* (Jonathan Cape, London, 1930), pp. 294–331.

73 Philip Wylie, *Generation of Vipers* (Rinehart, New York, 1955, 20th edn), pp. 194–217.

74   Patricia J. Campbell, *Sex Education Books for Young Adults, 1892–1979* (R. R. Bowker, New York, 1979), p. 61.
75   Kinsey et al., *Sexual Behavior in the Human Female*, pp. 16–17.
76   Barbara Ehrenreich, *Hearts of Men: American Dreams and the Flight from Commitment* (Anchor, New York, 1983), p. 18.
77   Gershon Legman, *Love and Death: a Study in Censorship* (Hacker, New York, 1963), p. 70.
78   Ehrenreich, *Hearts of Men*, p. 53ff.
79   Wini Breines, *Young, White and Miserable: Growing Up Female in the Fifties* (Beacon Press, Boston, 1992), pp. 70–83.
80   Gillis, *Youth and History*, p. 188.
81   Martine Segalen, *Historical Anthropology of the Family* (Cambridge University Press, Cambridge, 1986), pp. 139–50; Ellen K. Rothman, *Hands and Hearts: a History of Courtship in America* (Basic Books, New York, 1984).
82   Slater and Woodside, *Patterns of Marriage*, p. 113.
83   Angus Calder, *The People's War, 1939–45* (Pantheon, New York, 1969), p. 312.
84   Rickie Solinger, *Wake Up Little Susie: Single Pregnancy and Race before Roe v. Wade* (Routledge, New York, 1992), p. 220
85   Liz Heron, 'Dear Green Place' in *Truth, Dare or Promise: Girls Growing Up in the 1950s*, ed. Liz Heron (Virago, London, 1985), p. 163.
86   Beth Bailey, *From Front Porch to Back Seat: Courtship in Twentieth-century America* (Johns Hopkins University Press, Baltimore, MD, 1988), pp. 81–3.
87   Ibid., p. 26.
88   Sheila Rowbotham, 'Revolt in Roundhay', in *Truth, Dare or Promise*, ed. Heron, p. 206.
89   Mary Louise Adams, *The Trouble with Normal: Postwar Youth and the Making of Heterosexuality* (University of Toronto Press, Toronto, 1997).
90   Bloom et al., *The Grammar of Marriage*, p. 13.
91   Lisa Alther, *Kinflicks* (Random House, New York, 1975).
92   Joanne Meyerowitz, 'Women, Cheesecake and Borderline Material Responses to Girlie Magazines in the Mid-Twentieth Century United States', *Journal of Women's History*, 8 (1996), pp. 16–35.
93   Joan Jacob Brumberg, ' "Something Happens to Girls": Menarche and the Emergence of the Modern American Hygienic Imperative', *Journal of the History of Sexuality*, 4 (1993), pp. 124–7.
94   Bruno P. F. Wanrooij, 'Dollars and Decency: Italian Catholics and Hollywood (1945–1960)', in *Hollywood in Europe*, eds David W. Ellwood and Rob Kroes (Vu University Press, Amsterdam, 1994), pp. 246–50.
95   Breines, *Young, White and Miserable*, pp. 85–126.
96   Ibid., William Graebner, *Coming of Age in Buffalo: Youth and Authority in the Post-war Era* (Temple University Press, Philadelphia, 1990).
97   Legman, *Love and Death*, p. 77.
98   Solinger, *Wake Up Little Susie*, p. 109.

99   Frederic Wertham, *Seduction of the Innocent* (Rinehart, New York, 1953). On Wertham, see William W. Savage Jr, *Comic Books and America, 1945–54* (University of Oklahoma Press, Norman, 1990), pp. 95–103; James Gilbert, *A Cycle of Outrage: America's Reaction to the Juvenile Delinquent in the 1950s* (Oxford University Press, New York, 1986), pp. 91–108.

100 Wertham, *Seduction of the Innocent*, p. 190. Wertham, as director of the Quaker Readjustment Center, sought to 'cure' deviancy.

101 Ibid., p. 193. On opposition to Wertham's using comics as a 'whipping boy', see Frederic Thrasher, 'The Comics and Delinquency: Case of a Scapegoat', *Journal of Educational Sociology*, 23 (1949), pp. 195–8.

102 The film industry had in 1934 developed the Hollywood Production Code as a similar form of self-censorship. Daniel Lord S.J. and the Catholic League of Decency oversaw enforcement.

103 Martin Barker, *A Haunt of Fears: the Strange History of the British Horror Comics Campaign* (Pluto, London, 1984).

104 John d'Emilio, 'The Homosexual Menace: the Politics of Sexuality in Cold War America', in *Passion and Power: Sexuality in History*, eds Kathy Peiss and Robert A. Padgug (Temple University Press, Philadelphia, 1989), pp. 226–40.

105 Allan Berubé, *Coming Out Under Fire: the History of Gay Men and Women in World War Two* (The Free Press, New York, 1990), p. 25; and on Britain, see George Melly, *Rum, Bum and Concertina* (Weidenfeld and Nicolson, London, 1977).

106 Berubé, *Coming Out Under Fire*, p. 42.

107 Ibid., p. 19; John Costello, *Love, Sex and War: Changing Values 1939–45* (Collins, London, 1985), pp. 94–7.

108 Gordon Westwood [Michael Schofield], *Society and the Homosexual* (Dutton, London, 1952).

109 Berubé, *Coming Out Under Fire*, p. 259.

110 Estelle B. Freedman, ' "Uncontrolled Desires": the Response to the Sexual Psychopath, 1920–1960', in *Passion and Power*, eds Peiss and Padgug, pp. 203–16. Evidence suggests that Hoover was partly seeking to compensate for public suspicions about his own sexuality.

111 Adams, *The Trouble with Normal*, pp. 158–64.

112 Daniel J. Robinson and David Kimmel, 'The Queer Career of Homosexual Security Vetting in Cold War Canada', *Canadian Historical Review*, 75 (1994), pp. 319–45; Gary Kinsman, 'Character Weakness and "Fruit Machines": Towards an Analysis of the Anti-homosexual Security Campaign in the Canadian Civil Service', *Labour/Le Travail*, 35 (1995), pp. 133–61.

113 Robert G. Moeller, 'The Homosexual Man is a "Man", the Homosexual Woman is a "Woman": Sex, Society and the Law in Postwar West Germany', *Journal of the History of Sexuality*, 4 (1994), pp. 395–429.

114 *Memorandum of Evidence from the Ethical Union to the Department Committee on Homosexuality and Offences Related to Prostitution and Solicitation, April 1955* (Ethical Union, London, 1955), p. 3.

115 'Report of the Committee on Homosexual Offences and Prostitution, 1957', *Parliamentary Papers*, 14 (1956–7).

116 Michael Freeman, 'The Law and Sexual Deviation', in *Sexual Deviation*, ed. Ismond Rosen (Oxford University Press, Oxford, 1979), pp. 376–440.

117 The effect of the law was that prostitutes were arrested on a rota system, denied protection and prevented from having stable relationships as their partners had to prove they were not living on the proceeds of prostitution; see Cecil Rolph Hewitt, *Women of the Streets: a Sociological Study of the Common Prostitute* (Secker and Warburg, London, 1955), pp. 23, 112–13. The abolition of government-regulated prostitution in France in 1946 and in Italy in 1958 was heralded as ending the most glaring examples of Europe's sexual double standard.

118 Eva M. Hubback, *Population: Facts and Policies* (Allen and Unwin, London, 1945), p. 45.

119 In the United States contraception became a key concern of the Millbank Memorial Fund, the Scripps Foundation and the Rockefeller Foundation; see James Reed, 'Public Policy on Human Reproduction,' *Journal of Social History*, 18 (1985), pp. 392–5.

120 Tim Newburn, *Permission and Regulation: Laws and Morals in Post War Britain* (Routledge, London, 1992).

121 Carolyn Dean, *Sexuality and Western Culture* (Twayne, New York, 1996), p. 51.

122 Kinsey was largely oblivious to the gendered nature of sexual constraints. In discussing extra-marital sex, for example, he failed to note that the economically powerful partner in a relationship – the man – was in a better position to take risks, whereas the woman who sought sexual autonomy faced far greater dangers.

123 Kinsey was not interested in what sort of sexual type his subjects believed themselves to be. He rated his interviewees on the '0' to '6' scale – they were not allowed to rate themselves.

Chapter 9 'Sexual Revolution?': the Pill, Permissiveness and Politics

1 John Updike, *Couples* (Knopf, New York, 1968), p. 52.

2 Hans Simmer, 'On the History of Hormonal Contraception', *Contraception*, 1 (1970), pp. 3–27; 3 (1971), pp. 1–19; Nelly Oudshoorn, *An Archeology of Sex Hormones* (Routledge, London, 1994), pp. 112–19.

3 B. P. Wiesner, 'The Hormones and their Control of the Reproductive System', *Eugenics Review*, 22 (1930), pp. 19–26; Merriley Borell, 'Organotherapy and the Emergence of Reproductive Endocrinology', *Journal of the History of Biology*, 18 (1985), pp. 1–30.

4 James Reed, *From Private Vice to Public Virtue: the Birth Control Movement and American Society since 1830* (Basic Books, New York,

1978), pp. 352–53; J. B. Thomas, *Introduction to Human Embryology* (Lea and Febiger, Philadelphia, 1968), pp. 45–6.

5 Reed, *From Private Vice to Public Virtue.*

6 Carol Joffe, *The Regulation of Sexuality: Experiences of Family Planning Workers* (Temple University Press, Philadelphia, 1986). In Italy family planning clinics were not inspired by feminist concerns; see Lesley Caldwell, 'Italian Feminism: Some Considerations', in *Women and Italy*, eds Z. G. Baranski and S. W. Vinall (St Martin's Press, New York, 1991), p. 105.

7 Janine Mossuz-Lavau, *Les Lois de l'amour: les politiques de la sexualité en France (1950–1990)* (Payot, Paris, 1991), p. 47.

8 Dr Marie-Andrée Lagroua Weill-Hallé, *La Contraception au service de l'amour* (Editions Guy de Monçeau, Paris, 1966), p. 47.

9 Pierre Simon, *Rapport Simon sur le comportement sexuel des français* (Charron, Paris, 1972).

10 Mossuz-Lavau, *Les Lois de l'amour*, p. 49. The law was only fully applied in 1972.

11 Martine Segalen, '"Généreuse et raisonable": l'église et le contrôle de la fécondité dans les années 1950', in *Population et cultures: études réunies en l'honneur de François Lebrun* (University of Rennes, Rennes, 1989), pp. 127–36.

12 R. Christian Johnson, 'Feminism, Philanthropy and Science in the Development of the Oral Contraceptive Pill', *Pharmacy in History*, 19 (1977), pp. 63–77; Reed, *From Private Vice*, pp. 317–66.

13 Gigi Santow, 'Coitus Interruptus in the Twentieth Century', *Population and Development Review*, 19 (1993), pp. 767–92.

14 Harold Silver and Judith Ryder, *Modern English Society* (Methuen, London, 1985), p. 300.

15 Mary-Jo Bane, *Here to Stay: American Families in the Twentieth Century* (Basic Books, New York, 1976); Silver and Ryder, *Modern English Society*, p. 297.

16 Steven Seidman, *Embattled Eros: Sexual Politics and Ethics in Contemporary America* (Routledge, New York, 1992).

17 Michael Young and Peter Willmott, *The Symmetrical Family: a Study of Work and Leisure in the London Region* (Routledge, London, 1973).

18 Gay Talese, *Thy Neighbor's Wife* (Dell, New York, 1980).

19 Michael Anderson, 'The Emergence of the Modern Life Cycle in Britain', *Social History*, 10 (1985), pp. 69–88.

20 *The Essential Lenny Bruce*, ed. John Cohen (Ballantine, New York, 1967), p. 195.

21 Kristina Orfali, 'Un Modèle de transparence: la société suédoise', in *Histoire de la vie privée*, eds Philippe Ariès and Georges Duby (Seuil, Paris, 1987), vol. 5: *De la Première Guerre mondiale à nos jours*, pp. 595–602.

22 Laura Kipnis, 'Reading Hustler', in *Cultural Studies*, eds L. Grossberg, C. Nelson and P. A. Tricolet (Routledge, New York, 1992), pp. 373–91.

23   Angus McLaren and Arlene Tigar McLaren, *The Bedroom and the State: the Changing Practices and Politics of Contraception and Abortion in Canada, 1880–1997* (Oxford University Press, Toronto, 1997), pp. 134–8.

24   Jane Lewis and Kathleen Kiernan, 'The Boundaries between Marriage, Nonmarriage, and Parenthood: Changes in Behaviour and Policy in Postwar Britain', *Journal of Family History*, 21 (1996), p. 374.

25   Henri Leridon, *La seconde révolution contraceptive: la régulation des naissances en France de 1950 à 1985* (PUF, Paris, 1987); François A. Isambert, Paul Ladrière and Danièle Hervieu-Léger, *Contraception et avortement: dix ans de débat dans la presse (1965–1974)* (Editions du Centre national de la recherche scientifique, Paris, 1979).

26   Beth Bailey, 'Prescribing the Pill: Politics, Culture and the Sexual Revolution in America's Heartland' *Journal of Social History*, 30 (1997), pp. 827–56.

27   Eustace Chesser, *Unmarried Love* (Jarrolds, London, 1965).

28   Antoine Prost, 'Frontières et espaces du privé', *Histoire de la vie privée*, eds Ariés and Duby, p. 91.

29   Arlene Skolnick, *Embattled Paradise: the American Family in an Age of Uncertainty* (Basic Books, New York, 1991), p. 82.

30   Jean Claude Bologne, *Histoire de la pudeur* (Olivier Orban, Paris, 1986), p. 48.

31   Rickie Solinger, *Wake Up Little Susie: Single Pregnancy and Race before Roe v. Wade* (Routledge, New York, 1992), p. 217.

32   Barbara Ehrenreich, Elizabeth Hess and Gloria Jacobs, *Re-Making Love: the Feminization of Sex* (Doubleday, New York, 1986), p. 164.

33   Erica Jong, *Fear of Flying* (Holt, Rinehart and Winston, New York, 1973).

34   Alfred C. Kinsey, Wardell B. Pomeroy, Clyde E. Martin and Paul H. Gebhard, *Sexual Behavior in the Human Female* (W. B. Saunders, Philadelphia, 1953), p. 592.

35   Vern L. Bullough, *Science in the Bedroom: a History of Sex Research* (Basic Books, New York, 1994), p. 111.

36   William H. Masters and Virginia E. Johnson, *Human Sexual Response* (Little, Brown, Boston, 1966); and *Human Sexual Inadequacy* (Little, Brown, Boston, 1970).

37   Bullough, *Science in the Bedroom*, pp. 196–205.

38   Janice M. Irvine, *Disorders of Desire: Sex and Gender in Modern American Sexology* (Temple University Press, Philadelphia, 1990), pp. 67–94, 192–203; Leonore Tiefer, *Sex is Not a Natural Act and Other Essays* (Westview Press, Boulder, Colo., 1994).

39   Alex Comfort, *The Joy of Sex: a Gourmet Guide to Lovemaking* (Quartet, London, 1972); and for his depiction of business and military leaders as 'psychopaths' and 'licensed delinquents', see Alex Comfort, *Authority and Delinquency in the Modern State: a Criminological Approach to the Problem of Power* (Routledge and Kegan Paul, London, 1950).

40 Presumably because she lacked medical training there is not a single mention of Shere Hite in Bullough, *Science in the Bedroom.*

41 Nora Ephron, *Crazy Salad Plus Nine* (Pocket Books, New York, 1984), p. 72; Boston Women's Health Collective, *Our Bodies Ourselves* (Simon and Schuster, New York, 1971).

42 Nancy Friday, *My Secret Garden: Women's Sexual Fantasies* (Trident, New York, 1973).

43 Lynne Segal, *Straight Sex: Rethinking the Politics of Pleasure* (University of California Press, Berkeley, 1994), p. 317.

44 Paul Robinson, *The Freudian Left* (Harper and Row, New York, 1969).

45 Richard King, *The Party of Eros: Radical Social Thought and the Realm of Freedom* (University of North Carolina Press, Chapel Hill, 1973).

46 Matthew Russell, a doctor, quoted in Jonathan Green, *It: Sex since the Sixties* (Secker and Warburg, London, 1993), p. 11.

47 On race and sex tensions, see Simone M. Caron, 'Birth Control and the Black Community in the 1960s: Genocide or Power Politics', *Journal of Social History,* 31 (1998), pp. 545–70.

48 Deidre English, quoted in Alice Echols, *Daring to be Bad: Radical Feminism in America, 1967–1975* (University of Minnesota Press, Minneapolis, 1989), p. 43.

49 For an attempt to reclaim Freud, see Juliet Mitchell, *Psychoanalysis and Feminism* (Allen Lane, London, 1974).

50 Anne Koedt, 'The Myth of the Vaginal Orgasm', *Notes from the First Year* (New York Radical Women, New York, 1968).

51 Russell Jacoby, *Social Amnesia: a Critique of Conformist Psychology from Adler to Laing* (Beacon Press, Boston, 1975), pp. 106–9, 113–14; see also Christopher Lasch, *Haven in a Heartless World: the Family Beseiged* (Basic Books, New York, 1977); *The Culture of Narcissism: American Life in an Age of Diminishing Expectations* (Norton, New York, 1978).

52 Kate Millet, *Sexual Politics* (Doubleday, New York, 1970),

53 Shulamith Firestone, *The Dialectic of Sex: the Case for Feminist Revolution* (Bantam, New York, 1970).

54 On popular fears, see Barbara Seaman, *The Doctors' Case against the Pill* (Wyden, New York, 1969).

55 Theodore Zeldin, *France, 1848–1945* (Clarendon Press, Oxford, 1953), vol. I, pp. 359–60.

56 Italy's abortion campaign, begun in 1970, resulted in the reform of the law in 1978; Lucia Chiatola Birnbaum, *Liberazione della Donna: Feminism in Italy* (Wesleyan University Press, Middletown, Conn., 1986), p. 104.

57 Donna Harscha, 'Society, the State and Abortion in East Germany, 1950–1972', *American Historical Review,* 102 (1997), pp. 53–84.

58 Stevi Jackson, *Christine Delphy* (Sage, London, 1996), pp. 15–19.

59 Mossuz-Lavau, *Les Lois de l'amour,* p. 83.

60 Laure Adler, *Les Femmes politiques* (Seuil, Paris, 1993), p. 172. The final Veil law of 17 January 1975 allowed a woman, who was no more than ten weeks pregnant and could provide proof of the 'distress' it caused

her, to seek to have her pregnancy terminated in an authorized medical establishment. The bill was more restrictive than that passed in many neighbouring states, limiting intervention to the first ten weeks of gestation; in the United Kingdom intervention was permitted up until the twenty-fourth week.

61　On the observation that every feminist novel of the 1970s contained one 'obligatory abortion' scene, see Lisa Maria Hogeland, 'Sexuality in the Consciousness Raising Novel of the 1970s', *Journal of the History of Sexuality*, 5 (1995), pp. 614–20.

62　Susan Brownmiller, *Against our Will: Women and Rape* (Simon and Schuster, New York, 1975).

63　Angela Y. Davis, *Women, Race and Class* (Random House, New York, 1981), pp. 172–83.

64　Robin Morgan, 'Theory and Practice: Pornography and Rape', in *Take Back the Night: Women on Pornography*, ed. Laura Lederer (William Morrow, New York, 1980), pp. 125–32.

65　Echols, *Daring to be Bad*.

66　Ehrenreich, *Re-Making Love*, pp. 66–7.

67　Charlotte Wolff, *Love between Women* (Duckworth, London, 1971).

68　Sheila Jeffreys, *Anticlimax: a Feminist Perspective on the Sexual Revolution* (New York University Press, New York, 1991).

69　Echols, *Daring to be Bad*, pp. 104–5.

70　Ibid., p. 238. On Canada, see Becki Ross, *The House that Jill Built: a Lesbian Nation in Formation* (University of Toronto Press, Toronto, 1996).

71　Monique Wittig, *Les Guérillères*, trans. David Le Vay (Avon Books, New York, 1971).

72　Kate Millet, *Flying* (Ballantine, New York, 1975).

73　Adrienne Rich, 'Compulsory Heterosexuality and Lesbian Existence', in *Desire: the Politics of Sexuality*, eds Ann Snitow, Christine Stansell and Sharon Thompson (Virago, London, 1983), pp. 212–41.

74　Adrienne Rich, *Of Woman Born: Motherhood as Experience and Institution* (Norton, New York, 1976).

75　Lillian Faderman, *Odd Girls and Twilight Lovers: a History of Lesbian Life in Twentieth Century America* (Columbia University Press, New York, 1991).

76　Race created yet another divide; see Rochella Thorpe, '"A House Where Queers Go": African-American Lesbian Nightlife in Detroit, 1940–1945', in *Inventing Lesbian Cultures in America*, ed. Ellen Levin (Beacon Press, Boston, 1996), pp. 40–61.

77　Elizabeth Lapovsky Kennedy and Madeleine Davis, 'The Reproduction of Butch-Fem Roles: a Social Constructionist Approach', in *Passion and Power: Sexuality in History*, eds Kathy Peiss and Christina Simmons, with Robert Padgug (Temple University Press, Philadelphia, 1989), pp. 241–56; Becki L. Ross, 'Detaining the (Tattooed) Delinquent Body: the Practices of Moral Regulation at Toronto's Street Haven, 1965–1969', *Journal of the History of Sexuality*, 7 (1997), pp. 561–95.

78   Laud Humphreys, *Tearoom Trade: Impersonal Sex in Public Places* (Aldine-Atherton, New York, 1975).

79   Lee Edelman, 'Tearooms and Sympathy, or, The Epistemology of the Water Closet', in *Nationalisms and Sexualities*, ed. A. Parker (Routledge, New York, 1992), pp. 263–84.

80   The therapies tried out on Alan Turing, a brilliant mathematician who played a key role during the war in decoding German messages, contributed to his 1954 suicide; Andrew Hodges, *Alan Turing: the Enigma* (Burnett Books, London, 1983), pp. 468–75, 500–1.

81   Michael Schofield, *Sociological Aspects of Homosexuality: a Comparative Study of Three Types of Homosexuals* (Longman, London, 1965), pp. 167–70.

82   Ibid., pp. 175–94.

83   Gary Kinsman, *The Regulation of Desire: Sexuality in Canada* (Black Rose Books, Montréal, 1987), pp. 151–3.

84   On the reform campaign, see Jeffrey Weeks, *Coming Out: Homosexual Politics in Britain from the Nineteenth Century to the Present* (Quartet, London, 1977), pp. 168–78.

85   Stephen Jeffrey-Poulter, *Peers, Queers and Commons: the Struggle for Gay Law Reform from 1950 to the Present* (Routledge, London, 1991), pp. 82–8.

86   Ibid., p. 124; on reform in Canada, see Kinsman, *The Regulation of Desire*, pp. 164–72.

87   Antony Copley, *Sexual Moralities in France, 1780–1980: New Ideas on the Family, Divorce, and Homosexuality* (Routledge, London, 1989), p. 218.

88   Jean-Louis Bory and Guy Hocquenghem, *Comment nous appelez vous déjà? Ces hommes que l'on dit homosexuels* (Calman-Levy, Paris, 1977), pp. 215–19.

89   Mossuz-Lavau, *Les Lois de l'amour*, p. 201.

90   Bory and Hocquenghem, *Comment nous appelez vous déjà?*, pp. 220–1.

91   Ronald Bayer, *Homosexuality and American Psychiatry: the Politics of Diagnosis* (Princeton University Press, Princeton, NJ, 1987), pp. 70–81.

92   On the reform campaign, see Weeks, *Coming Out*, pp. 185–200.

93   Stephen O. Murray, *American Gay* (University of Chicago Press, Chicago, 1996), pp. 60–3.

94   M. Dannecker and R. Reiche, *Der gewöhnliche Homosexuelle* (Fischer, Frankfurt, 1974); A. P. Bell and M. S. Weinberg, *Homosexualities: a Study of Diversity among Men and Women* (Simon and Schuster, New York, 1978).

95   Bayer, *Homosexuality and American Psychiatry*, pp. 101–54.

96   Jeffrey Weeks, *Sexuality and its Discontents* (Routledge and Kegan Paul, London, 1985), p. 185.

97   The African-American writer James Baldwin disliked the notion of a 'gay' identity in part because he was black, in part because he represented an earlier generation that hoped to end all labelling.

98 Murray, *American Gay*, pp. 68–77.
99 Alan Sinfield, *The Wilde Century: Effeminacy, Oscar Wilde and the Queer Movement* (Cassell, London, 1994), p. 185.
100 Michel Foucault, *The History of Sexuality*, trans. Robert Hurley (New York, Pantheon, 1978), vol. 1: *An Introduction*.
101 Robert A. Nye, 'Michel Foucault's Sexuality and the History of Homosexuality', in *Homosexuality in Modern France*, eds Jeffrey Meyrick and Bryant T. Ragan (Oxford University Presss, New York, 1996), pp. 229–34.
102 Lesley Caldwell, 'Italian Feminism: Some Considerations', in *Women and Italy*, eds Z. G. Baranski and S. W. Vinall (St Martin's Press, New York, 1991), p. 155; Jane C. and Peter T. Schneider, *Festival of the Poor: Fertility Decline and the Ideology of Class in Sicily, 1860–1980* (Arizona University Press, Tucson, 1996).

Chapter 10 'Backlash': AIDS and the Sexual Counter-revolution

1 *Time*, 18 November 1991, p. 82.
2 Susan Faludi, *Backlash: the Undeclared War against American Women* (Crown, New York, 1991).
3 Igor S. Kon, *The Sexual Revolution in Russia: from the Age of the Tsars to Today*, trans. James Riordan (Free Press, New York, 1995), pp. 3–4.
4 Randy Shilts, *And the Band Played On: People, Politics, and the AIDS Epidemic* (St Martin's Press, New York, 1987).
5 Cindy Patton, 'Between Innocence and Safety: Epidemiologic and Popular Constructions of Young People's Need for Safe Sex', in *Deviant Bodies: Critical Perspectives on Difference in Science and Popular Culture*, eds Jennifer Terry and Jacqueline Urla (Indiana University Press, Bloomington, 1995), pp. 340–3.
6 Virginia Berridge, *AIDS in the United Kingdom: the Making of Policy, 1981–1994* (Oxford University Press, Oxford, 1996).
7 Anna Marie Smith, *New Right Discourse on Race and Sexuality: Britain, 1968–1990* (Cambridge University Press, Cambridge, 1994), pp. 15–66.
8 *Le Nouvel observateur*, 17–20 November 1986, pp. 38–47.
9 Ibid., 4–10 December 1987, pp. 38–49.
10 Gerard Zwang, *Histoire des peines de sexe: les malheurs érotiques, leurs causes et leurs remèdes à travers les âges* (Maloine, Paris, 1994), p. 308.
11 James W. Jones, 'Discourses on and of AIDS in West Germany, 1986–90', *Journal of the History of Sexuality*, 2 (1992), p. 441.
12 *Le Nouvel observateur*, 24–30 June 1988, pp. 20–4.
13 Jan Willem Duyvendak, 'From Revolution to Involution: the Disappearance of the Gay Movement in France', *Journal of the History of Homosexuality*, 2(3) (1995), pp. 369–85.

14 *Le Nouvel observateur*, 29 July 1983, p. 53; 11 November 1983, p. 47.
15 Christopher Robinson, *Scandal in the Ink: Male and Female Homosexuality in Twentieth-century French Literature* (Cassell, London, 1995).
16 *Le Nouvel observateur*, 30 October–5 November 1987, pp. 38–43; see also Jean-Paul Aron and Roger Kempf, *Le Pénis et le démoralisation de l'Occident* (Grasset, Paris, 1984).
17 *The Independent*, 7 December 1997, p. 9.
18 *Le Nouvel observateur*, 15–21 February 1996, p. 6.
19 Toronto *Globe and Mail*, 19 December 1996, p. 4.
20 Charlotte Wolff, *Bisexuality: a Study* (Quartet, London, 1977), pp. 102–3.
21 Edward King, *Safety in Numbers: Safer Sex and Gay Men* (Routledge, New York, 1994).
22 Harry Benjamin, *The Transsexual Phenomenon* (Julian, New York, 1966); Janice M. Irvine, *Disorders of Desire: Sex and Gender in Modern American Sexology* (Temple University Press, Philadelphia, 1990), pp. 237–9; Anne Fausto-Sterling, *Myths of Gender* (Basic Books, New York, 1992).
23 Christine Jorgensen's transformation had made the world of the 1950s aware of sex assignment surgery; Irvine, *Disorders of Desire*, pp. 257–66.
24 There was also the economic question of whether trans-sexuals had the right to demand that the public health system provide them with sex-change operations.
25 Marjorie Garber, *Vice Versa: Bisexuality and the Eroticism of Everyday Life* (Simon and Schuster, New York, 1995).
26 Terry Castle, *The Apparitional Lesbian: Female Homosexuality and Modern Culture* (Columbia University Press, New York, 1993), p. 12.
27 An English survey found that two-thirds of lesbians had only one sexual partner and none more than twenty, whereas 11.4 per cent of gay men had more than twenty and 3.9 per cent a hundred or more; Kaye Wellings, Julia Field, Anne M. Johnson and Jane Wadsworth, *Sexual Behaviour in Britain: the National Survey of Sexual Attitudes and Lifestyles* (Penguin, London, 1994), p. 213.
28 For an avoidance of issues pertaining to straight women, see Sheila Jeffreys, *Anticlimax: a Feminist Perspective on the Sexual Revolution* (New York University Press, New York, 1991).
29 Dean Hamer and Peter Copeland, *The Science of Desire: the Search for the Gay Gene and the Biology of Behavior* (Simon and Schuster, New York, 1994).
30 Simon LeVay, *The Sexual Brain* (MIT Press, Cambridge, Mass., 1993).
31 Alice D. Dreger, 'Hermaphrodites in Love: the Truth of Gonads', in *Science and Homosexualities*, ed. Vernon A. Rosario (Routledge, New York, 1997), p. 50.
32 *Edmonton Journal*, 18 June 1995, p. A2; and see Angus McLaren, *Our own Master Race: Eugenics in Canada, 1885–1945* (Oxford University Press, Toronto, 1990).

33 Philip R. Reilly, *The Surgical Solution: a History of Involuntary Steril-ization in the United States* (Johns Hopkins University Press, Balti-more, MD, 1991).

34 Montreal *La Presse*, 27 August 1997, p. B5.

35 Toronto *Globe and Mail*, 29 August 1997; see also *Le Monde*, 19 Novem-ber 1986, p. 13; Philippe Ehrenström, 'Eugénisme et santé publique: la stérilisation légale des malades mentaux dans le canton de Vaud (Suisse), *History and Philosophy of the Life Sciences*, 15 (1993), pp. 205–27.

36 Toronto *Globe and Mail*, 16 December 1997, p. A14.

37 Elisabeth Badinter, *X Y: de l'identité masculine* (Odile Jacob, Paris, 1992).

38 Kenneth Clatterbaugh, *Contemporary Perspectives on Masculinity: Women, Men and Politics in Modern Society* (Westview Press, Boul-der, Colo., 1997). Robert Bly's *Iron John* (1990), an unexpected best-seller, mocked as a back-to-boyhood fantasy of escape from mom via pop psychology, popularized the notion of a 'men's movement'.

39 David Blankenhorn, *Fatherless America* (Basic Books, New York, 1995); David Popenoe, *Life without Father* (Martin Kessler, New York, 1996).

40 Arlene Skolnick, *Embattled Paradise: the American Family in an Age of Uncertainty* (Basic Books, New York, 1991).

41 David Popenoe, *Disturbing the Nest: Family Change and Decline in Modern Societies* (Aldine de Gruyter, New York, 1989), p. 1.

42 Toronto *Globe and Mail*, 4 October 1997, p. A9.

43 Clatterbaugh, *Contemporary Perspectives on Masculinity*, pp. 177–93.

44 Warren L. Vinz, *Pulpit Politics: Faces of American Protestantism in the Twentieth Century* (SUNY Press, Albany, 1997), p. 177; John C. Green et al., *Religion and the Cultural Wars: Dispatches from the Front* (Rowman and Littlefield, New York, 1996).

45 Ian Mylchreest, '"Sound Law and Undoubtedly Good Policy": *Roe* v. *Wade* in Comparative Perspective', in *The Politics of Abortion and Birth Control in Historical Perspective*, ed. Donald T. Critchlow (Penn-sylvania State University Press, University Park, 1996), pp. 53–71.

46 Faye D. Ginsburg, *Contested Lives: the Abortion Debate in an Amer-ican Community* (University of California Press, Berkeley, 1989).

47 *Libération*, 28 June 1995, pp. 1–5.

48 Law reform in France had made contraception and abortion available yet they were still technically illegal; Michèle Le Doeuff, *Hipparchia's Choice: an Essay Concerning Women, Philosophy, Etc.*, trans. Trista Selous (Blackwell, Oxford, 1991), pp. 247, 269, 303.

49 For the context, see James Davison Hunter and Joseph E. Davis, 'Cul-tural Politics at the Edge of Life', in *The Politics of Abortion and Birth Control*, ed. Critchlow, pp. 103–24.

50 Milan Korcok, 'Physicians Targeted as Abortion Debate in US Turns Violent', *Canadian Medical Association Journal*, 152 (1 March 1995), pp. 727–30; for doctors' own accounts of the dangers they ran, see Carole Joffe, *Doctors of Conscience: the Struggle to Provide Abortion Before and After Roe v. Wade* (Beacon Press, New York, 1996).

51 For the argument that the abortion pill could be a panacea, see Lawrence Lader, *RU 486: the Pill that Could End the Abortion Wars and Why American Women Don't Have It* (Addison-Wesley, Reading, Mass., 1991); Marie Bass, 'Birth Control Business', *Women's Review of Books*, 11 (July 1994), pp. 20–2.

52 Ken Plummer, 'Intimate Citizenship and the Culture of Sexual Story Telling', in *Sexual Cultures, Values and Intimacy*, eds Jeffrey Weeks and Janet Holland (Macmillan, London, 1996), pp. 34–52.

53 Donald Alexander Downs, *More than Victims: Battered Women, the Syndrome Society, and the Law* (University of Chicago Press, Chicago, 1996).

54 Susan Estrich, *Real Rape* (Harvard University Press, Cambridge, Mass., 1987).

55 On the American Psychiatric Association's (DMS-III-R) invention of the 'Psaraphilic Coercive Disorder aka Rapism', when a man has no control since led on by woman, see Annette Lawson, *Adultery: an Analysis of Love and Betrayal* (Basic Books, New York, 1988), p. 388.

56 The interest in and ability to discuss incest was reflected in France by the appearance of films such as *Le Souffle au coeur* (1971) and *Beau-père* (1981). In the United States the 1990s saw the release of *Spanking the Monkey* and the media's fascination with film director Woody Allen's relationship with his adopted daughter.

57 Matthew Hugh Erdelyi, *The Recovery of Unconscious Memory: Hypermnesia and Reminiscence* (University of Chicago Press, Chicago, 1996).

58 The number of men entering Catholic seminaries fell by 85 per cent between 1993 and 1996; Philip Jenkins, *Pedophiles and Priests: Anatomy of a Contemporary Crisis* (Oxford University Press, New York, 1996).

59 Vern L. Bullough, *Science in the Bedroom: a History of Sex Research* (Basic Books, New York, 1994), pp. 263–4.

60 Robin Morgan, 'Theory and Practice: Pornography and Rape', in *Take Back the Night: Women on Pornography*, ed. Laura Lederer (William Morrow, New York, 1980), pp. 125–32.

61 Gloria Steinem, 'The Real Linda Lovelace', in *Making Violence Sexy: Feminist Views on Pornography*, ed. Diana Russell (Teachers' College Press, New York, 1993), pp. 23–31.

62 Dany Lacombe, *Blue Politics: Pornography and the Law in the Age of Feminism* (University of Toronto Press, Toronto, 1994).

63 US Department of Justice, *Attorney General's Commission on Pornography Final Report* (US Government Printing Office, Washington, DC, 1986).

64 The notion of women exploited by lustful men, employed by conservatives like Midge Decter, *The New Chastity and Other Arguments against Women's Liberation* (Coward, McCann and Geoghegan, New York, 1972) was taken up in the 1980s by some feminists. Germaine Greer evolved from the sexual libertarian of *The Female Eunuch* (MacGibbon and Kee, London, 1970) to the critic of birth control of *Sex and Destiny: the Politics of Human Fertility* (Harper and Row, New York, 1984).

65 Andrea Dworkin, *Pornography* (Penguin, London, 1981); Catharine MacKinnon, *Only Words* (Harvard University Press, Cambridge, Mass., 1993); for a critique of Rich, see Diana Fuss, *Essentially Speaking* (Routledge, New York, 1989), p. 47.

66 See also Susan Griffin, *Pornography and Silence* (Harper and Row, New York, 1981).

67 See the papers in Carole Vance (ed.), *Pleasure and Danger: Exploring Female Sexuality* (Routledge and Kegan Paul, London, 1984).

68 Lynne Segal and Mary McIntosh, *Sex Exposed: Sexuality and the Pornography Debate* (Rutgers University Press, New Brunswick, NJ, 1993).

69 Calvin Thomas, *Male Matters: Masculinity, Anxiety and the Male Body on the Line* (University of Illinois Press, Chicago, 1996).

70 Gayle Rubin, 'Thinking Sex', in *Pleasure and Danger*, ed. Vance, pp. 297–309.

71 Pat Califa, *Public Sex: the Culture of Radical Sex* (Cleis Press, Pittsburgh, 1994).

72 The same sorts of activists who opposed censorship also defended prostitutes' right to live the life they chose, be it at King's Cross or on 42nd Street, asserting that a self-conscious trading in sex actually was an advance of sorts. Sex workers, who wanted better working conditions rather than the end of their jobs, distrusted those who sought to ban prostitution. See Laurie Bell (ed.), *Good Girls/Bad Girls: Sex Trade Workers and Feminists Face to Face* (Women's Press, Toronto, 1985); Shannon Bell, *Reading, Writing and Rewriting the Prostitute Body* (Indiana University Press, Bloomington, 1994).

73 Naomi Wolf, *The Beauty Myth* (Morrow, New York, 1991).

74 Jacqueline Urla and Alan C. Swedlund, 'The Anthropometry of Barbie: Unsettling Ideals of the Feminine Body in Popular Culture', in *Deviant Bodies*, eds Terry and Urla, pp. 277–313.

75 *Le Nouvel observateur*, 23 March 1984, pp. 46–53.

76 A survey of a young sexually active North American group in the mid-1990s found that two-thirds had sex at least once a week; Paul Sachdev, *Sex, Abortion and Unmarried Women* (Greenwood Press, Westport, Conn., 1995), p. 87.

77 Wellings et al., *Sexual Behaviour in Britain*, pp. 42, 49.

78 Jane M. Ussher, *Fantasies of Femininity: Reframing the Boundaries of Sex* (Penguin, London, 1997), pp. 30–8.

79 Wellings et al., *Sexual Behaviour in Britain*, pp. 72, 97.

80 Sachdev, *Sex, Abortion and Unmarried Women*, p. 93.

81 Wellings et al., *Sexual Behaviour in Britain*, p. 57; Sachdev, *Sex, Abortion and Unmarried Women*, p. 105.

82 Cheryl D. Hayes, *Risking the Future: Adolescent Sexuality, Pregnancy and Childbearing* (National Academy Press, New York, 1987).

83 Kristin A. Moore, Margaret C. Simms and Charles L. Betsey (eds), *Choice and Circumstance: Racial Differences in Adolescent Sexuality and Fertility* (Transactions, Oxford, 1986), p. 127.

84 Marian J. Morton, *And Sin No More: Social Policy and Unwed Mothers in Cleveland, 1855–1990* (Ohio State University Press, Columbus, 1993); Annette Lawson and Deborah L. Rhode (eds), *The Politics of Pregnancy: Adolescent Sexuality and Public Policy* (Yale University Press, New Haven, Conn., 1993).

85 Moore et al., *Choice and Circumstance*, p. 127; Maris A. Vinovskis, *An 'Epidemic' of Adolescent Pregnancy? Some Historical and Policy Considerations* (Oxford University Press, New York, 1988), p. 25.

86 Susan McDaniel. 'Women's Role and Reproduction: the Changing Picture in Canada in the 1980s', *Atlantis*, 14 (1988), pp. 1–12; Carl Grindstaff, T. R. Balakrishnan and David J. Dewit, 'Educational Attainment, Age at First Birth and Life Time Fertility: an Analysis of Canadian Fertility Survey Data', *Canadian Review of Sociology and Anthropology*, 28 (1991), pp. 324–39. E. F. Jones et al., 'Teenage Pregnancy in Developed Countries: Determinants and Policy Implications', *Family Planning Perspectives*, 17 (March/April 1985), pp. 53–63; Surinder Wadhera and John Silins, 'Teenage Pregnancy in Canada, 1975–1985', *Family Planning Perspectives*, 22 (January/February 1990), pp. 27–30.

87 Toronto *Globe and Mail*, 26 September 1996, p. A1.

88 Sachdev, *Sex, Abortion and Unmarried Women*, pp. 113, 123.

89 Ibid., p. 160.

90 Vancouver *Sun*, 24 August 1996, p. 8A.

91 Dana Lear, *Sex and Sexuality: Risk and Relationships in the Age of AIDS* (Sage, New York, 1997).

92 Steven Seidman, *Embattled Eros: Sexual Politics and Ethics in Contemporary America* (Routledge, New York, 1992), p. 94.

93 Wellings et al., *Sexual Behaviour in Britain*, pp. 149–57; Toronto *Globe and Mail*, 19 February 1998.

94 Alfred Spira, *Sexual Behaviour and AIDS* (Avebury, Aldershot, 1994).

95 *Le Nouvel observateur*, 21–27 October 1993, pp. 4–14.

96 *Newsweek*, 2 June 1986, p. 55.

97 *Le Nouvel observateur*, 23–29 October 1987, p. 42

98 François de Singley, *Modern Marriage and its Costs to Women*, trans. Malcolm Bailey (University of Delaware Press, Newark, 1996), pp. 168, 192–3. Famous French unmarried intellectual couples included Louis Aragon and Elsa Triolet, Jean-Paul Sartre and Simone de Beauvoir, Philippe Sollers and Julia Kristeva.

99 *Le Nouvel observateur*, 15–21 February 1996, pp. 4–6.

100 Jane Lewis and John Welshman, 'The Issue of Never-married Motherhood in Britain, 1920–70', *Social History of Medicine*, 10 (1997), pp. 401–18.

101 Ussher, *Fantasies of Femininity*, p. 198.

102 Jean Duncombe and Dennis Marsden, 'Whose Orgasm is it Anyway? "Sex Work" in Long-term Heterosexual Relationships', in *Sexual Cultures, Values and Intimacy*, eds Weeks and Holland, pp. 220–38.

103 André Béjin, *Le Nouveau tempérament sexuel: essai sur la rationalisation et la démocratisation de la sexualité* (Editions Kime, Paris, 1990), p. 34.

104 One woman reported that she was angered rather than enlightened by her therapist showing her videos of ecstatic copulating couples. All she could identify with were the pimples on the actor's back; Irvine, *Disorders of Desire*, p. 131.

105 Janice M. Irvine, 'Regulated Passions: the Invention of Inhibited Sexual Desire and Sexual Addiction', in *Deviant Bodies*, eds Terry and Urla, pp. 314–37.

106 Michel Bozon and Henri Leridon (eds), *Sexuality and the Social Sciences: a French Survey on Sexual Behaviour* (Dartmouth Publishing, Aldershot, 1996), pp. 153, 295.

107 *Le Nouvel observateur*, 6–12 December 1990, pp. 9–10.

108 Wellings et al., *Sexual Behaviour in Britain*, p. 339; on racial differences and control of reproduction, see Dorothy Roberts, *Killing the Black Body: Race, Reproduction and the Meaning of Liberty* (Pantheon, New York, 1997), pp. 68–97.

109 'Breast Cancer and Hormonal Contraceptives', *The Lancet*, 347 (22 June 1996), pp. 1713–27; 'Breast Cancer and Hormonal Contraceptives', *Contraception*, 54, 3 (September 1996).

110 Toronto *Globe and Mail*, 27 November 1995.

111 *Maclean's*, 23 September 1985, pp. 61, 63; 12 January 1987, p. 36; Gary Kinsman, *The Regulation of Desire: Sexuality in Canada* (Black Rose Press, Montreal, 1987), p. 211.

112 Toronto *Globe and Mail*, 1 August 1996, pp. A1, 6.

113 Naomi Pfeffer, *The Stork and the Syringe: a Political History of Reproductive Medicine* (Polity Press, Cambridge, 1993), pp. 6–7, 35–6.

114 Edward F. Griffith, *The Childless Family: its Causes and Cure* (Kegan Paul, Trench and Trubner, London, 1939), p. 119.

115 George Ryley Scott, *Three Hundred Sex, Marriage and Birth Control Questions Answered* (T. Werner Laurie, London, 1941), p. 138.

116 *Orford* v. *Orford* (1921) 58 DLR 251.

117 Ronald R. Rindfus, S. Philip Morgan and Gray Swicegood, *First Births in America: Changes in the Timing of Parenthood* (University of California Press, Berkeley, 1988), p. 62.

118 Sarah Franklin, 'Postmodern Procreation: a Cultural Account of Assisted Reproduction', in *Conceiving the New World Order: the Global Politics of Reproduction*, eds Faye D. Ginsburg and Rayna Rapp (University of California Press, Berkeley, 1995), pp. 323–45

119 *Le Nouvel observateur*, 10 June 1983, p. 34.

120 Barbara Katz Rothman, *Recreating Motherhood: Ideology and Technology in a Patriarchal Society* (Norton, New York, 1988), pp. 159–68; Cynthia R. Daniels, *At Women's Expense: State Power and the Politics of Fetal Rights* (Harvard University Press, Cambridge, Mass., 1993).

121 A similar debate had earlier focused on the use of anaesthesia. In the 1920s women demanded 'twilight sleep'; in the 1970s they swung back to 'natural childbirth'.

122 Hilary Homans (ed.), *The Sexual Politics of Reproduction* (Gower, London, 1985), p. 11.

123 Margaret Marsh and Wanda Ronner, *The Empty Cradle: Infertility in America from Colonial Times to the Present* (Johns Hopkins University Press, Baltimore, MD, 1996).

124 Susan Sontag, *AIDS and its Metaphors* (Farrar, Strauss and Giroux, New York, 1988).

125 Ussher, *Fantasies of Femininity*, p. 239.

126 Cathy Schwitenberg (ed.), *The Madonna Connection: Representational Politics, Subcultural Identities, and Cultural Theory* (Westview Press, Boulder, Colo., 1993); Cornel West, *Race Matters* (Beacon Press, Boston, 1993), pp. 81–93.

127 Frank Mort, *Cultures of Consumption: Masculinities and Social Space in Late Twentieth-century Britain* (Routledge, London, 1996).

Conclusion

1 *The Times*, 2 January 1998.

2 Toronto *Globe and Mail*, 1 May 1998.

3 Michael Anderson, 'The Emergence of the Modern Life Cycle in Britain', *Social History*, 10 (1985), pp. 69–87.

4 Steven Seidman, *Difference Troubles: Queering Social Theory and Sexual Politics* (Cambridge University Press, Cambridge, 1997), pp. 109–64; Daniel Harris, *The Rise and Fall of Gay Culture* (Hyperion, New York, 1998).

5 Paula Bennett and Vernon A. Rosario II (eds), *Solitary Pleasures: the Historical, Literary, and Artistic Discourses of Autoeroticism* (Routledge, New York, 1995).

6 Harry Oosterhuis, 'Sexuality in the Netherlands: a Historical Overview', and Gert Hekma, 'Same Sex Relations among Men in Europe, 1700–1900,' in *Sexual Cultures in Europe*, eds Lesley Hall, Gert Hekma and Franz Eder (Manchester University Press, Manchester, 1999).

7 Vancouver *Sun*, 18 August 1996, p. A13.

8 Graham Heath, *The Illusionary Freedom: the Intellectual Origins and Social Consequences of the Sexual Revolution* (Heinemann, London, 1978); Christopher Lasch, *The Culture of Narcissism: American Life in an Age of Diminishing Expectations* (Norton, New York, 1978); André Béjin, *Le Nouveau tempérament sexuel: essai sur la rationalisation et la démocratisation de la sexualité* (Editions Kime, Paris, 1990)

9 Toronto *Globe and Mail*, 30 May 1998, p. A6; 20 July, p. A5.

10 Cleo Odzer, *Virtual Space: Sex and the Cyber Citizen* (Berkeley Books, New York, 1997).

11 Helpful theoretical approaches to these themes, suggested to me by Mariana Valverde, are Donna Haraway, *Simians, Cyborgs and Women: the Reinvention of Nature* (Free Association Press, London, 1991); Bruno Latour, *We Have Never Been Modern* (Harvard University Press, Cambridge, Mass., 1993).

Index